Applying the Rasch Model: Fundamental Measurement in the Human Sciences
Second Edition

D1215877

Applying the Rasch Model:
Fundamental Measurement in the Human Sciences
Second Edition

TREVOR G. BOND
Hong Kong Institute of Education

CHRISTINE M. FOX
University of Toledo

Routledge
Taylor & Francis Group
New York London

Routledge
Taylor & Francis Group
270 Madison Avenue
New York, NY 10016

Routledge
Taylor & Francis Group
2 Park Square
Milton Park, Abingdon
Oxon OX14 4RN

© 2007 by Taylor & Francis Group, LLC
Routledge is an imprint of Taylor & Francis Group, an Informa business
First published by Lawrence Erlbaum Associates,
Reprinted in 2010 by Routledge

International Standard Book Number-13: 978-0-8058-5461-9 (cloth)
978-0-8058-5462-6 (paper)
978-1-4106-1457-5 (e book)

Library of Congress Cataloging-in-Publication Data

Catalog record is available from the Library of Congress

Visit the Taylor & Francis Web site at
http://www.taylorandfrancis.com

and the Routledge Web site at
http://www.routledge.com

To Ben Wright,
Provocative, persistent, and passionate
TGB & CMF

Contents

Foreword

Then felt I like some watcher of the skies
When a new planet swims into his ken;

—John Keats, "On first looking into Chapman's Homer"

The first edition of this remarkable work arrived stealthily. Those of us in the know were aware that it was to be released at the 2001 AERA Annual Meeting in Seattle. When the Exhibitor area opened I headed for the Lawrence Erlbaum Associates booth and looked for the book. I purchased the very first copy. By the end of the AERA Meeting, "Bond & Fox" had sold out and was on its way to becoming an Erlbaum best seller.

And deservedly so. Rigorous measurement has been essential to the advancement of civilization since Babylonian times, and to the advancement of physical science since the Renaissance. But education, psychology, and social science have short-changed themselves by degrading measurement to the "assignment of numerals ... according to rule" (Stevens, 1959a, p. 25) and then acting as though one rule is as good as another. The essential rule in successful measurement is used ubiquitously for money, length, area, volume, weight, temperature—the things we deem most important to supporting life, liberty, and the pursuit of happiness. That rule is "one more unit means the same amount extra no matter how much there already is." This is exactly what Rasch measurement operationalizes for social science—and is what this book is all about.

Rasch measurement has appeared to be so complex and technical. Georg Rasch was a consultant mathematician and statistician. Though he used simple graphical techniques himself (Rasch, 1960, p. 71), he presented them in obscure algebra (1960, p. 173). In the following years, the utility of his conceptual breakthrough was lost in arguments over statistical niceties and the struggles of developing working software on the newly available computers. Benjamin Wright, the leading advocate of practical Rasch measurement, would convince audiences of the value of Rasch measurement. But even his books proved perplexing for the neophyte. It seemed that by the time the Rasch practitioner had become competent enough to write a book, those early hurdles that are always encountered in using an unfamiliar methodology were forgotten.

Trevor Bond and Christine Fox remembered, and wrote this book—now revised to excel its former self! Purists may decry the lack of technical sophistication within these pages—but that is exactly accords with the needs of the neophyte. This book filled a gaping void. Its success has motivated others to follow its lead, but so far, none has been so ruthless in rejecting the shackles of Greek letters, in-group jargon, statistical niceties, and the constraining historical precedents of a century of psychometrics.

Of course, history is important. The ideas underlying Rasch measurement go back to ancient Babylon, to the Greek philosophers, to the adventurers of the Renaissance. In fact, the fundamental mathematical relationship underlying the Rasch model was expressed by American philosopher Charles Sanders Peirce. Here is how he phrased it: "The combination of independent concurrent arguments takes a very simple form when expressed in terms of the intensity of belief, measured in the proposed way. It is this. Take the sum of all the feelings ["*logarithm* of the chance", i.e., log-odds] of belief which would be produced separately by all the arguments pro and subtract from that the similar sum for arguments con, and the remainder is the feeling of belief we ought to have on the whole. This is a procedure which men often resort to, under the name of balancing reasons." (Peirce, 1878, p. 709)

So, why, over a century after the publication of Peirce's article in a leading science journal of its time, is the arithmetic of log-odds regarded as obscure, technical, even fanatical, in Social Science? An answer is that Social Science has yet to regard rigorous measurement as crucial to progress.

The major conceptual transition in physical science was achieved with Isaac Newton's *Philosophiae Naturalis Principia Mathematica* [Mathematical Principles of Natural Philosophy] (1687). Prior to that work, physical science was chiefly devoted to describing phenomena. Arithmetical summaries were tentative and temporary. After Newton, his Laws of Motion were regarded as more reliable than the data. Astronomical observations that contradicted his Laws were challenged and brought into conformity with them. In contrast, Social Science has yet to advance to the point at which theory is regarded as more valid than data. But Newton's work was possible only because of the advances in physical measurement that preceded it. Good measurement leads to profound theory.

So what is the usual situation in Social Science? "Measures" are tentative and temporary descriptions. They are considered to be good if they explain the variance of interest, or correlate well with some other "measures," or predict well some outcome. If the "measures" are deemed unsatisfactory, then alternative methods of computing "measures" are investigated. This is the reverse of physical science. The measurement of weight and length follows strict rules. The extent to which weight explains variance, or correlates or predicts, is an experimental finding, not an aspect of measuring.

This book is the unusual situation in Social Science. It is a laborer to assist you in laying the foundation of truly scientific measurement upon which we can look forward to seeing the building of a skyscraper of breathtaking Social Science theory—theory which will be able to withstand the storms of contradictory data.

"Enter to Grow in Wisdom. Go Forth to Apply Wisdom in Service."[1]

—John "Mike" Linacre, University of Sydney, Australia

REFERENCES

Peirce, C.S. (1878). Illustration of the Logic of Science, by C.S. Peirce, Assistant in the United States Coast Survey. Fourth Paper: The Probability of Induction. *Popular Science Monthly,* pp. 705–718. Here from pp. 707–709.
Stevens, S. S. (1959) Measurement, Psychophysics and Utility, Chap. 2, in C. W. Churchman & P. Ratoosh (Eds.), *Measurement: Definitions and Theories.* New York: John Wiley.

[1] *Inscription on* **Flowers Hall,** *Huntingdon College, Montgomery, Alabama.*

Preface

At a *Quantitative Methods in the Social Sciences Colloquium* at the University of California Santa Barbara, the meeting chair introduced the topic, by referring, rather embarrassingly, to the first edition of Bond & Fox as an academic best-seller. He then provided the required empirical substantiation for his claim by circulating the latest Lawrence Erlbaum Associates catalogue with *Applying the Rasch Model* annotated just as announced: "Best Seller." Who would have imagined a book that was written primarily as a response to the perennial, frustrating question, "Can you tell me how you did that Rasch analysis?" could be so well received?

We have aimed our book at those who are studying quantitative research methods in the social sciences and, in particular, those who know they should be using the Rasch model but cannot work out the "How?" and the "Why?" We target graduate students in disciplines in education and psychology, but we intend to be relevant to those aiming to research across all human science disciplines. It seems that Rasch measurement is certainly on the uptake right across these disciplines: We aim to show our research colleagues how to get started and to give conceptually valid arguments for doing so.

Hardly a month passes without an unsolicited email from some corner of the world saying something like: I am really enjoying your Rasch analysis book, but I have a little question about page x. Last month's went like this: "After many years of dissatisfaction with traditional methods of analysing rating-scale data, I began a hunt on the basic assumption that someone somewhere must have developed newer, more satisfying methods. After finally encountering the name Rasch, and several more difficult months of trying to grasp the fundamentals . . . , I finally came across *Applying the Rasch Model.* I cannot tell you adequately what an enormous difference your book made. The graphical illustrations did wonders in furthering my understanding of measurement, the glossary was extremely helpful, and your pointing the reader to current software was a blessing."

With an audience containing colleagues such as that, it was difficult to resist putting together a second edition when the questions arose about whether one was on the way. Readers of the first edition will remember our rather heart-on-sleeve preface to that edition which gave personal accounts of how the authors succumbed to the lure of Rasch analysis and our thanks to those who helped us reach that point. Reviews of the first edition as well as solicited and unsolicited advice from colleagues and students pointed out some inadequacies of our first effort. But somehow, we had managed to write an appropriate book at just the right time. No doubt the bulk of our readers will be pleased that we resisted most of the urging by our more mathematically literate advisors to introduce the Rasch equations earlier–in the body of the text. Instead, we have attempted to improve conceptual clarity and accuracy and to leave the formal mathematical treatment of the models to Appendix A and to the array of texts whose authors are obviously better qualified to do that.

We have argued that thermometry rather than the meter rule might be a more apt analogy for those seeking parallels between what we are trying to do in the human sciences and what measurement in the physical sciences is like. We introduce that analogy towards the end of chapter 1 and continue to develop it as needed in this second edition; to that end, chapter 1 is substantially rewritten. A little confession is in order: We yielded a little to the suggestions of our mathematically literate critics and introduce the key Rasch equation in chapter 2 along with the ICC (Item Characteristic Curve). We did this in the illustrative context of an athletics high jump competition, so readers should not fear that we have forsaken clarity in order to quieten critics. The ICCs return in chapter 3 and in the new chapter 5. Chapter 5's new title, "Invariance: A Crucial Property of Scientific Measurement", exemplifies the new approach we have taken in the second edition. We no longer treat topics such as test linking and differential item functioning as merely functional aspects of psychometrics: We set them in the context of the more crucial measurement property, invariance of item, and person measures. We argue that measures must be invariant; if not, we want theoretically-driven explanations as to why. Chapter 8 on the many-facets Rasch model has now been supplemented by a very useful small empirical example with data set and control lines provided for those who grow confident after managing to repeat the analyses given in the earlier chapters. New examples in chapter 10 look at the growing use of student satisfaction data to hold universities and colleges accountable.

Collaboration with the *Winsteps* developer allows for the inclusion of a comprehensive CD with the second edition. Included is an introductory version of the latest *Winsteps* software, specifically targeted for the beginning Rasch analyst. While the software will take the same large data files as the commercially available version, the output files are constrained to show those figures and tables that are, in our opinion, best suited for the readers of our second edition. Data sets and more comprehensive versions of analysis controls are also provided. Appendix B takes a new approach to helping colleagues on the road to independence: We provide a step-by-step approach to analyzing the BLOT data set. Other material new to the second edition includes a focus on multidimensionality and Rasch factor analysis of residuals in chapter 12.

Needless to say, we remain deeply indebted to colleagues and students who have, in a variety of ways, required us to lift our game for the second edition. First and foremost amongst colleagues in this regard has been Mike Linacre, known by most Rasch users for his software *Winsteps* and *Facets*, but known to us for his unstinting support of our efforts. He graciously shared with us his retyped marginal notes from his dog-eared hardback first edition, a chapter-by-chapter commentary on strengths and weaknesses augmented by suggestions, advice and exemplars too many to acknowledge individually. He proactively worked with us on the free software CD and answered many technical and mathematical questions at a moment's notice. Thank you, Mike, you have been a generous model colleague. Kelly Bradley and her graduate students at Kentucky University have worked through the bulk of our second edition chapters. At short notice, Kelly volunteered her group to read critically the drafts. They have pointed to aspects needing clarification and to inconsistencies and errors that managed to escape us as we struggled to bring some sense of order to our electronic collaboration. Thanks to Kelly as well as to Shannon Sampson, Kenneth Royal, and Jessica Cunningham in particular for providing us with a perspective we might expect from a large section of our target audience. Lawrence Erlbaum Associates commissioned reviews of our revision plan form George Engelhard (Emory University), Kathy Green (University of Denver) and Randy Penfield (University of Florida); we are indebted to them for their insights and recommendations.

Other colleagues and students have helped us in more general but no less important ways. Along with those who are mentioned in the earlier preface, the following stand out: Terry Brown (Chicago) and Gerald Noelting (Quebec) will be sorely missed—both have died in the past few months. Magdalena Mok (Hong Kong), and fellow Australians, Rosemary Callingham, Peter Congdon, David Curtis, Juho Looveer, and Brian Doig all deserve special mention for their support. Italian colleagues Luigi Tesio (Milano), Enrico Gori (Udine), Silvia Ferrario (Veruno) and Guilio Vidotto (Padova) share highly appreciated passions from Rasch measurement and *cucina italiano*. Jack Stenner, Metametrics and Gage Kingsbury, NWEA, and Moritz Heene have contributed and supported in a variety of ways. Richard Smith, JAMPress, remains totally supportive of the publication of the collegial Rasch enterprise. Delegates to IOMW XII 2004 (Cairns), PROMS 2005 (Kuala Lumpur) and 2006 (Hong Kong) provided a wonderful context in which the ideas important to us and to this book could be discussed fruitfully. Our thanks to LEA editor, Debra Riegert, for her support of our endeavors.

So why would we spend time writing and then revising a book about what many consider just one of many analytical techniques that abound in the social sciences? Mark Wilson's review of our first edition made our point cogently for those "who might be otherwise perplexed at the motivation for writing a whole book about a topic that some might characterize as a an 'oversimplified special case' of an item response model ...."

The point of view in the Rasch approach to measurement is that one must start from a philosophy that establishes certain requirements of the items and the test as a whole, and these translate into requirements for the statistical model that one uses to scale the items—these requirements can then be satisfied by using items that adhere to the structure of the Rasch model. Thus, one's philosophy of measurement leads one to use a statistical analysis model that will guide the development and selection of items—the statistical model is being used as a means of quality control of the items. This is in contrast to the most common alternate approach where the statistical model is augmented by parameters that are designed to accommodate the characteristics of the item set—one could say that the statistical model is being used to describe the items.

Thus, in Wilson's words, one person's oversimplification is another person's strong measurement philosophy. Indeed, it is the attachment to a strong measurement philosophy that requires us to choose the Rasch model over others. Of course, others will not agree with us. But how is it that many in the human sciences continue to overlook the basic principle of measurement that children understand as necessary from just after they begin grade school?

—Trevor Bond
—Christine Fox

www.bondandfox.com

CHAPTER ONE

Why Measurement Is Fundamental

For more than half a century we in education, psychology, and the other human sciences have managed to delude ourselves about what measurement actually is. Every day, we rely both explicitly and implicitly on calibrated measurement systems to measure and cut timber, buy lengths of cloth, assemble the correct amounts of ingredients to bake a cake, and to administer appropriate doses of medicine to ailing relatives. So, how is it that when we go to our offices to conduct educational research, undertake some psychological investigation, or implement a standardized survey, we then go about treating and analysing those data as if the requirements for measurement that existed at home in the morning no longer apply in the afternoon? Why do we change our definition of and standards for measurement when the human condition is the focus of our attention?

Measurement systems are ignored when we routinely express the results of our research interventions in terms of either probability levels of $p < 0.01$ or $p < 0.05$, or better yet—effect sizes. Probability levels indicate only that A is more than B, that C is different from B, and effect size is meant to tell us by how much the two samples under scrutiny differ. Recently, a doctoral student was reporting the relationship between children's cognitive development (using a Rasch calibrated test), and their educational achievement based on a set of mandated state tests that have been Rasch calibrated for over two decades. Even though the differences in cognitive development and school achievement could be indicated clearly both in terms of the growth along the Rasch interval scale and in substantive terms according to which new abilities appear at specific Rasch estimated locations, it would have been a fruitless exercise to send the dissertation for examination without reporting those changes in terms of the now ubiquitous effect size estimation.

Instead of focusing on constructing measures of the human condition, psychologists and others in the human sciences have focused on applying sophisticated statistical procedures to their data. Although statistical analysis is a necessary and important part of the scientific process, and the authors in no way would ever wish to replace the role that statistics play in examining relations between

1

variables, the argument throughout this book is that quantitative researchers in the human sciences are focused too narrowly on statistical analysis, and not concerned nearly enough about the quality of the measures on which they use these statistics. Therefore, it is not the authors' purpose to replace quantitative statistics with fundamental measurement, but rather to refocus some of the time and energy used for data analysis on the construction of quality scientific measures.

It is at this point that adherents to Rasch measurement principles wheel out our regular whipping boy, S. S. Stevens (Stevens, 1946). For every one of us who has completed Psychometrics 101 or Quantitative Methods 101, Stevens's lesson remains ingrained forever in our psyche. In short, Stevens defines measurement as the assignment of numbers to objects or events according to a rule; and thereby, some form of measurement exists at each of four levels: nominal, ordinal, interval, and ratio. In spite of Stevens's personal claim to the contrary, we know that ratio-level measurement is likely to be beyond our capacity in the human sciences, but most of us do well enough by regarding the data that we have collected as belonging to interval-level scales. It remains puzzling that those who should set themselves up as scientists of the human condition, especially those in psychological and educational research, should accept, without apparent reflection, the veracity of the Stevens dictum. One reasonably might expect that those who see themselves as social *scientists* would aspire to be open-minded, reflective and, most importantly, critical researchers. In empirical science it would seem that this issue of measurement might be somewhat paramount. However, many attempts to raise these and related issues, the "whether our data constitute measures" issue, result in the abrupt termination of the opportunities for further discussion even in forums specifically identified as focusing on measurement, quantitative methods, or psychometrics. Is the attachment of our field to the Stevens definition of measurement merely another case of the emperor's new clothes? (Stone, 2002).

Measurement in the Stevens tradition chains our thinking to the level of raw data. Under the pretense of measuring, psychologists describe the raw data at hand. They report how many people answered the item correctly (or agreed with the item), how highly related one response is to another, and what the correlation is between each item and total score. These are mere descriptions. Although psychologists generally agree on what routinely counts as "measurement" in the human sciences, this usage cannot replace measurement as it is known in the physical sciences. Yet the flurry of activity surrounding all these statistical analyses, coupled with unbounded faith in the attributions of numbers to events, has blinded psychologists, in particular, to the inadequacy of these methods. Michell (1997) is quite blunt about this in his paper, entitled "Quantitative Science and the Definition of Measurement in Psychology," in which psychologists' "sustained failure to cognize relatively obvious methodological facts" is termed "*methodological thought disorder*" (p. 374).

Did Stevens really discover something special about measurement that has eluded our colleagues in the physical sciences? Will physicists eventually catch up with psychologists and their four levels of measurement? Or is it possible that as scientists specializing in the human sciences we might open our minds to the possibility that we haven't been measuring anything at all? Or if we have, it has been due as much to good intentions and good fortune as to our invocation of appropriate measurement methodology?

It is clear that in the social sciences the term "measurement" has a cachet not shared by the terms "quantitative" or "statistics." Check the response of colleagues if you ask them to forego the former title for either of the latter two. Perhaps we could learn a little about what measurement really entails if we could look at the development of measurement concepts amongst those in whom these developments are still taking place. Part of Jean Piaget's research agenda in Geneva was stimulated by discussions he had in Davos, Switzerland with Albert Einstein during a meeting in 1928 (Ducret, 1990, p. 61; Piaget, 1946, p. *vii*). Einstein counselled Piaget to examine the development of the concepts of speed, distance, and time in young children to see which of those concepts was logically primitive (i.e., if speed = distance/time, which of them could possibly develop before the others?). Piaget went on to examine the progressive construction of the concepts of length (and measurement) in children and reported those findings in 1948 (Piaget, Inhelder, & Szeminska, 1948). Piaget's assistants provided children with sets of materials to use in their investigations and through a series of loosely structured questions, asked children to develop a rudimentary measurement system for the materials (usually wooden dowels) provided.

The authors reported the following temporal and logical sequence in the acquisition of lineal measurement concepts in children:

1. Children classify the supplied objects into a class with at least one common attribute suitable for measurement (e.g., wooden rods) and put aside the rest (e.g., tumbler, ball etc.)

2. The next step is to seriate those selected objects according to the ordinal variation of that attribute (e.g., length).

3. Children then realize it is necessary to identify an arbitrary unit of difference between two successive lengths.(e.g. a small piece of rod, A, such that rod C – rod B = rod A). Their iteration of that unit is used to calculate length relationships, so that rod B = 2 × rod A; and rod B + rod A = rod C. The measurement attempt reveals that the generalized difference between any two adjacent rods, X_n and then next largest $X_{(n+1)}$, is the arbitrary unit, A.

4. In time, each child realizes that iterated units of measurement must be standardized across measurement contexts so all lengths can be measured against a common linear measurement scale.

Of course, it does not take Sherlock Holmes to detect the parallels between the outcomes of the investigations with young children and what we have learned from Stevens in our introductory college classes. For Piaget and the children, the hierarchical developmental sequence is classification, seriation, iteration, and then standardization. For Stevens, it was nominal, ordinal, interval, and ratio. The interesting, but crucial difference—which is well known to mature grade school children and seems to be ignored by many of us in the human sciences—is that *while classification and seriation are necessary precursors to the development of measurement systems, they are not sufficient for measurement.* The distinctive attribute of a measurement system is the requirement for an arbitrary unit of differences that can be iterated between successive lengths. School children are quick to insist that convenient lineal measurement units such as hand width and foot length are inadequate even for classroom projects; they demand the use of a standard length of stick, at least. And it is on this question that devotees of the Rasch models for measurement focus their attention: How do we develop units of measurement, which at first must be arbitrary, but can be iterated along a scale of interest so the unit values remain the same? This is the prime focus for Rasch measurement. The cover of a handout from the Rasch measurement Special Interest Group of the American Educational Research Association bears the motto: "Making Measures." Each cover of the *Journal of Applied Measurement* states the same objective in a different way: "Constructing Variables." It might be a very long time before those of us in the human sciences can happily adopt a genuine zero starting point for the measurement of math achievement or cognitive development, or to decide what zero introversion or prejudice looks like, but those who work painstakingly toward making measures so that the resultant scales have interval measurement properties are making an important contribution to scientific progress. These attempts at the construction of measures go beyond merely naming and ordering indicators towards the perhaps unattainable Holy Grail of genuine ratio measures.

It would not be too far fetched to claim that, in the eyes of some, the failure of traditional quantitative methods in psychology becomes obvious at the iteration of arbitrary unit (interval) phase; the "units" on most scales in the human sciences do not iterate. However, we can't help but infer that the problem is, in part, due to a certain confusion that seems to occur at the earlier classification (nominal) level. This occurs during the selection of the "object" of the quantification process. Most often, the questions, items, or indicators are included for pragmatic reasons, rather than for theoretical reasons; we just want to/have to collect these responses. On the other hand, when little children select those objects that can be measured on one scale, they group together those that have the particular dimension, prior to ordering them. In the human sciences, we have tended to put the indicators that interest us together and have no theory about which is acquired/displayed/achieved first, second or last.

In terms of Stevens's levels, the authors then would conclude that the nominal and ordinal levels are NOT any form of measurement in and of themselves. Admittedly, we concur that his interval and ratio levels actually would constitute genuine measurement, but the scales to which we routinely ascribe that measurement status in the human sciences are merely *presumed* to have measurement properties; those measurement properties are almost never tested empirically. It is not good enough to allocate numbers to human behaviours and then, merely to *assert* that this is measurement in the social sciences.

Up to this point in the chapter, the authors have ignored a crucial aspect of Stevens's definition (because we want to direct particular attention to it). Stevens reminded us that the numerical allocations have to be made "according to a rule," and therein lies the rub. What his definition fails to specify is that scientific measurement requires the allocations to be carried out according to a set of rules that will produce, at minimum, a resultant scale with a unit value that will maintain its value along the whole scale. Numerical allocations made "according to just a(ny) rule" produce many of the very useful indicators of the human condition we habitually use in our research; but only some of those would qualify as "measurement" so defined.

STATISTICS AND/OR MEASUREMENT

One regrettable consequence of the position of Stevens and others on this matter, is that statistical analysis has dominated social sciences to the almost complete exclusion of the concept of measurement. It does not follow that the aim of Rasch measurement proponents is to replace our use of conventional statistics. Rather, the aim is to provide social scientists with the means to produce genuine interval measures and to monitor the adherence of those scales to scientific measurement principles, so that Rasch estimates of ability/attitude/difficulty become the data for statistical analysis. In that way, the interval nature of data—a requirement for many of our most crucial and useful statistical analyses—is made explicit, not merely presumed. While statisticians in the social sciences might tend to resist Rasch measurement claims, the authors' vision of the future will see statistics and measurement playing much more complementary roles in the social sciences. As witnessed by the examples in the first edition of this text, Rasch calibrated scales are already having major impacts in measuring educational outcomes, psychological variables, medical rehabilitation, and standard-setting.

WHY FUNDAMENTAL MEASUREMENT?

Ben Wright (from the University of Chicago) would variously amuse, annoy, provoke, or enlighten members of his audience by taking a folding yard rule from his back pocket to illustrate the points he was making about using Rasch measurement. He would talk about scales in the human sciences as being like a yardstick made of elastic, as having segments made of rubber, or not being straight. The physical measurement analogy was useful both as a model to strive toward, and for exposing the weaknesses of inferior scale building techniques. The yardstick (or meter stick) makes obvious to us the properties of a fundamental measurement scale that is based on the extensive attribute of length. As grade school kids soon discover, they can concatenate lengths to show the additive relations in the physical linear measurement scale; they can put arbitrary "units" or rods together physically to add lengths.

This gives us great power when we match the properties of the system of natural numbers to reflect the iterative relations in adding units lengths together (100 cm. = 1 meter; 1000 m. = 1 kilometer, etc.). Consider how our predecessors used to line up locals to get lineal measures based on "feet" (*pieds* in French) and "thumbs" (imperial inches or *pouces* in French). It is worth checking the human role in the development of physical measures (Stone, 1998); the inordinate political, scientific, and personal difficulties in establishing the basis for the meter (Alder, 2002); and how the process for estimating the height of something as obvious and solid as Mount Everest was hailed "one of the most stupendous works in the whole history of science" even when the team had access to precisely calibrated measuring chains (Keay, 2000).

There are many lessons implied by reading the history behind Ben Wright's ruler. The first is that lots of arbitrary, local measures were used before they became standardized and interchangeable. (No tendentious comments here about how Americans cling to the imperial system of weights and measures, while the rest of the world embraces the metric system!) The second is that even when measures are standardized and apparently sufficiently reliable and precise, iterating the units in context to make estimates of physical size can still be a daunting task. Moral: If we think that making scientific measures in the human sciences is too difficult for us to persist, perhaps we don't know the history of the development of something as simple as the meter stick and how difficult it is to use that simple device for seemingly straightforward measurement tasks. Of course, critics of Ben's ruler analogy argue that we can't physically align bits of the human psyche together to produce measures, as we can with centimeters to make meters.

DERIVED MEASURES

Those in the physical sciences had already discovered that, although fundamental measurement is possible when units can be physically concatenated (as in weight, angles, time, etc.), these scales were in the minority, even in the physical sciences. The additive nature of other physical science measures—and density is an excellent exemplar—has to be discovered indirectly, rather than demonstrated in physical actions on concrete units. Adding one liter of water, mass one kilogram, and a density of one to another identical amount of water will give two liters of water with a mass of two kilograms but the density remains at just one. The units of volume and weight can be physically concatenated but not the unit of density – even though we can be scientifically correct in referring to substances as having twice, three times, or even half or one third the density of water. The density scale is derived from the constant ratio between mass and volume for any substance: 1.0 for pure water, 19.3 for gold, 1.7 for magnesium, and so forth.

So, if density is a derived measure, how did we go about measuring density in our school science classes? Well, if the science curriculum, text, orteacher were sensitive to the developmental bases of children's understanding of science, these experiments would not have taken place until much later than those exercises based on just measuring length, weight, and time. (Piaget discovered that children's conception of volume is constructed later than length, etc., and that density is not likely to be understood before the end of grade school or the start of high school.) So our high school science teacher gave us a collection of objects and had us measure the weight and the volume of each, then enter the values into

TABLE 1.1
Calculations of Density of Materials in Classroom Science Exercise

Mass / Volume	0.2 k	0.4 k	0.6k	0.8k	1.0k	1.2k
0.5 l	.4	.8	1.2	1.6	2.0	2.4
1.0 l	.2	.4	.6	.8	1.0	1.2
1.5 l	.13	.27	.4	.53	.67	.8
2.0 l	.1	.2	.3	.4	.5	.6
2.5 l	.08	.16	.24	.32	.4	.48
3.0 l	.07	.13	.2	.27	.33	.4

the cells of a class table so we could calculate the relative densities: Density = Mass / Volume. And if the teacher knew her job, she would have encouraged us to "discover" for ourselves that the density of any substance (e.g., copper) worked out to be the same, even though the sizes and shapes of copper objects varied considerably from group to group in the class room: Ah! The wonder of discovering not easily detected invariance (density) in the face of such obvious variation (weight and volume)!

Table 1.1 reveals not only the increasing fundamental measurement scale values from left to right in the top row (0.2, 0.4, 0.6 ... 1.2, etc.) and a similar additive scale for volume (0.5, 1.0 ... 3.0) going from top to bottom in the left hand column, but, as well, a derived measurement scale for density increasing diagonally (dotted line) from the lower left hand corner of the table to the top right hand corner.

So the physical scientists have fundamental (physically concatenating) measurement and derived (indirectly detected) measurement to cover all their measurable physical attributes of objects. Importantly for social scientists, in 1940, the Ferguson Committee determined that nothing in the world of psychological quantification had properties of either fundamental or derived physical measurement scales (Ferguson et al., 1940). Our current dependence on Stevens's four levels is indirectly attributable to the critique of those on the committee who espoused the physical science ideas of measurement. Coincidentally and unfortunately, Stevens's own attempts at the measurement of the perception of loudness had attracted the negative attention of the Ferguson committee, and the seminal work of prominent British physicist, N. R. Campbell, was instrumental in dismissing out

8

of hand the claims to scientific measurement of those involved in what we would loosely call psychometrics.

The response of Stevens was to redefine measurement for the benefit of psychologists: "Paraphrasing N.R. Campbell (Final Report, p. 340), we may say that measurement, in the broadest sense, is defined as the assignment of numerals to objects and events according to rules" (Stevens, 1946, p. 667). Stevens appealed to the authority of one of the sternest critics of his position, using what appeared to be reasonable reworkings of Campbell's own quotations to justify Stevens's now familiar, four levels of measurement in psychology: nominal, ordinal, interval, and ratio—each of which constituted some form of measurement.

CONJOINT MEASUREMENT

R. Duncan Luce and his colleagues have shown that both physicist Campbell and psychometrician Stevens were in error. Luce and Tukey (1964) argued that their conception of simultaneous conjoint measurement was a new type of fundamental measurement that subsumed the existing categories of fundamental (e.g., weight, volume) and derived (e.g., density, temperature) measurement from the physical sciences and, more importantly for us, paved the way for detecting measurement structures in non-physical attributes such as psychological constructs. Alluding back to the matrix of densities in Table 1.1, the key to measurement does not reside in the collusion of two fundamental measurement scales of weight and volume to produce a third, derived measurement scale for density which conserves the crucial properties of scientific measurement already inherent in weight and volume. According to Luce and Tukey the crucial indicator of an additive measurement structure in the data (for density and quite likely for some psychological attributes as well) is in the observable relationships between and amongst the matrix cells themselves.

Let's see the potential if we were able to apply some ideas from simultaneous conjoint measurement to an idea from educational or psychological testing. If we have some indicator of the two attributes (or facets) of a testing situation that can be ordered from least to most—let's say, ability of the candidates from least able to most able, and difficulty of the items, from least to most difficult, we could try to check whether the Luce and Tukey interval level scale measurement structures might exist in the ensuing data matrix.

Imagine that Table 1.2 is based on a relevant 100-item test given to a sample of 100 appropriate persons. Along the top row we have ordered some of our persons from the least able on the left (score 1 correct/99 incorrect) to the most able on the right (99 items correct/1 incorrect) and down the left hand column we have ordered our items from the most difficult (only 1 correct response/99 incorrect) to the least difficult (99 correct responses/only 1 incorrect). In essence, what Luce and Tukey require of us is to search Table 1.2 for the patterns of relationships between the cells; the same sorts of relationships that are evident in the weight/volume/density matrix of results for the derived measurement scale example in Table 1.1.

TABLE 1.2
Persons Ordered by Ability (Row) and Items Ordered by Facility (Column)

Items Persons	*p*	*q*	*r*	*s*	*t*	*u*	*v*	*w*	*x*	*y*	*z*	Ability
P												
Q												1/99
R												10/90
S												20/80
T												30/70
U												40/60
V												50/50
W												60/40
X												70/30
Y												80/20
Z												90/10
												99/1
Facility	1/99	10/90	20/80	30/70	40/60	50/50	60/40	70/30	80/20	90/10	99/1	

The mathematical axioms by which a data matrix can be tested for satisfying the requirements of the simultaneous conjoint measurement structures are, as we might imagine, rather complex. Researchers (e.g., Karabatsos, 1999b) work towards writing algorithms for computer software that could automate the processes, but a basic illustration or two might suffice by way of a conceptual introduction. Please take a moment for a fresh look at the relationship between the cells in the density matrix in Table 1.1 to try to find:

   a) What is the relationship between any cell and the one to its right in any row?
   b) What is the relationship between any cell and the one above it in any column?
   c) What is the relationship between any cell and the one diagonally to the right and above it?

Each cell in the density table (Table 1.1) has a value that is *less than*:

   a) the value of the cell to its right in the row (i.e., A < B);
   b) the value of the cell above it in the column (i.e., C < A);
   c) the value of the cell diagonally to the right and above it (i.e., C < B).

A little template summarizing those between-cell relationships can be represented as in Figure 1.1.

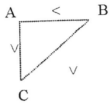

Figure 1.1.   Relationships between adjacent cells in a matrix of measures.

Check back through Table 1.1 for density calculations to see that those 'less than' relations hold between all adjacent pairs of cells as detailed in the template in Figure 1.1. Moreover, all those "less than" relations exist simultaneously.

THE RASCH MODEL FOR MEASUREMENT

Georg Rasch's formulation of his *Probabilistic models for some intelligence and attainment tests* (1960), quite independently of Luce and Tukey, saw the necessity for a similar set of relationships in the data matrix that ensued from using a well-constructed test. The principle he enunciated is delightfully straightforward:

> a person having a greater ability than another person should have the greater probability of solving any item of the type in question, and similarly, one item being more difficult than another means that for any person the probability of solving the second item is the greater one. (Rasch, 1960, p. 117)

A central feature of the Rasch model is a table of expected probabilities designed to address the key question: When a person with this ability (number of test items correct) encounters an item of this difficulty (number of persons who succeeded on the item), what is the likelihood that this person gets this item correct? Answer: The probability of success depends on the difference between the ability of the person and the difficulty of the item.

And this is what makes some Rasch measurement folk really enthusiastic about the scientific measurement possibilities for the Rasch model: the table of expected probabilities (see Table 1.3 for a snippet) generated using Rasch's formulation has the same set of "greater than/less than" relationships between the cells as does the density matrix in Table 1.1.

The Rasch model incorporates a method for ordering persons (e.g., from a sample of school children) according to their ability, and ordering items (e.g., from a diagnostic test of numerical computations) according to their difficulty. The theory of conjoint measurement applies whenever the levels of some attribute increase along with increases in the values of two other attributes. We can see from the snippet in Table 1.3, that levels of one attribute (probability of

TABLE 1.3
Table of Probabilities of Success When Ability Confronts Difficulty

Items Persons	p	q	r	s	t	u	v	w	x	y	z	Ability
P	.500	.866	.924	.949	.963	.973	.980	.986	.991	.995	.999	1/99
Q	.134	.500	.653	.741	.801	.847	.884	.915	.942	.968	.995	10/90
R	.076	.347	.500	.603	.682	.746	.801	.851	.896	.942	.991	20/80
S	.051	.259	.397	.500	.585	.659	.726	.789	.851	.915	.986	30/70
T	.037	.199	.318	.415	.500	.578	.653	.726	.801	.884	.980	40/60
U	.027	.153	.254	.341	.422	.500	.578	.659	.746	.847	.973	50/50
V	.020	.116	.199	.274	.347	.422	.500	.585	.682	.801	.963	60/40
W	.014	.085	.149	.211	.274	.341	.415	.500	.603	.741	.949	70/30
X	.009	.058	.104	.149	.199	.254	.318	.397	.500	.653	.924	80/20
Y	.005	.032	.058	.085	.116	.153	.199	.259	.347	.500	.866	90/10
Z	.001	.005	.009	.014	.020	.027	.037	.051	.076	.134	.500	99/1
Facility	1/99	10/90	20/80	30/70	40/60	50/50	60/40	70/30	80/20	90/10	99/1	

correct response) increase with the values of the two other attributes: item difficulty (facility) and person ability. Then, the purely ordinal relationships between the levels of probabilities are indicative of a quantitative measurement structure for all three. The template relationships from Figure 1.1 that held for the density table in Table 1.1, also apply for the Rasch expected response probabilities in Table 1.3. In fact, the required relationship is not quite so strict; it is "equal to or less than" ($\leq$) rather than just "less than" ($<$). The definitive exposition of the theory of simultaneous conjoint measurement is Krantz, Luce, Suppes, and Tversky (1971). While Narens and Luce (1986) and Michell (1990) provide simpler accounts, the most approachable is that of Michell (2003).

A SUITABLE ANALOGY FOR MEASUREMENT IN THE HUMAN SCIENCES

We can readily see why Ben Wright used a simple ruler (linear measurement) for his measurement analogy rather than the derived density scale. While the measurement principles underlying the ruler are the ideal to which we researchers in the human sciences should aspire, using the ruler as the key analogy does have some drawbacks that are not so helpful for many in the field.

The ruler can be used as an analogy for fundamental measurement only in situations where the actual objects can be physically concatenated. Not only does that seem a little far-fetched to apply to the study of human attributes, it is a principle that cannot work even with derived measures in the physical sciences such as density and temperature. The history of lineal physical measurement is so long and the ruler is so ubiquitous that often we do not readily see the parallels between the problems that befell the scale developers and the measurement problems that we in the human sciences currently face. We presume that the use of such standardized lineal measures is unproblematic and routinely error free, even though just a little reading and thought would reveal otherwise. With the exception of one major country, the use of the metric lineal measurement system is so routine that the progression in calibrations from millimeters, through centimeters, to meters and kilometers is taken for granted—all we need is a long enough ruler, or enough iterations of the shorter ruler.

Might thermometry—the measurement of temperature—be a more useful analogy for those of us who are trying to measure human attributes? The history of the thermometer is much more recent; there are written eye-witness accounts of the earliest efforts of Hookes, Galileo, and others. Temperature is not measured directly but instead is estimated by recording its effects on other substances such as mercury and colored alcohol. Scientists have theories about the way that certain substances behave in response to changes in temperature. We don't use just one prototypical thermometer across all (or even most) temperature measuring situations. In fact, most common thermometers have quite a limited scale range and restricted applications: A medical mercury thermometer is next to useless in the kitchen, unless the cook is thought to be sick. We know we can readily move between degrees Celsius and degrees Fahrenheit, while those with a smattering of high school physics can tell about degrees Kelvin. We understand that 0 °Celsius and 100 °Celsius are set at the freezing and boiling points of water for our convenience, not because these are the scientific ends of the temperature scale. We could start measuring temperatures at 0 °Celsius, Fahrenheit or Kelvin, depending on our purpose, or on a whim. The theory which posits 0 °Kelvin (−273 °Celsius) as absolute zero also suggests that actually measuring absolute zero temperature is itself impossible (Choppin, 1985).

We have no problems (other than feeling too cold) when negative temperatures are recorded: −10 °Celsius or "seven below" doesn't have us baffled about having a negative amount of temperature! No one principle of thermometer construction works across the temperature scale, that is, expanding liquids, bimetallic strips, and changes in electrical conductance all have limited applications. We all can use some thermometers effectively. But others require specialist knowledge and are used in specialist settings. Some quite functional thermometers are as cheap as chips and are virtually given away; others are expensive, delicate, and rarely even imagined by us ordinary folks. We know that any collection of thermometers will vary in their readings, even in the same room at the same time. In high stakes situations, when our child is very ill, we check the child's temperature two or three times in a row to make sure we got it right, but driving home from the hospital we will rely on the car's thermostat to turn on and off at 'round about' the correct temperatures to keep the engine running smoothly. We expect that we will get what we pay for in a thermometer: a couple of bucks for the car engine or the temperature in the living room; a few more bucks to control the temperature in the wine cellar; and a lot more in the operating theater for monitoring core body temperature during major surgery.

Our measurement endeavours in the human sciences might fit better with the thermometry analogy. While the whole scale (cf. temperatures from 0 °K to + ∞) might eventually represent development from before birth (even as far back as conception for some attributes) to death (even beyond for concepts of spirituality), each of us might work on just one small part at a time. The tasks/tests/schedules we develop are likely to be as specialized and as different as an infrared medical thermometer and the thermostat in a 1960 Ford Mustang. Some will be inexpensive and might have low-stakes consequences (just like the household thermometer); others will be high-cost, high-stakes and high maintenance (like that required to monitor and control the core temperature of a nuclear reactor, perhaps). We will acknowledge immediately that the accuracy and the precision of the test are likely to be cost/effort dependent, and that all estimates necessarily have error, but that those qualities will be appropriate to the decision making requirements. The names and sizes of our units might vary (as they do with degrees Celsius, Fahrenheit, and Kelvin). Yet, while many of our indicators will appear remarkably different and function in obviously different ways in a variety of apparently unrelated contexts, the eventual aim will be the calibration of the test and so forth on an underlying interval level measurement scale that has general applicability across a variety of human conditions (as for temperature).

It seems that the problems we have in human sciences for developing, standardizing, and converting measurement scales could appear a lot more tractable when viewed from the perspective of the major advances in thermometry in mere centuries. And the shortcomings of our attempts at scaling have obvious parallels in the variety of thermometers that are regularly in use even though many of them produce readings that are barely "good enough for government work!"

IN SUMMARY

Much is to be gained by learning about and reflecting on the problems that beset the development and scientific use of measurement scales in the physical sciences. Popular accounts by Alder (2002), Keay (2000), and Sobel (1996) are both readable and informative. It's reassuring to know we are not alone in our problems. Moreover, it also helps to understand a little how we came to fall so short of our reasonable expectations for scientific measurement in the human sciences. Michell (1999) provides a very readable account of key players, events, and apparent motivations. He also gives a potted introduction to the relationship between scientific measurement and the ideas of Luce and Rasch (Michell, 2003). While many in Rasch measurement do not agree with all of Michell's prognostications about measurement in our field, he certainly addresses many important issues that we hold in common, but rarely seem considered in other fora in our discipline.

In this chapter, the term *fundamental* was used in two different but equally important ways. Measurement of the sort we use in our daily lives—scales with iterative unit values—is fundamental to logical, empirically-based research in the human sciences. The properties of scientific measurement are most obvious in what is termed fundamental measurement in which attributes such as weight and length can be physically concatenated along the measurement scale. Many measurement scales in the physical scales are derived such that, although the measurement units can be iterated, the attribute itself (e.g, temperature and density) cannot be physically added together.

Luce and his colleagues have outlined the principles and properties of conjoint measurement that would bring the same sort of rigorous measurement to the human sciences as those in the physical sciences have enjoyed for a considerable time. Indeed, the fundamental and derived measurement systems of the physical sciences are special (restricted) cases of conjoint measurement; Luce termed conjoint measurement "a new type of fundamental measurement" (Luce & Tukey, 1964).

The Rasch models for measurement are currently the closest generally accessible approximation of these fundamental measurement principles for the human sciences. Of course, taking such an obviously chauvinistic approach risks alienating many of our colleagues in quantitative approaches to educational and psychological research. Even those completely dedicated to developing and using Rasch calibrated scales sometimes implore us to tread more softly, to be more circumspect, to appear less aggressive. The authors' championing of the Rasch model approach to measurement is not designed to be offensive; confronting, perhaps, but never offensive. It is disconcerting that colleagues who have such high standards for measuring water, cloth, and flour have much lower standards for dealing with math achievement, introversion, or cognitive development.

This book is an invitation (exhortation?) to set impossibly high standards for measurement in human science research and to work incrementally toward achieving those standards. We must remember that landing on the moon was once too far a goal.

CHAPTER TWO

Important Principles of Measurement Made Explicit

Imagine the competitors at an athletic meet as they ready themselves to participate in the high jump event for a state, national, or even international title. The winner, of course, will be the person who clears the highest setting of the cross bar. However, the competition requires the athletes to face a series of progressively higher settings of the cross bar until just the winner is left. This competition considers the difficulty of the jumps in terms of just one quantifiable empirical variable: the height of the bar above the ground. But that is a gross simplification; other variables (factors, facets, dimensions) invariably play a role: the competition surface; the air temperature; the prevailing wind (direction and strength); the relative humidity, or rain; the lighting (brightness, natural or artificial); even, the support (or lack of it) from the audience. What about the ability of the athletes? We take more notice of their latest competition results, than of any other relevant but usually dismissed indicator: each athlete's health status, recent injuries, suppleness relative to that state in other competitions, motivation, confidence, family or other personal circumstances, and so forth. Ignoring most of these influences on difficulty or ability while we try to predict which of the contestants is likely to succeed at each of the jumps in turn, we consider just two key influences for each jump attempt. For the indicator of the relative difficulty of each jump we use just the height of the bar; and for the ability of the athlete we refer only to the most recent results in competition. Interestingly, both the difficulty and the ability are expressed on the same scale: the meter scale of linear measure—ignoring all other likely influences.

If we could predict perfectly each outcome when a variety of athletes face a variety of jumps, we wouldn't even bother to hold the competition; we could award the medals on some summary of recent high jump performances. However, we cannot predict perfectly each athlete's performance, but we can make probabilistic estimates based on past performance. As the athlete lines up to jump each time the bar is raised, a group of spectators in the grandstand might like to estimate the chances each jumper has at being successful at each jump. They might consider all the variables mentioned above in estimating the probability of success for each attempt, but it is highly likely they would use only a few pieces of information in order to ease their cognitive load. Most likely, they would express their predictions in terms of chances/odds/probabilities rather than just "definitely will/ will not succeed." For example, they might make statements such as, "More than 50%"; "Less than 50%;" "Almost impossible to fail/succeed;" "Ah, about 60:40, I think!" We as researchers could make these predictions by making a simple calculation: Take the current jump height (jump difficulty, expressed in meters), the contestant's last competition result (athlete's ability, expressed on the same scale in meters) and compare the two. If jump difficulty and athlete ability (as estimated above) were the same, we could predict success: fail odds at 50:50, or, 50% probability of a successful attempt. As the ability of the jumper exceeds the difficulty of the jump (calculated on the simple meter scale alone), we would predict odds more and more in favor of success (60%, 70%, 85%)—according how big the ability—difficulty distance is in favor of the athlete (1cm, 2cm, 3cm). If the calculation shows the athlete to be at a disadvantage in the ability – difficulty comparison (e.g., –1cm, –2cm, –3cm, etc.), our predictions will decrease (to 40%, 30%, 15%, etc.) But few serious pundits would predict 0% or 100% for any competitive athlete for any reasonable competition height: Athletes we think of as certainties fail often enough, and a competitor with just an outside chance upsets the predictions often enough that we must make allowances for such human foibles.

Although this book emphasizes a particular version of one approach to the quantitative analyses of data from the human sciences, it raises a number of problems and principles endemic to the investigation of almost any human performance. The human abilities and task difficulties which we observe in the human sciences cannot be reduced conveniently to locations on existing scientific measurement scales (such as the meter scale in the high jump example). It seems reasonable to suggest that both qualitative and quantitative analyses of human observations are designed to yield summaries of those observations. The aim is to produce a shortened account of the results from the investigation sufficient to communicate the essence of the empirical data in a meaningful, useful, and valid way. Although it currently is the fashion to criticize quantitative approaches to developmental, psychological, and other human research for their reductionism, it is obvious that all summarizing methods do more or less injury to the phenomena under investigation, just as in the case of the high jump competition.

Admittedly, the summary of any complex human behavior in exclusively quantitative terms makes the reductionism obvious to all but the most hardened empiricist. The written summary of the same act in several sentences, or even paragraphs, also misses the mark in similar but perhaps less obvious ways. Neither Robert Parker's score of 93/100 nor a paragraph of suitably purple prose can capture adequately the experience of tasting an extraordinary wine. Each misses the point completely. But each summary (quantitative or qualitative) can summarize effectively aspects of the experience sufficiently for others to be tempted into purchasing and drinking a bottle of the same wine!

As we try to record an event to share with others, the original experience is damaged in a multitude of ways: via the orientation of the investigator, the adequacy of the observation schedule, the validity of the observations, and the completeness of the set of observations, and all this, before we look at the adequacy of the particular analytical devices along with the care and rigor of their use. The very act of focusing on any aspect of human experience immediately relegates all other aspects toward oblivion. The authors would argue that both quantitative and qualitative approaches have the same starting point: in observation. The extent of this common ground becomes evident in later chapters, where a synthesis of quantitative and qualitative approaches is demonstrated.

"All that can be observed is whether or not the specified event occurs, and whether the data recorder (observer or respondent) nominates (any particular) category as their observation" (Wright, 1996, p. 3). This is the basis of the results for all our investigations. In the grandstand we watch the athlete attempt the height of 1.75 meters and summarize all the drama, all the effort, as merely success or failure; green light/red light; ✔ or X. The test candidate might tick "false" on a response sheet, write a paragraph, or produce a journal. The observer might record that an appropriate word was inserted into a space in a sentence, note that "a" was the correct response to Item 17, or compose a particular phrase or statement to correspond to an identified segment of a video or journal record. In essence, all of our observations can be so depicted, whether qualitative or quantitative analyses are intended.

In the case of simple observations, the investigator might make a qualitative decision about whether the event was absent or present, whether it did or did not occur. As part of a more complex schedule, the investigator might decide whether a particular event was absent, whether it occurred to some extent or to a greater extent, or whether a complete display of the appropriate behavior was observed. In this way, all of our investigatory observations are qualitative, and the classification or identification of events deals with data at the nominal level. Nominal level data: We observe just those events that are the focus of our enquiry and not others. Ordinal level data: We record which of those observed events is better than another. When we start counting these events or observations, we apply numerical values to these events. This counting is the beginning of an expressly quantitative approach. Even in the first instance (presence/absence), we are dealing with ordinal data because we hold the presence of an event (a tick, a mark in the correct box, a "yes") as more valuable than the absence of that event (a cross, a mark in the wrong box, or a "no"). In the second instance (none/some/more/all) our data are much more evidently ordinal. Our counting of observations or events always remains on those levels. It is our attempt to make meaningful measures of those observations that constructs an interval scale, in which the distances between counts are made equal and meaningful. As a consequence, any analytical model that implicitly or explicitly makes assumptions about "interval" or "ratio" relations between the data points does so unjustifiably. Wright and Linacre (1989) developed these points more fully.

Recognizing the presence/absence of behavior and ordering observations along a none/some/more/all continuum presumes that some underlying theory is guiding those observations. Unfortunately, for many researchers in the human sciences, that theory often remains as implicit. Much of the research reported as exemplars in this volume shares common origins in expressly articulated explicit psychological theories. The researchers took to heart the advice of two of Piaget's closest *collaborateur*: If you want to get ahead, get a theory (Karmiloff-Smith & Inhelder, 1975).

Any investigator's record of qualitative observations represents nominal categories; focusing on some thing(s) and ignoring others. The investigator might then score these observations to organize them into a stepwise order of precedence according to the theoretical model used to generate the observational schedule. This presumption or expectation of meaningful ordering of data is at the very heart of any of those conceptions of humans that have developmental origins.

As a useful starting point, quantitative summarizing of qualitative observations can be achieved by simply assigning 1 (or ✔) for the presence of an occurrence and 0 (or X) for its absence, so that the data summary for Person A across all items is recorded as a row:

A 111000011001 or ✔✔✔XXXX✔✔XX✔

The data summary for Item d across all persons is recorded as a column:

d		
0	or	X
1		✔
0		X
1		✔
0		X
1		✔
0		X
0		X
1		✔
1		✔
0		X
0		X
0		X
0		✔

A teacher's record book or a complete record of a sample's performances on the items of a developmental test could look just like this. Typically, our preference for focusing on the performance of the persons, rather than investigating the performance of the items, has us rushing to express the results of the investigation as a raw score total for each person. We often do not make even that same crude summary for items. Therefore, in the matrix shown as Table 2.1, the last column entry for each person is the total raw score. The practice of using the raw score as the estimate of a person's ability on a test is ubiquitous in the human sciences.

TABLE 2.1

Data Matrix for 14 Selected Persons (A–N) on 12 Selected Items (a–l)

Persons	a	b	c	d	e	f	g	h	i	j	k	l	Raw Score
						Items							
A	✔	✔	✔	X	X	X	X	✔	✔	X	X	✔	6
B	✔	X	✔	✔	X	X	X	X	✔	X	X	X	4
C	✔	✔	✔	X	✔	X	X	✔	✔	✔	✔	✔	9
D	✔	X	✔	✔	X	X	X	X	✔	X	X	✔	5
E	X	✔	✔	X	X	✔	X	✔	✔	✔	✔	✔	8
F	✔	✔	✔	✔	X	X	X	✔	✔	X	X	✔	7
G	✔	X	✔	X	X	✔	X	X	✔	X	✔	✔	6
H	✔	X	✔	X	X	X	X	X	X	X	X	✔	3
I	✔	✔	✔	✔	X	X	X	✔	✔	X	X	✔	7
J	✔	✔	✔	✔	✔	✔	✔	✔	✔	X	✔	X	10
K	✔	X	✔	X	X	✔	X	X	✔	X	✔	✔	6
L	X	✔	✔	X	X	✔	X	✔	✔	✔	✔	✔	8
M	X	X	X	X	X	X	X	X	X	X	X	X	0
N	✔	✔	✔	✔	✔	✔	✔	✔	✔	✔	✔	✔	12

In keeping with a guiding principle adopted for the writing of this book, the authors have selected from some data actually collected to answer substantive questions from developmental or educational psychology. The data for chapter 2 are taken from a classroom mathematics test generated by a group of primary school teachers (Bond, 1996; Parkinson, 1996; Bond & Parkinson, 2007). The test was designed to make explicit the school's curriculum requirements for dealing with area-based concepts. Questions at the lower level required students to color the surface of, say, a square. Others required computations based on formulas such as area = length × breadth, and area = side^2. Advanced skills were tested by questions requiring calculations based on several formulas, added or subtracted, to give area measures of complex figures.

What then might we infer from the data matrix shown in Table 2.1? Of course, we can see that quite a range of person performances, from 0/12 (all wrong, Person M) to 12/12 (all correct, Person N), is evident. However, from this information alone, we cannot immediately draw any conclusions about the items, or about the interactions between the items and the persons.

Because the following steps (often implicit or omitted) can show us a lot about our data and introduce some crucial features of Rasch analysis, we should take each of them in turn. The authors would argue that researchers (and teachers) could learn a great deal about their testing procedures merely by taking time to inspect their raw data regularly in the following fashion. A simple spreadsheet on a microcomputer will do the job. The data matrix (i.e., the result of the theory-driven

TABLE 2.2

Selected Data Matrix With Persons Arranged According to Ability
(From Top to Bottom) and Items Arranged by Facility (From Left to Right)

Persons	c	i	a	l	b	h	k	d	f	j	e	g	Ability
N	✔	✔	✔	✔	✔	✔	✔	✔	✔	✔	X	✔	12
J	✔	✔	✔	X	✔	✔	✔	✔	✔	X	X	✔	10
C	✔	✔	✔	✔	✔	✔	✔	X	X	✔	✔	X	9
E	✔	✔	X	✔	✔	✔	✔	X	✔	✔	X	X	8
L	✔	✔	X	✔	✔	✔	✔	X	✔	✔	✔	X	8
I	✔	✔	✔	✔	✔	✔	X	✔	X	X	X	X	7
F	✔	✔	✔	✔	✔	✔	X	✔	X	X	✔	X	7
K	✔	✔	✔	✔	X	X	✔	X	✔	X	X	X	6
A	✔	✔	✔	✔	✔	✔	X	X	X	X	X	X	6
G	✔	✔	✔	✔	X	X	✔	X	✔	X	X	X	6
D	✔	✔	✔	✔	X	X	X	✔	X	X	X	X	5
B	✔	✔	✔	X	X	X	X	✔	X	X	X	X	4
H	✔	X	✔	✔	X	X	X	X	X	X	X	X	3
M	X	X	X	X	X	X	X	X	X	X	X	X	0
Facility	13	12	11	11	8	8	7	6	6	3	3	2	

qualitative observations) can be arranged so that the items are ordered from least to most difficult and the persons are ordered from least to most able (Table 2.2). This organized data table is termed a Scalogram (Guttman, 1944). The higher up the table one goes, the more able the persons (Person N: 12/12). The further right across the table one goes, the more difficult the items (Item g: only two persons are successful). The table then reveals some properties about the observations that will help to guide future data collection and the data analysis.

The simple task of ordering data from least to most occurrences (for persons and for items) is likely to show that the theoretical model used for the collection of the qualitative observations has not produced results entirely as anticipated. Usually, the first use of a test will not yield a complete set of distinctively useful observations. In the case of the observation schedule or items, some items might have no observations of presence (i.e., all zeroes were recorded, meaning every child "failed" on that item). Other items might not discriminate between the persons in the sample observed (i.e., all ones were recorded, meaning every child "passed" on that item). These items should be dropped temporarily from that data set because they are not useful discriminators of the substantive sequence under investigation with this particular sample. Subsequently, these items should be examined closely and perhaps improved, omitted, or used in other appropriate scales or with other samples.

Similarly, some persons might have no observations showing presence of the anticipated behaviors (all zeroes, meaning they "fail" all items; e.g., person M), or they might be more capable than this observation schedule predicted (all ones, meaning they "pass" all items; e.g., Person N). The results for these persons should be dropped temporarily also as inadequate. It is not possible to make satisfactory descriptions showing the progress of these persons along the continuum revealed by this qualitative observation schedule. All we can conclude definitively is that the persons had either too little ability to score on this test or more ability than needed for this test.

This procedure is not meant to disregard our intention to record that one child got everything right, or that another failed on all items for a particular sample or purpose. Rather, it reminds us that these results are quite insufficient for estimating ability. It should tell us that next time, when we construct subsequent versions of such a test, we will need to include some easier as well as some more difficult items of this sort to cover properly the range of abilities shown in a sample such as the one under investigation.

The authors' claim is that qualitative inspection of the data is a necessary prerequisite to meaningful quantitative analysis and, hence, should always precede it. We have discovered already how valuable information about the match or mismatch between the persons observed and the items used to observe them could guide our next investigation of this ability. We have been cautioned about the inadequate information we have about persons (in this case, Persons M and N). Strictly speaking, we temporarily should remove these cases from the data matrix and follow up with some extra data collection for these two. It is now revealed that we have some less-than-useful items (in this case, Item c). With the nonscoring Person M removed from the matrix, Item c is correctly answered by all. It might be a useful item for less able children, but not for this sample. For our next use of this test, we also have a guide to the difficulty level of further useful items.

The next step is to calculate item difficulties and person abilities (expressed as the fraction n/N, the item or person raw score divided by the total possible score). These fractions show more readily the ordinal relations among abilities on the one hand and among difficulties on the other, allowing us to make crude comparisons between the dispersions of difficulties and abilities in the observations (Table 2.3). The routine procedure in education circles is to express each of these n/N fractions as a percentage and to use them directly in reporting students' results. We will soon see that this commonplace procedure is not justified. In keeping with the caveat we expressed earlier, these n/N fractions should be regarded as merely orderings of the nominal categories, and as insufficient for the inference of interval relations between the frequencies of observations.

Just as theories about humans would predict, the data displayed in Table 2.3 show substantial variation in the presence of the targeted ability in the sample observed. They also show considerable variation in the facility or difficulty of the items that represent the observation schedule. Indeed, the very concept of a variable has variation at its heart. Immediately, the developmental nature of these observations is obvious in the way the presence of the observations (1s) change to

TABLE 2.3
Selected Ordered Data Matrix for Items
and Persons With Sufficient Information

Persons	i	a	l	b	h	k	d	f	j	e	g	Ability	n/N%
						Items							
J	1	1	0	1	1	1	1	1	0	1	1	9	82
C	1	1	1	1	1	1	0	0	1	1	0	8	73
E	1	0	1	1	1	1	0	1	1	0	0	7	64
L	1	0	1	1	1	1	0	1	1	0	0	7	64
I	1	1	1	1	1	0	1	0	0	0	0	6	55
F	1	1	1	1	1	0	1	0	0	0	0	6	55
K	1	1	1	0	0	1	0	1	0	0	0	5	45
A	1	1	1	1	1	0	0	0	0	0	0	5	45
G	1	1	1	0	0	1	0	1	0	0	0	5	45
D	1	1	1	0	0	0	1	0	0	0	0	4	36
B	1	1	0	0	0	0	1	0	0	0	0	3	27
H	0	1	1	0	0	0	0	0	0	0	0	2	18
Facility	11	10	10	7	7	6	5	5	3	2	1		
n/N%	93	83	83	58	58	50	42	42	25	17	08		

absences (0s) in the direction of increasing difficulty of the items (→) and in the direction of decreasing ability of the persons (↓).

Even at this level, the arrangements of some data points should cause us to reflect on the nature of these children's development made evident by these empirical manifestations of the underlying theoretical ideas. We should focus now on the patterns of success and failure revealed in the data matrix. Only of passing concern is the evidence showing that the intersection of the patterns of "success" and "difficulty" has a small zone of unpredictability associated with it. Typically, 1s do not change to 0s in a rigid, steplike fashion, either for persons or for items. It is reasonable to suggest that this pattern of responses reflects recently acquired or yet-to-be consolidated developmental abilities that might not be fully reliable in their display. Therefore, the data contained in the shaded cells of Table 2.3 should delay us no further.

Unlike the data patterns that display small zones of unpredictability, "unexpected" observations of presence (1) or absence (0) that seem more out of place (cells with data in bold type) are of greater concern. These unexpected observations will be of greater or lesser concern depending on their number and their location in the data matrix. Persons who score well on difficult items despite low overall total scores might have done so by guessing or cheating. Similarly, poor scores on easy items despite high overall total scores might indicate lack of concentration or guessing. Of course, the presence of other unexpected idiosyncratic circumstances, including particular person–item interactions, is always a possibility. Think of the high jump competition again. When the champion misses an early, easy jump or two, we suspect that it is due to nerves, or that the champ didn't take the jump seriously. For the past plodder who succeeds beyond all expectations, we might attribute that success to a new jumping technique, altered training regimes, or even chemical assistance. However unlikely such unexpected athletic performances are (based on the records), they are not impossible.

This brings to our attention an important principle guiding our use and interpretation of observational schedules and tests. Although some students (see Student A) perform in a strictly orderly fashion (raw score of 5 for Student A means exactly the 5 easiest items correct and the 6 hardest items incorrect), our observations of most human behaviors rarely show rigid steplike patterns of progression. The vagaries of our observational abilities, and those of human performance, ensure that rigid adherence to even precisely defined developmental sequences is the exception rather than the rule.

Similarly, Items that precisely separate more able from less able students, as Items i, e, and g appear to do, also are rare. It is more plausible that the sequence will be more or less predictable: that the likelihood of getting any question correct increases in line with the person's raw score. Of course, the lower a person's raw score is, the lower the likelihood of the person getting any question correct, or of meeting any of the observational criteria. Predicting success or failure is most hazardous where the 0s meet the 1s for any student. Obviously, in such cases, the response is almost equally likely to be successful or unsuccessful. A prediction of success is determined by how far the item is embedded in the student's zone of success. The further the item is embedded in the student's zone of success (the 1s), the more likely it is that the student will succeed on that item. Conversely, the likelihood of failure increases the further the item is embedded in the student's zone of failure (the 0s).

The pattern for Person A is almost too good to be true, but a closer look at the response patterns of the students gaining raw scores of 6 or 7 is illuminating. The patterns for Persons I and F are quite orderly enough according to the general principle of increased likelihood of success and failure just outlined. How could anyone who has sat for or written a test quibble about the little reversal of Items k and d? The response patterns for Persons E and L, however, do not match our expectations as easily. Although the unexpected failure on Item d might be overlooked, the unexpected failure on very easy Item a starts us wondering whether Person E's and Person L's understandings of area are directly comparable with those of C and I. However, we are not likely to be so equivocal when we try to interpret the success/failure patterns of Person K. The responses of Person K are so erratic and unpredictable in comparison with the general orderliness that is evident in the rest of the data matrix that it would be unfair to say that a raw score of 5 is a fair summary of Person K's ability to solve area problems.

The same argument can be applied just as readily to the performance patterns of items or observations. Responses to Items b and h seem orderly enough. It is possible to predict with a good deal of success any student's overall likelihood of doing well or poorly on the whole area test just by looking at that student's performance on Items b and/or h. But in looking at Item *d*, we see that it is not only a more difficult item but that the responses to it are so erratic, it is practically impossible to predict who will be successful with it and who will not. Success on Item d should be highly predictable for about the most able one third of the group, but the response pattern tells us that the difficulty rating for this item (0.42) cannot be taken at face value: High scorers C, E, and L failed on Item d, whereas low scorers D and B were successful. Now, the failure by C, E, and L on Item d might be due to those persons or due to Item d. The data themselves can't tell us. But since we note that d has more problems (unexpected performances on it) than do the persons, we would investigate Item d first. Something else is going on with this item, something different from the general response pattern that we see in the whole data matrix for area.

The next part of this procedure shows the inadequacy of treating raw scores of ability and difficulty directly as measurement scales. To illustrate the point, the ability fractions have been taken from Table 2.3 and their locations plotted along a continuum to see how the items and persons disperse (Fig. 2.1, left). Of course, the raw score fraction (0.45) corresponds exactly to the same raw score expressed as a percentage (45%). Many teachers and university professors would recognize the pattern shown for person abilities. They regularly see their students' results in this format as they go through the process of assigning grades. However, it is much less common for teachers or researchers to give even this very basic treatment to the test questions they use to produce these student grades.

The problem with using raw score fractions or percentages is that this procedure tends to clump students around the middle scores and does not adequately contrast the results of the more able and less able students. Earning a few extra marks near the midpoint of the test results, say from 48 to 55, does not reflect the same ability leap required for a move from 88 to 95 at the top of the test or from 8 to 15 at the bottom. The real problem here is that we routinely mistake the distances between fraction or percentage scores as having direct meaning, when all we really may infer from these data is the ordering of the persons or the items. We need a sound way of interpreting the size of the gaps between the scores, so that we are able to say, for example, "Betty shows more ability than Bill on this test, and by this much."

A simple mathematical procedure for better representing the relative distances between the raw scores has been available since the work of Thurstone in the 1920s. This procedure involves converting a raw score summary to its natural logarithm. Although such mathematical transformations to produce linear measures abound in the physical sciences, we have tended to avoid them, or even to be suspicious of them, in the human sciences; for example, the pendulum swing (http://web.mit.edu/aa-math/www/modules/node8.html). In addition to transforming the score from a merely ordinal scale to a mathematically more useful interval scale, a log odds scale avoids the problem of compression at the ends of the raw score scale due to its restricted range, leading to floor and ceiling effects. (Log odds: a *log*arithmic transformation of the *odds* of success.)

The first step in this procedure is to convert the raw score percentage into its success-to-failure ratio or odds. A raw score of 60% becomes odds of 60 to 40; 90%

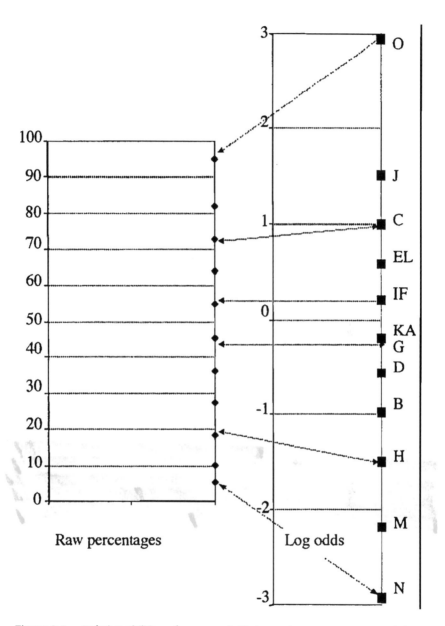

Figure 2.1. Relative abilities of persons A–H shown in raw percentages (left) and as log odds (right). More extreme persons' locations (M = 10%, N = 5%, and O = 95%) are added for purposes of illustration only.

becomes 90 to 10; 50% becomes 50 to 50; and so on. Then a spreadsheet command, or even many handheld calculators, can perform the elementary function of converting scores to their natural log odds. For Person L (64% or odds of 64 to 36), we enter 64/36, push the log function, and read off the result (+0.58). Try a few of these to get the hang of it: Ability odds of 55 to 45 for Person F become a log value of +0.20, and the odds of 45 to 55 for Person G become a value of –0.20. Using the data from the matrix, try a few other values or use a more familiar set of results to see what happens. Georg Rasch based his own work on this type of approximation (e.g., Rasch, 1980, p. 97).

We have included the logarithmic transformation of the person data on the righthand side of Figure 2.1. The relative placements (i.e., the ordinal relations) are, of course, the same as those on the left. The all-important order remains exactly the same. However, looking at the positions for the lower achievers on this test (those below the 50% level), we can observe that the distances between the person locations have been stretched out.

The distances between Persons D, B, and H (each only one raw score apart) are now considerably larger than the gaps between Persons F, L, and C (each one raw score apart as well). Now the scale we have for plotting the person and item locations approximates an interval scale, whereby the value of the scale is maintained at any position along that scale. It is only with an interval scale that we can begin to say how much more able Betty is than Bill, instead of merely saying that she is more able. Moreover, the effect becomes much more marked if we introduce some more extreme person abilities into these figures: A person with a 95% raw score becomes located at +2.94 on the log ability scale, whereas the low score of 10% translates as –2.2 and 5% becomes –2.94. The argument is that this wider distribution of person locations more fairly represents the increase in ability required to move from a score of 90% to a score of 95% as considerably greater than the ability difference between, say, a score of 50% and a score of 55%. This log-odds transformation of our raw data is a first approximation of the Rasch measurement scale that is the focus of this book. The Rasch model is an interesting model in that it follows from a small set of assumptions. The basic Rasch assumptions are that (a) each person is characterized by an ability, and (b) each item by a difficulty which (c) can be expressed by numbers along one line. Finally, (d) from the difference between the numbers (and nothing else) the probability of observing any particular scored response can be computed.

Up to this point, we have attempted to show that for a model to be useful for investigating aspects of the human condition represented in developmental and other theories, it needs to incorporate the following properties:

> It should be sensitive to the ordered acquisition of the skills or abilities under investigation (i.e., it should aim at uncovering the order of development or acquisition).
> It should be capable of estimating the developmental distances between the ordered skills or persons (i.e., it should tell us by how much Person T is more developed, more capable, or more rehabilitated than is Person S).

It should allow us to determine whether the general developmental pattern shown among items and persons is sufficient to account for the pattern of development shown by every item and every person.

The reader will not be very much surprised if we now go on to demonstrate that analyses based on Rasch measurement are particularly suited to investigations in the wide range of human sciences on exactly these grounds.

CHAPTER THREE

Basic Principles of the Rasch Model

This chapter presents a pathway analogy to explain the basic concepts of the Rasch model. Although the analogy is obviously and directly applicable to observations in developmental psychology, its relevance for the other measurement situations in the human sciences in which the Rasch model should be used is detailed in the following chapters. The high jump exemplar from the previous chapter will also be useful in introducing a formal statement of the Rasch model as well as the ideas of the Rasch item characteristic curve (ICC).

THE PATHWAY ANALOGY

Let us imagine a segment in children's development, such as the progressive attainment of the skills in drawing a reasonable human form or the progress toward realizing that two differently shaped glasses contain the same amount of juice. Although our underlying developmental theory for either of these two examples might define a single sequence of development that could be represented by the arrow in Figure 3.1, we would not expect our recorded observations of the development to be as perfect or precise as a straight line. Instead, what we need to be able to do is build a measurement tool (a set of tasks, a list of assessment criteria, or a series of questions) that will be empirically useful enough in practice to make a meaningful assessment of children's development of that ability.

What then will be good enough? Such a tool must represent our best effort to acknowledge both the role of that straight line in measurement theory and the diversions from this straight path that exist in the empirical reality of practice. Only the user will be able to tell that by experience, but the criteria by which usefulness can be gauged are built into the Rasch model and demonstrated in our analogy.

Whereas the arrow represents the unattainable ideal, the circular stepping-stones in Figure 3.1 represent a selection of the items (L, M, N, ... , U) in our test

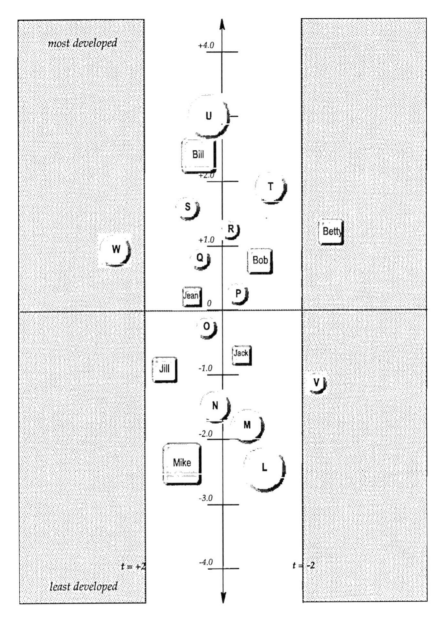

Figure 3.1   Developmental pathway for selected ersatz persons and items.

or observation schedule. The steps at the bottom of the path will suit the beginners, and those at the top will be reached only by the most developed children. Therefore, the different intermediary stepping-stones along the way will be useful for the varied levels of development we expect among the test takers. The distance of the step from the bottom of the path (A) represents its difficulty relative to the other items. This is our representation of item difficulty: Closer to the bottom is easier, further is more difficult. The idea is that each child will progress along the steps as far as the child's ability (development) will carry him or her. The child will use (master) the steps until the steps become too difficult. How far any child moves along the pathway will be our estimate of the child's development or ability. We have used little squares to represent how far each of the children has moved along the pathway. This is our representation of person ability.

This map of item and person relationships we have used to represent the pathway analogy contains a lot of basic information that is central to Rasch measurement, but which can be gleaned readily by attending to the basic difficulty/ability concepts mentioned earlier. Please look carefully at Figure 3.1 and try to answer the following questions (with reasons). All the answers can be derived directly from the figure without any extra knowledge of Rasch modelling. First, take a look at the positions of the round stepping-stones (item locations).

Is Item S (much) more difficult or (much) less difficult than Item N?
Which item is the most likely to be failed by the students?
Which item is the most likely to be passed by the students?

Now take a look at the positions of the squares that represent the person locations on the pathway (the item–person map of abilities and difficulties). With the Rasch model, the principles about items work with exactly the same logic for persons. According to the pathway representation of these data in Figure 3.1,

Is Bill (much) more able or (much) less able than Bob?
Which student is revealed as least able on this test?
Is Bill likely to have answered Item U correctly?
What would be more unexpected, that Bill will miss Item S or Item M?
Mike scored 1 on the test. Which item is most likely to be the one he got right?

The dotted lines in Figure 3.1, where white meets shaded, are meant to represent the edges of the pathway. Stepping-stones within these boundaries can be seen as useful steps on this particular pathway. Locations outside the boundaries must be interpreted cautiously—just as we would when stepping off a pathway into rougher country. Therefore,

Which items are not usefully located on the pathway in their present forms?
Which person is traveling to the beat of a different drum?
Is Bob's ability well measured by this test?
Jill scored 3 on the test. Which items did she most likely answer correctly?

From the representation of persons and items on the map, Item S is much more difficult than Item N, whereas Item U is the toughest on this test. Most of these children will not succeed on Item U. Item L, however, is very easy, in fact, the easiest on this test. Most children will get Item L correct. The map shows that Bill is considerably more able than Bob on this test. There is a fair-sized gap between the two. Bill is not likely to have succeeded on Item U. Persons who succeed on Item U usually need more ability than Bill shows. Bill has much more ability than required to succeed on Item M. For Bill, missing Item M would be a rare, but not impossible, event. However, because Item S is much tougher, much closer to Bill's ability level, we should not be surprised if Bill misses Items such as Item S from time to time.

Stepping-stones V and W are not located well enough on our pathway to be useful as they are, whereas Betty has not used the pathway in the same manner as the others. Bob's location fits well between the dotted control lines, indicating he has performed according to the model's expectations and thus is well measured. Jill is most likely to have succeeded with Items L, M, and N. Her location shows that she is more able than necessary to answer Items L, M, and N correctly at most administrations of this test.

In developing any test, our aim would be to put enough stepping-stones along the path to represent all the stepping-points useful for our testing purposes, between little development (A) and much development (Z). Of course, to do that, we would need to collect observations from enough suitable persons. Good data analysis requires more items and many more persons than we have included in Figure 3.1. We have merely selected some illustrative examples here. Also, with our emphasis on building and defining a pathway, we have concentrated on items and (unforgivably) tended to ignore persons at this point. Let us now turn our attention to some specific ideas and guidelines that will aid us in accomplishing this task.

Unidimensionality

Underlying the ideas about measuring development that have been raised so far is an important implicit principle. Unfortunately, this principle is so taken for granted in our use of measurement tools for size, weight, temperature, and the like that when it is made explicit, it causes concern for researchers in the human sciences who perhaps have not thought the matter through. In attempting to measure the physical attributes of objects, people, or the weather, scientists and laypeople alike take care to measure just one attribute of the target at a time. A rectangular solid has many attributes (e.g., length, breadth, height, weight, volume, density, and even hardness, to name a few), but all attempts to make meaningful estimations of the object under scrutiny focus on only one attribute at a time. This focus on one attribute or dimension at a time is referred to as *unidimensionality*.

Similarly, for people, height, weight, age, waist measurement, and blood pressure all are estimated separately. Perhaps we could envision a new scale for person size that incorporated both height and girth by starting with a tape measure at the toes, winding it around the left knee and right hip, under the left armpit, and up behind the head. No doubt we could become well practiced and reasonably accurate in making this measurement. We could perhaps even find some uses for it. But people designing airplane seats, hotel beds, and hatchways in submarines would soon revert to taking independent measures of, say, height and width in a sample of intended users, in which the dimensions are not confused with one another.

Another analogy illustrates confusions that can occur when two measures are confounded into one estimate. As we all know, the general practice for clothing manufacturers has been to establish sizes for their products to help consumers choose appropriate garments. This type of estimation system for determining generic shoe size as 9, 9½, 10, and so on confounds the two important attributes of shoe and foot size: the length and the width. On the other hand, for example, there have been very popular sizing systems for shoes in the United Kingdom, the United States, and Australia based on an alternative "fractional fitting" principle in which all shoes come in a variety of lengths and widths: 9A (quite narrow) . . . 9C . . . 9EE (very wide indeed). A little knowledge and experience with this system, in which the two key attributes, length and breadth, are estimated and reported separately, allows for much more confidence in predicting shoe size suitability.

The fractional fitting system has given way under the pressures of mass production, but one major U.S. running-shoe manufacturer boasts its "many widths for every shoe length" models, and specialist shoe manufacturers still use the system. However, even this system has its problems. For one, our confidence in this measurement system is lessened when, in certain situations, we determine that a particular shoe does not match the expectations we have of the shoe size scale. Similarly, the feet of some individuals do not match the model adequately, so that every shoe-buying attempt remains a tortuous, almost arcane process that relies more on persistence and chance than on anything at all "scientific."

Of course, even something as apparently simple as human foot and shoe size is oversimplified by the fractional fitting focus on length and width dimensions. Athletes, medical rehabilitation patients, and others who have specialist shoe needs, also take into account the height of the foot arch, the curve of the sole, and the height of the heel to get a better compromise between foot and shoe. Foot size is remarkably complex, and a single size scale that confuses length and width means "try before you buy" every time, even with sandals. Estimating the length and width dimensions separately makes the foot–shoe match much easier for most. It is sufficient for the task most of the time. Even so, we all recognize that foot size, like most physical and psychological attributes, is always much more complex than what we can capture through separate estimates of distinct attributes. Although the complexity of what we are measuring appears to be lost, it is through measuring one attribute at a time that we can develop both useful and meaningful composite descriptions.

We all are aware that the complexity of human existence can never be satisfactorily expressed as one score on any test. We can, however, develop some useful quantitative estimates of some human attributes, but we can do that only for one attribute or ability at a time. Confusing a number of attributes into a single generic score makes confident predictions from that score more hazardous and the score a less useful summary of ability or achievement. But carefully constructed tests that make good measurement estimates of single attributes might be sufficient for a number of thoughtfully decided purposes. For special or difficult situations, collecting additional estimates of other appropriate attributes is essential. Of course, qualitative data might be used to complement the quantitative results. Human beings are complex, multidimensional creatures to be sure. But whereas using height as a measure of a person is an obvious and convenient reductionism, in many cases useful predictions can be made about the suitability of doorway heights based on that estimate alone. And we would be naïve to think that this would be sufficient for every person.

The meaning of the estimates of person ability and item difficulty in the data matrix we have used thus far (see chap. 2) will be meaningful only if each and every question contributes to the measure of a single attribute (e.g., the ability to solve area problems). If the intention of teachers who test for this ability is not well implemented in each of the items, we might find that other attributes of the children's abilities are included in the measure and hence produce less meaningful test results. For example, one item might be predominantly a test of language comprehension. Another item might focus too much on interpretation of a complex geometrical drawing. Still another might be so poorly written that children find it difficult to understand the requirement of the examiner, and so on. Then, of course, the children must cooperate with the teachers' intention as expressed in the test. To the extent that they replace strategies based on the understanding of area with other strategies based on, say, simple recall, guessing, cheating, carelessness, use of a calculator, and so forth, the estimate of that child's ability to solve area problems will be confounded with other attributes not intentionally targeted by the teachers. The resultant score then is uninterpretable to the extent that these other abilities, and not the understanding of area, are manifested in the children's responses. It is here that the principles of unidimensionality require that our analytical procedures must incorporate a test of the degree to which persons and items fit our idea of the ideal unidimensional line.

Item Fit

A good measurement process in education, psychology, or the other human sciences will allow for the estimation of one ability at a time, and will not, intentionally or unintentionally, confuse two or more human attributes into one measure or score. Each of the items should contribute in a meaningful way to the construct/concept being investigated. It will be helpful here to reflect explicitly on how the Rasch model focuses on the key developmental ideas of "construct validity" and "order." First, *construct validity* focuses on the idea that the recorded performances are reflections of a single underlying construct: the theoretical construct as made explicit by the investigator's attempt to represent it in items or observations, and by the human ability inferred to be responsible for those performances. The data matrix that relates the items and the persons together in a coherent, integrated way is more likely to represent (i.e., fit) the construct under examination satisfactorily than one in which the relations appear serendipitous.

Of course, detecting this confusion might not be an easy matter, but for teacher-made tests and early drafts of potentially large-scale tests, it is useful to sit down with a few selected examinees after the test marking has been done to work through the questions with each examinee in turn to help determine the extent to which the intentions of the test writer are revealed in the students' responses. The ordered data matrix, as shown in chapter 2, would be a very good device for deciding which students and which questions might be worth closer scrutiny. Items or persons that do not adhere to the expected ability/difficulty pattern would be good starting points. That way, the quantitative and qualitative aspects of investigation get a chance to work together to improve test design.

Because visual inspection of a data matrix typically is not practical for assessing the impact of individual items or persons, Rasch analysis provides fit statistics designed to aid the investigator in making a number of interrelated decisions about the data (Smith, 1991a, 1992, 2000; Smith & Miao, 1994; Wright & Masters, 1982; Wright & Stone, 1979). Rasch analysis provides indicators of how well each item fits within the underlying construct. In Rasch measurement, the concept of fit is as a "quality-control mechanism" (akin to the use of fit in industrial statistics). Fit statistics indicate whether the researcher has completed a task of sufficient quality to allow that the output can be interpreted as interval level measures. This is a crucial aid for the investigator assessing the meaning of the unidimensional construct. That is, fit indices help the investigator to ascertain whether the assumption of unidimensionality holds up empirically. Items that do not fit the unidimensional construct (the ideal straight line as shown in Fig. 3.1) are those that diverge unacceptably from the expected ability/difficulty pattern (see Chapter 2). Therefore, fit statistics help to determine whether the item estimations may be held as meaningful quantitative summaries of the observations (i.e., whether each item contributes to the measurement of only one construct).

Notice in Figure 3.1 that the steps (e.g., Items, L, M, N) do not lie precisely along the theoretical straight line. We might get some of our items or observations close to perfect, but our aim is to place them close enough to the theoretical straight line to be good practical indicators of the hypothetical path from A to Z. Suppose we are developing a test of basic math skills. Items such as L, M, and N (easy items) might be simple addition problems, whereas Items T and U (difficult items) might be long-division problems. Stepping-stone items that are not close enough to the centerline to be part of this path, such as Items V and W in our drawn example, most likely do not follow this pattern. Perhaps these two items contain story problems that confound reading ability with math ability. The fit statistics then would indicate that these two items might be included better in some other related pathway. They will not be a useful part of the A–Z pathway until they fit a bit better. Perhaps we could try rewriting those items or expressing them some other way the next time we use this test. We could replace them or use them in some other test. At this stage, however, it could be more appropriate not to count the results of Items V and W in any child's test score. Our measure of children's math ability would be more meaningful if these results were not counted. At this point, novices might be given to despair of writing "good" items or collecting "good" data; they tend to throw out far too much, and finally decide to look for an analytical approach which is less demanding. Often the flaws in items that behave as Items V and W have, are too small to distort the measurement in any noticeable way. We could investigate that by making a couple observations go "missing" in the response column for Item V; that might fix the problem. Further, in this example, removing just one of those items, say, Item W, will shift the pathway toward Item V, and so Item V will now be on the pathway. In the end, those working in high-stakes assessment will be less tolerant of misfitting item and person performances. For the rest of us, using Rasch fit indicators should be an iterative learning experience: uncovering more about the variable, how it is revealed in person and item performances, discovering how our data collection can be better controlled, and so forth.

To help us to decide which items to include in our pathway, we could put a dotted line on each side of, and parallel to, our straight line as a check that the fit of our steps to the path is good enough for our purposes (e.g., something like 95% confidence lines). Indeed, some Rasch software outputs report item fit data in a graphic form, in just this way.

In each case, the analytical output would provide greater detail on how each item or performance met, or failed to meet, the model's expectations. Clearly, items whose estimations do not sufficiently "fit" the model require further investigation. Test construction and testing are always done for good reasons. Presumably then, there would always be sound theoretical grounds for including all of the items in an observation schedule and for using that schedule or check list to make observations of any particular person. Important insights into the theory or its expression in practice are likely outcomes of such deliberations. Our theories guide us in deciding what sort of items we should use and with whom we should use them. This Rasch-informed method can be contrasted with the often-used procedure of generating a huge net of possible items, and then trawling through very large, supposedly normal samples to find a set of items with acceptable statistical characteristics.

The Rasch model incorporates a theoretical idealization (or construct, or fiction) of the data's interrelations, an unachievable state that is mathematically represented as the ideal straight line shown in Figure 3.1. The Rasch model represents the concept of perfect "one attribute at a time" measurement, and hence we want to see whether reality (our data) adheres to that concept of a straight measurement line (psychometricians also refer to this fiction, or underlying construct, as a latent trait). Conversely, if the chief contention of this volume is accepted, then the outcomes of Rasch modelling can also reveal the suitability of the observation schedule as an expression of the substantive human sciences theory in empirical practice. That is, we can take the conventional approach and see this as a test of whether our data fit with our fiction. However, it is more useful if we complement this use with the idea of whether our construct, as expressed in developmental or other theory, fits with our data. Ideally, theory informs practice and practice informs theory, dialectically.

Difficulty/Ability Estimation and Error

In developing the mathematical representation of the straight line, the Rasch model specifically addresses the conception of order, an idea fundamental to any account of developing human ability and basic to the idea of measuring more or less of any human condition. Whereas order obviously is important in psychological theories of child development, it also is central to the arrangement of cells in a Likert response scale, easily detected in medical rehabilitation settings, and directly relevant to academic achievement where the difficulty of questions varies. Specifically, in the Rasch model, performances are attributed relative importance in proportion to the position they hold on the measurement continuum. For example, correctly worked-through long-division problems are attributed more importance in the assessment of advanced mathematical skill than correctly worked-through simple addition problems. The Rasch model thus incorporates an algorithm that expresses the probabilistic expectations of item and person performances when one construct is held to underlie the developmental sequence represented by the observation schedule (Wright & Stone, 1979).

When a data matrix reflects a successful attempt to implement a theoretically guided line of inquiry with a sample for whom that inquiry was appropriate, then a number of propositions are supportable. Two key propositions drawn directly from Rasch's basic principle quoted in chapter 1 are as follows:

> Persons who are more able or more developed have a greater likelihood of correctly answering all the items in the observation schedule (e.g., in Fig. 3.1, Bill is more likely than Bob to answer all the items correctly).
> Easier items are more likely to be answered or reached correctly by all persons (e.g., both Bob and Bill are more likely to answer Item L correctly than Item P, and more likely to answer P correctly than S).

These propositions are necessary for expressing unidimensionality of data, and they explicitly illustrate the concept of order in establishing that unidimensionality. Based on this logic of order, as an initial approximation, the Rasch analysis software programs perform a logarithmic transformation of the item and person data to convert the ordinal data to yield interval data (see, e.g., Fischer & Molenaar, 1995). These transformations represent the estimation of person ability and item difficulty detected in the data set (i.e., item and person placement along the single line of inquiry). Actual item and person performance probabilities determine the interval sizes. They are not introduced as *a priori* assumptions of the investigator, or of the analytical algorithm. To the extent that the set of observations adheres sufficiently to Rasch's mathematical model of expectations, it is held to be unidimensional (i.e., the single difficulty/ability continuum is sufficient to explain the patterns of item/person performances). A common misunderstanding is that misfit makes the Rasch estimates nonlinear. This is not the case. Most estimation algorithms used in Rasch analysis produce linear estimates on the basis that the data are unidimensional. The estimates themselves are forced to be unidimensional and linear, as the Rasch model requires. But, the Rasch estimates produced by the estimation might not match well the data in the matrix. Misfit means that the data are not a good match to the estimates, not that the estimates are nonlinear; they are linear but they are not a good summary of the data.

These person ability and item difficulty estimates, having been subjected to a log transformation (and several iterations of the estimation procedure), are displayed in computer output along a *logit* (log odds unit) scale. The logit scale is an interval scale in which the unit intervals between the locations on the person–item map have a consistent value or meaning. The Rasch model routinely sets at 50% the probability of success for any person on an item located at the same point on the item–person logit scale. Because Bob's logit ability estimate is equal to Item Q's difficulty estimate, Bob has a 50% chance of passing this item, for which he is equally matched. The probability of his success increases to almost 75% for a dichotomous item that is 1 logit easier (perhaps Item O) or decreases to about 25% for a dichotomous item that is 1 logit harder (perhaps Item T). The investigator now has more detailed information than that provided by just the data matrix alone on which to make judgments concerning the items, the persons, and the substantive theory that guided the investigation.

But how do we interpret the precision of these estimates? What is the good of item and person estimates if we do not know how good they are? Often our best intentions to realize our theoretical ideas as observation schedules or items go astray. Yes, the stepping-stones along the pathway might be located at an exact point along the pathway, but our figure gives each one a size as well. The difficulty location of any test item (stepping-stone) is located at a point, but always has a zone of imprecision, or error, associated with it. Small steppingstones (small error) suggest that we can locate their difficulty rather precisely. With the larger steppingstones (larger errors), the item locations are not as precise. Figure 3.1 shows that some of the items overlap, particularly at the extremes of the path where errors of location tend to be larger. Collecting more data is usually the easy remedy for item imprecision—find more appropriate persons to test. Reducing error in person estimates is more problematic especially when we want to separate persons into mutually exclusive groups like "still developing" and "mastered these skills". In that case we have to develop more of these appropriate items in order to improve precision of person estimates.

Figure 3.1 shows that Items O, P, Q, R, and S have relatively little error associated with their difficulty estimates, because ability estimates for a number of our test candidates (Jill, Jack, Jean, Bob, and Bill) are close to or targeted near the same level as those items. Thus, if Items Q, R, and S are, say, multiplication problems, this means that the ability of both Bill and Bob includes capabilities at or near the ability to solve multiplication problems. Hence their responses provide us with enough information to estimate the difficulty of those items more precisely. Items L, M, N, and U, on the other hand, have relatively large errors associated with their estimates. Because very few persons in our sample have ability levels equal to the difficulty estimates of these items (i.e., the bulk of our sample is too competent for the simple addition problems, but not up to the demands of Item U), estimating the difficulty of such items involves somewhat less statistical information, so we are left with more imprecision.

Each person's ability location on the map has an error estimate as well. Note that Bill's square is a bit larger than Bob's. Bill's ability estimate contains more uncertainty because there are not as many items in our observation schedule targeted at his level of ability. Bob, on the other hand, has more items close to his ability level, thereby providing more detailed information to estimate his ability level accurately. Mike has only one, or perhaps two, items directly relevant to him, so his ability estimate will be clouded by a larger error estimate.

All this does not mean that the steppingstones provided to measure some human ability along some pathway under investigation represent all or the only steps along that path. Development occurs, or ability develops, independently of our observing it in some organized manner via a test or observation schedule. The items we use are chosen for any one of a number of pragmatic or theoretical reasons from the almost endless population of possible relevant items. Therefore, a child's progress along the pathway can be pictured in any reasonable way: as little steps, large steps, skipping, or a mixture of these. However, the record of development produced by our observation of it, via a test or check list, will depend on which steppingstones the child succeeded in using and which the child did not use, on the day of the test, to progress as far as possible along the pathway.

Measurement of any human performance and the estimation of any ability depend on the cooperation of the subject being tested. We tend to assume that the person being examined cooperates with our intention, as revealed by the test instructions and items. However, we all know about some notorious practices of test takers that subvert our measurement intentions. Sometimes respondents just guess at some or all of the answers. Sometimes they copy from neighbors. Sometimes they even bring notes to crib. They also have been known to have lapses in concentration, give up partway through the testing, try to remember formulaic responses to problem-solving tests, and so on. Some even appear less than entirely motivated to complete our clever tasks or do not speak the test language well enough.

Despite all these well-known problems, we as psychologists, teachers, health professionals, and examiners tend to ignore the problems and just count the number of correct steps taken on the pathway (i.e., the raw score) as the indicator of ability. This is a time-honored strategy, but it could stand some serious reconsideration. A pathway is useful only to the extent that the vast majority of respondents use it in demonstrably similar ways. Betty, who scores 6/10 (getting Items L, O, R, S, T, and U correct on our test in Fig. 3.1), is not showing the same development as Bob, who scores a raw score of 5/10 by using Steps L, M, N, O, and Q. Therefore, if we want to plot Bob and Betty somewhere on the pathway, we must credit Bob with five, and Betty with six answers correct. We can locate Bob on the pathway well within the dotted lines, showing that his performance pattern fitted our developmental expectations sufficiently well. Betty is located outside the pathway's dotted lines (i.e., her response pattern does not fit the model). That is a warning to us: Even though Betty scores 6/10, her pattern for scoring those six marks was not orderly enough for us to claim that her performance fitted our expectations. Something else has contributed to Betty's score. We should not take 6/10 at face value as an indicator of Betty's development. If our path is set up according to Rasch's specifications, then we will want to check out Betty's result: Is she a guesser? Were the items she missed biased against her? Did she lose concentration on easy items that did not engage her? Of course, we cannot tell that from her score alone, but her misfitting location off the pathway suggests that 6/10 is not a representative score for her, and that we need to find out more.

Reliability

Suppose the investigator did not provide enough steps along the pathway. The first consequence would be that the locations of the steps would be less precise. More good items give more precise locations than fewer good items. Because we do not have many steps to separate the varying levels of development in our example, the children would tend to be distributed along the steps in clumps. This would not be a problem if the test were designed to provide merely a coarse-grained picture of the development being recorded. However, if we are involved in high-stakes testing to certify the sufficient development of skills in a critical medical setting, or to allow just certain schoolchildren to move on in a particular educational direction as the result of some testing or recording procedure, then coarse-grained measures will not suffice. The representation of the pathway, as test items or tasks, would require many more stepping-stones (items), each with a quite precise location, so that any person's location on the path could be located precisely. This would be of utmost importance at the point along the pathway where the "developed enough/not developed enough" decision is to be made (i.e., at the high-stakes cutoff score).

The Rasch measurement model provides indices that help the investigator to determine whether there are enough items spread along the continuum, as opposed to clumps of them, and enough spread of ability among persons. The *person reliability index* indicates the replicability of person ordering we could expect if this sample of persons were given another a parallel set of items measuring the same construct (Wright & Masters, 1982).

That is, given another set of the same number and distribution of items purported to measure the same construct, will Bill still be estimated as being more able than Bob, and Bob more able than Jean? Person reliability is enhanced by small errors in ability estimates, which in turn is affected by the number of targeted items. Then, in the make-believe example represented in Figure 3.1, we would expect person reliability to be fairly low. What we do have working for us in terms of person reliability is that our items are targeted at the ability level of our sample. This helps to give us confidence in our ability estimates. However, the shortcoming with this pathway example is the lack of many additional persons spread along the ability continuum. Person reliability requires not only ability estimates well targeted by a suitable pool of items, but also a large enough spread of ability across the sample so that the measures demonstrate a hierarchy of ability/development (person separation) on this construct (Fox & Jones, 1998). Therefore, high person reliability means that we have developed a line of inquiry in which some persons score higher and some score lower, and that we could expect consistency of these inferences.

The *item reliability index* indicates the replicability of item placements along the pathway if these same items were given to another sample of the same size that behaved the same way. For example, if other persons were given these same items, would the item estimates remain stable? For example, would Item P still be more difficult than Item N ? In Figure 3.1, we would expect a very low item reliability index because there are not enough people in the example at the lower ability levels. Therefore, Items L through P, for example, do not have enough information (and hence have large errors) to pinpoint their exact difficulty level accurately. We would need more children with lower math ability in the sample to estimate better the location of these easier items. Therefore, from high item reliability, we can infer that we have developed a line of inquiry in which some items are more difficult and some items are easier, and that we could expect consistency of these inferences. In summary, low item (person) reliability directs us to collect more data in order to reduce the error or imprecision of the estimates. However, achieving high item (person) reliability does not signal the end of the task. Having satisfied this criterion allows us to look elsewhere for other additional evidence that the measures are valid.

A BASIC FRAMEWORK FOR MEASUREMENT

The Rasch model provides a mathematical framework against which test developers can compare their data. The model is based on the idea that useful measurement involves examination of only one human attribute at a time (unidimensionality) on a hierarchical "more than/less than" line of inquiry. This line of inquiry is a theoretical idealization against which we can compare patterns of responses that do not coincide with this ideal. Person and item performance deviations from that line (fit) can be assessed, alerting the investigator to reconsider item wording and score interpretations from these data.

Each item difficulty and person ability is estimated on a logit scale, and each of these estimates has a degree of error associated with it. Estimation error decreases as information about difficulty and ability increases (i.e., when items and persons are appropriately targeted with the sample of items and persons at hand). These error estimates, coupled with item and person reliability estimates, indicate the stability and replicability of the item and person estimates. This information then guides the researcher in knowing how better to interpret and modify measures in the human sciences.

How then would these pathway features be represented in a Rasch analysis? Most Rasch software output includes a form of item–person map in which person ability and item difficulty relations are easily seen. However, representing all the Rasch concepts on one variable map as we have in Figure 3.1 can be very difficult,

TABLE 3.1
Ersatz Item Statistics for the Pathway in Figure 3.1

Item Name	Difficulty Estimate	Error of Estimate	Fit Estimate as t
U	+3.0	0.60	−0.3
T	+1.9	0.43	+1.3
S	+1.6	0.33	−0.9
R	+1.2	0.28	+0.2
W	+0.9	0.43	−2.6
Q	+0.8	0.30	−0.6
P	+0.2	0.30	+0.4
O	−0.3	0.28	−0.4
V	−1.1	0.30	+2.4
N	−1.5	0.43	−0.2
M	−1.8	0.45	+0.6
L	−2.5	0.60	+1.0

so estimates for fit and error usually are included in tables along with ability and difficulty estimates, as shown in Table 3.1. The depiction of estimate, error, and fit on one map was original with Bond and Fox (2001).

Item difficulty estimates are expressed in logits, in which a logit value of 0 is arbitrarily set as the average, or mean, of the item difficulty estimates. Thus, item O is near the average on the scale; Items L and N are easier, having negative logit scores; whereas Items R, S, and T have positive logit estimates, meaning that they are progressively more difficult. Those who are put off a little by negative logit values could refer to estimates of temperature, in which values below 0 are routine, depending on the climate in which you live. Seven degrees below 0, −7 °C, easily carries the message of just how cold it is. We address the issue of scale conversion in chapter 10.

Person ability is estimated in relation to the item difficulty estimates (e.g., the more negative the value, the lower the child's ability on this test). Bill's ability estimate of +2.3 makes him clearly "top of the class" on this test, even with the relatively imprecise nature of his estimate. Please take a few minutes to examine how each of the estimates in Tables 3.1 and 3.2 has been represented diagrammatically in Figure 3.1. It is the item–person map representation of Rasch modelling that is very attractive to both new and experienced users. The values of the key attributes being measured can be meaningfully interpreted at a glance. A picture paints a thousand words.

SO FAR . . .

Figure 3.2 is included to clarify the principles that we will use to construct the pathway variable maps and that readers will need to understand to interpret these maps in chapters 3 through 8.

TABLE 3.2
Ersatz Person Statistics for the Pathway in Figure 3.1

Person Name	Ability Estimate	Error of Estimate	Fit Estimate as t
Bill	+2.3	0.45	−0.6
Betty	+1.2	0.36	+2.8
Bob	+0.8	0.36	+0.8
Jean	+0.2	0.30	−0.8
Jack	−0.7	0.30	+0.5
Jill	−1.0	0.36	−1.6
Mike	−2.4	0.50	−1.0

Estimation (Difficulty, Ability, & Precision)

Both items (as circles) and persons (as squares) are located on the same map. The logit scale is an interval scale in which all logit units are of the same size.The highest values are located at the top of the map, and the lowest values are located at the bottom.

Each item and person is located along the logit scale according to its estimated value: More positive (higher) persons are more able, and more positive (higher) items are more difficult.

The measurement error of the item and person estimates is indicated by the size of the symbol: Larger symbols indicate greater error (in logits).

Estimated values are read vertically (only) on the logit scale for both estimates and errors.

Fit (Quality Control)

Items and persons that fit the model's expectations are located in the white zone.

Items and persons that do not fit the model are located in the shaded zone.

Fit values are read horizontally (only) on a standardized t scale.

Acceptable values (white) fall between −2.0 and +2.0 with sample sizes between about 30 and 300.

THE RASCH MODEL

While the Rasch model provides a mathematical framework against which researchers in the human sciences should compare their data, readers will not be surprised to learn that the formulations and calculations of the model are both more detailed and more exact than portrayed in the Pathway analogy. While the Rasch model guides us in doing exactly the sorts of things we have discussed in

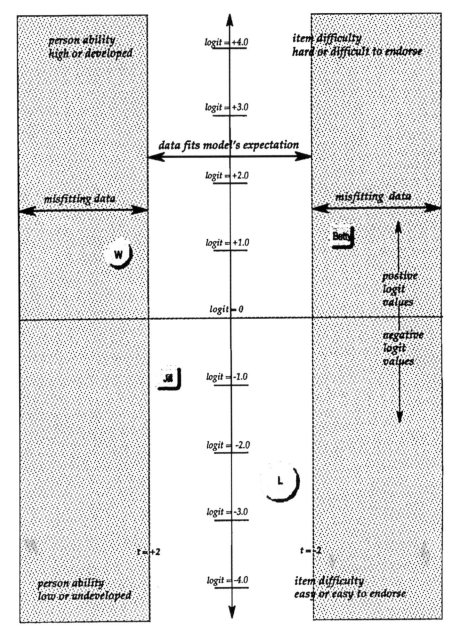

Figure 3.2. Principles used to construct the developmental pathway variable maps.

the previous two chapters, it is not simply a matter of setting up a Scalogram matrix for our data and then adding the raw scores for items and persons and hitting the 'natural logarithm' button on a calculator. The authors deliberately have kept the technical details of the Rasch model to Appendix A so that readers are faced with understanding the concepts (of scientific measurement and the Rasch model) before they are confronted with the mathematical formulations.

This approach seems to be just as bewildering for our mathematically sophisticated colleagues as it is appreciated by newcomers to the field. The psychometricians see the mathematics-free approach as self-evidently inferior; the novices see it as obviously user-friendly. There are tradeoffs in adopting that approach. However, referring to the high jump competition might help bridge the gulf (OK; it might help the novices and risk further alienating the experts).

The spectators in the grandstand had decided that, although there were potentially many, many variables involved in any and every high jump attempt during the competition, the most parsimonious and effective predictor of success or failure at each attempt was the relationship between the difficulty of the particular jump (expressed as height of the bar in meters) and the ability of the particular athlete faced with the jump (expressed as previous best competition jump, also in meters). The best indicator of the likely success of any athlete at any jump was the athlete ability minus jump difficulty difference; the probability of success is a function of the difference between the two key facets in the jumping equation:

Probability (conventionally written as P) of success (i.e. a result of 1 rather than 0) for athlete n facing jump i is a function of the difference between the athlete's ability (we use B) and the jump's difficulty (we adopt D); or

$$P_{ni}(x=1) = f(B_n - D_i) \qquad (1)$$

In English: The probability, when athlete n faces jump i, of a successful jump 1, is a mathematical function f of the difference between the ability of that athlete B_n and the difficulty of the jump D_i.

We can then imagine some possible outcomes of our mental calculations: where the ability—difficulty difference favored the athlete, the athlete would be more likely to make the jump; where the ability—difficulty difference favored the jump, the athlete would be likely to fail the attempt. The greater the ability—difficulty difference in favor of the athlete, the more and more likely the athlete would be to succeed; The greater the ability—difficulty difference in favor of the high jump bar, the more and more likely the athlete would be to fail at that attempt. So far, we haven't specified the exact nature of the mathematical function f. We could ask some statisticians for a bit of guidance there, but we have already reduced their options somewhat because we have estimated athlete ability and jump difficulty as points along a meter measurement scale.

A little table of some observed values as we are about start the high jump competition might help.

We could then develop a little look-up table that would be independent of any particular bar heights or athlete record, for any difference between bar height and

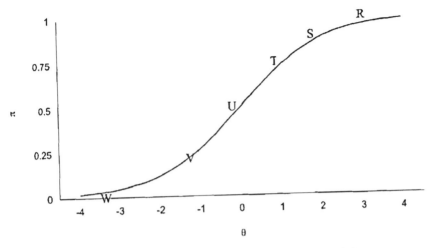

Figure 3.3. Predicting the likely success of all athletes at all high jump attempts.

athlete record, the function would yield the same probability of success or failure. In Figure 3.3, we have a graph based on that table to help with our predictions.

To make the chart in Figure 3.3 useful in predicting the likely success of all athletes at all high jump attempts, we have plotted the B_n–D_i differences in centimeters on the horizontal axis. As one moves to the right along the horizontal axis, the advantage is more and more in favor of the athlete (positive difference). As one moves to the left, the athlete is more and more disadvantaged (negative difference). The vertical axis shows the probability of success for any B_n–D_i difference. When the ability of the athlete matches exactly the height of the bar (B_n–D_i = 0), the graph predicts success for the athlete half (0.5) of the time. Athlete U from Table 3.3 would have that 50% prediction at height (c): no difference between the previous best competition jump and the height to be faced (both at 1.85m). Athletes R and S from Table 3.3 provide an instructive comparison: each is facing a jump (e) with a difficulty of 1.84m. Athlete R has an ability estimated at 1.87m (previous competition best) while Athlete S's ability is recorded at 1.86m. Might Athlete S beat Athlete R today? It is certainly possible. But who would have the higher probability of success? Our model tells us that Athlete R has a better than 75% prediction: Athlete R's best jump is 2cm better than the height being faced. For Athlete S, whose B_s–D_e difference is +3cms, the probability of success can be read from the y-axis as at over 90%. For Athlete W from Table 3.3 the prospects seem a little grim; much less than a 10% probability of jumping the bar set 3cms higher than Athlete W's previous competition best. Of course, it has been done—but not often. That is what the low probability is communicating. Note that it did not matter that the spectators were predicting the probable success for three different athletes for three different jumps: it is not raw ability or mere bar difficulty that is

TABLE 3.3
Some Ersatz Observed Values for High Jumpers

n	B	D	i	$B_n\text{-}D_i$
R	1.87m	1.84m	e	3cm
S	1.86m	1.84m	e	2cm
T	1.84m	1.83m	c	1cm
U	1.85m	1.85m	f	0cm
V	1.76m	1.77m	b	−1cm
W	1.70m	1.73m	a	−3cm

important, but the difference between the two. Then, for the subjects for whom this model is meant to hold (coached high jumpers) and the task for which it is relevant (important high jump competitions), this graph represents the relationship between odds of success on the one hand and the ability–difficulty difference on the other.

This logistic curve just presented is known as the response expectation curve of the Rasch model for dichotomous items (usually called the item characteristic curve or ICC). With logits (log odds units), rather than centimeters on the X-axis, to summarize the $B_n\text{-}D_i$ differences from any person–item pair from the pathway analogy (Fig. 3.1), we can read the predicted success probabilities when any person meets any dichotomous item on a Rasch modelled scale, simply by knowing the $B_n\text{-}D_i$ difference between ability and difficulty. The measurement theorem for the Rasch model requires that a data matrix from a test, and so forth, meet the probability expectations from the two formal statements of the Rasch model: the first as the formula (1) above, the second in graphical form (Fig. 3.3). For Georg Rasch, in his quest to develop measurement scales that generalized across all relevant persons meeting all appropriate items of the type under investigation, this is his summary of how items and persons should behave when they meet in a testing situation. This is not an assumption of the Rasch model, but a requirement. For measurement along an interval scale, where estimates of person abilities and item difficulties remain invariant, this is the elegant mathematical expression of the impossible to achieve in practice gold standard. Just as the theorem of Pythagoras states a perfect, but impossible to achieve, relationship between the lengths of the side of right-angled triangles, so Rasch's theorem states how persons and items should perform in concert in the perfect measurement world.

IN SUMMARY

An unidimensional interval level measurement scale can be constructed when ordinal relationships between two aspects of a human performance (say, person ability and item difficulty) are preserved in the third aspect (say, response probabilities);

Ability of any person is estimated conveniently from the total number of correct responses by calculating each person's success : failure odds;

Difficulty of any item is estimated conveniently from the total number of correct responses by calculating each item's success: failure odds;

The ordered item/person data matrix from any unidimensional test should reveal strong ordering of response probabilities between all pairs of adjacent cells;

The response probability for any person n attempting any item i is a function of the difference between the ability of the person (B_n) and the difficulty of the item (D_i);

Fit is a quality control principle used to help decide whether the actual item and person performances are close enough to the Rasch model's requirements to be counted as linear interval scale measures;

Differences between persons, between items, and between persons and items can be read directly from the interval level scale to make comparisons interpreted as "how much difference" exits between any two locations in probabilistic terms.

CHAPTER FOUR

Building a Set of Items for Measurement

It would be a useful starting point to consider that there exists a family of Rasch models for measurement (Andrich, 1988; Masters & Wright, 1984; Fischer & Molenaar, 1995; Rost, 1996). In this chapter the authors introduce the use of the simplest model, the model for analyzing dichotomous data. This was, in fact, the model with which Georg Rasch did his initial work. Since then, the procedures for performing dichotomous Rasch analysis have been developed further by a number of researchers (foremost among them Ben Wright from Chicago; Wright & Stone, 1979, and G. H. Fischer, 1974; Fischer & Molenaar, 1995), whereas others have extended the basic Rasch model to include analysis of Likert-type rating scales (David Andrich, Perth, Australia, 1978a, 1978b, 1978c; Earling Andersen, a student of Rasch, 1977), responses that could be given partial credit (Geoff Masters, Melbourne, Australia, 1982), and testing situations in which many facets other than just person and item needed to be measured (Mike Linacre, Chicago, 1989). In each case, many researchers justly could claim that they contributed to the development of the Rasch-family models. This is not the place to attempt a full picture of some of the rich history of the Rasch approach. Fischer and Molenaar (1999) provide a useful summary of the contributions of several key European contributors. However, the researchers cited are certainly amongst the most energetic proponents of Rasch measurement models. Each of these models from the Rasch family is more complex than the preceding one, but has the basic dichotomous model at its core. Therefore, if the researcher chooses not to use an added feature of any more complex model, it then collapses to the preceding, simpler model.

At the basis of all Rasch modeling is the model developed first: the model for analyzing dichotomous data, which are data that have simply two values, usually 0 and 1. It is easy to mistake this level of data as being "nominal," the sort of data we get when we categorize hair color as being brunette or blonde, or when we categorize a subject's sex as male or female. However, there is an important distinction concerning the data that are appropriate for analysis with the Rasch dichotomous model: The value of 1 is meaningfully greater than the value of 0, not merely different from 0. This might sound pedantic, but it is a very important point. If we allocate the code of 0 for the females in a sample, and 1 for the males, we intend just to differentiate them in terms of sex, showing that the sex of one group of respondents is different from that of the other group. However, when we use the code 1 to indicate the correct answer to a math problem and 0 as the code for the incorrect answer, we are saying something very different: Not only is the correct answer different from the incorrect answer, it also is better than the incorrect answer in a crucially important way. We regard the correct answer as superior to the incorrect answer, and we routinely regard children who give the correct answer as showing more ability than those who do not. Note then that Rasch modeling is appropriate only when we can impute some order in the allocation of scores such that 1 is better than 0 (as is a correct response versus an incorrect response). In a scale designed to measure rehabilitation after surgery, allocating 1 = pain free and 0 = some pain, develops an index of improved health status, whereas for an index of the progression of arthritis the same indicators would be given the reverse values: 0 = pain free and 1 = some pain. So, 1 = better health in the first example, but 1 = more arthritis in the second. Order does not apply to the case in which 1 (e.g., male) is merely different from 0 (e.g., female), but certainly not better.

Two important points should be mentioned here. The first point is that the codes 1 and 0 merely record our observation of what the child actually did or did not do in response to the test prompt, not what the child could or could not do. Although we all might try to make measures out of those performances that we actually observe and record, and we might do this just so we can make decisions about the people who make the performances, we do not have any magic insight into how competent each person really is. All we have recorded is what the child did or did not do in response to the test prompt, not what the child could or could not do if given another response opportunity.

The second point is that researchers can save themselves a bit of hair tearing in the future by remembering always to use the code of 0 to record the lowest level of performance on any test item. Although this is obvious in the 0 = wrong and 1 = right format, it is not as obvious in coding a rating scale or awarding part marks. With Rasch analysis, it is a convenient and common practice to allocate 0 to indicate the lowest level of response and 1 the next level above that and so on. One routinely used format for the collection of dichotomous data is the multiple-choice test. Such a test would have only one "completely correct" or "best" answer that would receive the score of 1 for that item, with all the other distractors or alternative answers receiving the score of 0, although a partial-credit scoring and model might also be arranged for multiple-choice data (see chap. 7).

ANALYZING DICHOTOMOUS DATA: THE BLOT

In keeping with an important premise of this volume, that the key worked examples will be derived from the research of developmentalists, educators, and others trying to solve actual measurement problems, the dichotomous data discussed in this chapter come from a test of cognitive development for adolescents: Bond's Logical Operations Test (BLOT; Bond, 1976/1995). The BLOT was developed to provide a test suitable for administration to whole class groups at a time, as a partial replacement for the individual interview technique developed and used by Jean Piaget and his colleagues in Geneva. The idea was to develop a multiple-choice test with response sheets that could be computer scored, so that a child's cognitive development could be categorized as more or less developed according to the total number of test items the child answered correctly. Of course, this general principle applies to most educational and psychological tests, as well as to health status check lists, so the principles outlined in the following discussion have far wider application than just to those interested in Piaget's idea of formal operational thinking.

One theme reiterated throughout this volume is that good tests have, as their basis, a very clear and explicit understanding concerning the line of inquiry the test is trying to put into practice—what was once termed construct validity. Of course, this understanding might be revealed in a number of different ways. It could be part of a general psychological theory explained in one or more textbooks by some renowned guru, or part of a treatise on the exact sequence of development during a certain period of life. It might derive from a set of curriculum statements in a particular subject area at the grade school or high school level, or it might just as easily be taken from detailed theoretical or conceptual analysis of a field of knowledge being tested (e.g., math or spelling). In medical settings, it might be the understandings of rehabilitation progress after stroke, gleaned by health professionals who reflect on the effects of their practice. A more encompassing concept of validity introduced by Messick (1995) is reviewed in relation to Rasch measurement in chapter 13.

In the case of the BLOT, the specifications for the items were taken one by one from chapter 17 of the textbook entitled *The Growth of Logical Thinking* (Inhelder & Piaget, 1958). In this chapter Piaget spelled out in detail each of the logical operations that he thought were central to mature thought. The test developer's task then was to represent each of these logical specifications as accurately as possible in multiple-choice test items that would make sense to preadolescents and adolescents without requiring any specific background knowledge. As can be imagined, some items were rewritten a number of times as a result of trial runs with high school students.

Here, the key role of the test developer in putting the substantive theory into measurement practice is clear. In this case, it might have been handy to have Professor Piaget write the items, but then he was not interested in this aspect of group assessment at all. In all test development, the success of the enterprise will be determined largely by how well the intentions of the theory writer, the classroom teacher, or the health specialist have been converted into items, not merely any items, but items such that the performances of the target audience will reveal exactly those intentions and not some other sort of ability. Clearly then, the test developer needs some detailed understanding of the substantive area of inquiry as well as a great deal of commitment to the implementing of that understanding into measurement practice.

The BLOT is a 35-item multiple-choice test that operationalizes item-by-item each of the schemas of the formal operational stage identified by Inhelder and Piaget (1958). Each item comprises an item stem of two to four short sentences followed by a set of four or five alternative responses. The students' responses are collected on computer scan sheets and computer scored. The following interpretation shows us the sense that Rasch modeling can make of the BLOT and allows us to determine how much faith we can place in the idea that adolescents' cognitive development can be represented by the total raw score on the BLOT.

Using the BLOT generates a data file that looks like the following sample:

```
11111111110110101011010111111011111
11111111111111111111111111101111111
11010111111111110111110111110101111
11111111111111111111110111111111111
11111111111101111110111111111111111
11111111111110111101011111111111111
11111111111101111110101111111111111
11111111111111111111111111101011111
11111111111111111111111101111111111
11011111011111101111101111000110111
11111110111111111111011011111101111
11111110111111111111111111101001111
11111111111111101111101011101111111
11111111111110111110111111111111111
11111111111110111110111111111111111
11111111111110111111011111101110111
etc.
```

Each row represents the performances of one student on the 35 BLOT items. Given the principle of dichotomous scoring, the 1s represent the correct answers and the 0s represent the incorrect answers: The score for Item 1 is in Column 1, for Item 2 in Column 2, and so on up to item 35 in column 35. With this example, there is no student ID. The file is set up in the input order of the students' results. Although the BLOT can be computer scored, this file was typed in as a Word (text-only) file by the investigator.

ITEM DIFFICULTY LOCATIONS AND ERRORS

For the first part of the interpretation, we have included the results of the item analysis only, as Figure 4.1. This is in exactly the same format as that described for the developmental pathway analogy introduced in chapter 3: easy items at the bottom and difficult items at the top. The error estimates for the item difficulty are

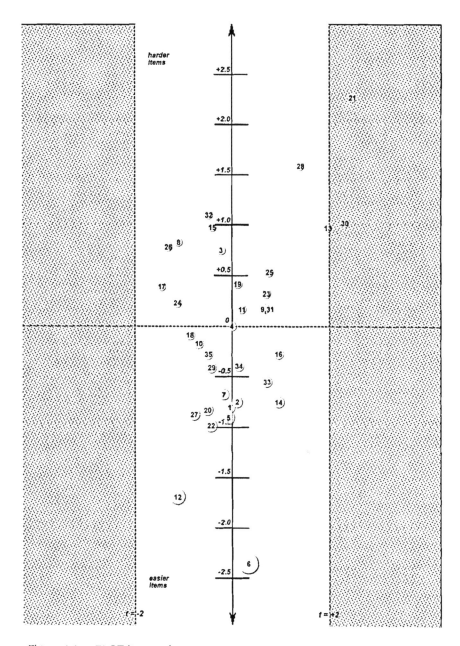

Figure 4.1.   BLOT item pathway.

shown by the error indicators attached to the item circle, whereas items that fit the Rasch model are located on the white pathway between the parallel dotted lines.

A number of ideas can be appreciated immediately as a result of trying to find meaning in Figure 4.1. First, it seems to represent some sort of developmental acquisition of ability: There are easy items, not-so-easy items, more difficult items, and even more difficult items. For example, Items 6 and 12 are the very easiest BLOT items, and Items 21 and 28 are extremely difficult in comparison with the others, whereas Item 4 sits exactly at the midpoint (0) on the item difficulty scale. Given the range of varying difficulties of BLOT items, we reasonably might expect that a group of suitable students would show a range of developmental abilities on this test. It is worth noting that the extremely easy items (6 and 12) have the least precise estimates, whereas the error estimates for the remaining 33 items are comparatively quite small.

A glance at the dotted lines reveals that the fit of the BLOT to the Rasch model's expectations is quite good. Locations for just two of the items (i.e., Items 21 and 30) do not seem to fit satisfactorily to the same developmental pathway as do the remaining items. Items 21 and 30, therefore, should be candidates for closer inspection before they are included routinely in students' BLOT scores in the future. This is good evidence for reasonably inferring that the ability underlying the BLOT items follows a single line of inquiry. The Piagetian conception of cog-nitive development seems to be a reasonable description of that line of inquiry, given its explicit use in the BLOT development phase.

Although the item difficulties span five complete units on the logit scale, Figure 4.1 shows that more than two logits of that development are represented by merely four items: Items 6 and 12 at the bottom of the scale and Items 21 and 28 at the top. However, from below −1 logits to above +1 logits, we have approximately 30 closely packed and overlapping items. The consequence of this is that we would find it very hard to locate persons precisely at the extreme ends of the scale represented by the BLOT items, but we could have a great deal of confidence if we had to make impor-tant decisions relating to students who perform in the −1 to +1 logits zone.

Although it is rather artificial to consider item performance separately from person performance, the purpose of this chapter is to demonstrate the develop-ment of a dichotomous test. At this point, suffice it to say that the distribution of person abilities among children who have been given the BLOT follows the same general pattern as that for items. The vast majority of person performances fit the Rasch model, whereas the distribution of persons along the ability scale is not as clumped as for items. This latter observation can be confirmed by referring to Figure 4.2: the item–person map for the BLOT analysis.

ITEM FIT

Table 4.1 includes the item statistics from a Rasch analysis of dichotomous BLOT data. For each item number, the estimate of item difficulty and its accompanying error estimate in logits are given. These should correspond in a one-to-one way

```
-----------------------------------------------------------------------------
LOT Person Ability Estimates        BLOT Item Difficulty Estimates
-----------------------------------------------------------------------------
  4.0
                  XXXXXXXXXXXXXXX


                  XXXXXXXX
  3.0

                  XXXXXXX

          XXXXXXXXXXXXXXXXXXXX          21
  2.0           XXXXXX
                XXXXXXX

                 XXXXX                  28
              XXXXXXXXX

              XXXXXXXXXXX               32
              XXXXXXXXXXX               30
  1.0            XXXXX                  13      15
              XXXXXXXX                   8      26
                                         3
                 XXX                    25
                 XXX                    17      19
              XXXXXXXX                  23
               XXXXXX                    9      11      24      31
   .0             XX                     4
                  XX                    18
                   X                    10
                   X                    16      35
                   X                    29      34
                   X                     7      33
                 XXX                     1       2      14
                                        20
 -1.0              X                     5      27
                   X                    22


                   X

                                        12
 -2.0
                   X


                                         6



 -3.0
-----------------------------------------------------------------------------
Each X represents    1 student
```

Figure 4.2   Item-person map for the BLOT analysis (QUEST).

TABLE 4.1
BLOT Item Difficulty Estimates With Associated Error Estimates for Each Item

Item	Difficulty Estimate	Error Estimate	Infit Mean Square	Outfit Mean Square	Infit t	Outfit t
1	−0.77	0.26	0.98	0.69	0.0	−0.8
2	−0.70	0.26	1.01	0.75	0.1	−0.6
3	0.74	0.2	0.98	0.9	−0.2	−0.5
4	0.00	0.22	1.00	0.88	0.0	−0.4
5	−0.98	0.28	0.98	0.76	−0.1	−0.5
6	−2.42	0.47	1.06	0.83	0.3	0.1
7	−0.64	0.25	0.97	0.65	−0.1	−1.0
8	0.85	0.19	0.91	1.00	−1.1	0.1
9	0.18	0.21	1.07	0.97	0.7	0.0
10	−0.19	0.23	0.92	0.68	−0.7	−1.1
11	0.18	0.21	1.02	0.96	0.2	−0.1
12	−1.76	0.36	0.69	0.24	−1.1	−1.5
13	1.00	0.19	1.16	1.32	2.0	1.8
14	−0.70	0.26	1.15	1.32	1.0	0.9
15	1.00	0.19	0.96	0.84	−0.4	−0.9
16	−0.30	0.23	1.13	1.03	1.0	0.2
17	0.39	0.2	0.87	0.75	−1.4	−1.2
18	−0.05	0.22	0.9	0.74	−0.9	−1.0
19	0.47	0.2	1.01	1.05	0.1	0.3
20	−0.84	0.27	0.91	0.81	−0.5	−0.4
21	2.33	0.2	1.27	1.75	2.6	3.4
22	−1.06	0.29	0.91	1.69	−0.4	1.4
23	0.35	0.21	1.06	0.92	0.7	−0.3
24	0.22	0.21	0.89	1.03	−1.1	0.2
25	0.51	0.2	1.07	1.26	0.8	1.2
26	0.78	0.2	0.89	0.75	−1.3	−1.4
27	−0.91	0.27	0.85	0.62	−0.8	−0.9
28	1.63	0.19	1.12	1.23	1.4	1.4
29	−0.46	0.24	0.94	0.71	−0.4	−0.8
30	1.07	0.19	1.19	1.15	2.3	0.9
31	0.18	0.21	1.07	1.55	0.7	2.0
32	1.14	0.19	0.96	0.85	−0.5	−0.9
33	−0.52	0.25	1.1	0.93	0.7	−0.1
34	−0.41	0.24	1	0.79	0.1	−0.6
35	−0.30	0.23	0.93	0.73	−0.5	−0.9

Note. Fit statistics are shown in their natural (mean square) and standardized forms (standardized as t).

with the pictorial representation in Figures 4.1 and 4.2, although only some of the BLOT items are numbered: the higher the difficulty estimate, the further up the pathway, and the larger the error estimate, the larger the imprecision associated with the stepping-stone. The output in Table 4.1 has been ordered in terms of descending item difficulty so the correspondences between estimate values (and errors) and map locations for items are more readily appreciated. However, the columns that contain the fit statistics are not so easily interpreted.

Generally speaking, fit statistics focus on two aspects of fit, each of which is routinely reported in both an unstandardized and a standardized form. The concept of fit is the subject of chapter 12. In Table 4.1, the two aspects of fit reported are item infit and outfit. In Figure 4.1, only one of the fit statistics (from the infit t column from Table 4.1 is used as the indicator of (mis-) fit. The unstandardized form is reported as mean squares, and the standardized form is reported as a t statistic, in which acceptable values are those routinely accepted for t (i.e., −2 to +2). The mean square is the unstandardized form of the fit statistic and is merely the mean, or average value, of the squared residuals for that item. The residual values represent the differences between the Rasch model's theoretical expectation of item performance and the performance actually encountered for that item in the data matrix. Larger residuals indicate an item with larger differences between how the item should have performed (i.e., Rasch model expectations) and how it actually performed (i.e., when the children took the test). Residuals are squared, following the usual statistical convention, to make all "actual minus expected" differences positive so they can be added to give a sum of differences.

In the standardized versions of fit statistics, the mean square value is transformed, with the sample size kept in mind, to produce a statistic with a distribution just like t. The "fit" issue will be raised again and again in this volume and everywhere that Rasch analysts gather to chat (e.g., see Smith, 2000). Note that the infit t value for each item is located in relation to the horizontal axis of the map; the vertical location represents the item difficulty in logits.

The infit and outfit statistics adopt slightly different techniques for assessing an item's fit to the Rasch model. The infit statistic gives relatively more weight to the performances of persons closer to the item value. The argument is that persons whose ability is close to the item's difficulty should give a more sensitive insight into that item's performance. The outfit statistic is not weighted, and therefore remains more sensitive to the influence of outlying scores. It is for this reason that users of the Rasch model routinely pay more attention to infit values than to outfit values. Aberrant infit scores usually cause more concern than large outfit statistics. Of course, outfit statistics do have meaning, and we return to the issues involved in interpreting infit and outfit statistics in chapter 12.

INTERPRETING RASCH ANALYSIS OUTPUT

To make this analysis work, you would need to tell your Rasch software:

The name of the data file and where it is located.

The format of the data: easy in this case, 35 items (one item per column usually is the default).

The type of analysis: easy again, the dichotomous model is the usual default.

The name and location for the output file.

Most versions of Rasch analysis software produce some form of the item–person map shown as Figure 4.2, in which the items are indicated by the item number, and each individual person's performance is represented by an "X." One delightful aspect about this Rasch representation of data analysis is that many of the person and item relations are shown in meaningful pictorial, or "map," form. First-timers often gasp when they see their very own data represented in the Rasch variable map format. More recently, this item–person representation of the variable in map-form has been termed a Wright map (e.g., Wilson, 2005).

The logit scale, which is the measurement unit common to both person ability and item difficulty, is displayed down the middle of the map in Figure 4.2. Because the logit scale is an interval scale, the equal distances anywhere up and down that scale are of equal size. Therefore, Item 15 is as much more difficult than item 4 as Item 4 is more difficult than Item 5. The distances between are equal (1 logit). Of course, the same equal-value principle applies to differences in person locations as well. Persons and items are located on the map according to their ability and difficulty estimates, respectively.

As a convenient starting point for the mapping process, the mean of the item difficulties is adopted by default as the 0 point. In this case, ignoring the error of measurement for a moment, Item 4 is calculated as having that exact difficulty estimate (0 logits), so it is located at the 0 point on the item–person map. Person locations are plotted so that any person has a 50% probability of succeeding with an item located at the same point on the logit scale. For example, a person with an ability estimate of 0 logits has a 50% probability of succeeding on Item 4. That same person would have a greater than 50% chance of succeeding on items less difficult than Item 4 (say, Items 18, 29, and 5) and a less than 50% probability of succeeding on items more difficult than item 4 (say, Items 17, 25, and 26). The 50% *limen*, or threshold, is adopted routinely by Rasch analysis, although some Rasch software allows for variations from this value to be specified. For example, those committed to the concept of mastery learning might want to use the 80% threshold that is used routinely in that field to indicate mastery.

With those basic principles in mind, we now can tell immediately from the Wright map in Figure 4.2 that the BLOT is too easy for a sample like this one. Just look where the persons are located in comparison with the items. First, the person distribution is top-heavy in comparison with the item distribution. Second, the top 50 BLOT performers (one third of this sample) are targeted by only two questions: items 21 and 28. The Rasch output tells us as well that three more candidates topped out on the BLOT with a perfect score of 35 of 35. From a general test-development perspective, this would be regarded as a serious inadequacy in a test. If this is the usual sort of target group for this test, then the test needs some more questions of a difficulty like that of Items 21 and 28 so the abilities of the high-fliers can be estimated more precisely. As well, we would need some even more difficult questions to raise the "ceiling" of the test.

A key point to remember, however, is that Rasch analysis item–person maps usually report the relations between the two key variables only: item difficulty estimates and person ability estimates. Other key parts of the analysis—the precision of those estimates (error), the fit of the items, the fit of the persons, the reliabilities of the person and item estimates—are reported in detail in the output tables. The variable map, represented as a pathway, on which both ability/difficulty estimates and their errors as well as fit indicators are represented is original with the authors (Bond & Fox, 2001), and now implemented in WINSTEPS (Linacre, 2006a).

For items we have the following information that is useful:

```
Summary of Item Estimates
■ ■ ■ ■ ■ ▪ ▪ ▪ ▪ ▪ ▪ ▪ ▪ ▪ ▪ ▪ ▪ ▪ ▪ ▪ ■ ■ ■ ■ ■ ■
Mean                      0.00
SD                        0.95
SD(adjusted)              0.92
Reliability of estimate   0.94


Fit Statistics
=========================
Infit Mean Square              Outfit Mean Square

   Mean     1.00          Mean       0.95
   SD       0.11          SD         0.31


       Infit t                  Outfit t

   Mean     0.09          Mean      -0.05
   SD       0.98          SD         1.10


0 items with zero scores
0 items with perfect scores.
```

We already know that the mean of item estimates is located at 0 logits (by default), and that the standard deviation for item estimates is nearly 1. We can confirm the latter by referring to the item–person map: The vast majority of items are located in the narrow band between +1 and −1 logits. The reliability of the item difficulty estimates is a very high .94 on a 0 to 1 scale. Item reliability can be interpreted on this 0 to 1 scale, much in the same way as Cronbach's alpha is interpreted, or it can be transformed to an item separation index, wherein the reliability is calculated as the number of standard errors of spread among the items (see Fox & Jones, 1998, Wright & Masters, 1982; or appendix A of this text for an explanation). Item reliability and item separation refer to the ability of the test to define a distinction hierarchy of items along the measured variable. The higher the number, the more confidence we can place in the replicability of item placement across other samples. Therefore, the item reliability index of .94 means that we can quite readily rely on this order of item estimates to be replicated when we give the BLOT to other samples for whom it is suitable.

The summary of fit statistics also can be informative. Unstandardized fit estimates (i.e., mean squares) are modelled by the Rasch algorithm to have a mean of 1. The actual unstandardized item fit statistics for the BLOT have their means very close to the expected 1, with the infit mean squares showing little spread from that ideal and the outfit mean squares show greater variation.

In the standardization of fit scores, the mean square values are transformed so they are distributed like *t*, with a mean of 0 and a standard deviation of 1. Therefore, we should not be surprised to see the preceding item mean squares transformed into near-0 values. But for how many of the BLOT items is this information applicable? The little note at the bottom of the output reminds us that all the BLOT items were useful for this sample. An item would not be useful for discriminating ability among members of this group if everyone were successful with it (item too easy) or everyone got it wrong (item too hard).

COMPARING PERSONS AND ITEMS

When we turn our focus toward the summary of person performances, we find that Rasch modeling has the distinct advantage of applying the same analytical logic, and therefore the same logic of interpretation, to persons as it does to items.

```
Summary of Case Estimates
Mean                         1.56
SD                           1.30
SD (adjusted)                1.17
Reliability of estimate      0.81


Fit Statistics
Infit    Mean  Square      Outfit  Mean   Square
   Mean          0.99         Mean        0.95
   SD            0.13         SD          0.46
           Infit t                   Outfit t
   Mean          0.13         Mean        0.10
   SD            0.58         SD          0.63
0 cases with zero scores
3 cases with perfect scores
```

The person ability estimate mean of +1.56 is the first indicator that this sample finds this test comparatively easy. Figure 4.3 is included to show three possible relations between item difficulty and person ability. The mean person estimate

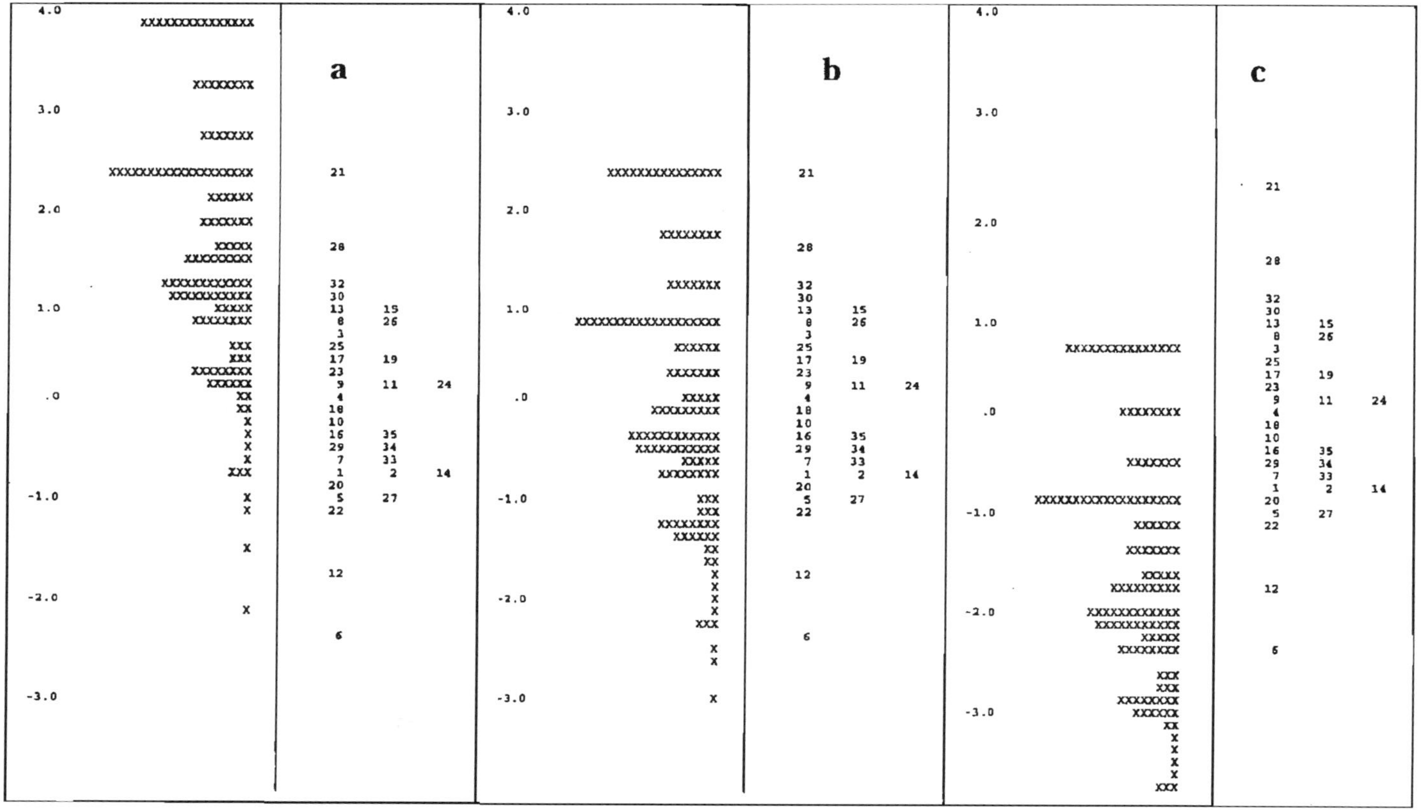

Figure 4.3. Item-person maps showing a test as (a) relatively easy for the sample, (b) well matched to the sample, and (c) relatively difficult for the sample.

(i.e., the group average) would be closer to 0 for a well-matched test (Fig. 4.3b). A tough test would yield a mean person estimate with a large negative value (Fig. 4.3c). The standard deviation of 1.30 for person estimates indicates greater spread of person measures or variation in those measures than with item measures. The reliability of the person ability estimates is high at .81, which is not as reliable as the item separations, but more than acceptable nonetheless.

This corroborates the targeting problem we identified from the Wright map. Although we can rely on this order of person estimates to be replicated when we give these persons another test like the BLOT, in the current analysis we have better information about the items than we do about the persons, so the item estimates are more reliable. In other words, the performances of 150 persons give us more good information about the 35 BLOT items than the 35 BLOT items give about the 150 persons. From consideration of the three distributions in the item–person maps of Figure 4.3, we could expect the best person separability index in Case b, where the match between items and persons is the best. In Case c, the difficult test, both item and person reliability would be lower: The least able persons have no items to distinguish between them, whereas the toughest questions have no persons sufficiently able to provide good information about them.

Again, the person fit summary statistics are equally good. The mean of the infit mean squares at 0.99 and the outfit mean squares at 0.95 are very close to the Rasch-modelled expectations of 1. Consequently, they produce standardized fit t values just greater than 0. The spread in, or variation of, modelled fit scores for persons (infit t $SD = 0.58$ and outfit t $SD = 0.63$) suggests that the vast majority of person ability estimates will have error estimates well inside the conventionally acceptable range of -2 to $+2$.

The logistic curve introduced in chapter 3 to summarize the prospects of high jumpers is extended in Figure 4.4 to represent some key aspects of the Rasch expectations of performances on the BLOT test. Figure 4.4 shows the item characteristic curves (or ICCs) for three BLOT items: Item 6, the easiest item to the left; Item 21, the most difficult BLOT item to the right; and Item 4, which it so happens, is conveniently located at the origin point of the BLOT item and person calibrations. You can check the location of the response expectation curves against the estimations in Table 4.1: The 0.50 expected score point on each curve should locate directly above the item estimate value from Table 4.1 (Item 6 at -2.42 logits, Item 21 at $+2.33$ logits and Item 4 at 0.00 logits). So Alain (ability -2.42 logits) has a 0.5 probability of selecting the correct answer on easiest Item 6. From that point is looks like it's all uphill for Alain as he faces the more difficult BLOT questions. Chrissie (ability = 2.33 logits) has a 50% probability of success on the toughest BLOT item (Item 21); for the other BLOT items, her probability of selecting the correct answer will increase as she meets easier and easier items. Bob (ability = 0.00 logits) has a 0.5 expectation of success on Item 4 (at the same location 0.0 logits); much higher probability on Item 6, but much lower on Item 21. Table 4.2 provides a helpful summary of the theoretical expectations of success for Alain, Bob, and Chrissie on dichotomous BLOT Items, 6, 4, and 21 based on the Rasch modelled relationships between the person abilities and the item

Item Characteristic Curves

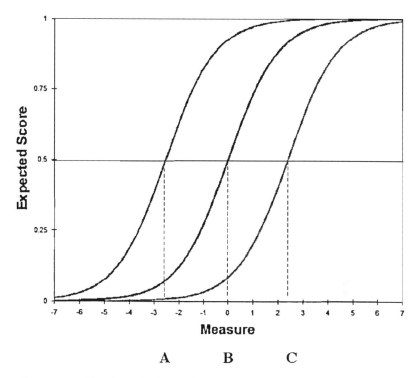

Figure 4.4. The theoretical ICCs for 3 BLOT items: 6 (easiest), 4 (0.0 logits), and 21 (hardest).

difficulties (only). It's worth taking the time to check out your understanding of those expectations. You can see the graphical representation of those relationships in the plot of ICCs in Figure 4.4, the Wright map in Figure 4.2, and the pathway map in Figure 4.1. (n.b. We'll return to the actual performance plots of BLOT items in chap. 5 when we discuss DIF and in chap. 12 on fit.)

THE PROBLEM OF GUESSING

It takes very little imagination to realize that some children faced with completing the BLOT during a high school science class might to resort to guessing answers to the items. Indeed, during the original development of the BLOT (Bond, 1976), it was important to demonstrate that ascribing formal operational thinking status to guessing would be highly improbable. The author went to the length of calculating the probabilities for achieving high BLOT scores by merely guessing.

TABLE 4.2
Rasch Modelled Expectations of Performances of Three Persons
on Three BLOT Items

Person	Alain (−2.42)		Bob (0.00)		Chrissie (+2.33)	
Item	B-D logits	Prob. Success	B-D logits	Prob. Success	B-D logits	Prob. Success
6 (−2.42)	0.00	0.50	2.42	0.91	4.75	0.99
4 (0.00)	−2.42	0.08	0.00	0.50	2.3	0.91
21 (+2.33)	−4.75	0.01	−2.33	0.09	0.00	0.50

We would be naïve to presume that test performances, especially those involving multiple-choice questions—MCQ—such as the BLOT, were free of such candidate behavior. It is more reasonable to think that where the student is required to choose the correct alternative answer (rather than to compose a response), the possibility of guessing exists. Indeed, some data analysis models (including IRT models) are touted as superior to the Rasch model explicitly because they are claimed to account for guessing behavior with their model parameters. Even accidental marks on a scan sheet might later be marked as "correct" by the computer. Children faced with many demands to respond to MCQs as part of regular school assessments might not always remain completely on task or fully motivated to work out every answer fully. The dichotomous Rasch model, on the other hand, models the relationship between two aspects of the testing situation—the ability of the candidates and the difficulty of the items. What's left over (the residual) is counted towards misfit. In contrast to models where a guessing parameter is included as an attribute of items, no such allowance is included in the Rasch model. Critics of the Rasch model claim this to be a fatal weakness.

Now, the problem with random guessing is that it tells us nothing about the ability of the candidate, and random answers might be mistaken as indicators of the ability being tested. However, research shows that random guessing is not ubiquitous and should be examined in context. Some candidates proceed by eliminating the alternative answers that are obviously wrong in their eyes, and then guess amongst the possibly correct alternatives not so eliminated. At least that sort of informed guessing does contain some information about candidate ability and item difficulty. Some candidates do not guess at all—they always try to work out the right answer. Others try to work out the answer when they feel they have the ability to do so, but resort to random (or pattern) guessing when they feel they do not. In that light, guessing is not merely an item property which is invoked of respondents by all or some (difficult) items; nor is it just a person property invoked by tests. More likely, guessing is one of a number of possible measurement disturbances that should not go undetected. Although we worry about the possibility of unearned success by lucky guessing, the reflective measurement practitioner should be also concerned with other possible candidate behaviors such as "sleeping" through the easy or early test items (getting them wrong), or "plodding" slowly through the test (and not reaching, or merely guessing at the items near the end of the test). Thus, the Rasch model provides a set of diagnostics for detecting these types of respondent behaviors, and informs the researcher as to the type of disturbance as well as the severity of it.

Difficulty, Ability, and Fit

"A(n) unique strength of the Rasch model is its requirement that the outcome of any interaction between person and item be solely determined by just two parameters, the ability of the person and the difficulty of the item. This requirement establishes a strong framework against which to test data for the presence of anomalous behavior that may influence the estimation of item and person parameters. The identification of anomalies is not restricted to guessing, but addresses any potential measurement disturbance." (Smith, 1993)

We could hypothesize, as did Waller (1973), "that when a guesser engages in random guessing, it is only on items that are too difficult for him" (see Gershon, 1992). Now, that implies the importance of the relationship already at the centre of the Rasch model—the relationship between person ability (B_n) and item difficulty (D_i), that is guessing is more likely when $B_n - D_i$ is large and negative. It also suggests something else about another key Rasch concept: fit. When $B_n - D_i$ is large and negative for any person × item combination, the expected probability of success is very low; an unexpected success (unearned success by random guessing) would result in large misfit for that item-person combination. We will return to the guessing/ability/difficulty issue in the chapter on fit, but two clarifications are worth reiterating: Under the Rasch model, estimates of ability and difficulty are based on the total number of correct responses (only), while the pattern of those responses is revealed in the indicators of fit. When guessing occurs, the patterns of success will not likely accord with expectations based on ability and difficulty alone—we will have detected an important indicator of a measurement disturbance.

THE THEORY–PRACTICE DIALOGUE

Of course, every test developer and user should try to discern what the results from the performance of the items and persons in practice have to say about the substantive theory being investigated, and should try to decide what the theory tells about the persons and items under investigation. This should always be seen as an ongoing dialectical process. It is not the authors' intention to bore the reader with mini-lectures on the detail of Piagetian theory, but to guide the reflective measurement practitioner, we have included just a little consideration of it here to indicate the sort of meanings that might be attributed to the results of the BLOT analysis shown earlier.

The analysis provides quite good evidence that the items work well together to represent one underlying path of inquiry or ability. Given that the specifications for the logical structure of each and every item were lifted directly from the Inhelder and Piaget (1958) text, this could be seen to confirm the idea that Piaget's model for adolescent intelligence is coherent in itself. At least psychometric evidence points to "something" and not "many things" as the object of inquiry. Moreover, whatever this ability is, it also is evident in the BLOT answering behavior of a bunch of suitable subjects: 150 adolescent schoolchildren.

Because both the items and the persons were shown to behave in sufficiently lawful and predictable ways, it is reasonable to conclude that this part of Piaget's theory and its instantiation in the BLOT are certainly worth the effort of continued refinement and investigation.

The ceiling effect on the BLOT continues to be an ongoing problem: The most cognitively developed kids top out on the test. Although that amounts to only 3 of the 150 tested for this chapter (at age 15), we reasonably could expect that more and more of these students would "hit the ceiling" as we tracked their development over time (Endler & Bond, 2001; Endler, 2004). This is further complicated to the extent that some Rasch analysis software routinely imputes an ability estimate for those who get a perfect score, whereas other software packages ignore the perfect scorers because they do not have enough information to provide an accurate estimate. Clearly, the BLOT needs more difficult items based on Piaget's specifications if we intend to use it to estimate accurately the cognitive development of our more intellectually able teenagers. If, however, its purpose is merely to separate those high school students with less cognitive development from those with more in order to provide developmentally appropriate learning experiences in, say, science and math, then adding more difficult items would not serve that end.

The spread of items, or the lack of spread, on the item–person map suggests that some of the BLOT items are psychometrically redundant: The area from 0 to −1 logits is saturated with items. It seems that a number of the particular intellectual skills incorporated into BLOT items are very much like other skills/items, and that it would not be necessary to include them all in a parsimonious test. Indeed, dropping some of the psychometrically redundant items in favor of more difficult items would remedy two of the apparent measurement deficiencies of the BLOT.

Of course, psychometrically redundant and theoretically redundant are two different but related perspectives on the theory–practice nexus: In the first round, the practice tells us that the conceptualization of the theory has a lot going for it, but that a more useful test could be developed by going back to the theory to find specifications for further item development and rationalization.

Software control files for this analysis and their explanations appear as follows:

QUEST:

```
title BLOT for Chapter Four
data bond87.txt
format items 5-39
est
```

```
show>>BLOT.out
show items>>BLOT.items
quit
```

Line 1 gives a name to the output.
Line 2 tells QUEST which file has the data.
Line 3 indicates that the BLOT responses are in columns 5 to 39.
Line 4 commands QUEST to perform a Rasch estimation.
Line 5 directs the general output to a file called BLOT.out.
Line 6 directs the item statistics output to a file called BLOT.items.

WINSTEPS:

```
& INST
TITLE='BLOT for chapter Four'
NI=35
ITEM1=5
NAME1=1
IFILE=BLOT.IF
&END
Item 1
Item 2
Item 35
END NAMES
11111111110110101101011111111011111
11111111111111111111111111101111111
11010111111111101110111111010111111 etc.
```

Line 1 contains a command that must begin every WINSTEPS file.
Line 2 provides a title for the output.
Line 3 indicates the number of items in the test.
Line 4 identifies the starting column for the data.
Line 5 identifies the starting column for the person identification number.
Line 6 directs the item statistics output to a file called Blot.if.
Line 7 indicates the end of the commands and the beginning of the item names.

Lines 8 to 10 give a line-per-item name. Only the first two and the last BLOT items are named here.

Line 11 indicates an end to the names.

Line 12, and so forth, ASCII data file, like the 0s and 1s shown earlier in the chapter, follows immediately after this line.

Bond&FoxSteps:
The complete data file, control lines, and tutorial for this analysis are preloaded into the Bond&FoxSteps software included on the accompanying CD.

CHAPTER FIVE

Invariance: A Crucial Property
of Scientific Measurement

*They do not understand the thrill of discovering an invariance of
some kind which never covers the totality of any situation. Social
studies will not become science until students of social phenomena
learn to appreciate this essential aspect of science.*

—*L. L. Thurstone (1952)*

We have already raised the idea that central to the concept of measurement is the
view that we must attempt to measure one single construct at a time. In chapter 4,
we gave an example of how this might be achieved in practice. A detailed theoretical description was taken as the starting point, and we used Rasch methodology as
the technique to examine how successful our attempt had been to implement that
construct into measurement practice.

It is a *prima facie* requirement of measurement outside the social sciences that
the values attributed to variables by any measurement system should be independent of the particular measurement instrument used (as long as the instrument is
appropriate to the purpose). Moreover, the calibrations of the measurement
instrument should remain invariant across any of its intended purposes. By
reflecting on the earlier thermometry analogy we would see it as crucial that any
one thermometer would give useful indications of the temperature across any
number of contexts for which the particular thermometer was appropriate—in
terms of its construction and the part of the temperature scale for which it was calibrated: For example, it would give useful readings of atmospheric temperature at
any place on earth where humans can live outdoors. Moreover, we expect that any
number of appropriate thermometers will yield usefully equivalent temperature
readings in any one context, for example the ambient temperature right now in

69

the wine cellar. For any one device, the readings will remain invariant across all suitable contexts. For any one context, all suitably calibrated devices will yield invariant readings. We expect that thermometers will be more or less accurate: The reading will provide a good match with the actual temperature; and that any thermometer's reading will have precision suitable to its purpose. So, two properties of measuring devices will impact on the invariance we routinely expect from scientific measurement. Does the estimate provided more or less match the actual state of affairs, that is, is it accurate? Does the estimate have a margin for error that is small enough for the purpose, that is, is it precise? Given our relatively brief history of attempting genuine measurement in the human sciences, it must be expected that our measurement attempts should fall somewhat short of those based on the physical sciences model. But, if measurement, rather than mere quantification, is going to be the hallmark of our research, then we are bound to attempt to overcome the obvious difficulties that lie in store.

However, in the human sciences, invariance of item and person estimates remains the exception rather than the rule. Interpretations of results from many tests must be made exactly in terms of the sample on which the test was normed and candidates' results for tests of common human abilities depend on which test was actually used for the estimation. This context-dependent nature of estimates in human science research, both in terms of who was tested and what test was used, seems to be the complete antithesis of the invariance we expect across thermometers and temperatures. Even if invariance is important, it is often claimed that IRT in general and Rasch measurement in particular, have not delivered on their promise to deliver the invariance that is a core scientific measurement property. Or, if invariance is sometimes important, then it is not necessarily always important: "...if the intention is to use a one-shot calibration at one point in time with one set of examinees, it is logically inconsistent to justify the use of an IRT model because model parameters possess the feature of *invariance*. Invariance refers to the identity of item and person parameters from *repeated* calibration for *perfect* model fit and is not needed in this case. Hence, it should not be cited as the *primary* reason for using such a model" (Kaplan, 2004, p. 87).

An important goal of early research in any of the human sciences should be the establishment of item difficulty values for important testing devices such that those values are sufficiently invariant for their intended purposes. (No reasonable user expects every thermometer to give readings that are both perfectly accurate and infinitely precise.) Further investigations then would involve the anchoring of the new results to the item values derived from that earlier research. It would be naïve, however, to expect that our early attempts will satisfy even the relative invariance principle on all appropriate occasions. In the same way as the Inspector of Weights and Measures would monitor the scales used by the local greengrocer, we should monitor continually that the item values continue to behave as expected, taking into account the error of measurement. Where the invariance principle is not instantiated in practice, we should be motivated to examine the reason for that inadequate behavior and avoid using any such item in the measure in its current form. "This is the main reason that validity is an evolving property and validation is a continuing process" (Messick, 1995, p.741).

Our attention to the validity of our measures should derive in the first instance from the principle of *invariance* of Rasch measures: estimates of item difficulty on the one hand and estimates of person ability on the other. Given that Rasch measurement instantiates interval level, rather than ratio level measurement, invariance of item, and person estimate values always remains relative. Individual Rasch analyses (by default) adopt the mean of the item difficulty estimates as the zero point on the calibration scale, so it is the differences between item estimates and person estimates, rather than those estimates *per se,* which should remain invariant across investigations.

PERSON AND ITEM INVARIANCE

While we easily see that the group of persons who took the test are a sample of the population of all possible test candidates, we less readily realize that the test items themselves are merely a sample of all possible test items. This is due, in no small part, to the relative ease of capturing a new sample of suitable test candidates and the relative difficulty of constructing a new sample of suitable test items. In Rasch measurement, as we have already seen, the principles and logic of analysis and interpretation for persons completely mirrors that for items. We have a constant reminder of the sample/population relationship for both items and persons, even though any sample's representativeness of the relevant population is far less crucial than is the case for true score statistics. In Rasch measurement, the general appropriateness of the sample, rather than its statistical representativeness of the population, is sufficient for stable item calibration. We take up the feature of person-distribution free item calibration in chapter 10.

Ben Wright's challenge to those claiming to have a good test was rather forthright and based on the simple requirement for invariance of estimates; an important measurement principle for any testing situation and quite easy to implement, even in the one-shot calibration exercise alluded to by Kaplan above. Divide your sample of persons in two according to their ability and conduct item estimations for the total test for each half of the sample in turn. The invariance principle requires that the relative difficulties of the items should remain stable across the two substantially different subsamples (within the constraints of the requirement for targeting items and persons). The corollary is also true: Divide your test into two and estimate the person abilities with each half of the test: Relative person ability estimates should remain invariant regardless of which half of the sample test items is used for the person estimation. In chapter 10 we will introduce the feature of parameter separation (see also Smith, 2001). This is the property of the Rasch model that supports direct comparisons of person ability and item difficulty estimates, that is, independently of the distribution of those abilities and difficulties in the particular samples of persons and items under examination.

COMMON ITEM LINKING

Figure 5.1, then, represents the results of finally taking up Wright's challenge—rather than merely repeating it as it was passed on to others. The data

Common Item Linking BLOT

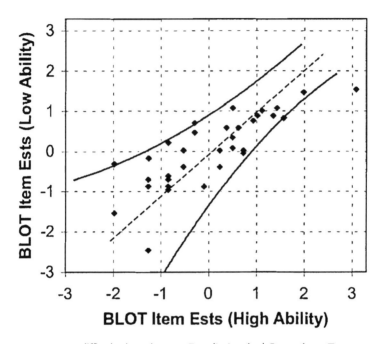

Figure 5.1.   Item difficulty invariance—Bond's Logical Operations Test.

from the 150 students who took the BLOT (the bond87.txt data set from chap. 4) were divided into two equally-sized subsamples. The first contained those with scores of 27–35 (High), and the second contained those who had raw scores of 5–26 (Low). Data from each subsample were analysed separately and the 35 item estimates (and SEs) for each group were imported into an Excel spreadsheet (Bond & Fox, 2001, pp. 62–65). The plot of item values (in Fig. 5.1) shows that, with the notable exception of Item 21, the item estimates of the BLOT items are invariant (within error); the dotted line is not a regression line, but the Rasch modelled relationship required for invariance (the 95% control lines are based on the SEs for each of the item pairs).

The simple first step is to plot the pair of calibrations for each item onto a simple scatter plot, using the Rasch-modeled ability estimate measures (in logits) for each item. Although the Rasch item measures are based exactly on the raw score totals for each half of the sample (High and Low), these modeled ability estimates contain much more information about the interval scale and the measurement errors associated with each of the measures. Those working in the application of fundamental measurement principles usually take care to distinguish between raw scores, usually regarded as counts, and Rasch-modeled ability estimates, which satisfy the requirements necessary to be regarded and used as measures. The difficulty estimates of items from each of the analyses with the High ability and Low ability subsamples of students are plotted on the corresponding x and y axes in Figure 5.1. Recall that both the calibrations are centered, by default, on the mean of the BLOT item values at 0.0 logits and that each item has two item estimates (D_x from the High ability estimation and D_y from the Low ability estimation) and corresponding error terms (see Table 5.1).

If we draw a diagonal line (45° or slope = 1) through the point representing the calibration means of D.x and D.y (0.0 logits), we would construct a line that represented the exact modeled relation between the two sets of item estimates if they remained completely invariant under perfectly precise (i.e., error-free) measurement conditions. In such a situation (unachievable in practice), all the plotted points (i.e., the D.x / D.y location for each of the 35 BLOT items) should lie exactly along this diagonal line. Usefully and realistically, Rasch modeling provides us with error estimates for each and every difficulty estimate, and we can use these to construct quality control lines (shown in Fig. 5.1) to see whether the distribution of the plotted ability points is close enough to the modeled relationship diagonal line for the measures to be regarded as sufficiently invariant (i.e., identical within the limits of measurement error).

The formula for constructing the control lines for a 95% confidence band around the diagonal through the mean estimates, derived originally from Wright and Stone (1979, pp. 94–95), is given as an Excel spreadsheet at the end of this chapter. Whereas some Rasch analysis software (e.g., WINSTEPS) will produce a graph of such comparisons on demand, anyone familiar with the graphing procedures in a spreadsheet can develop a worksheet that will import Rasch analysis output and use the pairs of item difficulty estimates to plot the locations and the associated pairs of error estimates to plot the control lines. Simple visual inspection will reveal whether enough of the points (i.e., 95% or more of them) lie within the control band. With only 1/35 BLOT item locations outside the control lines (i.e., 2.9%), it seems reasonable to argue that the item estimates may be regarded as remaining invariant in spite of coming from different subsamples.

Now, Item 21 is, by far, the most difficult BLOT item (see Figs. 4.1 & 4.2) The High ability subsample allows us to gauge the difficulty difference between Items 21 and 28 quite well. However, the 21–28 gap is well out of the range of the BLOT abilities shown by the Low ability half of the sample. This results in the 21–28 interval being underestimated with the Low ability group (the targeting problem). Given that 26/35 has been estimated as the bound between concrete operational and formal operational performance on the BLOT, the invariance of the item estimates (within error) helps affirm the integrity of the BLOT under Rasch analysis procedures and demonstrates that the BLOT Rasch intervalscale maintains its measurement properties across quite disparate subsamples (after Bond, 2004).

TABLE 5.1

BLOT Item Estimates and Errors Based on Split Half Subsamples. Errors
Increase Dramatically With Off-Target (High-Ability) Respondents.

BLOT item#	High-Ability Subsample		Low-Ability Subsample	
	Estimate	Error	Estimate	Error
1	−0.85	0.6	−0.74	0.29
2	−0.85	0.6	−0.65	0.29
3	0.93	0.31	0.73	0.25
4	0.23	0.39	−0.01	0.26
5	−1.27	0.73	−0.91	0.31
6	−1.27	0.73	−2.5	0.53
7	−1.98	1.01	−0.35	0.27
8	1.02	0.3	0.85	0.25
9	0.73	0.33	−0.01	0.26
10	−0.54	0.53	−0.01	0.26
11	0.73	0.33	−0.08	0.26
12	−1.98	1.01	−1.57	0.37
13	1.35	0.28	0.85	0.25
14	−0.1	0.44	−0.91	0.31
15	1.11	0.3	0.97	0.25
16	0.23	0.39	−0.42	0.28
17	−0.3	0.48	0.67	0.25
18	−0.85	0.6	0.18	0.25
19	0.37	0.37	0.55	0.25
20	−1.27	0.73	−0.74	0.29
21	3.08	0.25	1.5	0.27
22	−0.85	0.6	−1	0.31
23	0.5	0.36	0.31	0.25
24	−0.3	0.48	0.43	0.25
25	0.62	0.34	0.55	0.25
26	0.5	0.36	1.04	0.25
27	−0.85	0.6	−0.91	0.31
28	1.98	0.26	1.43	0.27
29	−0.54	0.53	−0.42	0.28
30	1.57	0.27	0.79	0.25
31	0.5	0.36	0.05	0.26
32	1.43	0.28	1.04	0.25
33	−0.54	0.53	−0.42	0.28
34	−1.27	0.73	−0.21	0.26
35	−1.27	0.73	−0.08	0.26

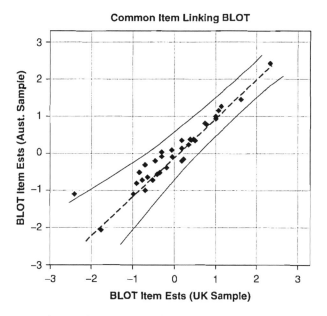

Figure 5.2.   Invariance of BLOT Item Difficulty across countries (UK u. Australia).

The invariance principle also applies where the same test (e.g., BLOT) was used in two unconnected testing situations (e.g., it has been used as a measure of cognitive development research projects in Australia and the U.S., as well as in the U.K.). Then, the measurement requirement is that the BLOT item estimates should remain invariant across analyses conducted in different countries. In Figure 5.2, the Dx values came from the research conducted in Australia (Stanbridge, 2001) and Dy are the BLOT values from chapter 4 collected from high school children in the UK, while each item estimate is tied to its corresponding error term. This should be regarded as a particularly rigorous internal validation technique, especially in comparison with, say, calculating test–retest correlations.

Having established the invariance of the test item values under such circumstances as those above, researchers might then capitalize on that invariant property by treating the item difficulty estimates as known calibrated values: a sort of within-laboratory decision to anchor the measurement scale so comparisons of values taken in different research contexts might be facilitated. Early development and refinement of thermometers underwent such procedures.

ANCHORING ITEM VALUES

Based on the evidence to date (e.g., Endler & Bond, 2001) it seemed reasonable to expect changes in the BLOT estimates of cognitive development for cohorts of adolescents as they undertook classroom interventions designed to impact on the understanding of science (Adey & Shayer, 1994). Indeed, even without such a program, it would be reasonable to expect that BLOT scores would change during the period in which this development has been specifically theorized (Inhelder & Piaget, 1955/1958). While many children's scores might be expected to rise over two or three years, those of others might remain rather flat; and some, might, indeed, decline. Failure to establish "known values" for the cognitive development scale (e.g., BLOT item estimates) would yield confounded results. Returning to the temperature analogy, 100° C on the Celsius temperature scale was calibrated to indicate the boiling point of pure water at sea level. Failure to fix that indicated position on the thermometer's scale before climbing Mont Blanc or Mount Everest would confound the effect of a crucial contextual variable (lower atmospheric pressure) if a new boiling point were independently calibrated in the new context alone. Rasch analysis software allows the user to input known values (e.g., as anchored item values) so output (e.g., person values) might be more validly compared across contexts.

Figures 5.3 and 5.4 then provide the bases for a very interesting comparison. The first of the Wright maps summarises the BLOT cognitive development variable for one class of high school students at the end of the CASE intervention in an Oregon school district (Endler, 2004). This Rasch analysis, using the dichotomous model is just another application of the analytical procedures used in chapter 4. The second Wright map is based on the exact same data but this Rasch analysis differed in one important way: The item difficulty values were not estimated during this analysis. At the beginning of the intervention project (some three years earlier), BLOT data were collected from a cross sectional sample of some 658 students from Years 6 to 11. The item difficulty estimates calculated during that analysis were then used as anchored known values, so that any child's BLOT estimate taken at any time during the intervention would be calibrated against a ruler that was fixed for the life of the project. While this allowed for valid comparisons between the estimates for children across year levels, cohorts, and time, it was essential for tracking the changes for any one child over the course of the longitudinal study. Note that while the distribution profiles both for case estimates and for item estimates remain the same across the two variable maps, it is the relationship *between* the case and item distributions that changes.

The exemplars above might be termed common-item linking: What links the data sets together are items that the data sets have in common. The High and Low ability students in Figure 5.1, the UK and the Australian sample in Figure 5.2, and the pre- and post-intervention samples in Figure 5.4 all have performances on the same 35 BLOT items in common. Showing these item values to be invariant allows comparisons between samples to be made directly. Given that the common items formed a complete test, the procedure might be termed common test linking: two samples having one test in common. This procedure could then form the basis for, say, measurement of scholastic performance across years: The Year 3 and Year 5 math tests each have 10 of 50 math items in common—presumably they would be among the more difficult items on the Year 3 test and the easier items on the Year 5 test. The items for which invariance of item difficulties can be established empir-

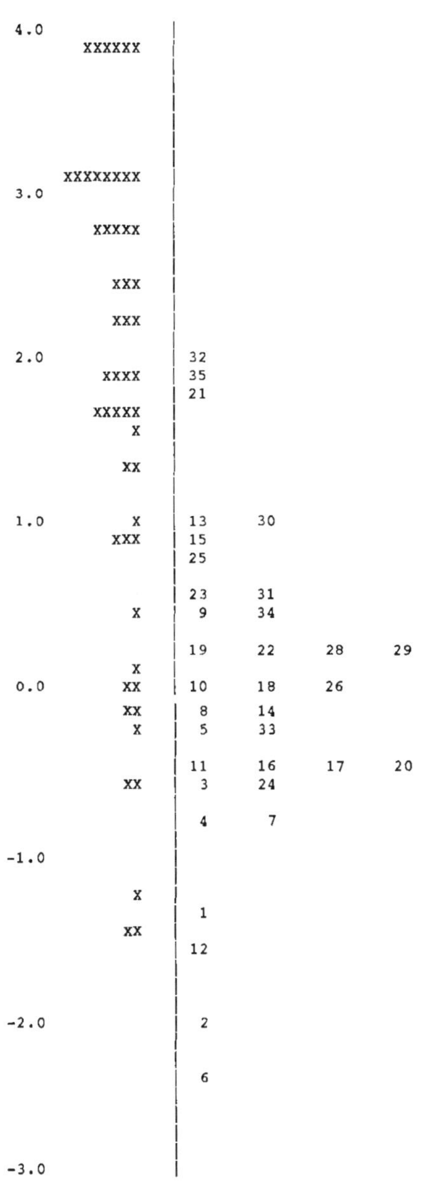

```
4.0                        |             4.0                          |
        XXXXX              |                    XXXXX                 |
                          |                                          |
                          |                                          |
                          |                                          |
      XXXXXXXX            |                                          |
3.0                        |             3.0 XXXXXXXX                 |
      XXXXX               |                                          |
                          |                    XXXXX                 |
     XXX                  |                                          |
                          |                   XXX                    |
     XXX                  |                                          |
2.0            | 32        |             2.0                          |
     XXXX      | 35        |                   XXX                   |
               | 21        |                                          |
     XXXXX     |           |                  XXXX                   |
       X       |           |                 XXXXX                   |
      XX       |           |                   X    | 21   32         |
               |           |                                          |
1.0     X      | 13   30   |                  XX                     |
      XXX      | 15        |             1.0        | 30              |
               | 25        |                        | 28              |
               |           |                   X    | 15              |
               | 23   31   |                 XXX    | 13              |
       X       | 9    34   |                        | 8    17   31    |
               |           |                   X    | 3               |
               | 19   22   28   29 |                | 9    26   35    |
       X       |           |                        | 19   25   29    |
0.0    XX      | 10   18   26 |                XXX   | 23              |
      XX       | 8    14   |             0.0   XX   | 11              |
       X       | 5    33   |                   X    | 10   22   34    |
               |           |                        | 5    20         |
               | 11   16   17   20 |                | 18              |
      XX       | 3    24   |                        | 7    33         |
               |           |                  XX    | 24              |
               | 4    7    |                        | 4    14   16    |
-1.0           |           |                        | 1    27         |
       X       |           |            -1.0        | 2               |
               | 1         |                   X    |                 |
      XX       |           |                  XX    | 12              |
               | 12        |                                          |
               |           |                        | 6               |
-2.0           | 2         |            -2.0        |                 |
               |           |                                          |
               | 6         |                                          |
               |           |                                          |
-3.0           |           |            -3.0        |                 |
```

Figure 5.3.   Wright map for Year 10 on
BLOT.

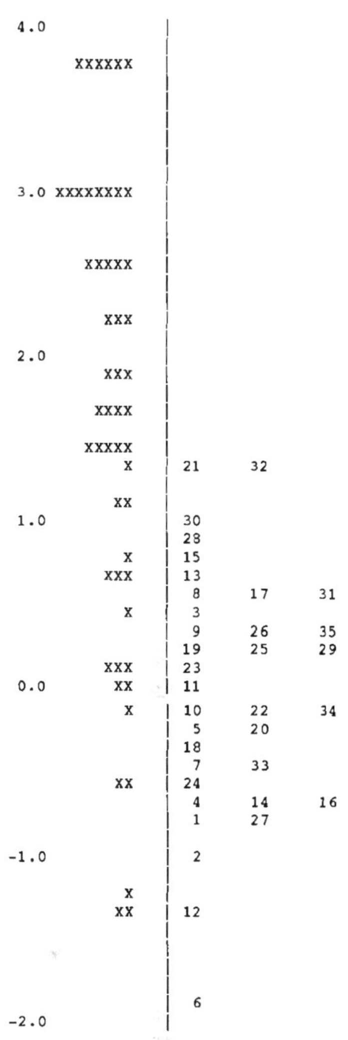

Figure 5.4   Wright map for Year
10 on BLOT (items anchored).

At the beginning of the intervention project (some three years earlier), BLOT
data were collected from a cross-sectional sample of some 658 students from
Years 6 to 11.

ically are then used as common items for linking the performance estimates for the Year 3 and Year 5 samples. Those link values might also be anchored so that comparisons can be made over time. Ingebo (1997) describes in detail how the crucial scientific principle of invariance of measures guided the use of the Rasch model in Oregon. They calibrated the large item banks for mandated assessment by using the principles of common item linking and anchoring described above. While Endler took the precaution of anchoring the BLOT item values to those calculated in the pre-intervention analysis, for the cohort-by-cohort analysis this ultimately proved unnecessary. As it happened, because of the adequately representational size of the cohorts, the BLOT item values showed no meaningful variations across the annual estimations (Endler, 2004).

LINKING USING PSEUDO-COMMON ITEMS

When the faculty evaluation system for providing *Student Feedback About Teaching* was developed for a major regional research university in Australia (Bond, 2005a), it was intended that such evaluations could inform high-stakes decisions concerning faculty hiring, tenure, and promotion procedures. Consequently, evaluations are reported as graphs (see Fig. 5.5) on which Rasch item measures allow for comparisons to be made between any teacher's feedback and that of the university benchmark (both estimates and errors are plotted). In order to provide some continuation with the results from the previously used "Evaluation of Teaching" methodology, data from the six items on that earlier

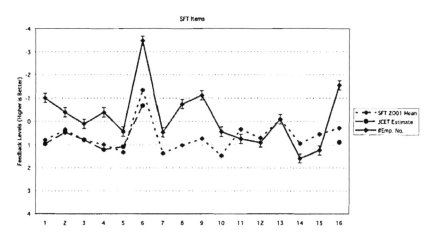

Figure 5.5.   Mean Rasch item estimates (with error bars) for 16 SFT items (benchmark: solid; one teacher: dotted) and for six pseudo-equivalent items (dashed) from the earlier JCET survey.

questionnaire which *most closely matched* similar items on the new SFT instrument were analyzed in the same fashion, that is, these were not common items, but the closest things to common items that could be used to examine links between the data sets. Rasch item estimates for the university's historical data on those six items were also plotted on SFT feedback graphs (as JCET estimates) so that staff applying for tenure and promotions, and the members of the university's promotions committee, might infer better the relationships between the current SFT results and those from the earlier JCET surveys. The comparison shown in the SFT reporting graph in Figure 5.5 does not satisfy the stringent measurement requirements of the Common Item Linking techniques outlined previously. However, the patterns of the plots for four of those six pseudo-common items show remarkable correspondence between the historical (JCET) and the new (SFT) evaluations. There is a noticeable discrepancy a measurable difference, between the "old" and the "new" feedback levels for Item 6 (teacher expertise) and Item 16 (teaching overall): They are lower in the historical data set. This seems congruent with the conditions under which each of the evaluation instruments was administered: Staff may elect to have the current SFT evaluation whereas the earlier JCET instrument routinely surveyed *all* university classes as well as those for which a staff member elected an evaluation. It seems reasonable that the teaching (Item 16) and expertise (Item 6) of teachers aiming for tenure and promotion might be better appreciated by their students than that of all teaching staff. Treating similar items as though they are the same, and therefore of invariant difficulty, allows for insights into the data that would not be possible with a less stringent data analysis model (after Bond, 2005a).

Rasch pseudo-common item linking of data sets has been used to remarkable effect in the area of health rehabilitation by Fisher (1997) and for college student evaluations of educational experience by Beltyukova (Beltyukova & Fox, 2002; Beltyukova, Fox, & Stone, 2004). One object of Fisher's research (Fisher, 2000) is the establishment of what he terms "universal metrics" for important aspects of human capital. The attempt at linking large data sets derived from quite disparate rehabilitation scales (e.g., Fisher, 1997) revealed the remarkable utility of the Rasch model in supporting the co-calibration of instruments across samples, in spite of differences in number and format of items. While the research did not mathematically formalize the measurement links between the physical functioning scales, it showed that "inter-laboratory" collaboration could be expected to yield a single scale for physical functioning along which person estimates derived from the individual indices could be scaled for comparative purposes. Beltyukova's research investigated the extent to which two nationally used instruments for assessing student satisfaction with colleges in the US could be scaled on a common quantitative metric. Seventeen apparently similar items with good Rasch measurement characteristics were used to provide pseudo-common item links between two large data sets: one derived from the College Student Survey, and the other from the Student Satisfaction Inventory. Rasch analysis of the combined data sets linked by the pseudo-common items showed the stability of the student satisfaction construct across the very different CSS and SSI instruments and samples (Beltyukova, Fox, & Stone, 2004, p. 67).

COMMON PERSON LINKING

Of course the converse of Ben Wright's challenge (invariance of item calibrations derived from splitting the person sample in two) should also hold true: splitting a sample of items (the test) into two, and calculating person ability estimates for each half test should yield person estimates that are invariant for all practical purposes (identical within error). That realization prompted further analyses of the BLOT data from chapter 4, the results of which are reported as a graph in Figure 5.6. The steps of the analysis remain the same as above, but some procedural and interpretative modifications are needed because of the asymmetry of the BLOT data matrix. The earlier split person–sample comparison yield two subsets of data for analysis: Each subset contained 75 person performances across 35 items. The current split-test comparison is based on two subsets of data each with 150 person performances on just 17 (or 18) items.

There are many ways to divide a test in half (easy half; hard half; first half; second half, etc.). For the investigation of the invariance of person estimates reported in Figure 5.6, the odd-numbered items (1, 3, 5 ... 35) provided the person

Common Person Linking BLOT

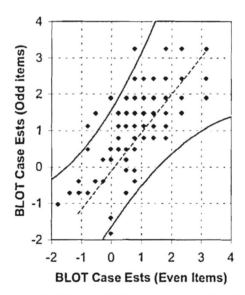

Figure 5.6.   Invariance BLOT case abilities estimated with half the items (odd vs. even).

estimates plotted on the y–axis and the even-numbered items (2, 4, 6, … 34) were used to estimate person abilities on the x–axis. Again the line (slope = 1) represents the error-free Rasch-modelled equivalence between the person estimates, but there is considerable dispersion away from that line. Has the investigation failed? Are Rasch person estimates not invariant even when drawn from two halves of the same test?

The answer to both questions is, no. First of all, there are not 150 plotted points on the graph. The usual Rasch estimation procedures do not calculate item or person estimates for perfect scores: Cases which scored 18/18 on the "odds" or 17/17 on the "evens" do not have two Rasch person ability estimates to plot. Figure 5.6 plots the 122 cases (from a total of 150) that had estimates calculated from each half-test. But the big difference between the BLOT person invariance graph in Figure 5.6 and the BLOT item invariance graph at the beginning of this chapter (Fig. 5.1) is the imprecision of the plotted estimates in Figure 5.6. In chapter 4, the analysis of the complete BLOT data set (150 cases and 35 items) yielded item estimates with errors of around 0.25 logits; that is the precision yielded with 150 cases. Errors for person estimates based on 35 BLOT items have errors that vary from about 0.40 logits to 1.03 logits for a score of 34/35 (little statistical information due to lack of items at that level). When the person sample was divided into low and high ability subsamples, precision for item estimates remained around 0.3 for the low group but varied up to about one logit for the high group (the targeting problem). When the BLOT test is divided into two (odds and evens), the person estimates so calculated plummet in precision: No SE is below 0.50 and many approach or exceed 1.0 logit. You can see in Figure 5.6 that the 95% control lines are widest apart at the top of the graph, where BLOT person estimates are the least precise (larger error terms). Still, very few of the person locations fall outside those control lines, supporting the notion that the person estimates will remain invariant (identical allowing for error) when each person's ability is estimated from each half of the BLOT (odd, then even items) in turn. In passing, we should note that the correlation between person performances is $r = 0.71$ (explaining a mere 50% of the variance in the person data). How can the Rasch measurement evidence be so strong while the correlation seems so modest? That is because the Rasch model provides us with more statistical information than can be used by a true score calculation such as correlation. For the true score model, each person's performance (X = the number right) is composed of a true score component (T) and an error component (E), neither of which can ever be known (i.e., $X = T + E$). But this proposition is tautologous; it can never be tested. All we ever have is X, and that is all that can be used for calculating correlations, factors, and so forth.

In Rasch measurement, a person's performance is represented by a number of components relating to quantity and quality. The Rasch quantity components include the person estimate *and* its error term. So the evidence in the linking graphs in this chapter incorporates both components (estimate and error) to reveal the extent to which the estimates may be regarded as invariant (i.e., not measurably different) across contexts. Correlation calculations, on the other hand, cannot take measurement error (precision) into account, so the ensuing *r* values are attenuated because they must ignore the (unknowable) errors. We might also continue to reflect on how much (unwarranted) faith we routinely put in test totals because our traditional statistical training blinds us to the possibility of estimating errors for individual persons. Seeing how error terms increase in size as the number of items decreases should encourage all those in Rasch measurement to be more circumspect about hard and fast interpretations based on just counts or estimates alone.

INVARIANCE OF PERSON ESTIMATES ACROSS TESTS: CONCURRENT VALIDITY

We should expect that when one latent trait or underlying construct is the subject of a variety of tests, person measures should remain invariant (within error) across those testing conditions. This is the idea that (loosely) underlies the almost routine demonstration of concurrent validity undertaken when a sample of candidates is given two tests and the resulting scores are correlated (notwithstanding the problems with correlations noted above). The long-term aim of a genuine measurement system in the human sciences should be access to a series of co-calibrated testing situations, such that the raw score or locally calculated person measure could be expressed on the single scale used worldwide. That might remind us of the analogy drawn from thermometry. Thermometers are used to estimate temperature *indirectly*, by observation of the effect of temperature on some testing variable: the length of an enclosed column of coloured alcohol, the resistance of a metal wire, the straightening of a bimetallic strip, and so forth. The units of temperature are not physically additive in the fundamental measurement sense and almost as many types of thermometer exist as there are temperatures to estimate. No one thermometer is useful for more than a few selective applications, and none measure over the full range of the temperature variable. Certainly, none do so without error. Temperatures are measured internationally, translations from °F to °C are routine, and temperature estimations are understood and compared after the most elementary sort of training in "test administration".

So the next step in achieving this end (after establishing the invariance of item and person performances as above) is addressed by one of the questions continually asked in psychological and other human sciences research: "Does this test measure the same construct as this other test?" This is one important technique in helping to establish the validity of a test. Although the core validity issue in test development revolves around the crucial question of construct validity (see Messick, 1995), test developers legitimately appeal to the psychometric overlap between a new test and an established and recognized test to claim that the new test has concurrent validity. It is, indeed, unfortunate that a combination of concurrent and face or content validity often is held as the only sufficient prerequisite for test development. Almost total reliance on the results of empirical data analysis techniques to resolve issues of validity have obscured the central role of construct validity in the human sciences. The authors return to this important issue in the closing chapter. Suffice it to say, here, that, *a priori*, the researcher must first be satisfied by an elaboration of the theoretical construct under examination in a pair of tests that they purport to measure the same construct. Of course, the answer to the question, "Do two tests measure the same construct?" involves another issue, "How could we tell if test A measures the same construct as test B?"

One purpose of a test A versus test B comparison might be to develop two forms of the same test so that we can use them validly as equally useful alternatives in a test–retest format. Why else would we want to develop a test that measures the same construct as an already existing test? Of course, there are a number of very pragmatic reasons. The new test might be shorter, offer a new format, or allow greater ease of administration, scoring, or interpretation. It might be more suitable to a particular target population or a particular testing context; it might be written in another language. It might provide greater precision around important high-stakes decision points, or it might help to prevent cheating, or to avoid the learning effect when tests are used more than once. On the other hand, it might just provide a useful, low-cost, quick-to-use, screening device when the high cost of high-power testing of all potential subjects is not warranted. For example, while the Family Strain Questionnaire (FSQ, Rossi Ferrario, Baiardi, & Zotti, 2004) is a structured interview administered, after referral, by qualified psychologists to caregivers of chronically ill patients, the short form of the Family Strain Questionnaire (FSQ-SF; Bond, Rossi Ferrario, & Zotti, 2005) was developed using Rasch analysis principles, so that it could be used routinely as a 10 minute screening device for signs of caregiver stress administered by home-care nurses or medical practitioners.

Inherent in all these possibilities is the theory–practice dialogue that is the important focus of all good measurement. Tests apparently quite dissimilar in format that measure the same construct will inform us about the theoretical construct we are investigating, as will apparently similar tests that cannot be accepted as measuring the same underlying trait. To illustrate a Rasch measurement approach to examining concurrent validity, we investigate the properties of another classroom test of formal operational thinking—this time, one developed in the United Kingdom. Then we use the linking procedures from Rasch modeling already introduced above to see whether this test can be judged to be measuring the same construct as that shown in the results of the Bond's Logical Operations Test (BLOT) analysis in the previous chapter.

THE PRTIII–PENDULUM

The Piagetian Reasoning Task (PRTIII–Pendulum) was developed in the United Kingdom (Shayer, Küchemann, & Wylam, 1976) to allow Piagetian reasoning tasks to be administered to whole class groups. Using the PRTIII, the teacher demonstrates a number of experiments in front of the class and, from time to time, the children make written responses to the questions posed on individual answer sheets. The teacher later codes each written answer from the child (a few words, sometimes a sentence or two) as 1 (correct) or 0 (incorrect) according to a set of scoring criteria (derived from chap. 4 of Inhelder & Piaget, 1955/1958), thereby producing the same sort of dichotomous data string for each child as that produced by the computer-scored BLOT results in the previous chapter. Any number of teacher-made tests adopt that general format of a written short-answer test given to a whole class at a time, with the teacher marking the answers right or wrong at a later time and reporting the total score as the test result. Any number of testing opportunities in the human sciences could adopt the same analytical approach profitably.

The PRTIII contains 13 items, which are scored dichotomously. The data we have for analysis in this section came from the very same 150 children who completed the BLOT in chapter 4. Of course, we took the usual testing precaution of ensuring that half of the children completed the BLOT first, with the other half completing the PRTIII before the BLOT, to neutralize any order effect.

The dispersal of the PRTIII items in terms of their difficulty locations, the error of those difficulty estimates, and the fit of those estimates to the Rasch model are illustrated using the pathway principle in Figure 5.7. The details of the item statistics for the PRTIII results from these 150 children are reported in Table 5.2. Item difficulties span a range from −3.17 logits for the easiest item (item 1) to +3.40 logits for the most difficult of the PRTIII items (Item 2). All of the PRTIII items fit within the conventional limits for the infit t statistic, in this case, ranging from +1.5 to −1.4. At this point, we should recall that Rasch analysis routinely adopts an arbitrary 0 point for each scale, usually the mean of the test's item difficulties.

TEST SCORE LINKING

Central to the demonstration that we need to use here is the notion that one sample of children has been the subject of two test administrations, each test of which is held to measure the same underlying construct. One very simple procedure could be adopted. We could reasonably regard all these items as attempts to measure the same underlying construct and just analyze the BLOT and PRTIII items together as one test. Such an analysis might easily be regarded as sufficient for the basic purpose of establishing whether two sets of items adhere to Rasch principles sufficiently to be regarded as measuring the same construct. If the principles espoused in chapter 4 allow us to regard the 35 BLOT items as measuring just one construct, then we could draw the same conclusion about the 48 BLOT and PRTIII items if they were Rasch-analyzed as one test. However, a possible problem with this technique is raised in chapter 12, whereas the procedures we demonstrate in this chapter are much more informative, based on the concept of measurement invariance that should be central to a wide range of measurement applications.

The key issue is whether the performances of students across both tests are similar enough to sustain the argument that the one dimension being assessed on each test is the same dimension for both tests. The estimates of students taking both the BLOT and the PRTIII are plotted on the corresponding x and y axes in Figure 5.8.

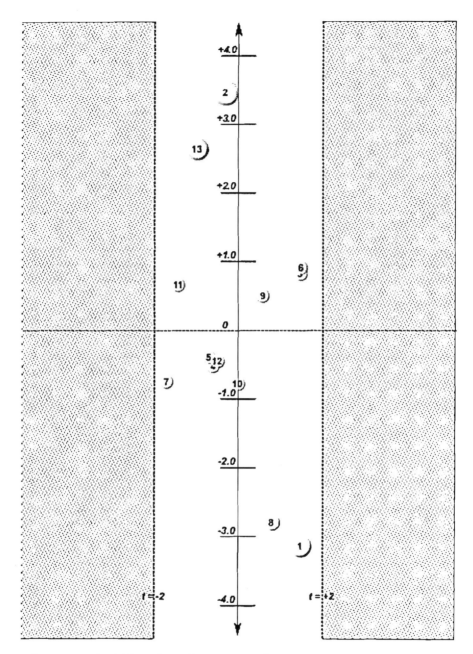

Figure 5.7. Variable pathway for PRTIII–Pendulum

TABLE 5.2
Item Statistics for PRTIII–Pendulum

PRTIII Item No.	Difficulty Estimate	Error Estimate	Infit Mean Square	Outfit Mean Square	Infit t	Outfit t
1	−3.17	0.30	1.26	1.08	1.4	0.3
2	3.40	0.44	0.91	0.64	−0.2	0.1
3	0.8	0.22	1.17	1.09	1.5	0.4
4	−0.61	0.21	0.94	0.98	−0.6	0.0
5	−0.37	0.21	0.93	0.90	−0.7	−0.4
6	0.94	0.23	1.17	1.30	1.5	1.0
7	−0.77	0.21	0.82	0.75	−1.8	−1.3
8	−2.81	0.27	1.10	3.01	0.7	2.6
9	0.53	0.22	1.04	1.30	0.4	1.2
10	−0.81	0.21	1.00	0.86	0.0	−0.6
11	0.67	0.22	0.85	0.72	−1.4	−1.0
12	−0.41	0.21	0.97	0.83	−0.3	−0.9
13	2.60	0.33	0.79	0.67	−1.0	−0.2

The only difference between the BLOT ability scale and the PRTIII ability scale is the difference in the arbitrary 0 points allotted to each scale during the Rasch analyses. First, take the mean ability score for the BLOT (B.x: ability estimate on test x) and for the PRTIII (B.y: ability estimate on test y) and plot that point on the graph.

The next point of interest in this comparison is the relative difficulty of the two tests being analyzed. Recall that each of the analyses we have used for this exercise was conducted separately. The origin of the scale developed for the BLOT (0 logits) was the mean of the BLOT item difficulty estimates, and the origin of the scale developed for the PRTIII (0 logits) was the mean of the PRTIII item difficulty estimates. If the tests were of the same average difficulty for these students, the BLOT 0 and the PRTIII 0 will be identical. Usually it would be the case that the mean ability on the BLOT and the mean ability on the PRTIII also will be identical (within error). Then the intercept of the diagonal line on the x-axis is the adjustment that must be made to the BLOT estimates to bring them to the scale of the PRTIII estimates. In this case, the BLOT estimates require an adjustment of −2 logits to align them with the PRTIII scale (i.e., the PRTIII is 2.28 logits more difficult for this sample than the BLOT). We already had some hint of that in the individual analyses. Whereas three students "topped out" on the BLOT with perfect scores, only one of them did so on the PRTIII. Conversely, six students scored 0 on the PRTIII, whereas the lowest BLOT score was 5/35. All prima facie evidence suggests that the students found the PRTIII tougher than the BLOT. If the two tests were both measuring the same ability *and* were of the same mean difficulty, at least 95% of the plotted points would lie within the control lines, and the diagonal line representing the modeled relations between the performances would

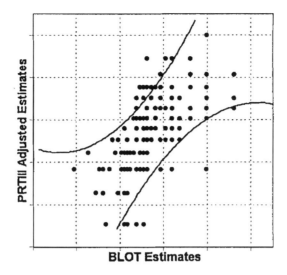

Figure 5.8.   Common person linking BLOT and PRTIII.

pass through the origin point of the graph. BLOT, however, was designed to mark the transition to formal operational thinking and contains a preponderance of easier items; the PRTIII has items that extend well into the upper limits of that Piagetian stage, and, the items are then, on average, more difficult.[1]

How much variation in person estimates can be expected depends on the size of the error estimates for each of the person ability locations. The error sizes depend on the amount of good information we have about person abilities. More items in a

---

[1] If, instead, we were to draw in a line of best fit for the data points in Figure 5.8, we could bring the temperature analogy to bear on interpreting the relationship between BLOT and PRTIII. Remember the Fahrenheit–Celsius scale relationship:

Fahrenheit$°$ = Celsius$°$ * 1.8 + 32

For this sample of persons:

BLOT: mean = 1.63   S.D. = 1.37
PRTIII: mean = −.65   S.D. = 1.89

The PRTIII = BLOT relationship is:

PRTIII = (BLOT - 1.63) * 1.89/1.37 − .65 or

PRTIII = BLOT * 1.38 − 2.90

Uncovering the 1.38 : 1 relationship between PRTIII logits and BLOT logits is a timely reminder that the logit is a probabilistic, not substantive, unit and that the length of the logit needs to be monitored. "Equating of the interval scales constructed from two tests is confirmed when plots of the measures of elements common to the tests follow an identity line stochastically. When this verification fails, a necessary step is to linearly adjust the relative lengths of the logits constructed by the two tests (and intended to be based on the same underlying variable) by the ratio of the observed standard deviations of the measures common to those tests, so that both tests measure in the same substantive units." (Linacre & Wright, 1989, p. 55)

test produce smaller measurement errors for persons taking the test. Equally, test items that are appropriately difficult for the sample produce tighter error estimates than poorly targeted items. Moreover, in Rasch modeling, the converse is also true: More persons produce less measurement error for items, and samples that are well chosen for the test yield better item difficulty error estimates.

A quick look at the item error estimates for the BLOT (Table 4.1) will show that they are approximately the same magnitude as the item error estimates for the PRTIII (Table 5.2), mostly about 0.20 logits. This is largely because we have 150 well-targeted persons to provide information about both the BLOT items and the PRTIII items. For PRTIII Item 2, however, the targeting of persons is not so good: The item is very difficult for these Year 9 students, and the error estimate "blows out" to 0.44 logits as a consequence. Now, let us apply the same logic to the person error estimates in Table 5.3. This table contains a slice of the person results from the analyses of the BLOT and PRTIII. Here we have results for 23 persons. Although 150 persons provided information about the test items, we have only 35 BLOT items providing information about the persons and a mere 13 PRTIII items, one of which is arguably not targeted on most of the sample. The person error estimates yielded by the BLOT are approximately 0.50 logits, whereas the PRTIII yields person error estimates approximating the 0.70 mark, confirming the claim that more good items provide more precise estimates of person ability than do fewer good items. The near extreme BLOT score of 34/35 for Person 59 produces a high ability estimate (+3.93 logits), but with low precision (error = 1.03 logits).

As outlined before, the statistics often used in human sciences research usually do not provide individual error estimates for each person and each item. Any dispersion of scores from the perfect diagonal is regarded as unmodeled or residual variance. As outlined before, test development approaches based on the inspection of correlations generally are less than adequate. Precision in measurement derives from the amount of good information we have on which to model the measures. Measurement error must be taken into account when correlation statistics are interpreted: The more information, the smaller the error and the higher the correlation must be. Conversely, a small circle of plotted points well within the control lines of Figure 5.9 could help to justify the assertion that two tests were measuring the same variable even though the correlation coefficient was "disastrously" low (Masters & Beswick, 1986).

Therefore, although plotting raw test scores, or counts, against each other might be more or less informative, the plotting of Rasch-modeled estimates of person ability, or item difficulty, can be far more useful when interpreted in the context of the precision (i.e., measurement error) of these estimates. The invariance of relative person ability, whether measured by the BLOT or the PRTIII, is good evidence to suggest that these tests can be used interchangeably. Invariance of person estimates and item estimates within the modeled expectations of measurement error over time, across measurement contexts, and so on, is a key Rasch measurement strategy. Moreover, it is crucial to genuine scientific measurement. Disturbances to expected invariance beyond the bounds imposed by modeled error in these situations can be adduced as evidence that our measurement expectations have not been sustained in practice: that tests we had developed as

TABLE 5.3
Raw Scores and Ability Estimates With Errors on the PRTIII
and BLOT for a Subsample of Students

Student ID No.	PRTIII Score (/13)	Ability Estimate	BLOT Error Estimate	Score (/35)	Ability Estimate	Error Estimate
58	8	0.69	0.70	29	1.83	0.48
59	9	1.20	0.74	34	3.93	1.03
60	7	0.22	0.68	28	1.62	0.45
61	3	−1.80	0.81	26	1.24	0.41
62	9	1.20	0.74	26	1.24	0.41
63	2	−2.54	0.92	29	1.83	0.48
64	9	1.20	0.74	31	2.36	0.56
65	8	0.69	0.70	31	2.36	0.56
66	7	0.22	0.68	31	2.36	0.56
67	0	Case has zero score		25	1.08	0.40
68	2	−2.54	0.92	26	1.24	0.41
70	3	−1.80	0.81	22	0.62	0.38
72	9	1.20	0.74	28	1.62	0.45
73	4	−1.21	0.74	27	1.42	0.43
74	9	1.20	0.74	31	2.36	0.56
75	2	−2.54	0.92	24	0.92	0.39
76	11	2.55	0.93	26	1.24	0.41
77	4	−1.21	0.74	30	2.07	0.51
78	7	0.22	0.68	23	0.77	0.38
79	3	−1.80	0.81	26	1.24	0.41
80	6	−0.24	0.68	26	1.24	0.41
81	8	0.69	0.70	32	2.71	0.63
82	7	0.22	0.68	33	3.17	0.75

useful alternatives are not that; that some test items are biased; that some test formats discriminate against some persons or group of persons; that some items are context dependent, and so on.

The principles we have described are more often used in testing situations to compare the abilities of two groups of subjects who are given the same test. Rasch modeling allows us to determine the relationships between two different groups of people who share performance on a common test. This is called common test linking. In the case of equating BLOT and PRTIII, however, the position was reversed: We had two groups of items (different tests) that had been given to the same sample (a single group of subjects). In this example, Rasch modeling was used to investigate the relations between the two tests. This benefit of Rasch modeling derives from an important principle: the computational logic applied to persons in relation to items is exactly the same as the logic applied to items in relation to persons. With experience in using Rasch analysis, the growing realiza-

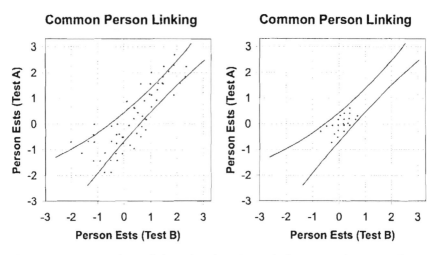

Figure 5.9.   (a) good correlation / low invariance (b) low / correlation good invariance

tion that these principles are exactly the same for items and for persons (e.g., estimates, errors, and fit are expressed in exactly the same units on a single scale for both) allows for considerable power and flexibility in addressing a range of problems that we must address when we try to solve practical measurement questions in the human sciences. Smith (2001) summarized the basic steps for co-calibration of test instruments while the key aspect of the conceptual basis for these procedures presented in Bond and Fox (2001), relies on earlier expositions (Wright & Stone, 1979; Masters & Beswick, 1986).

THE THEORY–PRACTICE DIALOGUE

How could two tests be so apparently different and still measure the same underlying ability trait? The PRTIII requires a teacher demonstration of pendulum experiments while students write their answers in sentences, which the teacher later carefully assesses with the use of a detailed marking key. The BLOT is machine-marked, multiple-choice testing in its plainest form, untouched by human hands. Although the PRTIII as a whole is measurably, more difficult than the BLOT, they both can be seen as two practical instantiations of the theoretical ideas expounded by Inhelder and Piaget (1955/1958). Both tests aim to be classroom measures of mature adolescent thinking that teachers could use to inform themselves about the relevance and suitability of particular learning experiences for their high school students.

    Given that Piaget's conception of formal operational thought is regarded by some as passé or even fatally flawed, the equivalence of the PRTIII and the BLOT, despite their distinct differences, suggests that there might be more to the underlying theory than meets the critic's eye. It is clear that selecting the correct operational answer from many distractors (BLOT) is much easier than constructing the correct written answer in the particular context of a high school physics experiment (PRTIII). The BLOT will provide a fine-grained analysis of the development of formal operational thinking, whereas the PRTIII will show just how developed that thinking can be. Test users who do not have the skills necessary to administer and grade the PRTIII can use the BLOT, but at the cost of the "ceiling effect" for the most able test takers. As would be expected, both tests have strong relations with high school achievement, especially in the area of science, in which most of the research has been carried out.

Measurement Invariance: Where It Really Matters

An *ex post facto* demonstration based on 150 students across 35 items hardly can be more than a demonstration of the invariance principle at work—apparently, it is in large scale empirical evaluations where our high expectations for measurement invariance are not demonstrated. Fan (1998) wrote the oft-cited report of a large-scale empirical investigation which concludes, *inter alia,* that Rasch measurement results are not worth the extra effort necessary to produce them.

In light of the previous argument and empirical evidence, Kingsbury's (2003) study of the long term stability of item parameter estimates in achievement testing has a number of important features. First, rather than using parameter estimates from a set of items used in a single test, it investigated the stability of item parameter estimates in two large item banks used to measure achievement in mathematics (> 2300 items) and reading (c.1400 items) with students from school years 2-10 in seven US states. (Sample sizes for the 1999–2000 school year item calibrations ranged from 300 to 10,000 students.) Second, the elapsed time since initial calibration ranged from 7 to 22 years. Finally, and most importantly (for these purposes), "the one-parameter logistic (1PL) IRT model (Wright, 1977) was used to create and maintain the underlying measurement scales used with these banks." While thousands of items have been added to these item banks over the course of time, each item has been connected to the original measurement scale through the use of IRT procedures and systematic Rasch measurement practices (Ingebo, 1997).

The observed correlations between the original and new item difficulties were extremely high (.967 in mathematics, .976 in reading), more like what would be expected if items were given to two samples at the same time, rather than samples separated by a time span from 7 to 20 years. Over that period, the average drift in the item difficulty parameters was .01 standard deviations of the mean item difficulty estimate. In Rasch measurement terms (i.e., focusing on impact on the measurement scales), the largest observed change in student scores moving from the original calibrations to the new calibrations was at the level of the minimal possible difference detectable by the tests, with over 99% of expected changes being less than the minimal detectable difference (Kingsbury, 2003).

These results, of course, are not fortuitous. Ingebo (1997) reported how the Portland Public School District and the Northwest Evaluation Association deliberately implemented the Rasch model to build the original calibrated item banks stimulated by an address at an Educational Testing Service seminar in 1967. "While his measurement ideas seemed far-fetched, Dr. Wright's experimental test data (were) so promising that the Portland Public Schools initiated inspection of Rasch measurement" (Ingebo, 1997, p.8). It seems now, that some three decades later, we also have the opportunity to decide whether the promised benefits of these "far-fetched" measurement claims would be worth the long-term effort necessary to build a Rasch based measurement system for, say, the SAT.

Failures of Invariance: DIF

The principle underlying the plots of person and item invariance across testing situations is exactly that underlying the detection of Differential Item Functioning (DIF). When an item's difficulty estimate location varies across samples by more than the modelled error, then *prima facie* evidence of DIF exists. Indeed, Scheuneman and Subhiyah (1998) from the National Board of Medical Examiners used merely an item estimate difference greater than 0.5 logits as the criterion for detecting DIF in a 250 item medical certification test given to over 400 candidates. Given that SE estimates are inversely proportional to sample size, we could safely expect that a difference of 0.5 logit might have both statistical and substantive meaning (i.e., a genuine measured difference) on this high-stakes test. Their very basic approach, based on the violation of the Rasch model's expectation of estimate invariance, detected about 80% of the items uncovered by the Mantel-Haenszel procedure. Moreover, they argued, when the examiner understands the substantive construct under examination, and is thereby able to posit reasonable hypotheses about the performances of subsamples of examinees, Rasch based indications of DIF are more directly comprehensible in terms of those group differences. When Tesio and colleagues (2002) collaborated across national boundaries (between Italy and the USA) and equated Rasch rehabilitation measures on the FIM^{TM}, they found the predicted invariance of item difficulty values across the two settings. They went on to reveal that variations in a few difficulty locations (i.e., DIF) reflected differences between an incentive-driven medical system in the US and a more family-based support system in Italy (Tesio, Granger, Perucca, Franchignoni, Battaglia, & Russell, 2002). Monitoring item calibrations is an important aspect of delivering Computer Adaptive Tests: Items showing displacement of difficulty estimates (DIF) usually are retired from the active item pool for diagnosis of the possible causes of the problem. Even with the demonstrably sound PRTIII, Shayer is always careful to recheck the item calibrations each time that task is used for a new sample: a routine and uneventful procedure that, for years, produced predictably unremarkable results. PRTIII item values were as good as set in stone. When a key item concerning the application of the classic *ceteris paribus* principle became slowly but measurably easier in relation to the remaining items, the DIF was attributable to the change in the national science curriculum which explicitly required teaching the "hold all things equal" principle of making a "fair test." Theory-informed testing requires explanation when the invariance required of sound measurement is not maintained.

Most of the interest generated by examining DIF took place in the era of the sex-bias of test items, especially in IQ or achievement testing. In more politically correct times we now refer to gender-related DIF; DIF is less emotive than bias. Two little illustrations from performances on BLOT Items 3 and 35 might be useful at this stage. This will help to show a particular depiction of DIF from a Rasch-measurement perspective as well as hinting how difficult the factors involved in responding to gender-related DIF in testing might be.

In the previous chapter we noted that the theoretical ICCs could be useful for understanding failures of invariance, such as DIF and understanding fit. The principles by which such actual performance versus expected performance graphs are constructed are covered in more detail in chapter 12. Suffice it to say here that the curved ICC in each graph shows the same form as the graph for the high jumper example in chapter 3 and for BLOT Items 6, 4 and 21 in the previous chapter. This is the graphical representation of the Rasch model's expectation of item–person performance. The line plots (continuous for males; dotted for females in Fig. 5.10) show how the two groups of students actually performed. In the left hand graph for BLOT Item 3, the plots of actual performances for boys and girls follow (more or less) the model's expected curve (the ICC). Certainly, there are now obvious differences in the patterns of the plots for boys and girls.

That's not the case for the plots on the right: the actual versus expected performances for boys and girls on BLOT Item 35. Now, for performances of boys and girls high on the BLOT scale (to the right), the performances for boys and girls are virtually identical. But look what happens below that level of BLOT ability (to the left): The boys' plot (continuous) shows their actual performances really exceed the model's ICC of expected performance (continuous line almost exclusively above the ICC); but the girls' plot (dotted) shows that they underperform on Item 35 when their overall BLOT abilities levels are taken into account. Moreover, and this encapsulates the very essence of gender-related DIF, boys out perform girls *of the same ability* level on Item 35.

The examination of gender-related DIF was undertaken for the first time (*mea culpa*) for this chapter. There seemed to be a number of potential DIF candidates amongst the BLOT items: Some items refered specifically to male or female characters or to gender-related activities. Surely the question about matching wide tires and wheels on a motor vehicle would favor the male "tappet-heads", but, no. So what about Item 35? In BLOT Item 34: "A mouse is trapped on a conveyor belt when it starts moving in direction (A)…" In the subsequent Item, 35 "The direction of the motion of the belt is then reversed. Which of the following would now keep the mouse near the mid-point? …" So why does BLOT Item 35 favor lower ability males over females of equal ability? Is there some reference to mechanical understanding in the context of reversing the conveyor belt that gives the lower ability boys an advantage? Or (tongue firmly planted in cheek) are the lower ability girls somehow disadvantaged by the prospect of the escaping mouse? The alternative hypotheses are not meant to offend, merely to suggest that the causes and potential remedies for DIF might not be obvious even when the patterns of the failed invariance are demonstrated clearly from the Rasch measurement perspective.

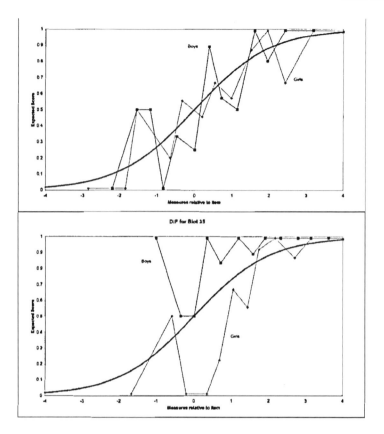

Figure 5.10.   Comparisons of boys' and girls' performances on BLOT items: 3 (no-DIF) and 35 (gender-DIF).

When we recall that the procedures for item and person estimation are mirrored, we must then also countenance the complementary situation of Differential Person Functioning: the examinee who performs differentially on two tests of the latent trait delivered in different contexts. Part of Bunting's research not reported in Bond and Bunting (1995) involved the equating of students' results derived from the individually delivered Piagetian interview of the pendulum task (Bond & Fox, 2001; chap. 7) with those from the PRTIII—a demonstrated class task of the same problem (Bond & Fox, 2001; chap. 5). While the common person linking procedure did not disconfirm the presence of a single underlying construct, two sets of results were noteworthy, especially in terms of reflecting on the underlying developmental theory. First, the individual Piagetian interview version of the pendulum task was, on average, about 2 logits easier for the sample than was the pencil and paper demonstrated class-task PRTIII—almost exactly the same difference and direction for the BLOT versus PRTIII comparison reported earlier (Bond, 1995; see Stafford, 2005, p. 333). Second, two of the DIF results highlight the complexities of measuring and understanding the complexities of the human condition. A male student, described by his teacher as coming from a male-dominated military family, scored much better on the PRTIII administered in the class setting by (older, male) Bond than he did in the individual Piagetian interview administered by (younger, female) Bunting. A female student performed much better in the individual Piagetian interview with Bunting than she did in the class group test where she seemed more focussed on her young male peer sitting (very closely) beside her. And, what is more, the person fit statistics in all four instances were quite unremarkable (Bunting, 1993). Now, reflect on that little theory/practice in context dialogue.

And, of course, while the many-faceted Rasch model can be used to measure the systematic severity or leniency of judges (raters), Differential Rater Functioning would alert us to the presence of rater bias—the rater who (un)wittingly changes severity according some group characteristic. One exemplar from the 2002 Winter Olympics in Salt Lake City had WINSTEPS/Facets Rasch software author Mike Linacre, quoted in the Canadian press (Strauss, 2002; www.rasch.org/rmt/rmt154a.htm) under the headline: "New scoring system would have iced the gold for the Canadians." Linacre's analysis revealed how the scoring of the French judge in the figure skating final changed in severity in a way inconsistent with the patterns of other judges or even the French judge herself. The French judge's DRF handed the gold to the Russian pair and caused a furore. The ongoing substantive question for those in the human sciences would be, how would the theory of construct/context/rater deal with that sort of evidence?

The following software control files are used in the analysis to yield PRTIII person estimates:

```
QUEST:
title PRTIII for Chapter Five
data bond87.txt
format name 1-3 items 41-53
est
show>>PRTIII.
outshow cases>>PRTIII.cases
quit
```

Line 1 gives a name to the output.
Line 2 tells QUEST which file has the data.

Line 3 indicates that the PRTIII responses are in columns 41 to 53.

Line 4 commands QUEST to perform a Rasch estimation.

Line 5 directs the general output to a file called PRTIII.out.

Line 6 directs the person statistics output to a file called PRTIII.cases.

The inclusion of the following line before the "quit" command in the chapter 4 QUEST control file will produce BLOT person estimates for the common person equating plot:

```
show cases>>BLOT.cases.
```

```
    WINSTEPS:
    &INST
    TITLE = 'PRTIII for Chapter Five'
    NI = 13
    ITEM1 = 41
    NAME1 = 1
    IFILE = BLOT.IF
    &END
    Item 1
    Item 2

    Item 13
    END NAMES
    etc.
```

PROCEDURE FOR COMMON PERSON LINKING
OF PRTIII AND BLOT USING EXCEL

1. Run PRTIII analysis in WINSTEPS or QUEST and obtain person ability estimates and error estimates. Import these measures, including the ID number, into an Excel spreadsheet. Do the same for BLOT.

2. Merge the two files by ID (column A) and obtain the file shown in Figure 5.11.

3. Compute the average of ability estimates for BLOT (column D) and PRTIII (column E) and obtain the file demonstrated in Figure 5.12.

    Average measure for BLOT = 1.6461
    D152 = AVERAGE(D2:D151)
    Average measure for PRTIII = −0.6323
    E152 = AVERAGE(E2:E151)

4. Calculate the difference between the two means:

    Difference = 1.6461 − (−.6323) = 2.2784 = 2.28
    = (D152-E152)

5. Adjust the PRTIII person measures by incorporating the mean difference, as shown in Figure 5.13:

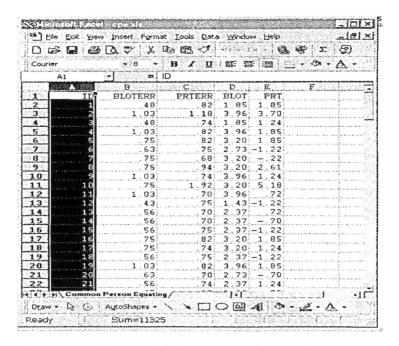

Figure 5.11.   The merged file from PRTIII and BLOT estimates.

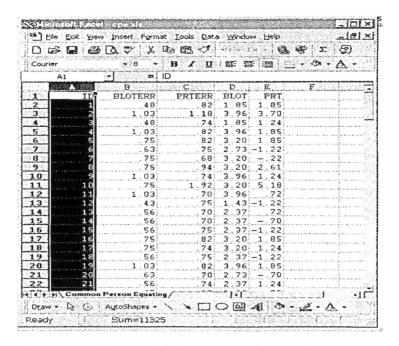

Figure 5.12.   Calculating the means of PRTIII and BLOT estimates.

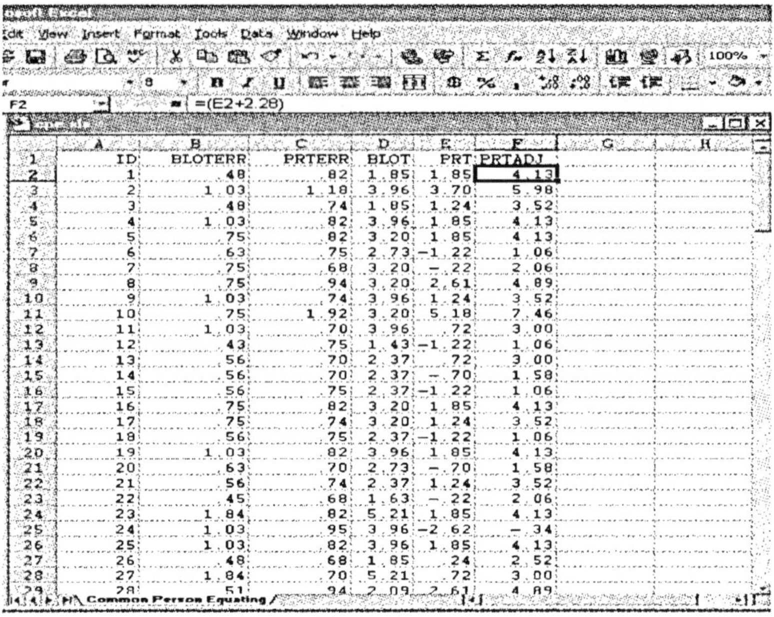

	A	B	C	D	E	F
1	ID	BLOTERR	PRTERR	BLOT	PRT	PRTADJ
2	1	.48	.82	1.85	1.85	4.13
3	2	1.03	1.18	3.96	3.70	5.98
4	3	.48	.74	1.85	1.24	3.52
5	4	1.03	.82	3.96	1.85	4.13
6	5	.75	.82	3.20	1.85	4.13
7	6	.63	.75	2.73	-1.22	1.06
8	7	.75	.68	3.20	-.22	2.06
9	8	.75	.94	3.20	2.61	4.89
10	9	1.03	.74	3.96	1.24	3.52
11	10	.75	1.92	3.20	5.18	7.46
12	11	1.03	.70	3.96	.72	3.00
13	12	.43	.75	1.43	-1.22	1.06
14	13	.56	.70	2.37	.72	3.00
15	14	.56	.70	2.37	-.70	1.58
16	15	.56	.75	2.37	-1.22	1.06
17	16	.75	.82	3.20	1.85	4.13
18	17	.75	.74	3.20	1.24	3.52
19	18	.56	.75	2.37	-1.22	1.06
20	19	1.03	.82	3.96	1.85	4.13
21	20	.63	.70	2.73	-.70	1.58
22	21	.56	.74	2.37	1.24	3.52
23	22	.45	.68	1.63	-.22	2.06
24	23	1.84	.82	5.21	1.85	4.13
25	24	1.03	.95	3.96	-2.62	-.34
26	25	1.03	.82	3.96	1.85	4.13
27	26	.48	.68	1.85	.24	2.52
28	27	1.84	.70	5.21	.72	3.00
29	28	.51	.94	2.09	2.61	4.89

Figure 5.13. Adjusting PRTIII measures by incorporating the mean difference.

Person ability estimates of PRTIII adjusted for BLOT
= person ability estimates of PRTIII + 2.28
PRTADJ:

```
F2 = (E2 + 2.28) then Fill Down.
```

6. Compute the paired 95% quality control lines: D–2*EBLOT:

```
G2 = ((D2+F2)/2-SQRT(B2*B2 + C2*C2))
```

D+ 2*EPRT:

```
H2 = ((D2+F2)/2 + SQRT(B2*B2 + C2*C2))
```

D+ 2*EBLOT:

```
I2 = ((D2+F2)/2 + SQRT(B2*B2 + C2*C2))
```

D– 2*EPRT

```
J2 = ((D2 + F2)/2 - SQRT (B2*B2 + C2 * C2))
```

By now, the working file should have the following variables added:

PRTIII adjusted ability estimates, and a1 (D –2*EBLOT), b1 (D + 2*EPRT), a2 (D –2*BLOT), b2 (D –2*EPRT), as demonstrated in Figure 5.14.

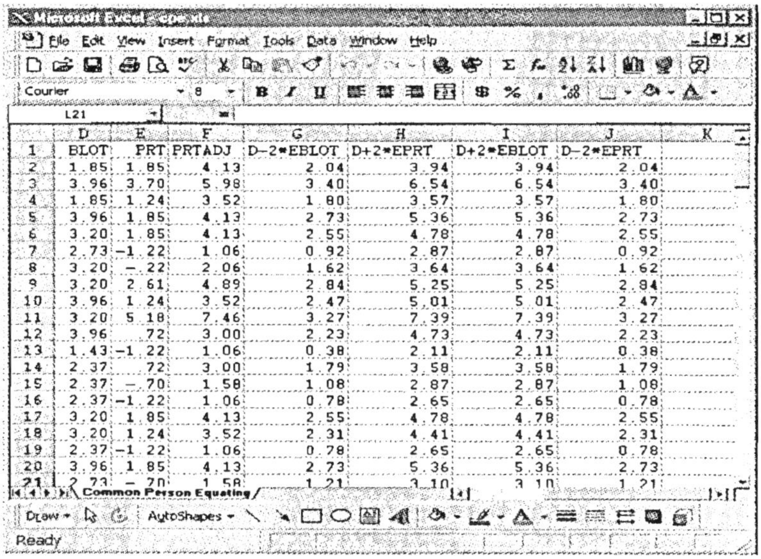

	D	E	F	G	H	I	J	K
1	BLOT	PRT	PRTADJ	D-2*EBLOT	D+2*EPRT	D+2*EBLOT	D-2*EPRT	
2	1.85	1.85	4.13	2.04	3.94	3.94	2.04	
3	3.96	3.70	5.98	3.40	6.54	6.54	3.40	
4	1.85	1.24	3.52	1.80	3.57	3.57	1.80	
5	3.96	1.85	4.13	2.73	5.36	5.36	2.73	
6	3.20	1.85	4.13	2.55	4.78	4.78	2.55	
7	2.73	-1.22	1.06	0.92	2.87	2.87	0.92	
8	3.20	-.22	2.06	1.62	3.64	3.64	1.62	
9	3.20	2.61	4.89	2.84	5.25	5.25	2.84	
10	3.96	1.24	3.52	2.47	5.01	5.01	2.47	
11	3.20	5.18	7.46	3.27	7.39	7.39	3.27	
12	3.96	.72	3.00	2.23	4.73	4.73	2.23	
13	1.43	-1.22	1.06	0.38	2.11	2.11	0.38	
14	2.37	.72	3.00	1.79	3.58	3.58	1.79	
15	2.37	-.70	1.58	1.08	2.87	2.87	1.08	
16	2.37	-1.22	1.06	0.78	2.65	2.65	0.78	
17	3.20	1.85	4.13	2.55	4.78	4.78	2.55	
18	3.20	1.24	3.52	2.31	4.41	4.41	2.31	
19	2.37	-1.22	1.06	0.78	2.65	2.65	0.78	
20	3.96	1.85	4.13	2.73	5.36	5.36	2.73	
21	2.73	-.70	1.58	1.21	3.10	3.10	1.21	

Figure 5.14. The complete working file.

7. Plot the obtained results in EXCEL using scatterplot. There are three series to be plotted: Series 1 contains BLOT ability estimates on the x axis and PRTIII ability estimates on the y

   Series 2 contains a1 on the x axis and b1 on the y axis.
   Series 3 contains a2 on the x axis and b2 on the y axis.

   The resulting graph is shown in Figure 5.8.

(Note: Values for a1 are in Column G, b1 values are in H, a2 values are in I, and values for b2 are in Column J.)

CHAPTER SIX

Measurement Using Likert Scales

The previous chapters have demonstrated how the basic features of Rasch modelling can be used to deal with simple right–wrong, or dichotomous, data. An extension of these principles allows us to extend the idea of Rasch modelling to polytomous (erroneously called polychotomous) data. One form of this approach to collecting data that has been around for a long time is the principle of the Likert scale (Likert, 1932), which usually is used to collect attitude data. Likert scales share a number of common features, regardless of which attitudes they assess, and with possible responses usually expressed in a format such as: SD (strongly disagree), D (disagree), N (neutral), A (agree), and SA (strongly agree). Similarly, each Likert scale item is provided with a stem (or statement of attitude) and the respondent is required to mark a response on the disagree–agree continuum, indicating the extent to which the statement in the stem is endorsed. An uneven number of response options might provide a "neutral" response at the mid-point while an even number of response options might force the respondent into choosing either a positive or negative response.

Interestingly, Likert scales are usually regarded by psychologists as a softer form of data collection, in which the researcher clearly acknowledges that the questions are requiring merely expressed opinions. This at least recognizes the inherent subjectivity involved in collecting information about any human condition (Hales, 1986). However, the standard methods for analyzing Likert scales then immediately disregard the subjective nature of the data by making unwarranted assumptions about their meaning. These assumptions are made in order to find a quick and easy way of producing some sort of overall score in terms of, say, computer anxiety, attitudes toward study, or endorsement of particular medical practices. We can easily show how it is both counterintuitive and mathematically inappropriate to analyze Likert data in the traditional way.

A standard display of Likert response options might take this form:

SD	D	N	A	SA
SD	D	N	A	SA
SD	D	N	A	SA
SD	D	N	A	SA
SD	D	N	A	SA

The coding for responses then could be treated in the following way:

1	2	3	4	5
1	2	3	4	5
1	2	3	4	5
1	2	3	4	5
1	2	3	4	5

where the higher number indicates a higher degree of agreement with the statement being evaluated. Five endorsements of the SA code by a respondent results in a satisfaction score of 25, five times the amount of satisfaction indicated by the respondent who endorses the five SD categories ($5 \times 1 = 5$), or almost exactly twice the satisfaction of someone who endorses two Ns and three SDs ($2 \times 3 + 3 \times 2 = 12$). If the Likert scale analyst, however, allocates the numerical codes 0, 1, 2, 3, 4 to categories SD, D, N, A, and SA as in another oft-used practice, then the arithmetic from that calculation is even more counterintuitive: five SAs = $5 \times 4 = 20$; five SDs = $5 \times 0 = 0$; and endorsing two Ns and three SDs yields a total score of $2 \times 2 + 3 \times 1 = 7$. The original coding yields scores 25:12:5 which, under the second coding, become 20:7:0. Even simple addition should be used only when the additive structure of the data has been demonstrated: It is not enough merely to allocate numbers to events according to a rule...

Whenever scores are added in this manner, the ratio, or at least the interval nature of the data, is being presumed. That is, the relative value of each response category across all items is treated as being the same, and the unit increases across the rating scale are given equal value. These assumptions are conveyed when the data analysis treats SA = 5 as having a value five times greater than that of SD = 1, and does so for each and every item on the scale. On the one hand, the subjectivity of attitude data is acknowledged each time the data are collected. Yet on the other hand, the data are subsequently analyzed in a rigidly prescriptive and inappropriate statistical way (i.e., by failure to incorporate that subjectivity into the data analysis).

It is more than likely that the stem

20. I am so afraid of computers I avoid using them. SD   D   N   A   SA

indicates much higher levels of computer anxiety in educational situations than does the stem

19. I am afraid that I will make mistakes when I use my computer. SD D N A SA

Indeed, the children who respond SA on the "mistakes" stem might routinely endorse N on the "avoid using" stem, yet traditional analyses of the SA responses to each of the stems will contribute exactly five points to the overall computer anxiety score. A more realistic representation of the way that a sample of grade school children might actually use these two stems could be something like this:

	Less Anxious	More Anxious
20. Avoid using	SD D N A SA	
19. Mistakes	SD D N A SA	

where any move to the right indicates more anxiety overall.

From this example, we can see that endorsing SA on "avoid using" should indicate a higher level of anxiety on the overall computer anxiety scale. This makes intuitive sense: Students who report that they "strongly agree" with avoidance of computers due to fear seem to show much higher levels of the underlying "computer anxiety" construct than those who merely "strongly agree" with a fear of making mistakes.

Already, the parallels can be seen between the Rasch approach to Likert scale data and what we have detailed in the previous chapters. In particular, the Rasch model allows the item difficulty of each stem or question to be based on the way in which an appropriate group of subjects actually responded to that stem in practice. Given that the subject might possibly endorse one of many response categories on a Likert scale, rather than make just the right/wrong distinction possible under the dichotomous model, the application of the Rasch model to these polytomous data will be a little more complex. In a manner similar to that used for dichotomous data, the Rasch model establishes the relative difficulty of each item stem in recording the development of computer anxiety from the lowest to the highest levels the instrument is able to record. Therefore, each item will be accorded a difficulty estimate. Rasch modelling also will establish the pattern in the use of the Likert scale categories to yield a rating scale structure common to all the items on the scale. So the Rasch Rating Scale model (RSM) has just one extra feature over the model for dichotomous data: as well as reporting person estimates and a threshold estimate for each item, it provides, in addition, one set of rating scale thresholds that is common for all of the items.

In Figure 6.1, we have represented the locations of five Likert stems and five respondents drawn from a much larger number of stems and respondents on a make-believe anxiety scale. Of course, we have used the pathway analogy introduced earlier, so the principles of Rasch analysis interpretation will remain the same as before. Indeed, before reading any further, the reader should take a few minutes to try interpreting the key attributes of the items and the persons in Figure 6.1: 1.1 = Item 1, Threshold 1; 1.2 = Item 1, Threshold 2; and so on.

The locations of the persons, as indications of how much anxiety they revealed in their responses, are indicated by the squares as previously. The location of the square indicates the person estimate (in this case, the amount of anxiety), and the

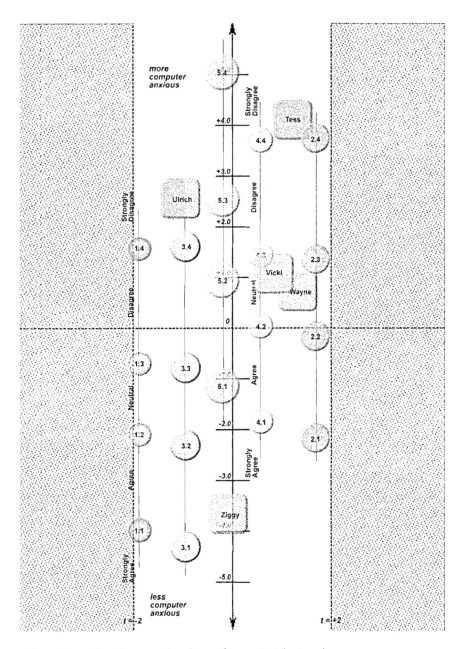

Figure 6.1.   Developmental pathway for ersatz Likert scale.

error estimates show the amount of imprecision for that location. It will be easy to recognize Tess as the most anxious person because she has the highest location on the logit scale. Ziggy is shown as the least anxious of all. Although the locations for Vicki and Wayne would be different in terms of just the person estimates alone, the size of the associated error estimates means that no meaningful difference in the anxiety levels reported by these two persons may be inferred.

The items, however, indicate a rather more complicated representation than we are accustomed to observing with dichotomous data. For dichotomous data, each item was represented on the developmental pathway (and in the computer printout) as having a single item estimate, with an associated error estimate. For rating-scale data, not only does each item have a difficulty estimate, but the scale also has a series of thresholds. This is the level at which the likelihood of being observed in a given response category (below the threshold) is exceeded by the likelihood of being observed in the next higher category (above the threshold). For clarification, these are often termed Rasch–Andrich thresholds that apply to the RSM. The alternative conceptualization, Rasch–Thurstone threshold, was described by Masters for the Partial Credit model (see the following chapter), but is often generalized to the RSM. Although it might seem a little strange to talk about failure and success on Likert attitude scales, we can easily see the appropriateness of, say, failure to agree with, or even better, failure to endorse, any particular response category. Similarly, success can be interpreted as agreement with, or better still, endorsement of, a particular response category. For the polytomous data we have collected with our Likert scale, we will need a number of thresholds for the anxiety scale to show the progression:

$$SD \rightarrow D \rightarrow N \rightarrow A \rightarrow SA.$$

Therefore, what we represented in earlier chapters with dichotomous items as

one item threshold estimate

showed how the item difficulty estimate indicated the threshold between the two possible response categories on an item. With the rating scale model, this now is represented as

SA
Fourth threshold estimate
A
Third threshold estimate
N
Second threshold estimate
D
First threshold estimate
SD

because four thresholds are needed to separate the five possible response categories on the Likert scale. But more than just that, the Rasch rating scale model does not presume the size of the step necessary to move across each threshold. It detects the threshold structure of the Likert scale in the data set, and then estimates a single set of threshold values that apply to all of the item stems in the scale.

Going back to Figure 6.1, it is obvious that the thresholds for any one item (e.g., 1.1, 1.2, 1.3) are not spread equidistantly. Some steps (say, from Threshold 2 to Threshold 3) require smaller increases in anxiety than other steps (say, from Threshold 1 to Threshold 2). However, the step structure (the pattern of the thresholds across items) is identical for every item in the Likert scale. We can see, as well, that the relative difficulty of the items also varies as it did for the dichotomous data examples. Item 1 is much easier to endorse than Item 5, for example. We can see now that even a response of SA on Item 3 indicates only a modest amount of anxiety on the overall pathway, whereas an A response for Item 5 indicates more anxiety than can be detected by Item 3 at all. The traditional statistical analysis of Likert scale data is based on the *a priori* arrangement of the response opportunities as a rectangular, ordered block, as shown on the questionnaire. However, the locations of the step thresholds in Figure 6.1 do not corroborate this traditional presumption. First, the locations for those scale positions, as revealed in the reality of practice, show that the increase in anxiety implied by the move from SD to N is less than the increase required by the move from N to A. Second, it shows that the item stems themselves also vary in the level of anxiety that they can actually detect.

We can use the Wright map representation of the anxiety variable to show what sort of anxiety responses are likely to be made by persons with overall high, medium, and low anxiety levels as reported by their use of this scale. Please take a moment to examine Figure 6.1, trying to determine for high-anxious person Tess, mid-anxious person Vicki, and low-anxious person Ziggy what categories (SD D N A SA) each is likely to have endorsed for items 1 to 5, respectively. The Rasch model treatment of Likert scale data is intuitively more satisfactory and mathematically more justifiable than the traditional "allocate 1, 2, 3, 4, 5 and just add them up" approach. The Rasch model explicitly recognizes the SD D N A SA and the subsequent coding 1 2 3 4 5 as ordered categories only, in which the value of each category is higher than that of the previous category, but by an unspecified amount. That is, the data are regarded as ordinal (not interval or ratio) data, and we use the Rasch model to transform the counts of the endorsements of these ordered Likert categories into interval scales based on the actual empirical evidence, rather than on some unfounded assumption made beforehand. The adding of raw scores to yield a person or item total score in Rasch measurement is justified only for those items which adhere to the model's requirements: They must pass the quality control criteria first. These quality control criteria are the Rasch reliability and validity diagnostics.

Therefore, in the Rasch rating-scale model, developed in the work of David Andrich (Andrich, 1978a, 1978b, 1978c) and Earling Andersen (Andersen, 1977), the finer detail of the item structure is shown. The analyses provide both an item estimate for each Likert stem as well as a set of estimates for the four thresholds that mark the boundaries between the five Likert categories: SD D N A SA. By analyzing the data in this manner, we can see immediately that the items do not carry the same relative value in the construct under investigation. In Figure 6.1, Item 3 can differentiate between the lower levels of anxiety, whereas information from Item 5 is useful in differentiating respondents who have moderate to high anxiety levels. Item 2 works in the midrange of this attitude construct, whereas Item 4 works best from midrange to higher levels, and Item 1 on this rating scale is a low-to-mid anxiety item. It can be seen, then, that a good Likert-style instrument relies on the incorporation of item stems varying in degree of difficulty, as for a test composed of dichotomous items. How the construction of step estimates for a Likert scale are conceptualized under the Rasch model might be seen easily in the ersatz data set given in Table 6.1.

The ersatz data in Table 6.1 summarize the responses of 40 persons to a 7-item Likert scale, in which the respondents were requested to indicate their degrees of agreement along a 5-point scale: SD, D, N, A, and SA. In the rows, the response information for each of the items has been recorded. The Item Counts column

TABLE 6.1
The Bases for the Estimation of Item Difficulties
and Thresholds for Ersatz Likert Scale Data

	SD (1)	D (2)	N (3)	A (4)	SA (5)	Item Counts	Possible (40 × 5)	%
Item 1	5	8	11	10	6	$5\times1+8\times2+11\times3+$ $10\times4+6\times5=124$	200	62
Item 2	9	7	10	9	5	$9\times1+7\times2+10\times3+$ $9\times4+5\times5=114$	200	57
Item 3	9	8	9	10	4	$9\times1+8\times2+9\times3+$ $10\times4+4\times5=112$	200	56
Item 4	7	9	9	8	7	$7\times1+9\times2+9\times3+$ $8\times4+7\times5=119$	200	59.5
Item 5	3	4	11	12	10	$3\times1+4\times2+11\times3+$ $12\times4+10\times5=142$	200	71
Item 6	5	9	9	9	8	$5\times1+9\times2+9\times3+$ $9\times4+8\times5=126$	200	63
Item 7	12	13	8	4	3	$12\times1+13\times2+8\times$ $3+4\times4+3\times5=93$	200	46.5
Category counts	50	58	67	62	43			
Possible (7 × 40)	280	280	280	280	280			
%	17.9	20.7	23.9	22.1	15.4			

shows how the responses in each category were added to produce a count for each item. That information would be used as the basis for the estimation of item difficulties. In the columns, the response information for each Likert response category has been recorded. The latter information would be used as the basis for the estimation of the rating scale thresholds, and that set of threshold values would be applied identically to all of the items on the scale. In other words, the thresholds are estimated once for all items. In the cases of both item difficulties and thresholds, the estimation is based on the proportion of the actual responses to the total possible responses. These proportions for items and response categories are shown as the percentage entries, which are the basis on which the transformation into log odd units or logits take place.

  So it is not merely the range of anxiety detected by the SD D N A SA categories that is important. To make a good instrument, it is necessary to use a collection of item stems that also tap into a range of anxiety levels. It is then rather useless to use a statistical procedure that treats all items as having the same value and all SAs as worth 5 on the final score. In the hypothetical example of Figure 6.1, responses of SA on Items 4 and 5 indicate higher levels of the underlying construct than SAs on Items 1 and 3. Although it is possible that the endorsement of SA for Item 5 might really indicate five times the anxiety detected by the endorsement of SD on Item 3, it is quite clear that SA on Item 3 cannot be treated as indicating five times more anxiety than SD on Item 4. There is a considerable anxiety scale increase between SD on Item 3 and SA on Item 5, but there is not nearly so large a gap between SD on Item 4 and SA on Item 3. We need to use Rasch modelling to help us construct a measure of the underlying construct, and then to interpret each person estimate as the measure of the person's revelation of that latent trait as indicated on the assessment instrument.

PRACTICAL IMPLICATIONS

What then would we need to do to make a Rasch analysis of a rating scale work, given that we have used or developed a Likert-style instrument designed to investigate a single dimension of an attitude or opinion, and have administered that instrument to a suitable sample of appropriate persons? First, we should note that moving from a dichotomous to a polytomous Rasch model should prompt us to reconsider what might constitute a suitable sample of persons for a rating scale analysis. As always, we would need a sample varied enough in the presence of the underlying psychological construct that all the response options for all of the items will be used. However, given that a typical Likert scale has, say, five response opportunities (e.g., SD D N A SA) rather than just two (✔ or ✗), we will need proportionately more persons in our sample to achieve the same density of data for each response opportunity. It should be recalled that the precision of the estimates depends on the amount of good statistical information. Whereas 40 persons might yield, say, 25 ✔ and 15 ✗ responses on a dichotomous item, those same 40 persons might yield 6 SDs, 8 Ds, 12 Ns, 9 As, and 5 SDs on a Likert-format item.

The immediate consequence would be less measurement precision (i.e., larger error estimates) at each of the item thresholds as a direct result of the thinner spread of the 40 responses across the five response categories. But the person estimates would be more precise, as any given number of polytomous items will always provide more statistical information than the same number of dichotomous responses. Problems might be further compounded if the full range of response opportunities was not used by the persons in the sample. The interpretation of a Likert data matrix containing empty cells in the data set (i.e., those with zero responses) is not unambiguous using the rating scale model. Such empty cells might be a result of not using a sample large enough to estimate effectively the difficulty for every category threshold, or it might be the result of using numbers or types of response categories that are inappropriate for the construct. These and other related issues are canvassed in chapter 11.

We then would indicate to the Rasch software the number of items we were attempting to analyze as well as the range of responses encountered in the data file. Whereas most simple statistical summations of Likert responses use the SD = 1, D = 2, N = 3, A = 4, and SA = 5 coding system, it is a good practice, at least in the beginning, to use a coding system that is a logical extension of that used for dichotomous data, thus starting with zero: SD = 0, D = 1, N = 2, A = 3, and SA = 4. In both instances, 0 is used to record the minimum level of the construct detected by the item, and 1 indicates the next detectable level. In both instances, 1 indicates detection of more of the underlying construct than 0 does.

With dichotomous data, we exhaust the response opportunities at that point. Even a mathematics professor will get the same code of 1 for a correct response to the item $3 + 4 = \square$ as does the little child in Year 2 who responds correctly that $3 + 4 = 7$. The item $3 + 4 = \square$ cannot differentiate the professor's mathematics ability from that of the child. With the Likert format, we have a larger, but still finite, number of ordered categories, to use in detecting gradual increases in the underlying construct. Most importantly, the ordinal nature of the category relations SD < D < N < A < SA is conserved exactly in the use of the coding numerals 0 < 1 < 2 < 3 < 4.

Indeed, some Rasch software for rating scale analysis will require the use of 0 as the indicator of the lowest detectable category in the data set. In other software, the codes will be treated automatically as though 0 was used for the lowest category (i.e., by default). The possibilities for confusion and misunderstanding can be compounded further when other Rasch modelling techniques are used. It is possible to avoid being caught unaware by routinely using 0 for the lowest detectable category and 1 for the next higher detectable category, with 2, 3, and so on being used as appropriate. In passing, we should note again that 0 has a different meaning from "blank" in Rasch modelling: Whereas 0 is routinely used to indicate the presence of the lowest detectable category (e.g., wrong or SD, say), "blank" indicates the absence of a recorded response (i.e., missing data). Although sometimes it might be a reasonable inference to treat "blank" as 0 in dichotomous data (i.e., as ✗ rather than ✔), the problem of how "blank" should be treated in a Likert data file is not so easily resolved. Should it be treated as the lowest detectable category, SD? Why? As this person's average score for the rest of the items? Why? As the person's modal response? Why? As the average or modal response for all other persons on this item? Why? These are the imputation procedures routinely used in the traditional approaches to analyzing Likert scale data. Our assertion is that the best inference concludes that somehow the respondent did not respond to the item. It should be left blank. The Rasch model has no problem accommodating such missing data.

ANALYZING RATING SCALE DATA: THE COMPUTER ANXIETY INDEX

In this worked example based on King and Bond (1996), we have tried to determine the extent to which grade school children's Likert scale responses to the Computer Opinion Survey (Simonson, Maurer, Montag-Torardi, & Whitaker, 1987) could be used to construct a measure of computer anxiety. The Computer Opinion Survey consists of 26 positively or negatively worded Likert-type items developed from a larger number of items considered by its authors as indicative of a person's feelings of anxiety toward computers. As each stem has six response options (1 = strongly agree, 2 = agree, 3 = slightly agree, 4 = slightly disagree, 5 = disagree, 6 = strongly disagree), the possible range of the CAIN (Computer Anxiety INdex) scores extends from 26 (i.e., 26 answers each having a low anxiety value of 1) to 156 (i.e., 26 answers each having a high anxiety value of 6) for a complete response set. Following the principles set out in the Test Administrator's Manual (Montag, Simonson, & Maurer, 1984), negatively worded items are scored in the reverse direction (6-5-4-3-2-1), and the CAIN for each respondent is calculated by adding all the raw scores across the 26 items: adopting the scoring technique that is ubiquitous in Likert scale use in the human sciences.

The authors of the Computer Opinion Survey claim that the CAIN scores have the usual high statistical estimates of reliability and concurrent validity for investigating computer anxiety (King & Bond, 1996; Montag et al., 1984; Simonson et al., 1987). The investigation of the CAIN (King & Bond, 1996) was prompted by the counterintuitive results from an earlier investigation (King, 1993), which showed by using conventional statistical procedures that a sample of 120 year 7 students made pre- to post-test gains in computer anxiety after being exposed to greater than usual numbers of microcomputers in normal classroom environments over a period of 9 months.

Figure 6.2 provides the item-map representation of responses that a large sample ($n = 372$) of year 7 students made to the Computer Opinion Survey. The display is in the format of the pathway analogy introduced earlier. The figure is a little cramped given that it represents the item difficulties, error estimates, and item fit estimates for each of the 26 Computer Opinion Survey items while, for illustration purposes, it also represents the pattern of the five threshold locations for (only) a number of items.

At this point in the chapter, we have provided a map of all 26 items to show the bases of the decision to include just some of these items in a subsequent analysis. A perusal of the details in Figure 6.2 will lead to the inference that a number of

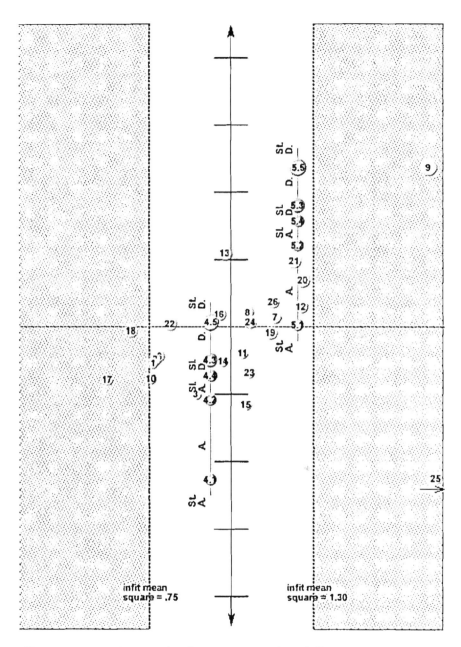

Figure 6.2. Developmental pathway representation of all 26 CAIN items (some with associated threshold estimates).

111

the items do not appear to be revealing the same construct (computer anxiety) that the others seem to be tapping. Which items are they? What is the evidence of inadequate fit?

The map for the Computer Opinion Survey items also provides *prima facie* evidence for the claim made earlier in this chapter that as a general rule, Likert attitude or opinion items are likely to vary in terms of their difficulty, agreeability, or endorsability. Which are the easier Computer Opinion Survey items for these grade school students to endorse? With which items is it more difficult to agree? How does the plotting of the five-item threshold values for items 4 and 5 on the map provide evidence for varying item difficulty? The location of those threshold estimates reveals a basic problem with the Computer Opinion Survey for this sample. The thresholds between *slightly agree, slightly disagree,* and *disagree* (thresholds 3 and 4) are quite confused. Not only are the thresholds very close together, their locations do not increase according to the logical order principle required by the Rasch measurement model. At this point we would conclude only that the category *slightly disagree* is nonmodal for this sample. It is not necessary to conclude that the category ordinal structure is incorrect. Issues related to rating scale design are canvassed in chapter 11.

A section showing the output of the Rasch item estimates for the Computer Opinion Survey items is included as Table 6.2 so the detail of the map locations can be confirmed more easily. In this instance, the Rasch output was requested with the items listed in item difficulty order rather than the order in which the items appeared in the test (i.e., question 1 to question 26). This makes it possible to start at the top of the table and at the bottom of the map to check the correspondences between the difficulty estimates and the item locations.

Items 1, 10, 17, and 18 fall to the left side of the satisfactory fit zone in Figure 6.2 (suggesting possible item redundancy), whereas items 9 and 25 fall to the right side "misfit" zone (indicating erratic response patterns). In Figure 6.2, the unstandardized infit mean square values, rather than the standardized infit *t* values, are plotted. Issues related to the interpretation of fit are canvassed in chapter 12. When King and Bond (1996) calculated Rasch computer anxiety person estimates for these data, they decided to eliminate the misfitting items and perform a second analysis using just the 20 fitting items, with the aim of getting more valid person computer anxiety measures from the Computer Opinion Survey responses. Although we take the idea that our test respondents are "sampled" from the total possible population of persons for granted, we tend not to view our tests, checklists, or Likert prompts as "sampled" from the total possible population of items. Given that the logic and techniques of modelling item responses in Rasch analysis are specifically and completely interchangeable with the logic and techniques of modelling person responses, it is useful to remember that our particular test items are selected from the total population of possible items in the same way that our particular test respondents are drawn from the total population of possible persons.

Figures 6.3 and 6.4 introduce complete person–item (Wright or variable) maps for the computer anxiety analysis referred to earlier. It will be recalled that we introduced this representation of the data in chapter 4 when we looked at the idea of the

TABLE 6.2
Item and Threshold Estimates (With Fit Statistics)
for All 26 Computer Anxiety Index Items

Item #	Difficulty Error	Taus					Infit Mean Square	Outfit Mean Square	Infit t	Outfit t
		1	2	3	4	5				
9	0.78	−0.67	−0.09	0.18	0.09	0.49	1.55	1.46	4.1	3.1
	0.07	0.03	0.03	0.03	0.04	0.08				
13	0.63	−0.67	−0.09	0.18	0.09	0.49	0.92	0.72	−0.7	−2.3
	0.06	0.03	0.03	0.03	0.04	0.08				
21	0.55	−0.67	−0.09	0.18	0.09	0.49	1.17	1.03	1.6	0.3
	0.06	0.03	0.03	0.03	0.04	0.08				
20	0.42	−0.67	−0.09	0.18	0.09	0.49	1.25	1.33	2.4	2.5
	0.06	0.03	0.03	0.03	0.04	0.08				
26	0.26	−0.67	−0.09	0.18	0.09	0.49	1.08	1.08	0.8	0.7
	0.05	0.03	0.03	0.03	0.04	0.08				
12	0.23	−0.67	−0.09	0.18	0.09	0.49	1.23	1.14	2.4	1.2
	0.05	0.03	0.03	0.03	0.04	0.08				
8	0.17	−0.67	−0.09	0.18	0.09	0.49	0.96	0.88	−0.5	−1.1
	0.05	0.03	0.03	0.03	0.04	0.08				
16	0.16	−0.67	−0.09	0.18	0.09	0.49	0.91	0.89	−1.1	−1.0
	0.05	0.03	0.03	0.03	0.04	0.08				
7	0.15	−0.67	−0.09	0.18	0.09	0.49	1.09	1.14	1.0	1.3
	0.05	0.03	0.03	0.03	0.04	0.08				
24	0.10	−0.67	−0.09	0.18	0.09	0.49	1.01	1.00	0.2	0.0
	0.05	0.03	0.03	0.03	0.04	0.08				
22	0.09	−0.67	−0.09	0.18	0.09	0.49	0.80	0.72	−2.6	−2.8
	0.05	0.03	0.03	0.03	0.04	0.08				
5	0.08	−0.67	−0.09	0.18	0.09	0.49	1.15	1.10	1.8	1.0
	0.05	0.03	0.03	0.03	0.04	0.08				
18	0.03	−0.67	−0.09	0.18	0.09	0.49	0.70	0.67	−4.2	−3.5
	0.05	0.03	0.03	0.03	0.04	0.08				
19	0.01	−0.67	−0.09	0.18	0.09	0.49	1.07	1.10	0.9	0.9
	0.05	0.03	0.03	0.03	0.04	0.08				
11	−0.08	−0.67	−0.09	0.18	0.09	0.49	0.95	1.02	−0.7	0.3
	0.04	0.03	0.03	0.03	0.04	0.08				
6	−0.11	−0.67	−0.09	0.18	0.09	0.49	0.78	0.80	−3.2	−2.1
	0.04	0.03	0.03	0.03	0.04	0.08				
2	−0.13	−0.67	−0.09	0.18	0.09	0.49	0.77	0.84	−3.3	−1.6
	0.04	0.03	0.03	0.03	0.04	0.08				
14	−0.14	−0.67	−0.09	0.18	0.09	0.49	0.92	0.91	−1.2	−0.9
	0.04	0.03	0.03	0.03	0.04	0.08				
1	−0.15	−0.67	−0.09	0.18	0.09	0.49	0.77	0.99	−3.5	−0.1
	0.04	0.03	0.03	0.03	0.04	0.08				

(continued)

TABLE 6.2 (*Continued*)

Item #	Difficulty Error	Taus					Infit Mean Square	Outfit Mean Square	Infit t	Outfit t
		1	2	3	4	5				
23	-0.24	-0.67	-0.09	0.18	0.09	0.49	1.01	1.10	0.1	1.1
	0.04	0.03	0.03	0.03	0.04	0.08				
10	-0.27	-0.67	-0.09	0.18	0.09	0.49	0.76	0.86	-3.8	-1.6
	0.04	0.03	0.03	0.03	0.04	0.08				
17	-0.28	-0.67	-0.09	0.18	0.09	0.49	0.63	0.64	-6.2	-4.4
	0.04	0.03	0.03	0.03	0.04	0.08				
4	-0.37	-0.67	-0.09	0.18	0.09	0.49	0.88	0.95	-1.8	-0.5
	0.04	0.03	0.03	0.03	0.04	0.08				
3	-0.39	-0.67	-0.09	0.18	0.09	0.49	0.85	1.02	-2.4	0.2
	0.04	0.03	0.03	0.03	0.04	0.08				
15	-0.49	-0.67	-0.09	0.18	0.09	0.49	1.00	1.00	0.1	0.0
	0.04	0.03	0.03	0.03	0.04	0.08				
25	-1.01	-0.67	-0.09	0.18	0.09	0.49	2.10	2.43	13.0	11.6
	0.04	0.03	0.03	0.03	0.04	0.08				
Mean	0.00						1.01	1.03	-0.3	0.1
SD	0.38						0.30	0.34	3.6	2.9

sample of persons being properly targeted by the sample of items. Both figures show the distribution of person estimates along the logit scale for the variable on the left side. Figure 6.4 derives from WINSTEPS output and plots the item difficulty estimates for all 26 CAIN items (i.e., one difficulty estimate per item). Figure 6.3 derives from QUEST output and plots the threshold estimates for the 20 CAIN items included in the final analysis (i.e., five threshold estimates per item).

It is also worth noting that the versions of item–person maps routinely seen in Rasch analysis output from the regular analysis software programs (e.g., QUEST, WINSTEPS) focus on the relative distributions of item difficulty and person ability estimates only. These maps do not try to include item fit and person fit representations on the same map as we have with our pathway map in which the white pathway between the dotted lines is meant to indicate sufficient fit.

In Figure 6.3, we can discern that the targeting of this sample's computer anxiety levels has not been well accomplished by the current version of the Computer Opinion Survey. Three aspects of the graphic evidence help to demonstrate this. First, the "tail" of the distribution of persons (each X represents two persons here) hangs considerably below the lowest levels of item thresholds. In other words, some 60 of these school students have computer anxiety levels so low that they are barely detected at the extreme low range of the measure. The computer anxiety levels of these persons will be measured very imprecisely by the Computer Opinion Survey. Second, and conversely, at least the A and SA categories of most items are located well above the locations of the most computer-anxious persons

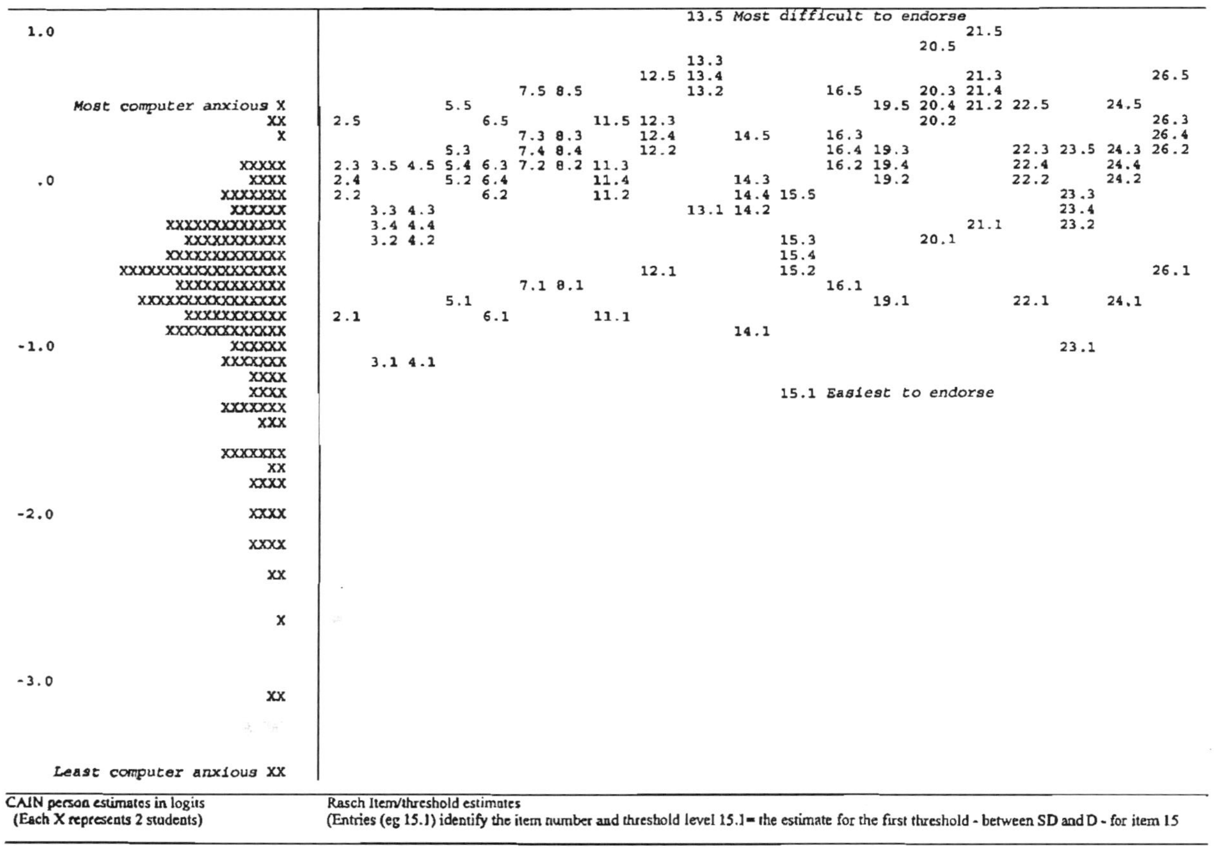

Figure 6.3 — Computer anxiety estimates map (rotated)

```
1.0
                                                    13.5 Most difficult to endorse

                                                           21.5
                                                    20.5
     Most computer anxious X
                           X                                                                           26.5
                                                              21.3
                                                              21.4
                                        12.5   13.3  16.5  20.3  21.2  22.5        24.5          26.3
                                 7.5 8.5 12.4  13.4        20.4                                  26.4
                      5.5  6.5   11.5 12.3 13.2       19.5 20.2                                  26.2
                         7.3 8.3
.0   2.5        3.5 4.5  7.4 8.4  14.5       16.3 19.3        22.3  23.5          24.3
          XXXX     5.3 6.3 7.2 8.2 11.3       16.4 19.4        22.4  23.3          24.4
           XXX     5.4 6.4      11.4          16.2 19.2        22.2  23.4          24.2
          XXXXX    5.2 6.2      11.2 14.3 15.5                      23.2
        XXXXXXX  3.3 4.3        13.1 14.4
      XXXXXXXXX  3.4 4.4             14.2
     XXXXXXXXXXX 3.2 4.2
    XXXXXXXXXXXX                     15.3       20.1 21.1
   XXXXXXXXXXXXX                     15.4
    XXXXXXXXXXX                      15.2
     XXXXXXXXXX  2.1   5.1 6.1  7.1 8.1 12.1  16.1 19.1        22.1              24.1     26.1
      XXXXXXX
      XXXXX
-1.0  XXXXX     3.1 4.1              14.1
      XXXX
       XXX                                    15.1 Easiest to endorse
      XXXXXXX
        XX
-2.0  XXXX
      XXX
       XX
        X
-3.0
       XX

     Least computer anxious XX
```

CAIN person estimates in logits
(Each X represents 2 students)

Rasch Item/threshold estimates
(Entries (eg 15.1) identify the item number and threshold level 15.1 = the estimate for the first threshold - between SD and D - for item 15

Figure 6.3. Computer anxiety estimates for the large sample of 11 and 12 year olds and associated item category thresholds for 20 CAIN items.

115

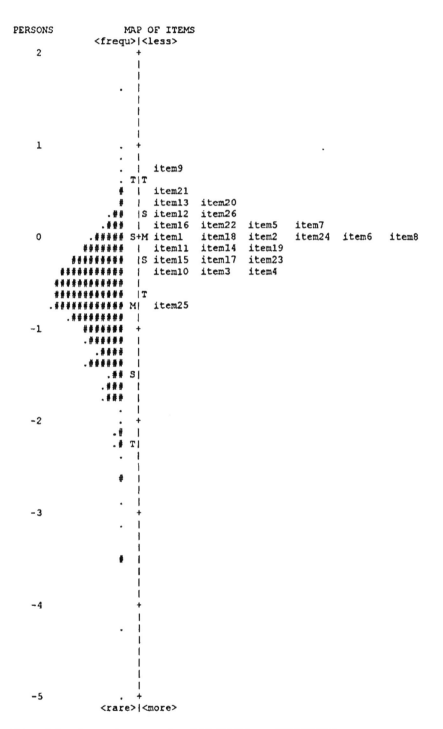

Figure 6.4.   Person-item map for all 26 CAIN items (WINSTEPS).

in this sample. We need a sample of respondents who are much more computer-anxious than this group if we want more than very imprecisely measured item difficulty estimates for the Computer Opinion Survey. Finally, the bulk of the persons are not located opposite the bulk of the items. The distribution of person anxiety estimates in Figure 6.3 is centered around a mean value of –0.80 logits. Compared with the mean value of 0 logits routinely adopted for items, the anxiety levels of these persons are, on average, considerably lower than the anxiety levels of these items. Further administrations of the Computer Opinion Survey would be warranted with either persons who are more computer-anxious than these, with items that detect lower levels of computer anxiety, or preferably with both.

Figure 6.3 shows, and the values in Table 6.2 confirm, that Items 3, 4, 14, 15, and 23 are the easier-to-endorse items. Not only are the SD categories (i.e., below the first thresholds, 3.1, 4.1, 14.1, etc.) easier for the low-anxiety persons to endorse, but the SA categories for the same items (i.e., above the fifth thresholds, 3.5, 4.5, 14.5, etc.) become endorsable at lower levels of computer anxiety than even the fourth threshold of other items such as 20 and 21 (20.4, 21.4). Indeed it is as easy to endorse Item 15 at the highest anxiety (strongly agree) level (i.e., above 15.5) as it is to respond "slightly disagree" to Item 13 (i.e., above 13.2).

The tabular output from the Rasch analysis for Likert-type items is necessarily more complicated than the tables for dichotomous items. Although we could expect to see a single difficulty estimate for each item, we also would expect to see values and errors for each of the response thresholds. In Table 6.2, we see that each of the 26 Computer Opinion Survey items has a single-item difficulty estimate as well as five threshold difficulty estimates (and error estimates) recorded. However, just one set of fit statistics is included for each item, just as we are used to having with dichotomous data. A little slice of the person statistics output (Table 6.3) shows that the person estimates, errors, and fit indices remain the same in the Rasch analysis for Likert-type data. In this example, each person has a single computer anxiety estimate expressed in logits (derived from the logarithmic transformation of the odds based on that person's total raw score on the 20 Computer Opinion Survey items), an error (or imprecision) estimate for that anxiety level, and both unstandardized and standardized fit estimates. The fit estimates warn us when the person estimate should not be regarded as a fair summary of that person's computer anxiety. The fit statistics for this section of the person output look very good, although we would want to be a bit circumspect about accepting the computer anxiety estimate of 0 logits for Person 81 (infit $t = -2.79$; outfit $t = -2.69$) at face value. (Perhaps Person 81 used only one or two of the available response categories.) The interpretation of fit is taken up more comprehensively in chapter 12.

The detailed threshold output is very helpful to our understanding of the variable under investigation, in terms of both the structure of the Likert-scale items and the direct interpretation of any person's most probable response to each item, given that person's location. However, for other purposes, such as using the linking procedures described in chapter 5 or comparing the response levels of two groups taking the same test, all that item information becomes unwieldy. What is needed is the single difficulty estimate and associated error for each rating scale test item. How

TABLE 6.3
Excerpt From Person Estimates on 20-Item Computer Anxiety Index (CAIN)

Name	Maximum Possible Score	Estimate	Error	Infit Mean Square	Outfit Mean Square	Infit t	Outfit t
81	48 100	0.00	0.16	0.44	0.44	−2.79	−2.69
82	7 100	−1.85	0.37	1.27	1.13	0.65	0.41
83	15 100	−1.13	0.25	0.67	0.70	−0.72	−0.63
84	25 100	−0.66	0.19	1.28	1.18	0.85	0.59
85	27 100	−0.59	0.19	1.28	1.20	0.90	0.65
86	5 100	−2.18	0.44	1.01	0.82	0.22	−0.14
87	19 100	−0.91	0.22	0.79	0.92	−0.45	−0.07
88	30 100	−0.49	0.18	0.51	0.60	−1.83	−1.33
89	35 100	−0.34	0.17	0.85	0.95	−0.47	−0.05
90	26 100	−0.62	0.19	1.14	1.31	0.50	0.91
91	16 100	−1.07	0.24	1.06	0.87	0.28	−0.16
92	46 100	−0.05	0.16	0.90	0.91	−0.30	−0.26
93	15 100	−1.13	0.25	0.71	0.95	−0.59	0.04
94	8 100	−1.72	0.35	1.13	0.95	0.41	0.08
95	18 100	−0.96	0.23	0.55	0.64	−1.19	−0.87
96	23 100	−0.73	0.20	0.70	0.93	−0.80	−0.08
97	20 100	−0.86	0.21	0.91	1.00	−0.11	0.15
98	27 100	−0.59	0.19	1.00	1.21	0.10	0.67
99	11 100	−1.42	0.29	0.96	0.91	0.07	−0.04
Mean		−0.80		1.05	1.05	−0.12	−0.09
SD		0.69		0.63	0.66	1.64	1.61

could such a concept be interpreted in practice? If we go back to the depiction of the response categories that we used at the beginning of this chapter, we can introduce a necessarily naïve view of the Likert item difficulty/endorsability concept and then amplify it with what we have learned from the successful application of Rasch measurement principles to rating scale analysis.

The simplistic version has the response categories set up in the standard format with a little caret (^) to indicate the balance point for that item:

1.   SD   D   N   A   SA
                                         ^

The sample's responses to this first item are so regularly distributed across the five categories that the balance point for the item, its difficulty or endorsability, is in the N category. For the next item, many more respondents have endorsed the SD and D categories rather than the A and SA categories, so the balance point for that item is better represented thus:

2.   SD   D   N   A   SA
                            ^

Item 2 is more difficult for the sample to endorse. It takes all the N, A, and SA category responses together to balance the D and SD responses. Item 3 is evaluated rather differently by the sample:

3.   SD   D   N   A   SA
                                      ^

Heavy use of the A and SA categories relative to the other three response items indicates that this item is much easier for this sample to endorse. The bulk of the sample "agrees" or "strongly agrees" with the statement in Item 3.

When the response balance points for these items are aligned (after all, this is just one sample responding to all of these items), the comparative display of item difficulties relative to the one sample of persons has the following appearance:

1.   SD   D   N   A   SA
2.   SD   D   N   A   SA
3.   SD   D   N   A   SA
easy to endorse   ^   difficult to endorse

Item 1 is moderately difficult for this sample to endorse, and Item 2 is more difficult to endorse, whereas Item 3 shows as easier to endorse. The balance-point concept works a bit like a teeter-totter or seesaw. Both the number of persons endorsing the category and the distance of the category from the balance point will determine the effect of response distributions on item difficulty. Imagine the effect of the following possible variations in response distribution for the three preceding items. What would be the effect on the difficulty of Item 3 if a few of the respondents were moved to N from A, or if the same number were moved to SD from D, or to SD from SA? Although we cannot definitively predict the effect of these category distribution changes in the absence of more complete information about sample size and distribution, the balance-point principle predicts that the last move (SD < SA) would cause the greatest increase in item difficulty, whereas the N < A move (closest to the fulcrum) would cause a minimal difficulty increase.

The Rasch measurement approach to rating scale analysis as it is applied to Likert-type items uses all the foregoing information in estimating overall item difficulty estimates. The reduction of apparent detail in summarizing four or five threshold points per item in just one item difficulty estimate and one error estimate per item is not performed by discarding information, but by modelling all the relevant information according to its location along the item scale.

Figure 6.4 provides a person–item map using the item estimates, rather than threshold estimates, from rating scale analysis. Each item estimate can be regarded as the balance point for the response distribution across that item's categories, and of course the variation of item difficulty estimates shows the difficulty of the items relative to each other and, in the case of the item–person map in Figure 6.4, relative to the person distribution. Rasch overall item difficulties for polytomous items are usually set according to the balance point at which the highest and lowest categories are equally probable (Wright & Masters, 1981).

The tables of Rasch item outputs for rating scales routinely contain two aspects that distinguish the output from that generated by the other members of the family of Rasch models: Every item has its overall estimate of item difficulty, whereas all items share a threshold structure that is common to all items. This is obvious in Table 6.2, where repeating the identical threshold structure values for every item is redundant, but done to emphasize this distinctive feature of the RSM. The item difficulty estimates vary from item to item, but the threshold structure modelled by the Rasch analysis of the empirical data is common to all items. Figure 6.4 shows the overall item difficulties (the first column) from Table 6.2, whereas Figure 6.3 combines that information with the threshold estimates (the taus for five thresholds) to show the item/threshold structure of the Computer Opinion Survey results. The reader can confirm that the item and threshold values displayed graphically in Figures 6.2, 6.3, and 6.4 actually are those generated by the Rasch analysis as shown in Table 6.2. Of course, Figures 6.3 and 6.4 do not display fit information.

The original developers of Likert scales such as the CAIN easily could complain that considerable injury has been done to their work when items are deleted from the analyses and levels of anxiety are reported by person estimates rather than raw scores. After all, the items were put there for very good reasons: content and face validity, and so on. But the very act of adding all the responses to get a total raw score presumes that the responses of all items contribute to the underlying construct and that they contribute equally. This preliminary attempt to use the Rasch model to construct a measure of computer anxiety using the CAIN data suggests that such presumptions are not warranted in this case: Not all items contribute to the same latent trait, and of those items that do, they do not all contribute equally.

Of course, analyses of rating scales rarely remain at the uncomplicated level reported by King and Bond (1996) and discussed in this introductory chapter. Chapter 11 shows how quite sophisticated considerations of Likert response categories and Rasch-based analyses of rating scale data can be conceptualized. However, the continuing fundamental thrust of this volume is the prerequisite necessity: First of all, the researcher must construct a measure and understand the meaning of that measure in practice; then, go on to use all the usual statistical techniques after that.

Control file for QUEST:

```
Title CAIN Analysis ALL ITEMS
data CAIN.dat
codes 0123456
recode (123456) (012345)
recode (012345) (543210)
!5,7,9,11,12,14,18,19,20,21,22,23,24,25
```

```
format items 3'-28
estimate rate
show!stat=tau>>CAINshow.doc
show items!stat=tau>>CAINitem.doc
show cases>>CAINcase.doc
quit
```

Title line gives a title "CAIN Analysis ALL ITEMS" to each output file.

Data names the data file as "CAIN.dat."

Codes indicates which codes in the file are valid.

First recode statement changes 1 to 0, 2 to 1, 3 to 2, and so forth, for all items so each minimum response is a 0.

Second recode statement changes 0 to 5, 1 to 4, 2 to 3, and so forth, for Items 5, 7, 9, 11, 12, 14, 18, 19, 20, 21, 22, 23, 24, and 25 (the negatively worded items), so higher scores always represent more anxiety.

Format indicates the columns in the data file where the responses for the 26 CAIN items are located.

The "estimate" command is appended with "rate" to indicate the use of Andrich's rating scale model.

Show commands include the qualifier "!stat=tau" to request output according using Rasch- Andrich thresholds, and to direct the output to files that will open with a word processor.

Control file for WINSTEPS:

```
; This file is Cain.CON
&INST TITLE="RS analysis of CAIN data"
NI=26
NAME1=1
ITEM1=3
CODES=123456
Newscore=654321
RESCORE=00001010101101000111111110
TABLES='1111111111111100110000'
;IDELQU=Y
&END
item1
   item2
   item3
   item4
   item5
   item6
   item7
   item8
   item9
```

```
item10
item11
item12
item13
item14
item15
item16
item17
item18
item19
item20
item21
item22
item23
item24
item25
item26
end names
```

Codes indicates which codes in the file are valid.

Newscore statement changes 1 to 5, 2 to 4, 3 to 3, 4 to 2, and 5 to 1.

Rescore changes the coding in newscore for Items 5, 7, 9, 11, 12, 14, 18, 19, 20, 21, 22, 23, 24, and 25 (the negatively worded items) so higher scores always represent more anxiety.

Note: In this WINSTEPS example, 1 not 0 is used to indicate the lowest response category.

Bond&FoxSteps:

The complete data file, control lines, and tutorial for this analysis are preloaded into the Bond&FoxSteps software included on the accompanying CD.

CHAPTER SEVEN

The Partial Credit Rasch Model

There can be no doubt that the extension of the Rasch model for simple dichotomous data into the rating scale model (Andersen, 1977; Andrich, 1978b) has had an enormous impact on Rasch modelling. The rating scale model is now used routinely for the analysis of Likert scale data (chap. 6), but Andrich originally intended it for another purpose. It was first intended for use in the evaluation of written essays. It would assist the examination process by producing measures from values applied to qualitative essay rating scales by examiners. However, it also paved the way for all the Rasch models that involve data with more than two values (0, 1).

The rating scale model requires that every item in a test have the same number of response categories, as we have come to expect from Likert scales. The items can have 3, 4, 5, or even 6 response opportunities, but nevertheless, the number of response options must be the same for every item on the test. That requirement suggests some unexpected difficulties that might occur even with Likert scales, especially during their development or early use. Just because the response form provides, for example, five response opportunities for each item, this does not ensure that all five response categories actually will be used in practice by the persons in the chosen sample. In spite of the researcher's intention to collect data for all five categories on all items, the data set might reveal different numbers of categories that were actually used for some items (we take up this and related problems in chap. 11). Moreover, we can easily envisage other testing situations in which it would be more useful not to be restricted to having the same number of response opportunities for every item.

Geoff Masters from Melbourne (Wright & Masters, 1982) is usually acknowledged as the developer of the model routinely called the partial credit Rasch model (PCM). The partial credit model specifically incorporates the possibility of having differing numbers of response opportunities for different items on the same test. Consider the possibility of tests in which one or more intermediate levels of success might exist between complete failure and complete success (i.e., partially correct answers). For this reason, the partial credit model is highly applicable in educational and other testing situations in which "part marks" are awarded for partial success. However, a very important Rasch principle must be observed in the awarding of part marks. Whereas school teachers might give two marks here, a half mark here, and one mark there, to give a total of 3.5 (part marks) out of a possible 5 for aspects of a partially correct solution to a math problem, Rasch modelling principles require that the part marks be awarded in an ordered way, so that each increasing value represents an increase in the underlying ability being tested.

For example, the ordered values 0, 1, and 2 might be applied to an item as follows: 0 = totally wrong, 1 = partially correct, and 2 = completely correct; values 0, 1, 2, and 3 might be used with another item thus: 0 = totally wrong, 1 = partially correct, 2 = almost completely correct, and 3 = completely correct. So, is there a limit to the number of partial credit steps between complete failure and complete success on an item? Of course we should recur to the guiding theory we are using. What does it tell us about the number of ordered steps between failure and success? Those who start with an explicit theoretical orientation will decide the number of steps on the basis of the guiding theory. For those with a more pragmatic bent, it will be necessary to develop a "part marks" schedule based on conceptual analysis, or by reflecting on observation of candidates' performances. In any empirical situation such as a test, a marking key, or an observation schedule, eventually we will be limited to the number of meaningful steps that are useful in discerning the display of the varying ability levels we find in our sample. An extreme case might be the use of visual analog scales (VAS) in psychophysical and medical research, such as requiring subjects to indicate along a 10-cm scale just how much pain they feel in arthritic joints. Routinely, the score is read from the scale in millimeters, but there is no empirical evidence at all that respondents can meaningfully discriminate among the 101 response intervals on the scale. The same issues arise with the use of percentages as raw data.

AN EXAMPLE FROM DEVELOPMENTAL THEORY

It is the application of the partial credit Rasch model to cognitive developmental data that has paved the way for original conceptions of how fundamental measurement principles might be meaningfully applied in unexpected settings. Let us take a well-known problem from Piaget's work, often called conservation of matter, an interview task often used with, for example, 3- to 7-year-olds, and therefore quite unsuitable for a written task format. A child judges two balls of playdough to have the same amount. Then one of them is rolled out into a snake or sausage shape right in front of the child's eyes. The child then is asked to judge again. The question is something like, "Does the snake have more playdough than the ball; does the ball have more playdough than the snake; or do they have the same amount of playdough?" Anyone who has watched young kids share a cupcake, pour drinks for friends, or gladly swap little coins for bigger ones will know that whereas adults often do not "see the problem" here, it is only during the grade school years that children develop the understanding that the amount of playdough, amount of juice, or number of sweets will remain invariant no matter how the objects are rearranged.

Piaget's approach was to claim that the child who consistently conserves shows qualitatively superior thinking to the child who does not, backing his claim with detailed logical analyses of the child's inferred thinking patterns. When we psychologists first tried to quantify our replications of this qualitative research, we adopted "0 = didn't conserve", "1 = did conserve" as the task performance summary. Hindsight has shown this to be rather naïve. The extent of the trivialization that routinely went on can be imagined: Little Johnny is interviewed for 15 minutes on three conservation tasks (amount of playdough, amount of juice, and number of sweets each suitably rearranged) and is scored like this: 1, 1, 0 (conserves playdough and juice but misses number). Betty and the psychologist chat and play together for 20 minutes, and her efforts are scored 0, 1, 0; whereas Jane scores 1, 1, 1 after a mere 10 minutes of concentrated effort on her part. After an equally brief encounter, it seems Bill remains enchanted with the magic that makes things more or less, just by moving them around (0, 0, 0). Then we would compound our errors by adding the scores up for each child: 2 for Johnny, 1 for Betty, and 3 for Jane, whereas Bill scores 0 however you look at it. Often we would take this even one step further and, claiming that 2/3 was enough to describe Johnny and Jane as "conservers" and Betty and Bill as "non-conservers." Consequently, if the purpose of the research was to relate cognitive development in kids to their mathematics scores, there was no meaningful result. That is hardly surprising!

Seen through the lens provided by the partial credit Rasch model, the opportunities for serious and sensitive measurement seem to multiply very productively. First, we could see that it would not be necessary to have just 0 and 1 (dichotomous) scoring. We could also have 0, 1, 2 or 0, 1, 2, 3 if we found suitable criteria to score against. Not only could we have "items" with two or three criteria for scoring (i.e., not the dichotomous model), but we are not constrained to the same number of steps for each item (i.e., not the rating scale model). Even more, we could mix dichotomous and polytomous items in the one test. Moreover, instead of providing a single overall score for each task or complete interview, we could see each task addressing a number of key aspects, each of which could be scored. Thus, the playdough task could be broken down into the following subtasks: (a) judges initial equivalence: no = 0, yes = 1; (b) conserves after snake transformation: no = 0, yes = 1; (c) uses "longer" appropriately: never = 0, sometimes = 1, consistently = 2; (d) gives reasons based on perception = 0, by rolling the snake back into a ball = 1, saying "You didn't add or take away anything" = 2, claiming "It's always the same no matter what you do" = 3.

Therefore, for the string of criteria or items a, b, c, d, for just the first test (playdough task), we could end up with Johnny's scores of 1, 1, 2, 2; Betty's 1, 1, 1, 1; Jane's perfect response string 1, 1, 2, 3; and Bill's 1, 0, 0, 0. It can be seen how we have now discriminated differences between Betty and Bill (both received 0 for playdough with dichotomous scoring), and between Jane and Johnny (both scored 1 in the dichotomous situation). Remember the ordered data matrix from chapter 2? We can do it again (see Table 7.1).

TABLE 7.1
Ordered Data Set for Four Children on Four
Polytomous Items

Criteria	a	b	c	d
Bill	1	0	0	0
Betty	1	1	1	1
Johnny	1	1	2	2
Jane	1	1	2	3

In Table 7.1, we see the same sort of evidence for developmental sequences that we saw in the sorted dichotomous data in Table 2.2. Being on guard about making unwarranted inferences from the data, we merely observe that we have recorded ordered increases in response levels (i.e., 0 < 1< 2 < 3, etc., or ordinal data). Further, we refrain from drawing unwarranted equivalences between the values of 1 for items a and b, between the scores of 2 for items c and d, and so forth. All we are entitled to say from these data categorizations is that for item a, 0 < 1, and for item b, 0 < 1. We may not claim that 1 (on a) = 1 (on b), or that 2 (on c) = 2 (on d). We use Rasch modelling to estimate those relations, the intervals between those ordered values, during the analysis process.

The data used to demonstrate the use of the partial credit Rasch model in this chapter have been chosen for a number of important reasons. We could have chosen a routinely used written mathematics or science achievement test, an essay scoring guide, or a medical rehabilitation example, as long as it offered the possibility of grading responses as partly correct. Many scoring situations would suffice, as long as the grading principle represented by the following responses is implemented: "wrong—partly correct—right" or "fail—some progress towards mastery—more complete response—mastery." However, with the current example, we can learn something about the partial credit model while we open our eyes to the range of possibilities for quantifying what traditionally has been seen as qualitative data in the human sciences.

If we return to the response probability curve that we introduced in Figures 3.2 and 4.4 (for dichotomous items) then the expectations for the responses to the question about "judging initial equivalence" would take the same form, all children would have a better than 50% probability of scoring 1 (= yes). We need to modify our graph a little if we want to model the curves for a polytomous response oppurtunity (e.g., 0, 1, 2 for uses "longer" appropriately). Figure 7.1 shows those relationships.

Low ability students (such as Bill) are more likely (i.e., probability exceeds 50%) to score 0 where scored on this question. High ability students (e.g., Johnny and Jane) have a greater than 50% likelihood of scoring the highest score for this item (uses "longer" consistently = 2). Betty's ability level predicts, however, that she is more likely to score 1 (rather than 0 or 2).

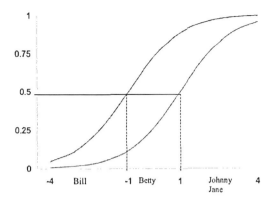

Figure 7.1.   Response probabilities for three response opportunity polytomous item (c).

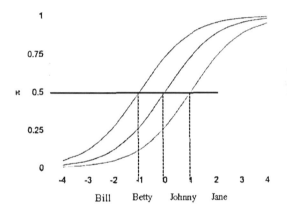

Figure 7.2.   Response probabilities for polytomous item with four response opportunities (d).

To model the curves for a polytomously scored item which has four response oppurtunities (e.g., gives reasons: 0, 1, 2, 3) a third threshold curve must be added to the figure. Figure 7.2 shows those relationships with the most probable responses to that item reflecting the scores shown in Table 7.1.

Shayer, Küchemann, and Wylam (1976), from the University of London, had a number of reasons for developing the Piagetian Reasoning Task (PRTIII–Pendulum) for classroom use. The PRTIII–Pendulum we used in chapter 5 was one of the demonstrated class tasks that they developed to replace administration using the traditional Piagetian interview technique. The U.K. researchers wanted data collection devices that could be administered to whole classes at a time, whereas Piaget's technique was a one-on-one interview. They wanted tasks that could be used by interested school science teachers, whereas Piaget claimed that his interviewers needed one year of daily practice to become competent. They wanted tasks that could yield quantifiable data, whereas Piaget's work was notorious for its uncompromisingly qualitative approach. Well, the Rasch model cannot change the Piagetian requirements for superior interview skills or make it possible to interview 30 schoolchildren simultaneously, but it can make wonderfully quantitative what is regarded traditionally as qualitative data. It can construct interval scale measures on which a whole range of the usual statistical techniques can be meaningfully employed. Indeed, the following piece of research, first reported in Bond and Bunting (1995), was inspired exactly by the existence of the partial credit Rasch model (Stafford, 2005).

CLINICAL INTERVIEW ANALYSIS: A RASCH-INSPIRED BREAKTHROUGH

Bond and Bunting (1995) reported in much more detail than necessary here the direct replication of the pendulum task using the Genevan interview technique as reported in chapter 4 of *The Growth of Logical Thinking From Childhood to Adolescence* (Inhelder & Piaget, 1955/1958). The child is presented with a pendulum apparatus consisting of an adjustable string suspended from a fixed point and a series of weights: 40 g, 80 g, 100 g. When given a demonstration of the apparatus and provoked by an initial question such as, "Can you show me what causes the pendulum to swing more or fewer times in some short time interval?" the child is encouraged to experiment with the apparatus to determine which of the variables (weight, length, push, angle) affects the period of oscillation. The child is asked to "think out loud," and the interviewer asks prompting questions, seeks clarification, and challenges the child's conclusions as seems appropriate. No, this is not your usual standard test or even structured interview![1]

What was original with Bond and Bunting (1995) in this work was the detailed scoring table (Table 7.2) developed exactly from chapter 4 of Inhelder and Piaget (1955/1958). These performance criteria are far more comprehensive than any developed before, including those of Bond (1976/1995), Shayer et al. (1976), and others, resulting directly from a detailed rereading of the key chapter with the possibilities opened up by partial credit Rasch modelling as the key stimulus. This probably sounds as though an excess of missionary zeal is sneaking in here, but the important claim is that when we see the old world of data through new eyes (in this case, Rasch modelling), completely new possibilities open up. We could

---

[1]The standard view of the Piagetian method can be summarized adequately by Wallace (1965): "Results obtained by such a flexible procedure as the *méthode clinique* do not lend themselves to statistical treatment" (p. 58). Indeed, even Piaget himself subscribed to that view. As a consequence, standardized individual interview procedures were developed, class tasks such as Shayer's (Shayer, Küchemann, & Wylam, 1976) were substituted, or pencil-and-paper tests such as Bond's (1976) were written to provide the sort of data amenable to statistical analyses.

TABLE 7.2

Ordered Performance Criteria for 18 Aspects of the Pendulum Interview Task

	IIA Early Concrete	IIB Mature Concrete	IIIA Early Formal	IIIB Mature Formal
1	1.1 Able to accurately serially order lengths			
2	2.0 Unable to accurately serially order weights	2.1 Able to accurately serially order weights -2.4		
3	3.1 Able to accurately serially order push -2.4			
4	4.1 Establishes inverse relation between length and frequency or oscillation -2.4			
5	5.0 Unable to manipulate some variables	5.1 Able to vary all factors -2.4		
6	6.0 Does not make inferences. Limited to observations	6.1 Makes inferences based only on observed concrete correspondence -2.4	6.2 Makes inferences going beyond observations, without needing to test all possibilities $+0.4$	
7		7.0 To test for length, manipulates incorrect variable and in an unsystematic manner	7.1 Manipulates incorrect variable, but makes logical deductions by inference to results on earlier experiments -1.0	7.2 Systematically manipulates lengths to test for their effects $+0.9$

(continued)

129

TABLE 7.2 (*Continued*)

IIA Early Concrete	IIB Mature Concrete	IIIA Early Formal	IIIB Mature Formal
8	8.0 Manipulates incorrect variable and is unsystematic in testing for weight	8.1 Manipulates incorrect variable, but makes logical deductions by inference to results on earlier experiments −0.7	8.2 Systematically manipulates weights to test for their effects −0.7
9	9.0 Manipulates incorrect variable and is unsystematic in test for push	9.1 Manipulates incorrect variable, but makes logical deductions by inference to results on earlier experiments −0.3	9.2 Systematically manipulates impetus to test for the effect of push +0.7
10 10.0 Makes illogical deductions about the role of length (including illogical exclusion of length in favor of weight or impetus)	10.1 Excludes the effect of length (because of inaccurate observations) −1.2	10.2 Logically deduces positive relation of affirmation or implication for the role of length +1.1	10.3 Deduces equivalence of length and frequency of oscillation
	11.1 Makes illogical deductions about the role of weight (either illogical exclusion or positive implications)	11.2 Logically deduces a positive relationship of *affirmation* or *implication* for weight, based on inaccurate observations	11.3 Excludes the role of weight

(*continued*)

	.0	.1	.2	.3
12	12.0 Preoccupied with the role of impetus as the cause of variations in the frequency of oscillation. Illogical deduction of positive implication −	12.1 Testing results in the illogical exclusion of the role of push	12.2 Logically deduces a positive relation of affirmation or implication for push, based on inaccurate observations +1.7	12.3 Excludes the role of push +2.9
13	13.0 Does not produce combinations of length with other variables 0.1	13.1 Produces combinations of different lengths with different weights or pushes to test for effects −2.1	13.2 Produces sets of combinations of lengths with various weights and pushes to test for their effects +1.40	
14	14.0 Does not produce combinations of weights with other variables	14.1 Produces combinations of different weights to test with different lengths to test for their effects −1.6	14.2 Produces combinations of different weights with different pushes to test for the effects −+1.1	14.3 Produces combinations weights with various lengths and pushes to test for their effects +1.1

(continued)

TABLE 7.2 (Continued)

	IIA Early Concrete	IIB Mathure Concrete	IIIA Early Formal	IIIB Mathure Formal
15		15.0 Does not produce combinations of push with other variables	15.1 Produces combinations of different pushes with various lengths, to test for their effects $+1.0$ 15.2 Produces combinations of different pushes with different weights, to test for their effects $+1.2$	15.3 Produces combinations of various pushes with lengths and weights to test for their effects $+2.14$
16			16.0 Unsystematic method	16.1 Systematically produces all combinations, using the method of varying a single factors, while holding all else constant $+1.4$
17			17.0 Unable to exclude the effect of weight	17.1 Logically excludes the effect of weight $+2.4$
18			18.0 Unable to exclude the effect of push	18.1 Logically excludes the effect of push $+3.1$

have made a similar claim in the previous chapter for developing measures via the rating scale model, but the claim would not have been original. Many already have developed scores for Likert scales, even if they have made the "measurement" claim erroneously. Although the vast majority of standardized psychological and educational testing falls into the dichotomous tradition (of, say, IQ scores) or Likert scales (personality assessment; Michell, 1986), the PCM allows for meaningful quantification in a virtually untouched category of human sciences research, in which the data are neither dichotomous, nor do they have some fixed number of response categories.

Therefore, when seen through the eyes of the PCM and not from the usual dichotomous/Likert viewpoint, the distinctive feature of the 15 tasks in Inhelder and Piaget (1955/1958) is their careful construction of problems that are relevant and interesting to a wide sample of children. Because the focus of the work was to monitor the progress from the logical thinking of childhood to that of adolescence, children's responses to these tasks are not classified as merely right or wrong. Children's solutions are, almost invariably, partially correct, and that whole domain of partially correct answers, whether it is in mathematics problem solving, essay writing, or medical rehabilitation, is the focus of the PCM.

SCORING INTERVIEW TRANSCRIPTS

Table 7.2 is a scoring guide that illustrates some important key features for those wishing to implement PCM in new testing situations. Across the top of the table, we can see the increasingly complex substages of thinking displayed: IIA (early concrete operational thought), IIB (mature concrete thought), IIIA (early formal operational thought), and, finally, IIIB (mature formal thought). The invariant *order* of stages is a critically distinctive feature of Piaget's work, just as order is the key requirement of Rasch measurement. Down the table, we have the 18 different aspects of solving the pendulum problem that Bunting found identified in the focus chapter. It is clear that lower level aspects of the problem (e.g., 1, 3, and 4) would be scored dichotomously: 1 for meeting the performance criterion and 0 for failing to meet it. Similarly, Aspects 7, 8, and 9 have three identifiable levels of performance each and will yield ordered polytomous data: Criteria 7.0, 8.0, and 9.0 indicate the lowest observable levels of performance on these aspects and should be scored 0.

Criteria 7.2, 8.2, and 9.2 indicate complete success on those aspects of the problem and will be scored 2. Because 7.1, 8.1, and 9.1 show partial success, they will attract the score of 1, somewhere on the ordered pathway between complete failure (0) and complete success (2).

Aspects 10 and 12 then have four ordered performance category levels and will be scored 0, 1, 2, and 3. Yet there is more: Although 16, 17, and 18 are to be scored dichotomously, successful performance on these aspects is supposed to reflect the highest level of mature thinking available to adolescents and adults. Clearly, the score of 1 here is meant to be of greater importance than the 1 scored for successful performances on Aspects 1.1, 2.1, 3.1, and 4.1. The much-lauded and much-criticized flexibility in administration of the task is not a problem for

Rasch modelling. Any aspects of the problem that are not actually encountered during the interview (omitted inadvertently or deliberately) are regarded as "missing data," and the data file has blanks recorded at those points. (The Rasch family of models can make do with less than complete data sets for either items or persons. It can provide estimates of ability and difficulty based on the available data. Of course, measurement precision declines as available information decreases.)

As a procedural point, all of the interviews ($n = 58$) of the high school students were videorecorded and transcribed. A matrix based on Table 7.2 was used for the recording of each child's performances, and the data string for each child recorded the score on each aspect of the problem (18 data points for each child), in which higher scores indicate more advanced performances. For example, the scores in column 14 (of the sample response strings that follow) indicate that Student 21 satisfied Criterion 14.1 from Table 7.2, whereas Student 65 performed to the requirements in criterion 14.3.

> 111111000212010000 Student 21 (least successful case)
> 111112212323132111 Student 65 (most successful case)

Ordered Performance Criteria for 18 Aspects of the Pendulum Interview Task

To perform a PCM analysis on the data file generated from this investigation, we need to indicate the following to the Rasch analysis software: The number of "items" and their location in the data file. In this case there are 18 items in columns 1 to 18. What the valid codes are in the file. Codes 0, 1, 2, 3 cover all the response possibilities here. We took the care always to use 0 as the code for the lowest possible observable response category for each item. The estimation procedure should use the PCM. For some software, this is the default estimation procedure for polytomous data. For example, in QUEST, the PCM is used with polytomous data unless the qualifier "estimate rate" is used to constrain the threshold estimates to be the same for all items, as discussed in chapter 6.

PARTIAL CREDIT MODEL RESULTS

Figure 7.3 displays the item estimates and fit statistics from the partial credit analysis of the *méthode clinique* interview data from the pendulum problem, using the pathway principles adopted earlier in this text. Figure 7.3 combines features of the displays from the dichotomous data analyses in chapters 4 and 5 and some features from the rating scale analysis of polytomous data in chapter 6.

First, the fit of items ($-2 < $ infit $t < + 2$) is displayed using the parallel dotted lines. In this case, all the 18 items fit the Rasch model sufficiently according to this criterion. They are all located between those lines. For each of those items that were scored dichotomously (1, 2, 3, 4, 5, 16, 17, and 18), one item difficulty estimate per item is plotted, indicating the threshold at which the probability of scoring 0 or 1 is 50%. For those items that are scored polytomously (0, 1, 2 or 0, 1, 2, 3), either two

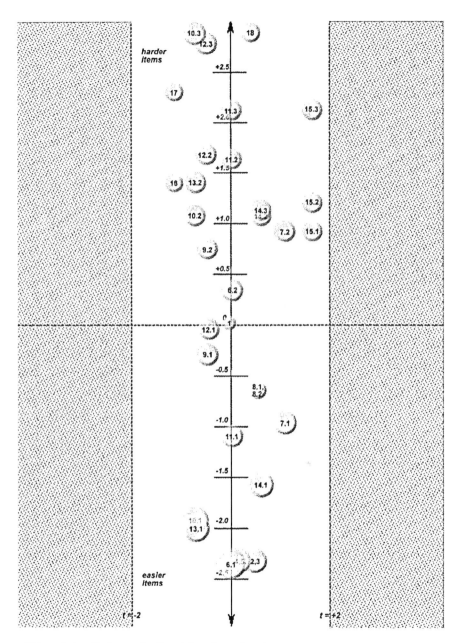

Figure 7.3. Pathway for Pendulum interview items.

or three difficulty thresholds are plotted. Three response categories (0, 1, 2 for Item 6) are separated by two thresholds (e.g., Estimate 6.1 separates the likelihood of scoring 0 on Aspect 6 from the likelihood of scoring 1 on Aspect 6; Estimate 6.2 separates the most probable response zones for scores of 1 and 2 on Aspect 6), whereas four response categories (0, 1, 2, 3) are separated by three threshold estimates (e.g., Aspect 12: four response categories with three estimates). Therefore, the item map in Figure 7.3 will show a number of item estimate formats:

		More likely to score 2 than below 2	More likely to score 3 than below 3 *Threshold estimate 12.3*
More likely to score 1 than zero.		*Threshold estimate 6.2*	More likely to score 2 than below 2
		More likely to score '1' than below 1.	*Threshold estimate 12.2*
Estimate threshold for 1			More likely to score 1
More likely to score 0		*Threshold estimate 6.1*	*Threshold estimate 12.1*
		More likely to score 0	More likely to score 0
Item 1		**Item 6**	**Item 12**

The format shown depends on the number of threshold estimates needed to separate the response categories in Table 7.2. While QUEST can handle up to 10 ordered response categories per item (0, 1, 2, 3, 4, 5, 6, 7, 8, 9), WINSTEPS PCM allows 100 ordered categories (0–99, so even percentages can be used as data). But whether any particular testing situation can make practical and meaningful use of 10 or more response categories is an empirical question discussed in chapter 11.

As we would expect from a task designed to elicit partially correct responses from a broad band of respondents, say, 5- to 18-year-olds, the pendulum task items cover a span of nearly 6 logits from the least difficult (6.1 at −2.41 logits) to that with the criterion most difficult to satisfy (a score of 1 on Item 18 at +3.12 logits). Given that this groundbreaking research was conducted by one undergraduate student in a very short time, and that each individual interview takes a considerable time to plan, implement, transcribe, and score, a rather small sample size of 58 students was used. As a result, the error estimates for the items and thresholds remain large, even unacceptably large in some instances. Three factors that were mentioned before have an influence on the size of error estimates. All other things being equal (and they never are), imprecision will increase for items when items are off target for the population, when the number of response categories per item increases, and when the sample is small. But SEs for persons will be smaller when 18 polytomous items (rather than 18 dichotomous items) comprise a test. Take a moment to look at the item error estimates in Table 7.3 and identify the more imprecise item difficulty locations (yes, they have the larger error indicators in Fig. 7.3). Then take a look at the complete item–person map in Figure 7.4 to see which of the preceding influences have contributed to the large error estimates you have identified.

TABLE 7.3
Item Estimates for Pendulum Interview Task

Item	Difficulty Estimate	Error Estimate	Infit t	Outfit t
1		Item has perfect score		
2	−2.36	0.73	+0.3	+0.5
3	−2.36	0.73	+0.3	+0.5
4	−2.36	0.73	+0.1	−0.4
5	−2.36	0.73	+0.1	−0.5
6.1	−2.41	1.25	0.0	−0.2
6.2	+0.36	0.63	0.0	−0.2
7.1	−0.97	0.72	+1.0	+0.6
7.2	+0.92	0.53	+1.0	+0.6
8.1	−0.65	0.30	+0.6	+2.3
8.2	−0.65	0.30	+0.6	+2.3
9.1	−0.28	0.59	−0.5	−0.3
9.2	+0.72	0.55	−0.5	−0.3
10.1	−2.03	0.94	−0.3	−0.2
10.2	−1.23	1.08	−0.3	−0.2
10.3	+3.10	0.66	−0.3	−0.2
11.1	−1.19	1.08	0.0	+0.3
11.2	+1.65	0.55	0.0	+0.3
11.3	+2.14	0.64	0.0	+0.3
12.1	−0.03	0.66	−0.7	−0.7
12.2	+1.73	0.52	−0.7	−0.7
12.3	+2.88	0.55	−0.7	−0.7
13.1	−2.06	0.53	−0.8	−0.9
13.2	+1.44	0.53	−0.8	−0.9
14.1	−1.56	0.64	+0.7	+0.5
14.2	+1.07	1.00	+0.7	+0.5
14.3	+1.13	0.55	+0.7	+0.5
15.1	+0.97	0.75	+2.0	+1.8
15.2	+1.27	0.49	+2.0	+1.8
15.3	+2.22	0.49	+2.0	+1.8
16	+1.41	0.47	−1.3	−1.0
17	+2.33	0.47	−1.4	−1.5
18	+3.02	0.51	−0.7	−1.1

```
- - - - - - - - - - - - - - - - - - - - - - - - - - - - - - - - - - - - - - - -
                         X      |
      4.0                       |
                                |
                                |
                         X      |   10.3                    18
      3.0                       |
                                |          12.3
                         X      |                    17
                       XXX      |   11.3      15.3
      2.0          XXXXXXX      |
                   XXXXXX       |   11.2  12.2
                    XXXX        |       13.2          16
                    XXXX        |                            15.2
      1.0             XX        |   10.2    14.2  14.3
                   XXXXXXX      |                       7.2  15.1
                    XXXX        |                            9.2
                   XXXXXX       |
                   XXXXXX       |                   6.2
       .0                       |         12.1
                        XXX     |
                         X      |                            9.1
                         X      |                      8.1  8.2
     -1.0                       |                      7.1
                         X      |   11.1
                                |
                                |       14.1
     -2.0                       |   10.1
                                |       13.1
                                |   2   3   4   5   6.1
```

Figure 7.4.   Item–Person map for Pendulum interview.

INTERPRETATION

What guidelines do these considerations provide for sample selection for further research using the pendulum task? First, we need to give the task to a larger sample, but what sort of larger sample? When we see that the items at the extremes of the difficulty range are dichotomous items, but that they have error estimates about the same size as those for the threshold estimates in the polytomous Items 11, 12, and 13, we should conclude that the next sample should include both more able persons on the pendulum task to make estimates for 16, 17, and 18 more precise, as well as less able persons to enhance the precision of Items 1, 2, 3, 4, and 5.

This is in keeping with what we already know: Inhelder and Piaget (1955/1958) designed this task for use with a broad age range (say, 5–18 years), whereas the breadth of the sample for this study was restricted deliberately to 12- to 15-year-olds, for two important reasons. First, it was the transition from concrete to formal thought that Bunting was investigating, not early concrete or mature formal thinking. Second, the investigation sought to avoid compounding the measurement of cognitive development with other age-related variables such as amount of education or exposure to formal science instruction. An increase in sample size would implicate both of these variables, as well as the possibility, indeed likelihood, that the team of interviewers/scorers necessary to administer the task to a larger sample would not do their work with the consistency that investigator aimed to achieve with the $n = 58$. The many-facets Rasch model that we introduce in chapter 8 addresses the issues of rater behavior and has the promise of modelling the effects of such influences.

First, we must acknowledge that empirical results such as these, derived from small and restricted samples, hardly can do more than point the way to the undoubted promise of larger scale investigations, although there are some hints in these results that show the possibility for theory–practice dialogue. In this case, the data from the pendulum task, at its first iteration, demonstrate sufficient adherence to the Rasch measurement specifications to be regarded as producing measures of cognitive development. These results are not bad for an explicitly qualitative approach that has faded from favor, in part, for not yielding suitably quantifiable results using traditional statistical approaches. Those who are interested can refer to the research report (Bond & Bunting, 1995) to see the correspondences, and lack of them, between interpretations derived from Piaget's theory and the empirical results. If those results hold in further investigations, some fine-tuning of the underlying theory will be required. Although that report recommended that future replications of the task include the provision of a suitable timing device for accurately assessing the pendulum's swing, this conclusion was derived from the opportunity that the interviewer had to pursue children's responses actively in the interview situation, not as a result of the Rasch analysis. We are not suggesting that Rasch modelling is the universal panacea for measurement in the human sciences. Nothing replaces thoughtful theory–driven research.

The use of Rasch modelling in the Bond and Bunting (1995) research showed the value that the concept of order has within a framework of unidimensionality. Interpretations of item and item step order as well as person order are clearly central in developmental and educational research, with clear implications for measuring physical skill acquisition and medical rehabilitation as well. Hand in hand with a clear concept of the variable under examination is the Rasch concept of unidimensionality. Although this might seem a little esoteric to some, the point is an important one in the application to Rasch measurement, especially in novel settings.

In an address to the Rasch Special Interest Group (SIG) at the American Educational Research Association (AERA), Keeves (1997) reminded the audience of the primary role of unidimensionality in the longitudinal testing of educational achievement such as the international studies regularly being conducted by the International Association for the Evaluation of Educational Achievement (IEA). For the sort of scaling and equating required for these efforts, he indicated:

> Fulfillment of the requirement of unidimensionality is a matter of degree not just a matter of kind as Bejar (1983, p. 31) has pointed out:
>
>> Unidimensionality does not imply that performance on items is due to a single psychological process. In fact, a variety of psychological processes are involved in responding to a set of test items. However, as long as they function in unison—that is, performance on each item is affected by the same process and in the same form—unidimensionality will hold.
>
> Thus a science test can involve physics, chemistry, or biology content and test different skills, knowledge, understanding, application and analysis (to use the terms of the Bloom taxonomy, in the tradition of the University of Chicago) provided the processes involved operate in concord, the requirement for unidimensionality will be satisfied. This demands empirical testing as well as logical analysis. (Keeves, 1997, p. 4)

This provides an interesting context for the interpretation of Rasch modelling results in terms of the theory–practice dialogue. If our aim is to put into systematic practice a particular conception of one psychological or educational construct at a time, our success at that is represented empirically by the development of a unidimensional test. The unsuccessful aspects of that attempt, especially in terms of inadequate item fit, or item disorder, require us to revisit our theory-driven intentions or our effort to operationalize the theory into practice via a test, an observation schedule, or a marking scheme. Items should be included in tests because very good reasons exist for having them there. Test developers should be committed to the items they develop: Item misfit then signals to the investigator "Think again!" not the usual "Throw it out!"

When both our theoretical considerations and our empirical evidence suggest to us that our efforts to develop a test of some underlying latent trait have been successful, then evidence of misordered items or persons suggests that refinement of our ideas is necessary. As a principle that can be applied more generally in test development and use, however, we have indicators of both unidimensionality and order that beg for interpretation in the context of the theory that generated the test and the practical situation that produced the results.

Control file for QUEST:

```
Title PCM Analysis of Piagetian Interview data
Data chap7.dat
Format items 17-34
Codes 01234
```

```
Est
show item>>PCMitem.doc
show cases>>PCMcase.doc
Quit
```

Title line gives a title, "PCM Analysis of Piagetian Interview data," to each output file.

Data names the data file as "chap7.dat."

Format indicates the columns in the data file where the responses for the 18 interview codes are located.

Codes indicates which codes in the file are valid.

The "estimate" command performs partial credit analysis as the default for polytomous data.

Show commands direct the output to files that will open with a word processor.

Control lines for WINSTEPS:

```
&INST
TITLE="PCM Analysis of Piagetian Interview Data"
NI=18
ITEM1=17
CODES=01234
GROUPS=0
&END
Item1
Item2
. . .
End Names
```

The first line is required by WINSTEPS.

Title line gives a title to the output file.

NI is the number of items to be analyzed.

ITEM1 is the column number where the data begin.

Codes lists the possible codes for the responses.

Groups = 0 specifies partial credit analysis.

Bond&FoxSteps:

The complete data file, control lines, and tutorial for this analysis are pre-loaded into the Bond&FoxSteps software included on the accompanying CD.

CHAPTER EIGHT

Measuring Facets Beyond Ability and Difficulty

Many of those who use other statistical methods for analysis in the social sciences tend to criticize the Rasch measurement approach for being simplistic. How could any human abilities seriously be regarded as unidimensional? Surely, even in the simplest forms of testing (e.g., color in the bubble multiple-choice testing) shouldn't we make some allowance for guessing, lack of concentration, and the like?

The response is that the Rasch approach is simple, not simplistic: The aim is to develop fundamental measures that can be used across similar appropriate measurement situations, not merely to describe the data produced by administering Test *a* to Sample *b* on Day *c*. Rasch modeling addresses itself to estimating properties of persons and tests that go beyond the particular observations made during any testing situation. Wright (1998b) summarized it succinctly: "I don't want to know which questions you answered. I want to know how much . . . you know. I need to leap from what I know and don't want—to what I want but can't know. That's called inference."

So far, we have focused on just two aspects of the measurement situation, on just two facets of the single underlying dimension being measured: One facet is the level of ability or attitude expressed by the person, whereas the second facet is the level of difficulty or endorsability of the item, stem, or prompt. The testing situation, therefore, can be viewed as an opportunity to collect data, some observable evidence of the interaction between the person and the test that provides empirical evidence about the existence of a latent trait revealed in the test items and any person's performance on them.

Of course, it does simplify matters quite remarkably to regard the person simply in terms of which items were "bubbled" on a computer scan sheet, and to regard the discipline of, say, mathematics in terms of 150 multiple-choice stems with four response options each. Surely, reading ability plays a part, along with the person's motivation, propensity to guess, and the like. Surely, some items are more clearly written; some have better diagrams; some are based on everyday experiences, whereas some are a little esoteric. Undoubtedly this is the case, but Rasch modeling works from the principle that the key predominant underlying attribute of the measurement situation is the latent trait expressed in the items, elicited from the candidates, and recorded in the performances when each test candidate and each test item interact. To the extent that the test performances are driven primarily by the person's ability and the item's difficulty, the Rasch model principles hold. Any aberrant performance, either by items or persons, would be flagged by the fit statistics for closer monitoring.

However, we easily can imagine measurement situations in which other aspects of the testing situation routinely interpose themselves between the ability of the candidates and the difficulty of the test (e.g., when judges are used to evaluate test performances in terms of performance criteria). The most notorious of these usually occurs at Olympic Games time, for example, in the platform diving or gymnastics sections of the summer games, or the figure skating competition of the winter games. Even the least-informed of us sit stunned in front of our television screens at what appears to be, shall we say, inconsistent behavior among and between judges. The TV score cards usually show the country of origin for each judge, and many of us shake our heads in disbelief at what appear to be obvious, and repeated, discrepancies between judges' score cards. Two general properties of judges' behavior seem worthy of note. The first is that some judges seem to be more lenient or more severe than other judges, right across the board. The second, the one that gets us the most riled, is what we would call bias, judgment that seems to be more lenient or more severe depending on the competitor, the competitor's country, that country's political alliances, and so on.

Why then, in important evaluation situations, do we continue to act as though the judge, rater, or examiner has merely a benign role? On a personal level, we might try to avoid the tough marker, complain that some judges are biased against us, or avoid the examiner's specialist topic, but we might as well face it; in high-stakes testing, we often have the suspicion that the marker, not the candidate or the test, might mean the difference between pass and fail, that the scorer rather than the performance determines silver, not gold.

Does this then not show the inadequacy of the fundamental Rasch principle of unidimensional measurement? Do we not need to consider more than just the test and the candidate? Well, no and yes, in that order! Clearly, we have suggested here that rater severity, at least, needs to be taken into the equation. This chapter argues that many other facets of the testing situation profitably can be considered as key aspects of the measurement process. Moreover, we show how the many-facets Rasch model, developed in the work of Mike Linacre of Chicago, successfully models these more complex situations, and does that successfully, all within the Rasch model's requirement for measurement along one dimension at a time. In the conceptualization of the many-facets Rasch model, the raters are regarded as independent experts who apply their understanding to rate person performances. They are not seen as human clones who are merely implementing the scoring rubric; expected to behave in machine-like manner.

A BASIC INTRODUCTION TO THE MANY-FACETS RASCH MODEL

Let us reconsider our earlier proposition that person ability and item difficulty are the key contributors to the performances that we wish to measure. If we had a little logit scale of item difficulty, it might look like this:

```
. . . . . . . . 1 . . . . . . . . 2 . . . . . . . . 3 . . . . . . . . 4 . . . . . . . . 5 . . . . . . . . 6 . . . . . .
easier                                                                          harder
```

so that a person who is successful on harder and harder items has ability located further towards the "harder" end of the scale

```
. . . . . . . . 1 . . . . . . . 2 . . . . . . . 3 . . . B . . . . . . 4 . . . . W . . . . 5 . . . . . . 6 . . . . . .
easier                                                                          harder
```

Here Bill has 1 logit less ability than Wendy. Now consider that their performances, say short written answers to questions, are rated by two different judges, one who generally is tough, and another who generally is more lenient:

```
. . . . . . . . 1 . . . . . . . 2 . . . . . . . 3 . . . . . . . B W . . . . . . . 5 . . . . . . . 6 . . . . . . . .
easier                                                                          harder
```

Now the ability estimates for Bill and Wendy are so close that they cannot be meaningfully separated by this testing situation. We can guess that Bill got the easy judge, whereas Wendy got the tough one. If the situation were reversed, we could have expected a result such as the following:

```
. . . . . . . . 1 . . . . . . . . 2 . . . . . B . . 3 . . . . . . . . 4 . . . . . . . . 5 W . . . . . 6 . . . . . .
easier                                                                          harder
```

It seems reasonable to presume that the examiners are not behaving in a random or precipitous way. They do know their area of expertise; they can discriminate better from lesser displays of ability; they both understand and use the marking guide sensitively and diligently; and both would be able to argue the "correctness" of the scores they give. As examiners, one is routinely tougher, and one is routinely easier.

Let us imagine giving a small set of short-answer examination papers for candidates Charles, Jenny, Bill, Wendy, and Harry to examiner Tough and then to examiner Easy for rating. Look at the outcome:

Judge Easy:

```
. . . . . . . . 1 . . . . . . 2 . . . . C . . . . 3 . . J . . . . . B . . . . . . 5 W . . . . H . . 6 . . . . . . .
less ability                                                                    more ability
```

Judge Tough:

. . . . 1 . . . C . . . 2 . . J . . . . . B 3 . . . . 4 W . . . . H . . 5 . . . . . . 6. . . . . .
less ability   more ability

We will put the pass mark at 3 on this scale. Greater than 3 is a passing grade. Judge T will fail both Bill and Jenny, but Judge E will give each of them a passing grade. Sure, you might be happy if Judge T (rather than Judge E) were accrediting your future brain surgeon, but what if the testing result was that your kid just missed the entrance cutoff for college? Either way, if we were serious about measurement of ability in a judged situation, we would want to be sure that passing or failing depended more on ability than on luck of the draw with examiners. We could fire one of the examiners, but which one? Better than that, we could give one or both of them some retraining in use of the marking guide. Even better still, we could model the difference in the severity of the judges, check the probability that the differences are systematically applied by each, and use all the available information we have to decide the cutoff point for the test.

WHY NOT USE INTERRATER RELIABILITY?

We can imagine that the interrater correlation shown in the preceding example will be just about perfect (i.e., +1), although the effects on passing or failing at the level of 3 would be quite different depending on which judge the candidate had. Try it. Use your spreadsheet or calculator to work out the correlation between the following sets of scores:

Candidate	Judge Easy	Judge Tough
a	7	6
b	6	5
c	5.5	4.5
d	5	4
e	4.5	3.5
f	4	3
g	3.5	2.5
h	3	2
i	2	1

The correlation is +1.0 (perfect), but Judge T fails Candidates f, g, h, and i, whereas Judge E fails only Candidates h and i.

A candidate in any of the preceding situations has to be considerably more able to get the same rating from the severe judge than a less able candidate would receive from the lenient judge. Because we have a complete set of data for raters, we can conclude that Judge T is just one 1 logit harder on candidates than Judge E: Adjusting Judge E's ratings by one logit to the left or Judge T's ratings by one logit to the right reveals the general consistency in the judging behavior. Therefore, the problem with intercorrelations between judge ratings is that they can demonstrate only consistency among the rank orders of candidates. They do not tell us anything about the severity or leniency differences between judges (i.e., judge discrepancies in difficulty levels). In standard settings it has been effectively demonstrated (e.g., Plake, 1998; Stone, 2001) that judges simply seem obliged to disagree. Short of attempting to force normative interrater agreement by iteration, it seems a rather hopeless situation merely to calculate rater agreements. Would it not be better to model the measurement relationship between raters and to monitor the Rasch quality control mechanisms to ensure raters, like items and persons, are performing consistently?

When we understand that raters involved in the evaluation process might influence the location of person ability estimates, we can imagine how various other facets of human performance measurement might intervene in that process in a scientifically lawful (i.e., measurable, and therefore accountable) way. We might want to determine whether the short form and the standard form of a test treated candidates equally, and, if not, how much they differed. While we are looking at the test facet, we could consider whether parallel tests actually produced equivalent measures of candidates. If we routinely change our accreditation or entrance tests to keep them secure, we would want to monitor whether we could rely equally on all forms of such tests. Likewise, if we reasonably harbor a suspicion that some attributes of the candidates are consistently important aspects of their performances, we could examine one or more facets related to candidates, such as gender, first language, cultural grouping, and the like.

RELATIONS AMONG RASCH FAMILY OF MODELS

We can now enlarge our understanding of Rasch's original (i.e., two-facets) model that the probability of any correct response is a function of the ability of the person and the difficulty of the item (i.e., probability = function of (ability–difficulty)), to include other additional facets of the examination process. The probability of any correct response is a function of the ability of the person and the difficulty of the item, with allowance made for the severity of the rater, and for which particular form of the test was taken (i.e., probability = function of (ability– difficulty–rater–test)).

Linacre's (1992) conception of the many-facets Rasch model shares an interesting property with the rating scale and partial credit models: When the extra facets (e.g., rater, test, or candidate) are not required to model the added complexities of the measurement situation, then the equation conflates to the basic two-facets Rasch model: probability = function of (ability–difficulty).

DATA SPECIFICATIONS OF THE MANY-FACETS RASCH MODEL

Interestingly, evaluations and examinations that do not adopt the many-facets Rasch model to deal with the "rater severity" problem, deal with the role of the examiner in two remarkably contrasting manners. The first, of course, is just to ignore the problem: All grades or scores are taken at face value, and no attempt is made even to check whether the scores assigned by raters differ at all. The second approach goes to the other extreme: It requires that all examiners grade the same set of papers in an attempt to ensure that all raters assign the same grade to any one paper. A less demanding practice of examiner pairing is widely used to provide some check on rater behavior. Of course, as we have seen, correlation indices are not indicators of this exact agreement intention, and interrater agreements of 90% mean little if agreement, say within one grade level, is counted as perfect. Although it might not be necessary for all examiners to score all tests, the subset of double-, triple-, or quintuple-marked papers must be large and must be graded by all (two, three, or five) examiners. Any paper not marked by all those examiners cannot be used to check rater behavior.

Now, with the Rasch model, we can take advantage of a property of the model that we have come across before. The Rasch model is quite robust in the face of missing data: It does not require a perfectly complete matrix of values as the starting point for calculations. True score-based statistics require a complete data set, so perfectly good data often are discarded because the set is incomplete, or some inauthentic datum (e.g., an average or typical score) is interpolated into the gap. On the other hand, the Rasch model requires only sufficient density of data to permit the calculations. Where the data matrix is empty, no information is interpolated. Therefore, a data set to detect rater severity effects does not require the very costly procedure of having all five judges rate all 500 papers. Provided the examiners' rotation roster is carefully thought out to provide sufficient links through the data set, it should not be necessary for any paper to be assessed by more than two examiners. The many-facets Rasch model's approach to monitoring the rater severity effect provides for the most parsimonious allocation of double-marking that is consonant with the calculation of rater effect estimations. Indeed, single-marking is all that is required if examinees each provide more than one piece of work to be assessed. The important element is that some suitable link(s) be provided across the sets of examinees, items, and raters. Linacre provides quite detailed requirements for minimal marking schedules in a number of places (Linacre, 1997; Lunz & Linacre, 1998).

Of course, given what we already know about the density of the data submitted for Rasch analysis, that more targeted data will produce more precise estimates than less data, we can be sure that the scoring roster requiring all raters to grade all questions for all candidates will produce the most precise estimates of ability, difficulty, and rater severity. The point is that a complete scoring roster can be too demanding, too expensive, or too time-consuming, or it often can be just plain impractical in a practical examination situation. The robust nature of the Rasch model in the face of missing data means that sufficiently accurate estimates of these three facets can be calculated with much less demanding (i.e., substantially incomplete) marking rosters.

Linacre (1997) displayed three judging rosters for ratings from the Advanced Placement Program of the College Board. The complete judging plan of 1,152 ratings illustrates the ideal plan for both conventional and Rasch analysis. This complete judging plan meets the connection requirement between all facets because every element (essays, examinees, and judges) can be compared directly and unambiguously with every other element.

A much less judge-intensive plan of only 180 ratings also is displayed, in which less precise Rasch estimates can be obtained because the facet-linking overlap is maintained. The Rasch measures would be less precise than with complete data because 83% fewer observations are made. Linacre's final table reveals the minimal judging plan, in which each of the 32 examinees' three essays is rated by only one judge. Each of the 12 judges rates eight essays, including two or three of each essay type, so that the examinee–judge essay overlap of these 96 ratings still enables all parameters to be estimated unambiguously in one frame of reference. Of course, the saving in judges' costs needs to be balanced against the cost of low measurement precision, but this plan requires only 96 ratings, 8% of the observations required for the complete judging plan. Lunz et al. (1998) reported the successful implementation of such a minimal judging plan (Linacre, 1997).

RATING CREATIVITY OF JUNIOR SCIENTISTS

An incidental part of a study commissioned by the US Navy provided Guilford (1954) with a set of ratings data via which he introduced some innovative approaches to the examination of and adjustment to ratings of examinees by a panel of experts. (Linacre, 1992, chapter 10), The data, summarized in Table 8.1 revealed how three senior scientists (Avogadro, Brahe, and Cavendish for our purposes) rated seven junior scientists (1–7) on five traits of creativity (a–e).

TABLE 8.1
Ratings of Seven Junior Scientists on Five Creativity Traits by Three Senior Scientists (after Guilford, 1954, p. 282)

		Hard			Creativity Traits									Easy		
		Trait e			Trait c			Trait b			Trait a			Trait d		
Examinee	Judge:	A	C	B	A	C	B	A	C	B	A	C	B	A	C	B
High	2	5	5	2^g	5	5	5	7	7	7	9	7	8	8	7	7
	5	5	7	3	7	7	3	7	7	4	9	9	2^f	8	7	2^f
	7	5	7	4	5	7	5	7	7	3	7	7	3	5	5	5
	1	3	3	3	3	5	4	5	5	5	5	5	6	5	7	6
	3	1	5	6^f	3	5	3	3	5	5	3	3	4	7^g	5	6
	4	3	1	5^f	1	3	4	3	3	6	7	5	5	3	3	5
Low	6	1	3	2	3	3	6^f	5	3	4	3	3	4	5	5	4

^{g} most unexplained ratings according to Guilford's descriptive model
^{f} most unexpected ratings according to many-facets Rasch analysis (using FACETS software)

Ratings were awarded on a rating scale which ranged from 1 to 9, with 9 meaning most creative. Following the principle established in Tables 4.1 and 5.2 of this volume), the data from Guilford's table has been ordered to show examinees in descending order of performance, and items in descending order of difficulty, left to right. Examiners also appear in order of leniency: in general, Scientist A gives higher ratings than does Scientist B, who is more lenient than Scientist C.

Most examples of many-facets Rasch analysis contain so many examinees, raters, or both, that it is often difficult to conceptualise how the data matrix might actually appear on paper (i.e., in two dimensions). Guilford's published exemplar provides the essentials for a many-facets conceptualization of his data. It is small enough that it can be easily transformed into a format that the reader can analyze and interpret. (Minifac is a free version of FACETS [Linacre, 2006b] software available at www.winsteps.com and included on the accompanying CD.) Helpfully, Guilford provided his own interpretation of rater behavior based on the light shed on the problem by analyses conducted under true score theory.

Guilford (1954, pp. 282–288) developed a descriptive model based on treating the senior scientists' ratings of junior colleagues as linear measures of performance. For later comparison, it is useful to record what conclusions Guilford came to from the results of his analyses. First of all, he detected evidence of judge–examinee interaction, in which he concluded that Judge A tended to overvalue Examinee 5, Judge B tended to overvalue Examinee 4 but undervalued Examinees 5 and 7, and Judge C tended to overvalue Examinee 5 and undervalue Examinee 4. Thus Judge B disagreed with Judges A and C about Examinees 4 and 5. Were judge–item interaction significant, then Judge A would tend to see examinees higher on Item a and lower on Items c and e than the other judges. In the raw data, Judge B's ratings correlated negatively with those of both Judges A and C, but, after removing explained effects, Guilford found that all judges' ratings then correlated positively. Unfortunately, the existence of the highly significant judge–examinee interactions indicates that there is no way of inferring how each of the senior scientists will use the creativity rating scale traits to judge the next junior scientist to join the group. That means that although Guilford's descriptive analyses, as all of those derived from true score theory, might help to clarify the relations, the findings cannot generalize beyond the current data set.

Given that the data array must represent more than just the two facets of analysis conducted using the dichotomous, PCM, and RSM Rasch models (items and persons), the structure of the data file must, in this case, represent three facets in a two-dimensional (i.e., flat text file) format. The data file below contains all of the data needed for the analysis, ordered according to the display in the original Guilford (1954) chapter. Each data line contains, first, identifiers for the facets (e.g., 1, 3, 1 indicates 1 = first Judge A, 3 = third Junior Scientist c, and 1–5 indicates values for Items 1–5 will follow) and then introduces the ratings (from 1–9) for 5 items or indicators: 3, 3, 3, 7, 1; that is, the ratings given by 1 (first Judge A) to 3 (third Junior Scientist c) on 1–5 (the five traits of creativity, numbered 1 to 5) are 3, 3, 3, 7, 1, and so forth.

```
Data=
1,1,1-5,5,5,3,5,3
1,2,1-5,9,7,5,8,5
1,3,1-5,3,3,3,7,1
1,4,1-5,7,3,1,3,3
1,5,1-5,9,7,7,8,5
1,6,1-5,3,5,3,5,1
1,7,1-5,7,7,5,5,5
2,1,1-5,6,5,4,6,3
2,2,1-5,8,7,5,7,2
2,3,1-5,4,5,3,6,6
2,4,1-5,5,6,4,5,5
2,5,1-5,2,4,3,2,3
2,6,1-5,4,4,6,4,2
2,7,1-5,3,3,5,5,4
3,1,1-5,5,5,5,7,3
3,2,1-5,7,7,5,7,5
3,3,1-5,3,5,5,5,5
3,4,1-5,5,3,3,3,1
3,5,1-5,9,7,7,7,7
3,6,1-5,3,3,3,5,3
3,7,1-5,7,7,7,5,7  ;
```

The many-facets Rasch model to be estimated considers the ability of the candidate, the difficulty of the item, and the difficulty of the rating category over the previous category (i.e., a RSM for items) and the severity of the judge. Guilford's analysis consisted of a sequence of analytical steps in which relevant information from earlier analyses were incorporated where appropriate into later analyses. In the many-facets Rasch model procedure, the facets are estimated concurrently so that they might be considered separately. The control lines given at the end of this chapter will allow the interested reader to replicate this analysis with FACETS (or the free Minifacs) software package. The pathway in Figure 8.1 shows estimates, errors and fit indicators for the main facets: raters, examinees, and traits.

Although not included here, the FACETS tables for this analysis show unremarkable fit statistics, that is, the ratings (Scale 1–9), items (Traits A–E), judges (Senior Sci, A, B, C) and junior scientists (A–F) perform sufficiently predictably to be able to be considered in a single Rasch measurement frame of reference. Given that, the Wright map of the Scientific Creativity variable is instructive (Fig. 8.2). When the many facets are estimated simultaneously, the information about any one facet can be read off the map, all other facets taken into consideration. All other facets considered (i.e., item and category difficulty as well as judge severity), Betty is the most creative junior scientist (+0.66 logits, error. = 0.18), while Fred (−0.29; 0.19) is the least creative. While the criteria for indicators Daring (est. − 0.29; err. 0.15) and Attack (est. −0.27; err. 0.15) are the easiest to satisfy, it takes a

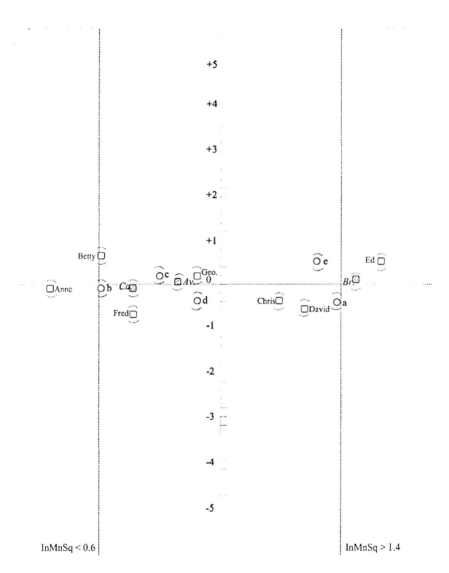

Figure 8.1.　Pathway of the many-facets Rasch analysis of scientists' ratings.

```
All Facet Vertical "Rulers".
-----------------------------------------------------------------------
|Measr|+Junior|-Traits               |+Junior|-Senior sci|+Junior |Scale|
-----------------------------------------------------------------------
+   1 +       +                     +       +           +        +(9)  +
|     |       |                     |       |           |        | 7   |
|     |       |                     |       |           |        |     |
|     |       |                     |       |           |        | --- |
|     | 2     |                     | *     |           | Betty  |     |
|     |       | Enthusiasm          |       |           |        |     |
|     | 5     |                     | *     |           | Edward | 6   |
|     | 7     |                     | *     |           | George |     |
|     |       | Clarity             |       | Brahe     |        | --- |
|     |       |                     |       |           |        |     |
*   0 *       *                     *       * Avogadro  *        * 5   *
|     | 1     | Basis               | *     | Cavendish | Anne   |     |
|     | 3     |                     | *     |           | Chris  | --- |
|     |       | Attack      Daring  |       |           |        |     |
|     |       |                     |       |           |        | 4   |
|     | 4     |                     | *     |           | David  |     |
|     | 6     |                     | *     |           | Fred   |     |
|     |       |                     |       |           |        | --- |
|     |       |                     |       |           |        |     |
|     |       |                     |       |           |        | 3   |
+  -1 +       +                     +       +           +        +(1)  +
-----------------------------------------------------------------------
|Measr|+Junior|-Traits              | * = 1 |-Senior sci|+Junior |Scale|
```

Figure 8.2.   Wright map for the many-facets Rasch analysis of scientists' ratings (from FACETS; Lincare, 2006c).

higher level of Scientific Creativity to be judged as having Enthusiasm. Senior Scientist B (est. −0.24; err. 0.12) can be seen as just measurably more demanding than Scientist C (est. −0.09; err. 0.1), but not Scientist A (est. 0.04; err. 0.1). The latter two senior scientists (A & C) are equally demanding of junior scientists when they rate them on the 9 category, 5 indicator Scientific Creativity scale.

So, is everything "hunky-dory" as they say in the classics? Well, no. If we take the principle of measurement invariance (from chapter 5) seriously, we would require that the creativity estimates of junior scientists should remain invariant across judges (especially after we have already taken into account the differences in judge severity). In Figure 8.3, taken directly form the FACETS output, we have plotted the creativity of each junior scientists as judged by senior scientists A and C on the horizontal axis against that candidate's estimate as judged by senior scientist B, alone. The modelled identity line is dotted in the FACETS figure.

Estimated measures of junior scientist creativity are not invariant across senior scientist ratings. Clearly, while Judge B is marginally more severe than the others, it is more important to note that Judge B's ratings vary too much from those of Judges A and C to be considered part of the same measurement system. We saw a hint of that in Table 8.1 above: While Guilford (1954) concluded that judges A and B each produced one of the most unexplained ratings in his analyses (indicated by the

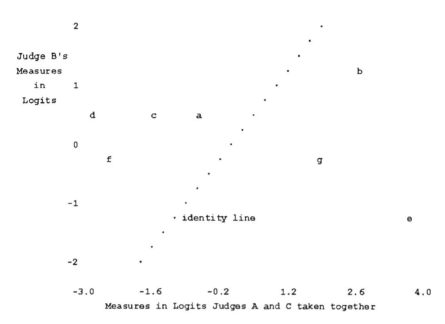

Figure 8.3.   Judge B's candidate measures plotted against those of Judges A and C together. An approximate expectation line is drawn in. Points are identified by junior scientist code (a–f).

superscript g in Table 8.1), the many-facets Rasch analysis attributed all five most unexpected ratings to Judge B (indicated by the superscript f). Seems that the Navy examinations board might seriously consider retiring Senior Scientist B from the scientific creativity judging panel. The control file for this many-facets Rasch analysis is given at the end of chapter 8. More detailed consideration of this analysis is given in chapter 10 of Linacre's (1992) expository text on the many-facets Rasch model.

MANY-FACETS ANALYSIS OF EIGHTH-GRADE WRITING

The many-facets Rasch model exemplar included here is taken from the work of Engelhard (1992, 1994), in which he examined rater severity and other aspects of the writing ability assessment in the high-stakes Eighth Grade Writing Test administered annually to all eighth-grade students in the state of Georgia. Each student was asked to write an essay of no more than two pages on a writing task randomly assigned from a set of eight topics (labeled a–h). The 1,000 marked scripts were selected randomly from the spring 1990 cohort of examinees, with 82 raters (or essay markers) having graded the essays. The essays were graded "by two raters, on each of the following five domains: content/organization, style, sentence formation, usage and mechanics," using "a four-category rating scale (ranging from *inadequate* [1] to *minimal* [2] to *good* [3] to *very good* [4]) . . . The final rating

pattern used to estimate student writing ability consists of 10 ratings (2 raters ×
5 domains = 10 domains)" (Engelhard, 1992, p. 177).

Of course, reliance on rater allocation of grades on five criteria across assigned
topics in a high-stakes statewide educational assessment requires that the raters
grade with the same severity, that the essay topics be equally demanding, and that
the grades across domains reflect similar ability. Indeed, raters for the Georgia
writing tests must meet rigid training and testing requirements. The estimated
interrater reliability for this set was .82, which is comparable with the usual
requirements of state education authorities. The essay topics were constructed
with the explicit intention of producing tasks of equal difficulty.

Engelhard's (1992) many-facets Rasch analysis of the writing assessments used the
following facets: essay writing ability (B), the difficulty of the assigned writing task
(T), the severity of the rater (R), the difficulty of the writing domain (D), and the difficulty of the rating scale step (F). Engelhard's conception of his measurement problem would take the following form: probability = function of (B–D–T–R–F).

As expected, the writing ability estimates of the 1,000 students varied considerably: Raw scores from 10/40 to 39/40 yielded estimates that varied from a low of
−6.84 logits to a high of +7.07 logits. Figure 8.4 (Engelhard, 1992, p. 179) reports
the estimates for raters (R), tasks (T), and domains (D).

The map of the task difficulty (T) facet shows that the examiners' intention to produce eight essay writing prompts of equal difficulty has almost been realized: The
most difficult writing task (c, "all-expense-paid trip"; estimate = +0.12; error = 0.06)
is measurably more difficult than the easiest task (b, "experience that turned out
better"; estimate = −0.16; error = 0.06). Therefore, although these writing
prompts/tasks show small, statistically significant differences in difficulty, for all
practical purposes, the prompt writers have succeeded in producing essay-writing
topics of approximately equal difficulty. In the absence of evidence showing such
empirical equivalence of task difficulty, students' final grades would be fairer if
their scores were adjusted to account for the differential difficulty of writing tasks.

The calibrations for writing domains (D) show greater variation in difficulty.
Whereas the domains of content/organization, usage and mechanics, style, and
sentence formation could be regarded as equally difficult, allowing for the error
of the estimates, the style domain was the most difficult at +0.50 logits (error =
0.05). Sentence formation, with a difficulty estimate of −0.28 (error = 0.05), was
significantly easier to score well on.

The plots of rater severity in Figure 8.4 tell a much more varied tale, however.
A group of approximately 20 raters (located around the 0 origin of the scale)
could be regarded has having graded the essays with the same middling severity
(allowing for measurement error). However, the remaining 60 raters are spread
across more than a 3.5-logit severity range, with the most severe rater (11) estimated at +1.78 logits (error = 0.66) and the most lenient rater (19) estimated at
−1.74 logits (error = 0.48).

Engelhard (1992, p. 177) pointed out that these raters were highly trained.
They had to undergo rigorous training and then qualify by achieving at least 62%
perfect agreement and 38% adjacent category agreements to become operational
raters. During the actual essay grading period, unidentifiable "validity" papers

	Raters	Writing Tasks	Domains
	Severe	*Hard*	*Hard*
+2.0			
.	11		
.			
.			
+1.5			
.	101 82		
.			
.	106 77 66		
+1.0			
.	35 18		
.	110 3 61 96 60 63		
.	31 65 79		
.	120		
+0.5	41 23 48 53		S
.	32 20 72 100		
.	103 14		
.	80 105 69 45 74 16		
.	7 75 52 70 40 34	d c	
0.0	85 102 93 71 58	g h f a e	M
.	114 113 21		C/O U
.	94 64	b	
.	12 119 73 118 37		SF
.	4 95 112 90 104 49		
-0.5	116 51 57 97		
.	24 76 111 86 26		
.	59		
.	27 44 115 55		
.			
-1.0	109 117		
.			
.	6		
.			
.	89 87		
-1.5			
.	25		
.	19		
.			
.			
-2.0			
	Lenient	*Easy*	*Easy*

Figure 8.4. Calibrations of rater severity, writing task, and writing domain difficulties (from Engelhard, 1992).

were included in each packet of 24 essays for grading so that rater agreement was continuously monitored. Every essay was graded by two raters, with papers showing large between-rater discrepancies being rescored by a third rater. The high interrater reliability mentioned earlier (.82) reveals how successful rater training and monitoring was when monitored through the eyes of conventional statistics.

Despite these remarkable efforts, the measurement of rater severity, using the many-facets Rasch model, reveals that variation in rater severity still could have a remarkable effect on student writing assessment scores. Table 8.2 has been derived from Engelhard's (1992) Table 5 (pp. 185–186) to show the impact of the variations in rater severity on the observed and expected ratings of essay writing for four selected students. Students 43 and 522 from this sample received identical total raw scores of 27/40 when their completely identical ratings across five writing domains by two raters were added together. They even shared a common rater (106), who is shown in Figure 8.4 as a moderately severe rater (estimate = +1.13), well above the mean. However, the essay of Student 43 received its other ratings from a lenient rater (26, estimate = −0.65 on Fig. 8.4), whereas the second rater for Student 522 was another severe rater (82, estimate = +1.29). The Rasch ability estimates of writing ability in the right column are based directly on the identical raw scores (27/40 for Students 43 and 522), but incorporate allowances for the unequal severity of the rater pairs derived from the modelled estimates of rater severity plotted in Figure 8.4. Relying on raw scores alone would cause the analyst to underestimate the writing ability of Student 522 by a considerable amount (1.99 −1.16 = 0.83 logits).

Similarly, Students 621 and 305 received completely identical ratings yielding equal raw score totals of 22/40 each. The essay of Student 621 was graded by two severe raters (82, estimate = +1.29; and 66, estimate = +1.06), whereas the 22/40 of student 305 came from a severe rater (61, estimate = +0.81) and a lenient rater (55, estimate = −0.85). This was a tough break for Student 621 because relying on raw scores alone and ignoring rater severity would have underestimated that student's writing ability by more than 1 logit this time (0.08 − [−1.18] = 1.26 logits).

It should be kept in mind that the pairs of raters for each preceding essay were in perfect accord with their allocation of grades for each essay (i.e., interrater reliability would be high for these essays). They met or exceeded the stringent agreement demands of the assessment system. However, the many-facets Rasch modeling of the essay-grading data, made possible because raters could be linked together across common essays, showed very considerable differences in rater severity. The range of rater severity in this tightly monitored grading system (more than 3.5 logits) clearly overwhelms the difficulty differences in the allocated writing topics and the variations across the writing domains. More importantly, differences in rater severity have the potential to confound severely the essay-writing ability estimates of these eighth-grade students. The fit statistics of these raters and ability estimates suggest that these effects are not the result of erratic judge behavior. The judges performed very consistently, well within the Rasch model's stringent expectations. However, the judges are consistently more or less lenient than each other, so much so that it would be unfair not to adjust students' final grades according to the allocation of examiner pairs.

TABLE 8.2
Observed and Expected Ratings for Selected Students

Domain				Domain							
S	SF	U	M	C/O	S	SF	U	M	Raw Score	Infit Mean Square	Ou M Sqi
Rater 26				Rater 106							
3	3	3	3	3	3	3	2	2	27	0.9	0
Rater 82				Rater 106							
3	3	3	3	3	3	3	2	2	27	0.9	0
Rater 66				Rater 82							
2	3	2	3	2	2	2	2	2	22	0.6	0
Rater 55				Rater 61							
2	3	2	3	2	2	2	2	2	22	0.5	0

Organization; S = Style; SF = Sentence Formation; U = Usage; M = Mechanics.

Engelhard (1992) further pointed out that misfitting raters could be identified. Their apparently erratic grade allocations could be identified by student essay number. Therefore, the essay could be reexamined, and the occasional inconsistencies of these examiners could be monitored more effectively. When the grade allocations of overfitting raters were examined, they typically showed little variation of grade allocation within essays (e.g., giving 444444, 33333, or 22222 across the five writing domains), indicating a holistic rather than an analytic approach to essay evaluation. In a later paper based on a section of similar eighth-grade essay-grading data (15 raters across 264 compositions), Engelhard (1994) showed how the many-facets Rasch model could be used to reveal typical rater errors other than severity, such as halo effect, central tendency, and restriction of score range.

RASCH MEASUREMENT OF FACETS BEYOND RATER EFFECTS

We could go a little further with this many-facets Rasch model study to investigate whether some other facets of essay-writing assessment could be profitably modelled.

The many-facets model allows all the relevant facets of a measurement situation to be modelled concurrently but examined independently. What is termed "differential item functioning" (DIF) in the less complex models of the Rasch family can be generalized to the concept of "differential facet functioning" (DFF) in this model to detect whether the invariance expected under the model's requirements actually are instantiated empirically or whether some sort of bias exists.

The basic Rasch measurement model is both strict and simple. It prescribes two attributes that matter when the interaction between a person and an item is modelled: the ability (agreeability) of the person and the difficulty (endorsability) of the item. We have illustrated, however, several instances in which it might be more reasonable to determine whether test responses are affected by other sources of systematic variance in the data collection situation such as the time of the test, the particular task, or the severity of the judge. We could regard these additional facets as decompositions of the original single Rasch difficulty facet, for example, in which a number of aspects of the examination process contribute to the difficulty that the candidates face in revealing their abilities. In these demonstrably more complex circumstances, we then can estimate the extent of those influences on the quality of our measures. The values for these separate facets, created on the same logit scale as person ability and item difficulty (i.e., in the same manner as thresholds are represented), are estimated while the parameter separation so fundamental to the construction of sound and reproducible measures is maintained. The many-facets Rasch model provides for the simultaneous estimation of facet parameters so that they may be examined separately. Whether the many-facets model is the most suitable for any particular analyses requires consideration. For example, do the judges actually interact in the examining process (as in an oral exam) or as mere observers of the performances. In the end, one must ask whether the model used provides a sufficient measurement summary of the examination occasion.

In the face of these developments, further reliance on interitem correlations between judges as the criterion for high-quality ratings is, at best, ill informed. Interjudge correlations tell us only about the consistency between judges in their rank ordering of candidates, and consistency is a necessary but not sufficient condition for producing valid ratings. We need to know whether the judges' ratings (or different tasks or examination timings, for example) result in the same decisions for candidates of the same ability. But how can we know this without estimating the relative severity of the different judges? We cannot, yet we need exactly this type of information to make valid, equitable comparisons among respondents. Without separately estimating such relevant individual facets, these sources of systematic variance go unmonitored, confounding our efforts to construct useful measures, and hence biasing important decisions.

FACETS control file for ratings of Scientific Creativity by senior scientists.

```
Title = Ratings of Scientists (Psychometric Methods p.282 Guilford 1954)
Facets = 3            ; three facets: judges (senior scientists), examinees
(junior scientists), items (traits)
Inter-rater = 1       ; facet 1 (senior scientists) is the rater facet
Positive = 2 ; examinees (junior scientists) have greater creativity with
greater score
Non-centered = 1      ; examinees and items are centered on 0 logits,
judges are allowed to float
Model = ?B,?B,?,R9 ; judges, examinees and items produce ratings with
maximum rating of 9.
    ; A bias/interaction analysis, ?B,?B will report interactions between
facets 1 (judges) and 2 (examinees)
Labels =
1, Senior scientists ; name of first facet: judges
 1 = Avogadro  ; names of elements within senior scientist facet
 2 = Brahe
 3 = Cavendish
*
2, Junior Scientists ; name of second facet: examinees
 1 = Anne
 2 = Betty
 3 = Chris
 4 = David
 5 = Edward
 6 = Fred
 7 = George
*
```

```
3, Traits        ; name of third facet: items
 1 = Attack
 2 = Basis
 3 = Clarity
 4 = Daring
 5 = Enthusiasm
*
 Data=
 1,1,1-5,5,5,3,5,3
 1,2,1-5,9,7,5,8,5
 1,3,1-5,3,3,3,7,1
 1,4,1-5,7,3,1,3,3
 1,5,1-5,9,7,7,8,5
 1,6,1-5,3,5,3,5,1
 1,7,1-5,7,7,5,5,5
 2,1,1-5,6,5,4,6,3
 2,2,1-5,8,7,5,7,2
 2,3,1-5,4,5,3,6,6
 2,4,1-5,5,6,4,5,5
 2,5,1-5,2,4,3,2,3
 2,6,1-5,4,4,6,4,2
 2,7,1-5,3,3,5,5,4
 3,1,1-5,5,5,5,7,3
 3,2,1-5,7,7,5,7,5
 3,3,1-5,3,5,5,5,5
 3,4,1-5,5,3,3,3,1
 3,5,1-5,9,7,7,7,7
 3,6,1-5,3,3,3,5,3
 3,7,1-5,7,7,7,5,7  ; last line of data, and end of file
```

Minifac:
The complete data file, control lines and tutorial for this analysis are pre-loaded into the Minifac software included on the accompanying CD.

CHAPTER NINE

Development, Education, and Rehabilitation: Change Over Time

One fundamental benefit from constructing measures of human science variables is that the estimates derived from Rasch procedures are located on an interval scale where the unit value of the scale is maintained at all points along the scale. A visual display of this interval scale, such as Rasch item–person maps, more completely conveys the nature of the relations between the item difficulties and the person abilities. Consequently, the construction of mathematically meaningful measurement intervals into what is otherwise merely ordinal data paves the way for a closer investigation of the results. Following the example of the physical sciences, we claim that statistical analyses will be effective only if fundamental measures have been constructed in the first place. Moreover, such measures provide the means by which researchers can focus on the changes that occur over time.

Even the most naïve conceptions of human development, school learning, physical rehabilitation and a host of conditions investigated in the human sciences, have at their core, the idea of change over time. Without adequate reflection, we might assume that the changes are always for the better: more strength, more height, more words spelled correctly, more shoulder flexibility following therapy, and so on, but of course that is not necessarily the case. While a disease might develop in predictable ways over time, health professionals see the condition of the patient deteriorating. Still, both are complementary aspects of change over time, and the use of invariant, interval measures of the crucial underlying human variables will be central to monitoring change as well as in attempting to detect the impacts of concomitant events such as diet, instruction, surgery, drugs or physical therapy. While the pediatrician might use a set of height and weight tables to compare any one child's status with some appropriate normative benchmark, more important to monitoring the health or developmental status will be the profile of the changes between visits over time. The premature baby might remain frighteningly below benchmark indicators for months and months while the parents remain delighted at the gains in height, weight, and on other developmental indicators.

In this important sense, the indicators we routinely use for assessing school achievement remain counterintuitive at best. At worst, they are potentially destructive without appropriate accompanying evidence based on invariant measurement scales. Letter grades and percentages on any child's school reports remain persistently and depressingly uniform across school years (B, A, B, B, A, B; 78%, 82%, 75%, 73%; 87%, 71%, etc.) in spite of huge investment of resources, time, and effort by the state, schools, teachers, and the children themselves. Even with norm-referenced and benchmark referenced outcome indicators, achievement levels are reported as virtually static while demands at each new school year become more and more sophisticated. One of the important direct consequences of the development of Rasch measurement scales for educational achievement has been the growing call for focus on growth in achievement over time, rather than the reporting achievement at any one point in time (Masters, 2004; Griffin, 2004; Cronin, Kingsbury, McCall, & Bowe, 2005; Gori, 2006; Bond, 2005). In spite of its being a truism, it is nevertheless worth reiterating: *It is impossible to measure change with a measure that changes.*

So while development over time is central to aspects of psychology, education, and health, stage-like development has been one of the major themes in developmental psychology, and one that remains controversial to this day (Fischer & Dawson, 2002). The stage notion in cognitive development is associated mainly with the work of Jean Piaget and his coworkers, but the concept exists in other theoretical viewpoints such as the classic work of Sigmund Freud, Lawrence Kohlberg's stages of moral development, and Abraham Maslow's hierarchy of needs. In general, changes occurring during development result in the construction of each new stage, which integrates the preceding stage while being qualitatively more sophisticated than its predecessor.

This raises both the notion of development *per se* and that of discontinuity in stage-like development. Given the apparently continuous and gradual nature of human development, principles from the Rasch models for measurement can be considered to suggest how empirical developmental data could be arranged so that evidence for stages might be revealed. In order to illustrate how Rasch item measures might be analyzed statistically to detect stage-like qualities of development, we have selected an example based on cognitive tasks developed by Noelting and his collaborators. Noelting's study was inspired by Piaget's qualitative framework research, but each task involved a collection of individual items with various degrees of complexity (Noelting & Rousseau, in press). The structure of each item corresponded to a form of thinking characterizing a stage of cognitive development.

SHOWING DEVELOPMENTAL STAGES CROSS-SECTIONALLY

An example of the items comprising the three tasks is shown in Figure 9.1. The mixing juices (MJ) task (Noelting, 1980a, 1980b) consists of assessing which set of

a) Mixing Juices (MJ)

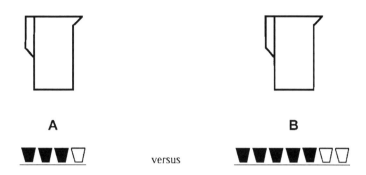

A   **B**

versus

b) Caskets Task (CT)

Of these three inscriptions, two are FALSE, one is TRUE

c) Coded Orthogonal Views (COV)

Item	Coded drawing	Legend

3		1,2
3		2
3	3	2,3

1 = cube on 1st layer
2 = cube on 2nd layer
3 = cube on 3rd layer

Figure 9.1.   The three Noelting tasks.

165

glasses will have a stronger concentration of juice after the liquids are mixed in a beaker. The caskets task (CT) derives from a logical puzzle by Smullyan (1978) and involves propositional logic. It consists of statements about the presence or the absence of an object in the caskets. Only one object exists, and it must be in one casket. The aim is to discover the casket in which the object is hidden. Finally, the coded orthogonal views task (COV; Gaulin, Noelting, & Puchalska, 1984; Noelting, Gaulin, & Puchalska, 1985) involves the drawing and coding of a three-dimensional object composed of cubes. The task concerns the reproduction of three-dimensional objects on a paper using coded drawing. Subjects are asked to draw an outline of the object from a frontal point of view, using signs in appropriate locations to account for the third dimension. An item is mastered if it is possible to reconstruct the object from the subject's drawing, which includes a coding system and a legend.

Criteria for cognitive developmental stages were established in Noelting's (1982) previous work from an analysis of children's behavior on each task. The criteria were then used to examine the correspondence between qualitative and quantitative stage characteristics. The cognitive developmental range covered by the tasks included the intuitive, the concrete, and the formal operational stages. Because the sample reported here consists of late adolescents and adults, data concerning the concrete operational and formal operational stages only are analyzed here. Previous Rasch analyses of data collected with the three tasks have shown a good intratask fit of items to the model's requirements. The data reported here come from an experiment conducted by Brunel, Noelting, Chagnon, Goyer, and Simard (1993), using versions of MJ, CT, and COV comprising 18, 16, and 7 items, respectively. The tasks were submitted to a sample of 350 subjects ranging in age from 16 years to adulthood. The written answers collected during group administration of the tasks were scored dichotomously according to stage criteria for each task.

The Rasch analysis of the data from the three tasks together is shown in Table 9.1. Items range on the difficulty scale from −5.97 logits for the easiest item to +4.61 logits for the most difficult item (a late formal item of COV). The spread of subjects on the same scale goes from −2.79 logits to +6.76 logits, with a person ability estimate mean +1.74 logits higher than the mean item difficulty estimate, which is centered routinely on 0 logits. Four items (COV2, COV3, COV4, and COV5) present infit and outfit values beyond the conventionally acceptable range for a t distribution (between −2.00 and +2.00), whereas negative fit values for items MJ15, MJ16, and CT10 indicate less variation in performance than expected.

EVIDENCE OF DISCONTINUITY

The item–person map of the cognitive development trait shows gaps between item difficulty allocations on the logit scale. One way to assess the significance of the empirical gaps could be to perform t tests between successive pairs of items along the logit scale (Fig. 9.2). The items are labeled by stage and located by task in different columns. The item hierarchy of difficulty presents some gaps. The

TABLE 9.1

Rasch Analysis of the Three Tasks: Item Statistics

Item		Logit Measures		Fit statistics		Item		Logit Measures		Fit Statistics	
Name	Stage	Difficulty	Error	Infit t	Outfit t	Name	Stage	Difficulty	Error	Infit t	Outfit t
COV7	3C	4.61	0.20	0.0	-0.2	CT9	2C	-0.78	0.18	-0.7	-0.5
MJ19	3C	4.13	0.17	-1.4	-1.6	MJ9	2B	-0.85	0.19	0.8	-0.5
MJ18	3C	4.01	0.17	-1.0	-1.6	MJ10	2A	-1.15	0.20	0.0	-0.9
CT18	3B	3.55	0.15	0.3	0.6	CT8	2B	-1.23	0.20	-0.1	-0.1
CT16	3B	3.41	0.15	2.0	1.0	CT7	2A	-1.27	0.21	-0.1	0.4
MJ16	3B	3.30	0.15	-2.8	-2.3	CT4	2A	-1.45	0.22	-0.8	0.2
COV6	3B	3.26	0.15	-0.3	0.4	CT6	2A	-1.71	0.23	-1.7	-1.5
MJ15	3B	3.16	0.14	-3.5	-2.7	CT3	1B	-2.08	0.26	-0.3	0.4
CT17	3B	3.12	0.14	1.7	0.1	CT2	1B	-2.15	0.27	0.4	1.8
CT15	3B	3.10	0.14	-0.1	-0.4	CT5	1B	-2.15	0.27	-0.4	0.9
MJ13	3A	2.48	0.13	-1.5	0.1	MJ8	1C	-2.23	0.28	-0.3	-1.3
MJ14	3A	2.48	0.13	-1.1	0.3	MJ5	1B	-2.31	0.29	0.0	1.2
COV5*	3A	2.41	0.13	4.0	3.3	COV1	2B	-2.31	0.29	-0.1	0.7
COV4*	3A	1.95	0.13	3.9	2.9	MJ6	1C	-2.58	0.31	0.0	-0.8
COV3*	2C	0.51	0.14	3.1	1.7	MJ7	1B	-2.58	0.31	0.1	0.8
MJ12	2B	0.30	0.15	-1.3	-1.7	MJ4	1C	-3.37	0.43	0.0	0.9
CT12	3A	0.22	0.15	-1.7	-1.4	CT1	1A	-4.12	0.59	0.2	1.9
COV2*	2C	-0.02	0.16	2.6	2.4	MJ2	1A	-5.26	1.01	0.0	-0.2
MJ11	2B	-0.10	0.16	-1.2	-1.4	MJ3	1A	-5.26	1.01	-0.1	-0.6
CT10	2C	-0.44	0.17	-2.4	-0.9	MJ1	0	-5.97	1.42	—	—
CT11	3A	-0.59	0.17	1.3	0.6						

*Does not fit the Rasch model ($t > 2.0$).

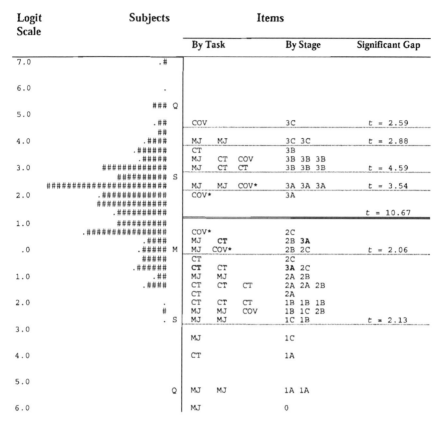

Figure 9.2. Map of subjects and items on the logit scale for the three Noelting tasks. The 3A items of caskets task with a concrete operational difficulty level are in bold. Items marked by * do not fit ($t > 2.0$).

results show seven statistically significant gaps in the scale, with the widest gap ($t = 10.67$) separating the concrete and the formal operational stages (stages 2 and 3 in Figure 9.2). These results provide a quantitative empirical demonstration of the qualitative changes that occur in thought processes during development, with the crucial passage from the concrete stage to the formal operational stage showing as the largest gap.

Smaller, but still significant, gaps in item difficulties show the locations of less comprehensive intra-stage developmental changes in thinking. Therefore, the qualitative discontinuity postulated between concrete and formal stages is supported quantitatively. The major gap obtained between 14 concrete level items and 14 formal level items indicates that the addition of a new component is not mastered gradually, but takes the form of a new organization. The size of this gap between stages demonstrates the important cognitive change associated with the passage from one stage to the next as compared with the within-stage transitions. The application of Rasch modelling to these data has opened a whole new world of analysis to Noelting and his colleagues, resulting in a complete new book (Noelting & Rousseau, in press) based on the interpretation and re-theorizing of his work, which has its basis in Rasch modelling of data from a lifetime of such testing.

MODELING AND MEASURING DEVELOPMENTAL DISCONTINUITY

Indeed, the measurement of stage-governed development is of such importance that it has been a focus of Mark Wilson (University of California, Berkeley), who has developed the Saltus model (a latent group model) from the basic Rasch model to detect discontinuity in development (Wilson, 1985). While the Saltus model might not be regarded strictly as a member of the Rasch family of models for measurement, its treatment of ability and difficulty is well grounded in principles central to the issues raised in this volume. Two key papers by Wilson (1989) and Mislevy and Wilson (1996) cover the key theoretical and technical issues in the application of the Saltus model. The term "Saltus," from the Latin meaning "leap," is designed to represent Wilson's conception of the relatively abrupt changes in the relative difficulty of items for a person who moves from one stage to the next. Although the tradition in developmental and other research had been to use Guttman scalogram analyses, Wilson (1989) summarized:

> This technique, derived from attitude questionnaires, assumes that there is just one item per level and assigns subjects to levels according to the following criteria. (a) A subject is in level n if he or she has responded correctly up to and including the item representing level n and has failed the remainder of the items: Such a response is said to be scalable. (b) A subject with any other response is of a *nonscale* type. (p. 277)

A far more realistic method would involve the development of a testing situation having many items or tasks at each of the developmental levels or stages, with the expectation that as a person moves into a new stage, discontinuity in development would be marked by a rather rapid transition from passing no, or few, tasks to passing many or most tasks indicative of the new level. Indeed, the Guttman requirements for ordinal scaling rarely are met even with continual refinement of testing procedures. There will always be some error in our recorded observations of human behavior. Some errors will be the result of deficiencies in our observation methods, whereas others will result from the nature of human behavior itself: the role of individual differences and the sheer unpredictability of humans. Under these pervasive conditions, Guttman scaling, while fundamentally correct on the crucial issue of order but ignoring the equally important aspect of stochasticity, has much more stringent requirements about human performance than the developmental theories it is being used to assess (Kofsky, 1966; Wilson, 1989).

The results from Noelting and Rousseau (in press) reported earlier in this chapter reveal what Wilson terms *segmentation,* prima facie evidence for first-order developmental discontinuity: When tests with many items at each level are submitted to Rasch analysis, items representing different stages should be contained in different segments of the scale (Fig. 9.2), with a nonzero distance between segments, and, of course, the items should be mapped in the order predicted by the theory. When item estimates are being tested for segmentation, the idea of a segmentation index must reflect the distance between the levels in terms of the errors of measurement of the item difficulty estimates. Given that the *t* test used to calculate the between-stages differences in the Significant Gap column in Figure 9.2 is the ratio of the "difference between adjacent item estimates" and the "sum of the measurement errors for those two items," then Noelting's results provide evidence of stage-like developmental discontinuity (Noelting, Coudé, Rousseau, & Bond, 2000; Wilson, 1989).

The more subtle type of leap that the Saltus model uniquely is designed to detect and model (i.e., second-order developmental discontinuity) can be appreciated readily from consideration of the following Saltus principles. Although the Saltus method can be applied to a number of hierarchical developmental levels in one analysis, the key points are encapsulated more easily in a situation of less complexity: one in which person abilities and item difficulties can be seen as representing either of two developmental levels, as shown in Table 9.2.

In this simple example, the cases at each level are considered as randomly sampled from a normally distributed population (with a specific mean and standard deviation for that level). The Saltus model is simpler than many other similar models—it estimates a much smaller number of parameters. It focuses on the amount (measured in logits) that each set of items "shifts" in difficulty when encountered by persons in each level. For each group of subjects in turn, we shall presume to view the two types of items from their perspectives. In each situation, we summarize the ability levels of the persons at a certain level by the mean of the ability estimates and summarize the difficulty levels of the items at a certain level by the mean of the difficulty estimates. The vertical arrow indicates increasing person ability or item difficulty (see Fig. 9.3).

First, we present the perspective of the lower level group:

For the lower ability group, the easy items look easy enough but the harder items look much tougher. The detail of the reasoning is that from the perspective of the mean ability of the lower level subjects (ß Group I) the mean difficulty of

TABLE 9.2
Subjects and Items Grouped for Saltus Example

Stage	Subject Groups	Item Types
Higher level	Higher level subjects II	Higher level items B
Lower level	Lower level subjects I	Lower level items A

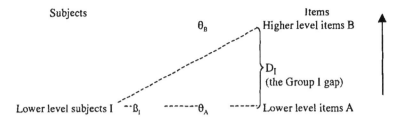

Figure 9.3a.   Group I subjects regard items grouped for Saltus example.

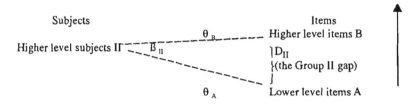

Figure 9.3b.   Group II subjects regard items grouped for Saltus example.

the lower level items (θ_A) appears to be relatively easy, whereas from that same perspective (β_I), the mean difficulty of the higher level items (θ_B) appears to be hard (i.e., $[\theta_B] - [\beta_I] > [\theta_A] - [\beta_I]$). Wilson refered to the difference between these two values as D_I (the Group I gap): $D_I = ([\theta_B] - [\beta_I]) - ([\theta_A] - [\beta_I])$. Figure 9.3a represents the relative difference in difficulty between higher (θ_B) and lower (θ_A) items for the lower level group of persons (β_I), and Figure 9.3b represents the perspective of the higher level group.

For those in the higher level ability group, all items look relatively easy. From the perspective of the mean ability of the higher level subjects (β_{II}) the mean difficulty of the lower level items (θ_A) appears to be relatively easy, and the mean difficulty of the higher level items (θ_B) appears to be relatively easy as well (i.e., $[\theta_B] - [\beta_{II}] > [\theta_A] - [\beta_{II}]$). Wilson refered to the difference between these two values as D_{II} (the Group II gap): $D_{II} = ([\theta_B] - [\beta_{II}]) - ([\theta_A] - [\beta_{II}])$. This represents the relative difference in difficulty between higher (θ_B) and lower (θ_A) items for the higher level group of persons (β_{II}). The asymmetry index, $D = D_I - D_{II}$, is used then in the Saltus model to detect a less immediately obvious form of developmental discontinuity. So Saltus is designed to estimate: the mean and standard deviation of each level's sample; the proportion of the total sample at each level, and the difficulty calibration of each item at each level. In turn, some of the parameters are estimated while others are held steady until the process converges. From the final estimates, the probability that any particular person belongs to any particular level can be computed—as revealed in the example from Draney (1996) that follows.

Therefore, a positive asymmetry index (i.e., $D_I \gg D_{II}$) indicates that the item types are closer together in item difficulty terms for group II than for group I, and a large $D_I - D_{II}$ difference is the indicator of second-order developmental discontinuity: Type B items are much harder than type A items for subjects in Group I (i.e., their probability of success on Type B items is low). Once the leap is made across the developmental levels (i.e., for subjects in Group II), the difference between the two item types becomes much less.

When the asymmetry index is 0, second-order developmental discontinuity has not been detected, and the principles of the basic Rasch model can be applied to the detection of first-order developmental discontinuity (as in the Noelting example). Wilson (1989) claimed that the further the asymmetry index is from 0, the greater the need for the Saltus model to interpret what the Rasch model could detect only as misfit. Importantly, Saltus results include both a probability of a person being in each stage and a location in each.

A SALTUS EXAMPLE

The data for the example given here from the work of Draney (1996) are also from a set of responses to Noelting's (1980a, 1980b) MJ task for assessing proportional reasoning, which were administered to a group of 460 subjects ranging in age from 5 to 17 years. Although the Noelting MJ task contains 20 items that are scored dichotomously, Draney raised an important issue regarding the Rasch modelling of such items. When subsets of dichotomous items are essentially replications of one another, there sometimes is the concern that the requirement of local independence of items, necessary for Rasch models, will be violated. Local independence requires that the success or failure on any item should not depend on the success or failure on any other item. This might not be the case when several questions relate to the same test premise. One method used to deal with this possibility is to group such related dichotomous items together into what could be called "superitems" (Wilson, 1989; Wilson & Iventosch, 1988). The person's score on any superitem is the summed scores of its individual subitems. Thus, a superitem is polytomous (i.e., if there are three items in a superitem, the subject might get 0, 1, 2, or 3 of them correct). This was the approach used in the Saltus modelling of the MJ data reported here (Draney, 1996).

Although the MJ task comprises three hierarchical groups of items (intuitive, concrete operational, and formal operational items), which, in the analysis reported at the start of this chapter, yielded information about three hierarchical groups of children (intuitive, concrete operational, and formal operational thinkers), the Saltus analysis reported here compares the set of intuitive superitems to the set of concrete operational superitems. Although the analysis uses only those six items (three for intuitive and three for concrete), all 460 members of the sample were included. In this case, the Saltus-based hypothesis is that the difference in difficulty between the intuitive and concrete items should be much greater for children in the intuitive stage than for those in the higher (concrete or formal operational) stages. To model this expectation, the youngest children were classified into the lower Saltus group (Group I) and all of the older children into the upper Saltus group (Group II). The Saltus parameter, or asymmetry index, $D = DI - DII$, describing the difference in difficulty between Group I and Group II, is predicted to be positive, indicating a developmental discontinuity between the intuitive and the operational stages of cognitive development (Draney, 1996).

TABLE 9.3
Average Mixing Juices Subitem Difficulties for the Intuitive Versus Concrete
Operational Saltus Comparison

Developmental Substage	Average Difficulty
Concrete 2c	+3.50
Concrete 2b	+3.12
Concrete 2a	+0.53
Intuitive 1c	−1.22
Intuitive 1b	−2.33
Intuitive 1a	−3.79

Table 9.3 reports the average item difficulty estimates for each of the intuitive (1a, 1b, 1c) and concrete (2a, 2b, 2c) substages described by Noelting. Difficulties are ordered hierarchically across the greater than seven logit range.

The interpretation of item difficulties and mean abilities for Saltus groups is easier when these locations are displayed in the form of the item–person map that we have used in earlier chapters. Figure 9.4 provides the item–group map of the MJ intuitive versus concrete Saltus analysis. The logit scale is shown on the left side of the figure. The column to the right of this contains the mean abilities of the two person-groups, with a range of one standard deviation on either side of each group mean. The mean ability estimate for the intuitive group (M1) is located between the upper and lower limits of the +1 standard deviation range (S1), as it also is for the operational group (M2 and S2). Following the display principles in Figures 9.3a and 9.3b, the difficulty levels for the items as seen by group I are shown in the section labeled Items From Group I Perspective, as they also are for items as seen by Group II. More difficult item steps and more able persons are toward the top of the logit scale, and less difficult item steps and less able persons are toward the bottom of the scale.

In this figure, the effect of the Saltus parameter is clear. The intuitive item difficulties are held fixed for both groups, but from the perspective of the intuitive group subjects, the concrete items seem to be much more difficult indeed (large DI gap). The higher ability of the operational Group II means that this group does considerably better on the intuitive items than does Group I, but from the perspective of the operational group subjects, the concrete items seem to be not difficult at all (small DII gap). The Saltus parameter (or asymmetry index, $D = DI − DII$) describing the relative difference in difficulty between Group A and Group B items is estimated at +2.99 logits (error = 0.003), both large and positive as predicted by the preceding account based on Draney (1996).

Table 9.4 provides the observed response strings, the probabilities of intuitive group membership, and the estimated abilities with standard errors for a subset of the sample chosen to be representative of typical persons. Persons who tend to score 0 on all of the concrete items, such as Persons A and B, are given a greater

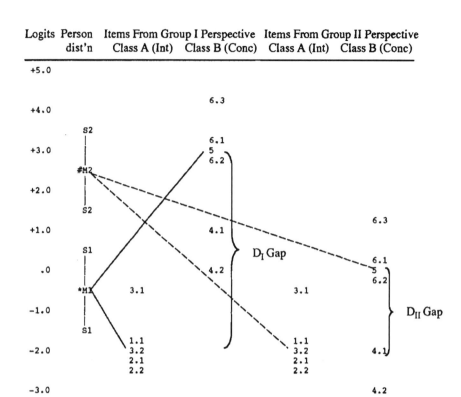

Logits	Person dist'n	Items From Group I Perspective		Items From Group II Perspective	
		Class A (Int)	Class B (Conc)	Class A (Int)	Class B (Conc)

*M1 (S1) shows average ability (with standard deviation) for group I (intuitive) thinkers.
#M2 (S2) shows average ability (s.d.) for group II (concrete & formal op'l) thinkers.

Figure 9.4.   Item–group map of intuitive versus concrete Saltus
analysis of mixing juices.

174

TABLE 9.4
Exemplar Persons for the Mixed Juices Intuitive Versus
Concrete Saltus Comparison

Person	Response String	Probability of Belonging to Group I	Ability I	Standard Error I	Ability II	Standard Error II
A	000000	1.00	−3.02	0.68	−2.30	0.57
B	222000	1.00	−0.30	0.69	−0.28	0.61
C	222100	1.00	0.19	0.70	0.10	0.63
D	212200	0.97	0.19	0.70	0.10	0.63
E	222001	1.00	0.19	0.70	0.10	0.63
F	222213	0.00	2.79	0.71	2.85	0.89
G	222212	0.01	2.28	0.72	2.11	0.82
H	222102	0.68	1.22	0.73	0.97	0.70
I	222210	0.68	1.22	0.73	0.97	0.70

than 0.99 probability of being in the intuitive group (I), regardless of scores on the intuitive items. Even persons such as C or D, who score either one or two on the easiest of the concrete items (Superitem 3), also are placed into the intuitive group, with a probability between 0.97 and 0.99. Even Person E, someone who answers one of the subitems of concrete superitem 6 correctly while missing all of the other concrete items, is classified in Group I ($p = 1$). Persons who tend to answer most, or all, of the concrete items correctly are placed into the operational group (II). Students such as Person F, whose score on all six items is perfect, has a higher probability (> 0.99) of being in the higher group (Group II) than Person G, who misses only one possible point on the concrete items.

Although the classification of Person H, who scores two out of three on the last concrete item, misses Item 5, and scores one out of two on (concrete) Item 4, is more equivocal (Group I classification has 0.68 probability), in the sample of 460 persons there are only 17 such persons, or less than 5%. Response strings like that of Person I (scores 0 on concrete Superitem 6, but does well on all the other items) all have Group I membership probabilities of 0.68.

LONGITUDINAL ANALYSES

It is unfortunately true that whereas development routinely encompasses at least the idea of change over time (part of the life span), genuine longitudinal research designs in developmental psychology or educational achievement, for example, remain the exception rather than the rule. Cross-sectional studies, in which subjects across an age range are tested for development or achievement simultaneously, comprise the vast majority, whereas longitudinal studies, in which a cohort of subjects is tested repeatedly as the subjects age, remain in the minority.

Longitudinal studies are more expensive. Repeated studies risk challenges to validity such as mortality, whereas the publish-or-perish prerogative pushes for short-term rather than long-term research commitment. Of course, longitudinal studies, which involve invariant, interval level (e.g., Rasch) measures of developmental attributes or educational achievement, are even scarcer on the ground. Although statistical analyses will never be replaced by the development of measures, statistical analyses based on measures have the potential to answer these questions more meaningfully than before.

LONGITUDINAL DATA: THE SHORT HAUL

Data for a study by Endler (1998) were collected over a 5-year period to investigate the progressive changes in the Piagetian level of cognitive development in a cohort of students during the course of their secondary education. Estimates of cognitive development were based on responses to Bond's Logical Operations Test (BLOT; Bond, 1976/1995; see also chaps. 4 and 5). All data collected from the Years 8, 10, and 12 cohorts were used to provide three separate empirical developmental accounts of the students in the year groups of 1993, 1995, and 1997. Figure 9.5 plots the track of the mean ability estimate for the cohort over the 5-year span. The graph depicts results that support the commonly understood progress of cognitive development across the adolescent years. Moreover, the use of the Rasch logit as the measurement unit allows us to make direct visual comparisons about the relative size of the developmental changes. By and large, early adolescents (as 13-year-olds in eighth grade) are, on the average, at the stage of mature concrete operational thought (Stage IIB). By the time their 15th birthdays have rolled around, as 10th graders, they show early formal operational thought (Stage IIIA), and by the time they are ready to graduate from high school (as 17-year-olds in the final year 12), mature formal thought (Stage IIIB) is in evidence. The addition of measurement error bars (in logits) for each of the mean ability estimates makes the significance of the size of change (compared with size of error) directly appreciable. The graph of these summary data portrays continued but modest change over the 5-year period as the developmental rule.

More importantly, however, the individual developmental profiles of particular students tested on more than one occasion over the 5-year period were tracked individually to trace each child's intellectual growth over time. These longitudinal results, shown in Figure 9.6, clearly show periods of rapidly developing formal operational thought along with periods of relatively little change. Given that this plotting of cognitive ability measures shows how developmental spurts occur at different periods, the longitudinal/cross-sectional contrast reveals the inadequacies of empirical accounts of cognitive development that rely on cross-sectional summaries alone. Individual growth summaries based on the use of interval measures show that the matching of educational strategy to intellectual abilities is a much more complicated task than cross-sectional data or group longitudinal trends possibly could reveal.

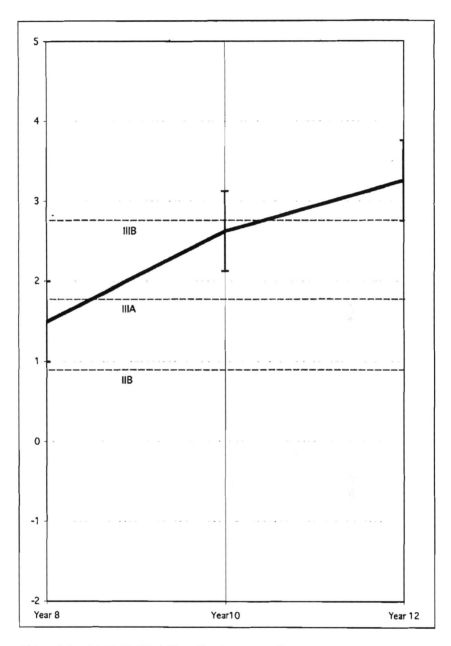

Figure 9.5.   Mean BLOT ability estimates across 5-year span.

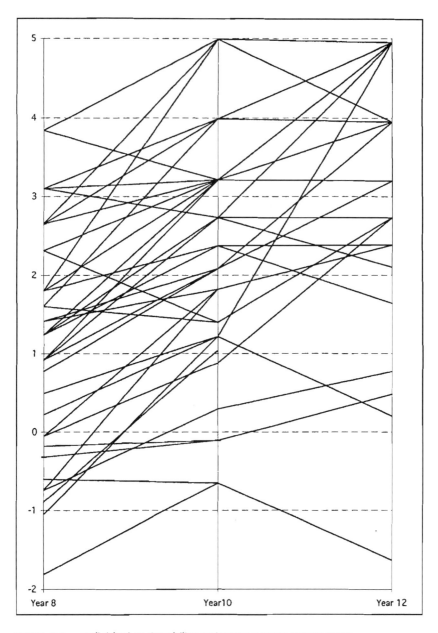

Figure 9.6.   Individual BLOT ability estimates across 5-year span.

ESTIMATES FOR PERFECT SCORES

Technically speaking, Rasch modelling cannot provide estimates for perfectly good (all ✔s) or completely failing (all ✗s) scores. As detailed in chapter 3, Rasch estimates are based on probability of success to probability of failure ratios. Whereas 80% success has 20% failure from which to construct a ratio, 100% success has 0% failure, and 0% success has 100% failure. Then, the 100/0 fraction produces an infinitely large estimate, and conversely, 0/100 yields an infinitely small result.

In keeping with that requirement, the QUEST software used in the Endler (1998) study does not provide Rasch ability estimates for perfect scores (all 1s, or all 0s). However, users of the BLOT would expect that the performances of many students would show ceiling effects during adolescence. Many students "top out" on the test with a perfect score of 35/35. Whereas the ceiling effect itself can result in underestimation of ability and growth, removing all 35/35 perfect scores from the data sets for Figures 9.6 and 9.7 would be even more misleading. Wright (1998) provided guidelines for the extrapolation of approximate measures for perfect scores. Endler (1998) chose to adopt the conservative approach that "(n)o extreme score extrapolation can be less than one logit" (Wright, 1998a), adding 1 logit to the +3.99 logits (for 34/35) to give the +4.99 logits estimate for 35/35 on the BLOT used to construct the preceding figures. More recent versions of QUEST developed at ACER for supporting the PISA international comparisons of educational achievement use Warm's (Warm, 1985) Weighted Likelihood Estimator (WLE) to provide estimates for perfect scores.

WINSTEPS Rasch software routinely provides an approximate estimate for perfect scores using an almost-perfect score as the basis for its estimation. That procedure yields an estimate of +5.16 logits for a perfect BLOT score in place of the +4.99 used by Endler (1998). Linacre (1999b) advised: "The measure for an extreme score is estimated as the measure for (maximum score −x) or (minimum score + x) in which 0.5 $\geq x \geq 0$. The default for WINSTEPS is 0.3. This takes the position that the extreme score is only barely extreme." The estimate from WINSTEPS of +5.16 logits is based on the fraction 34.7/0.03 (i.e., on a BLOT score of 34.7 out of a possible 35).

LONGITUDINAL DATA: THE LONG HAUL

Dawson's (2000) Rasch modelling of data collected by Armon (1984) to investigate the longitudinal development of moral judgment and ideas of the good provides an excellent exemplar of Rasch measures used to address the existence and nature of stage-like change in persons over time. Dawson argued that Rasch measurement, using the partial credit model, was well suited to answer questions about whether development is step-like or gradual, about the relation between development in different domains, and about the relations between stages assessed with different data collection instruments, all of which are seen as difficult for traditional quantitative methods even to address.

In her longitudinal study of moral reasoning and evaluative reasoning about the good, Armon interviewed a total of 42 individuals (19 males and 23 females) on four separate occasions: 1977, 1981, 1985, and 1989. The youngest commencing subject was 5 years of age, whereas the oldest was age 86 years on the final interview occasion. At each occasion, three dilemmas from the Moral Judgment Interview (MJI; Colby & Kohlberg, 1987) were used to assess moral reasoning along with Armon's (1984) Good Life interview which includes questions about the good life, good work, good friendship, and good person. The interviews were open ended. They were administered individually to each participant, tape-recorded, and transcribed, with seven participants missing two out of four interviews. Both the Colby and Kohlberg and the Armon scoring systems produce scores that can be reported as global stage scores (GSS) ranging from 1 to 5 in increments of one half stage (Armon, 1984; Colby & Kohlberg, 1987). All the interview examples in each of the five domains for each participant were scored individually and averaged, using a standard weighting system (Armon, 1984). This resulted in a single score for each participant in each domain (i.e., five scores per person per test time).

The Rasch analyses reported in Figure 9.7 were conducted on the pooled longitudinal and cross-sectional data. All observations were treated as independent, giving an n of 147 separate observations from the total number of 42 participants. This effectively increased the analytical power. This is a useful and permissible strategy when a study design involves more than two test times separated by relatively long intervals (Rogosa & Willett, 1985; Willett, 1989). More importantly for this exemplar, the longitudinal information incorporated into the Rasch estimation analysis in this way shows that any age differences reflect actual individual trends rather than mere statistical artifacts.

The item–person map in Figure 9.7 presents a thorough and comprehensive display of the results from the analysis, with the logit scale represented as a long vertical gray band toward the right of the figure. Estimates for individuals (represented by case numbers) at each of the four times of testing are in separate columns to the left of this band, arranged in ascending order from left to right. Tracing the developmental trajectory of the developmental trajectory for each individual then is simply a matter of joining the appropriate identification numbers.

Conservative, qualitatively judged locations for individuals with 0 scores (all items scored Stage 1) have been added to the bottom of the logit scale, whereas locations for individuals with perfect scores (all items scored Stage 5) have been added to the top of the logit scale. The few case numbers shown in bold indicate that their performance patterns did not fit the model. Table 9.5 shows the actual scores, infit mean squares, and standardized t infit values for those individuals. Dawson (2000) argued that although cases 35 and 26 (twice) had scores across items that were very similar, too similar to fit the Rasch model, these cases were not problematic from her theoretical perspective because the similarity of their scores is consistent with the hypothesis that individuals tend to think in structurally similar ways across these different contexts.

To the right of the logit scale are the item estimates for the good life, good work, good friendship, good person, and moral judgment, respectively. Dawson

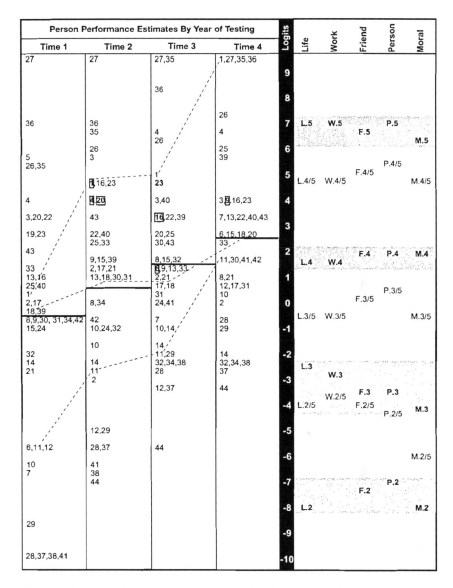

Figure 9.7.   Map of person performance estimates by year of testing.

181

TABLE 9.5
Moral and Evaluative Reasoning:
Person Performances That Do Not Fit the Model

		Actual Scores					
ID No.	Year	Good Life	Good Work	Good Friendship	Good Person	Moral Judgment	Infit Mean Square	Infit *t*
26	1977	4.5	4.5	4.5	4.0	4.5	0.18	−2.18
35	1977	4.5	4.5	4.5	4.0	5.0	0.18	−2.18
26	1989	4.5	4.5	4.5	4.5	4.5	0.90	−2.91
1	1989	4.0	4.0	3.5	5.0	3.5	3.97	+2.58

(2000) has helpfully added large horizontal gray bands to indicate the approximate range for each level of reasoning from Stage 2 to Stage 5 across the five items. With the exception of moral judgment at Stage 2.5, stage scores across items cluster within relatively narrow bands of the logit scale, indicating that individual stage scores across all five items appear to measure the same level of reasoning. Not only does this provide evidence for structural coherence across test contents, it also allows interpolation of stage boundaries and stage-wise progress onto the interval logit scale. The Stage 2.5 exception seems to be a consequence of the greater immediate relevance of a concrete moral dilemma, as opposed to the abstract concept of "good," for young children. There is an absence of any result in the distribution of the stages that would suggest that the developmental level in any one testing context item progresses more rapidly.

Finally, four narrow horizontal gray bands show the means of the person performance estimates at each of the test times. Mean development in this group over the course of the study spanned 4 logits, or approximately one full stage. An analysis of variance (ANOVA) comparing means at the four test times indicates that mean stage advance is significant: $F(3, 144) = 7.29, p < .001$.

In Figure 9.7, the developmental trajectories of three of the subjects have been made more obvious by the simple technique of joining the person estimates across the four data-collection occasions for Subjects 1, 11, and 18. In spite of the large differences in starting and ending locations for Persons 1 and 11, their developmental profiles show remarkable similarities in pattern/slope. While Persons 1 and 18 start at similar locations, their endpoints are quite different. However, Persons 11 and 18, who end up at about the same developmental point, have dramatically different starting points 12 years earlier. Nevertheless, for all three cases, the profiles are quite comparable: growth in period one, consolidation in period two, followed by more growth in period three.

Variations on the item–person map principle of representing the variable of interest have particular applications in the investigation of stage-like development of human abilities and attributes. The use of a genuine interval scale with such data allows for more informative results from these analyses. In the studies described in this chapter, the logit-scale person measures then were used as the input into a variety of statistical analyses for examining developmental trends.

CHAPTER TEN

The Rasch Model Applied Across the Human Sciences

DICHOTOMOUS ANALYSIS OF CHECKLISTS

We have already lamented that the large majority of empirical studies do not include the deliberate construction of a variable before performing the statistical analysis. Raw scores, or counts, are treated as measures, and analyses often are conducted at the item level rather than the variable level. For example, the ubiquitous checklist is an item format commonly used in surveys, particularly in the discipline of health education. A researcher who wished to know respondents' perceived barriers to getting involved in determining public health policy might ask them to check all statements that apply to them. Some of the options offered to the respondent might include the following: lack of time, lack of money, involvement not personally gratifying, and so on (Boardley, Fox, & Robinson, 1999).

The usual way to analyze data such as these is at the item level: Whether the respondent checked the item (a dichotomous answer) is investigated with regard to respondent characteristics such as sex, ethnicity, or level of education, usually with a chi-square analysis. Another common technique is to treat the items as a pseudoscale (i.e., by summing the total number of items checked by each respondent). In this example, scores could range from 0 to 8. Thus, subjects with higher counts are treated as having "more perceived barriers" to involvement than those with lower counts. As probably can be ascertained by now, these types of data analyses do not consider the pattern of responses, nor do they provide any understanding of the data at the level of the policy involvement variable. How then can Rasch analysis of checklist data provide a better alternative to these two options?

Boardley, Fox, and Robinson (1999) were interested in understanding what personal characteristics were related to the public policy involvement of nutritional professionals. Using the dichotomous Rasch model, the investigators constructed an involvement variable from a checklist of activities to create an interval-level measure in which higher estimates meant more involvement and lower estimates meant less involvement. These measures (the Rasch logit estimates) then were used in subsequent statistical analyses to determine whether certain groupings of persons differed significantly on involvement.

Figure 10.1 shows a WINSTEPS (Linacre & Wright, 2000) person–item map for the public policy involvement variable. As expected, the items with fewer checks indicate higher involvement items, such as volunteering as an elected official or serving as a public official, whereas the items with more checks indicate lower levels of involvement, such as voting. Both the items and the persons span a large logit range (approximately 7 logits), indicating that a variable from more to less involvement was clearly defined. When the distributions of the sample are compared with the distribution of items, it is clear that this sample is less involved than the mean involvement level defined by the items in the checklist.

A noticeable gap in the variable definition appears between "voted for a candidate or proposal" and "gave money to a campaign or official." This gap in the variable occurs just where many of the respondents are located. Thus, differentiation in public policy involvement is inadequate at this lower level of involvement. This is further reflected in the person separation statistics (a rather low 1.34).

This variable construction provided a better understanding of the analysis in several ways. First, the variable of public policy involvement was constructed, allowing for inferences to be made at the variable, not the item, level. Second, not only could the investigators visualize a continuum of involvement, but they also could measure individuals along that continuum. Third, suggestions for scale improvement were highlighted by the analysis. For example, the gap in the variable along the low involvement levels suggested the addition of activities requiring more involvement than voting, but less involvement than giving money. Inclusion of such items (e.g., reading relevant newspaper articles, discussing policy issues with colleagues, reading political brochures, or attending public hearings) might help differentiate those people at the bottom of the scale.

Although a post hoc Rasch analysis might not always be fruitful, this analysis was a considerable step forward for researchers in this field of health education, a step toward conducting analyses at the variable level rather than the item level. It also shows the flexibility of the dichotomous Rasch model in its application to checklist analysis, in addition to its usual use with the multiple-choice format.

CLIENT SATISFACTION ANALYSIS[1]

Rasch modeling of Likert scale data has paved the way for more sensitive, powerful, and meaningful analysis of customer satisfaction data. Bond and King (1998,

---

[1]Disclaimer: Reproduced with the permission of the Queensland Department of Education. All inquiries concerning the original material should be addressed to the Copyright Officer, PO Box 33, Albert Street, Brisbane, Q 4002, Australia.

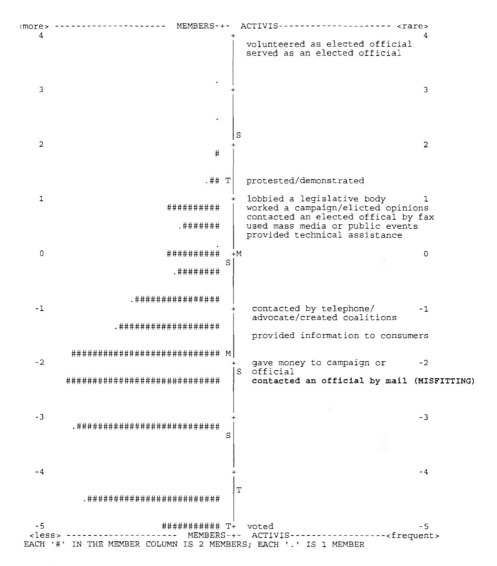

```
:more> -------------------- MEMBERS-+- ACTIVIS-------------------- <rare>
    4                                 +                                   4
                                      |   volunteered as elected official
                                      |   served as an elected official
                                      |
                                      |
    3                              .  +                                   3
                                      |
                                      |
                                   .  |
                                      |S
    2                                 +                                   2
                               #      |
                                      |
                             .## T|   protested/demonstrated
    1                                 +   lobbied a legislative body      1
                         ##########   |   worked a campaign/elicted opinions
                                      |   contacted an elected offical by fax
                          .#######    |   used mass media or public events
                                      |   provided technical assistance
                               .      |
    0                    ##########  +M                                   0
                                      S
                          .########   |
                                      |
                 .##############       |
   -1                                 +   contacted by telephone/         -1
                                      |   advocate/created coalitions
               .#################     |
                                      |   provided information to consumers
        ############################ M|
   -2                                 +   gave money to campaign or       -2
                                      |S  official
        ############################  |   contacted an official by mail (MISFITTING)
                                      |
                                      |
   -3                                 +                                   -3
        .##########################   |
                                      S
                                      |
                                      |
   -4                                 +                                   -4
                                      |T
        .########################     |
                                      |
   -5                ########### T+  voted                               -5
   <less> -------------------- MEMBERS-+- ACTIVIS------------------<frequent>
EACH '#' IN THE MEMBER COLUMN IS 2 MEMBERS; EACH '.' IS 1 MEMBER
```

Figure 10.1. Person–item map for public policy involvement variable.

2003) reported on the competing demands of a School Opinion Survey of client satisfaction involving approximately 36,000 parents and 45,000 students and carried out over 1,200 government schools in one state in Australia. The framework used to guide questionnaire construction was Moos's (1979) scheme for classifying human environments. The final 20-item School Opinion Survey parent and student forms (Bond, King, & Rigano, 1997) were designed after feedback from the administration of trial forms. Recommendations to the group representing state peak educational bodies that oversaw instrument development were supported by the results of Rasch modeling. This analysis showed that the 20 items with the best Rasch psychometric indices were also the 20 items rated most important by the trial samples.

One of the specified outcomes of the School Opinion Survey contracted research project (see also Bond & King, 2003a, 2003b; King & Bond, 2003) was the establishment of state parent and student satisfaction benchmarks. In a very large state education system, in which accountability of both the system as a whole and of individual school sites was to be undertaken in terms of quantitative outcomes, the benchmarks provided two complementary functions. The first function focused on the accountability of the individual education unit in which the role of the client satisfaction benchmarks would act as the standard against which satisfaction at any single school site could be compared. The second function focused on the education system as a whole, in which the benchmarks were to facilitate the tracking of changes in client satisfaction with public education over time. The contracted requirement that all state schools (more than 1,200 of them) were to be involved in the sample and would receive individual reports precluded the use of population proportional sampling.

To develop the satisfaction benchmarks for the School Opinion Survey project, Rasch analyses were performed by setting the mean of the persons, rather than the mean of the items, as the starting point (0 logits) for the calibration. The item difficulties, or endorsability, then were plotted in relation to the mean satisfaction level (0 logits) for the benchmark group (i.e., how easy it was, on the average, for the members of the benchmark group, parents or students, to endorse each of the 20 School Opinion Survey items). For example, if, from the standpoint of the group average, an item was plotted as "more difficult to endorse" than another, then that group was judged to be less satisfied on that item. Each statewide satisfaction benchmark, then, consisted of 20 item difficulty estimates, one for each School Opinion Survey item, and an accompanying error value for that estimate.

Table 10.1 shows the state benchmark item difficulty estimates when the mean satisfaction level of all responding parents (approximately 36,000) was set as the origin (0) of the Rasch analysis calibration: The higher the item estimate, the more difficult that item was for the group to endorse and the less satisfied the group was on that item. By way of an interpretative note, all of the item estimates are negative (below 0 logits), so the sample of parents found it relatively easy to agree with the 20 School Opinion Survey items.

Table 10.2 shows the corresponding state benchmark item difficulty estimates when the mean satisfaction level of all responding students (> 40,000) was set as

TABLE 10.1
Item Estimates for All Parents ($n = 35,928$)

Item No.	Estimate Logits	Error	Infit Mean Square	Outfit Mean Square
1	−1.637	0.008	0.95	0.97
2	−1.472	0.009	1.09	1.09
3	−1.273	0.007	0.88	0.89
4	−1.474	0.007	0.85	0.89
5	−1.411	0.007	0.73	0.76
6	−1.450	0.007	0.98	1.00
7	−1.352	0.007	1.02	1.04
8	−1.544	0.008	0.85	0.88
9	−1.587	0.008	0.92	0.94
10	−1.351	0.007	0.87	0.88
11	−1.280	0.008	0.82	0.84
12	−1.319	0.007	0.65	0.68
13	−1.334	0.008	0.81	0.83
14	−1.445	0.008	0.93	0.94
15	−1.747	0.008	0.71	0.77
16	−0.804	0.007	1.48	1.43
17	−0.615	0.007	1.62	1.53
18	−0.642	0.007	1.32	1.28
19	−1.560	0.008	1.16	1.18
20	−1.543	0.008	1.72	1.53

the starting point (0) of the Rasch analysis estimation procedure. Again, the higher the item estimate, the more difficult that item was for the group of all students to endorse and the less satisfied the group was on that item. For example, the single positive value in the estimates column for item 18 means that the student sample had the most difficulty endorsing that item on the School Opinion Survey student form.

In Figure 10.2, the benchmark estimate for the parents as a whole (from Table 10.1) is plotted along the heaviest line, representing the item difficulty estimates in graphic form. Furthermore, the statewide samples of parents and students were divided to produce 12 data sets, six each for parents and students. This was carried out according to the agreed-on notion of establishing benchmarks in which generally comparable schools would be grouped to allow fairer and more meaningful school-versus-benchmark comparisons to be undertaken and reported. Benchmarks were estimated and constructed separately for six groups of comparable schools. Figure 10.2 also shows the relative benchmark item satisfaction estimates for the parents for each of the six groups of comparable schools.

TABLE 10.2
Item Estimates for All Students ($n = 40,371$)

Item No.	Estimate	Error	Infit Mean Square	Outfit Mean Square
1	−0.736	0.007	0.91	0.91
2	−0.487	0.006	1.01	1.01
3	−0.635	0.006	0.93	0.93
4	−0.448	0.006	0.95	0.96
5	−0.731	0.006	0.86	0.87
6	−0.656	0.006	0.98	0.99
7	−1.023	0.006	0.98	1.00
8	−0.457	0.006	0.98	0.99
9	−0.790	0.006	0.98	1.00
10	−0.631	0.006	0.92	0.93
11	−0.850	0.006	0.76	0.78
12	−0.033	0.006	0.96	0.96
13	−0.558	0.006	0.87	0.88
14	−0.730	0.006	0.84	0.87
15	−0.250	0.005	1.22	1.19
16	−0.110	0.005	1.18	1.16
17	−0.111	0.005	1.19	1.17
18	−0.137	0.006	1.40	1.36
19	−0.706	0.006	1.08	1.09
20	−0.424	0.005	1.11	1.10

Rasch measurement showed that satisfaction with public education varied meaningfully across different types and sizes of schools. Consequently, school-versus-state benchmark comparisons that did not account for the wide variations in satisfaction level by school type would systematically give an advantage to some groups of schools over others.

"PERSON-FREE" ITEM ESTIMATES

The requirement that all state schools were to be involved in the sample precluded the use of population proportional sampling. In the smallest schools, the whole target population (parents and Year 7 students) of each school was surveyed. At larger education sites, samples were selected using alphabetical groupings by family name, with fewer groupings being required for larger schools.

The Rasch modeling property of measurement invariance (see chap. 5) was verified empirically when calculation of identical benchmark estimates resulted from the construction of simulated population proportional samples using sample-to-population ratio weightings. Given that educational assessment and evalu-

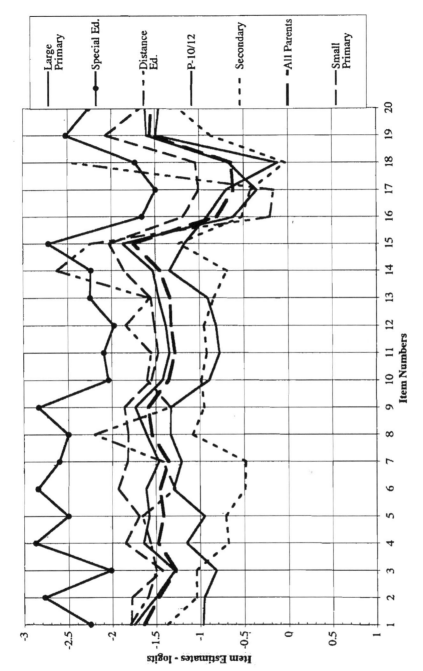

Figure 10.2. Benchmark satisfaction item estimates for parents.

189

ation has been informed by true-score statistical presumptions since its inception, it should be expected that those enamored with traditional principles might be more than a little skeptical of some claims made for the Rasch family of measurement models. Often, the most difficulty is expressed concerning the assertion that the Rasch family of models produces what are commonly referred to as "person-free" estimates of item difficulties and "item-free" estimates of person abilities. This is, of course, a direct consequence of the development of invariant, interval-scale fundamental measures: The use of the shorthand descriptors, "person-free" and "item-free" estimates raises some eyebrows in social science circles. Invariant Rasch measures can be seen as the natural consequence of two complementary Rasch measurement principles. The first is the calculation of item difficulty estimates that are independent of the distribution of abilities in the particular group of persons for whom the items are appropriate. The complement is the calculation of person ability estimates that are independent of the distribution of difficulties of the particular set of items used for the estimation. In that case, we should prefer "person-distribution-free" over "person-free" and "item-distribution-free" over "item-free" because some, rather tendentiously, seem to understand "person-free" to mean that no empirical person responses are required.

To confirm that the properties of the Rasch model (sample-free measures of item difficulty) were maintained with these data sets, a probability proportional to size sample was constructed for each parent and student benchmark by weighting every person's responses according to the size of the school target population and the number of responses from that school.

Weighted versus unweighted benchmark comparisons were reported for all 12 groups of clients. Except for two cases, in which the weightings for parents from larger schools depressed the satisfaction levels previously calculated, the benchmark comparisons provided empirical confirmation for the Rasch specific objectivity claim. Given that the two exceptions did not meet the model's requirements, the lower benchmarks were used for 1997 comparisons, and a recommendation was made for the modification of comparable school groups in subsequent surveys. Examples of weighted versus unweighted benchmark comparisons are shown in Figures 10.3 (no difference) and 10.4 (Parents in larger school settings were less satisfied).

STUDENT SATISFACTION AT UNIVERSITY

Student satisfaction surveys are now key parts of the mechanisms used by colleges and universities as part of wider efforts to demonstrate accountability to their institutional charters. Many tertiary educational institutions have developed in-house survey techniques for investigating students' satisfaction with a variety of aspects of college life. In the US, two national instruments focusing on student satisfaction—the College Student Survey (CSS) administered by the Higher Education Research Institute at UCLA and the Student Satisfaction Inventory (SSI) available through the USA Group Noel-Levit—are well endorsed by their use right across the country. In Australia, the Course Experience Questionnaire (CEQ) is

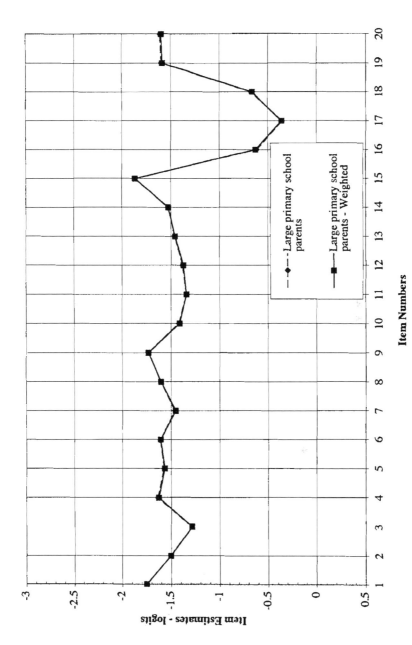

Figure 10.3. Weighted versus unweighted benchmark estimates for large primary school parents.

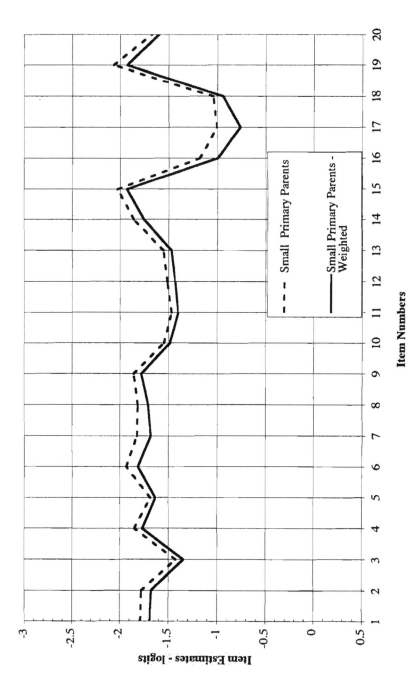

Figure 10.4.   Weighted versus unweighted benchmark estimates for small primary school parents.

used routinely to survey graduating students from Australian universities expressly so that intra- and inter-university comparisons can be made. Generally speaking, the reliance on true score theory in the development of these survey instruments and the analytical techniques routinely used in reporting their results makes genuine across-campus comparisons or the tracking of satisfaction changes across time just about impossible (Beltyukova & Fox, 2002; Curtis & Keeves, 2000).

The "Student Feedback about Teaching" (SFT) is a Rasch-based Likert-style indicator of student satisfaction that can be used to inform such high stakes decisions as faculty tenure and promotion. It was developed at a large regional university in Australia as part of that university's response to recently legislated requirements of accountability in the Australian university system. That university's existing in-house, paper-based "Evaluation of Teaching" instrument (JCET) was developed using the factor-analytic approaches almost ubiquitous in this field. Reports contain simple arithmetic means of item responses and for groups of items identified by factor analysis. Early steps in the development of the SFT approach involved online surveys of students, academic and administrative staff to ascertain the relative importance of individual JCET and CEQ prompts that were in use at the time. Further, the surveys also elicited suggestions for other items that might be used in providing information appropriate for the evaluation of teaching. The existing JCET data bank, developed from many years administration of the "Evaluation of Teaching" survey was analyzed using Rasch measurement techniques first trialled in the School Opinion Survey project above (Bond & King, 2003a, 2003b; King & Bond, 2003) to investigate the coherence of item and person performance.

At the time of writing, the SFT consisted of a core of 16 prompts, with the opportunity for staff electing to receive feedback about their teaching to select other prompts from a large bank of supplementary items. Data used to calculate the original SFT feedback benchmark (Bond, 2004) focused on the teaching of 30 members of the university's teaching staff. The Partial Credit Rasch Model (PCM; Wright & Masters, 1982) was used to estimate how difficult it was, on average, for the sample of more than 2000 students to endorse each of the SFT items. Following the principles used to develop the graph in Figure 10.3, the estimates and errors were plotted to represent a benchmark for all teachers, against which feedback estimates for each individual teacher might be compared. Separate PCM analyses of the data set for each teacher in turn were undertaken in order to estimate how difficult it was, on average, for the students in that teacher's classes to endorse each of the 16 SFT items for that teacher. For early SFT rounds, teachers at this university received summaries of their students' feedback as follows: (a) a table of the incidences and percentages of responses in each response category for each SFT prompt; (b) a graph which compared that teacher's feedback estimates with the benchmark feedback estimates for each SFT item (Fig. 10.5); and (c) a copy of the qualitative responses written by the students in the space provided on the back of the scannable SFT form.

The latest version of the SFT feedback processes implements a number of automation processes that streamline the analysis and reporting procedures while

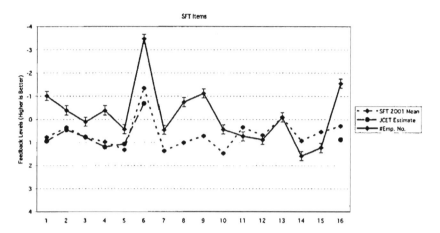

Figure 10.5.   Mean Rasch item estimates (with error bars) for 16 SFT items (benchmark: solid; one teacher: dotted) and for six pseudo-equivalent items (dashed) from the earlier JCET survey.

keeping the strengths of the Rasch measurement principles. While the university uses online data collection procedures for the low-stakes SFS (Student Feedback about Subjects) surveys, the much higher rate of response with the "form delivered in class" approach confirmed the paper-based collection of student responses. While individual Rasch analyses continue to be used for quality control and generation of the university benchmark, SFT data assembled from the scanner files are imported into a purpose-built Excel spreadsheet to develop reports for individual teachers. Estimates of individual teacher's feedback levels for the 16 SFT items are calculated using a linear transformation derived from the separate Rasch analyses used to generate estimates in the first iterations of the SFT system. Error whiskers for each location are based on sample size. Graphs are now automatically generated for classes where the number of student responses exceeds five and appear automatically as downloadable .gif files available through the university's secure "Staff Online" website.

The latest SFT feedback graph in Figure 10.6 reveals a number of interesting features. The most obvious plots are the two (solid) lines that provide the most direct summary of feedback to the teacher. The figure reveals this teacher to have feedback levels that are measurably higher that the university benchmark levels on all 16 SFT items. The benchmark levels are based on all the SFT data collected over the first four years of the SFT administration (2001–2004). For comparative purposes, the original SFT university benchmark for first semester, 2001 (reported in Bond, 2005) is plotted as a dotted line. Data about the six items from the earlier JCET questionnaire that most closely matched similar items on the new

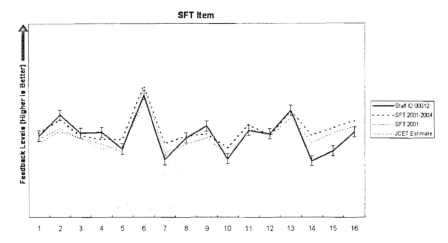

Figure 10.6.   SFT report Graph 2005 shows increase in benchmark values against Likert scale response options.

SFT instrument were analyzed using the Rasch model (see chap. 5). Rasch item estimates for the historical data on those six items are also plotted on SFT feedback graphs so that staff applying for tenure and promotions, and the members of the university's promotions committee, might better infer the relationships between the current SFT results and those from the earlier "Evaluation of Teaching" surveys. Figure 10.6 reveals a small but detectable increase in benchmark feedback levels over the 4 years on implementation for all SFT items except Item 6 (teacher expertise). The plots for four of the six JCET items show remarkable correspondence between the historical and the new SFT evaluations, with evaluations for Item 6 (teacher expertise) and Item 16 (teaching overall) lower in the historical data set. Why would that be? Current university staff may elect to have an SFT evaluation whereas JCET routinely surveyed all subjects. Is it reasonable to infer that the teaching and expertise of teachers aiming for tenure and promotion might be better appreciated than that of all university teaching staff? The logit scale that appeared on earlier SFT graphs (Bond, 2005a) has disappeared and in its place, the background of the graph contains colored bands to represent the response options on the JCET form: On average, teaching staff at this university are rated as "More than Acceptable" on all SFT items with Item 6 (teacher expertise) regarded as close to "Outstanding" in the eyes of responding students.

DEMOGRAPHIC VARIABLES IN STUDENT SATISFACTION

In Australia, the Course Experience Questionnaire (CEQ, mentioned earlier) is a survey instrument of 25 items that is administered annually to a cohort of students who have graduated from all of the nation's universities. It surveys graduates about the quality of the courses that they have recently completed. Important in this context, CEQ results are used to compare courses and institutions. Factor analysis identified five factors (clear goals, good teaching, appropriate assessment, generic skills, appropriate workload) among responses to 24 Likert-type items with five ordered response options from *strongly disagree* to *strongly agree*. The methods of analysis and reporting of comparative CEQ data code each item response option, then provide means and standard deviations both for items and for subsets of items. Methods similar to this are typical in Likert-style survey analyses (see chap. 6 and the note on JCET above). The reanalyses of CEQ data from 1996 (Curtis & Keeves, 2000) were premised on the authors' concern that traditional analyses treat the data as "interval and that a particular response option indicates the same level on the underlying trait for all items. Our concern is that graduates' responses are ordinal and therefore should be analysed differently." (Curtis & Keeves, 2000, p.74) Moreover, "if policy decisions are to be based on the results of the survey or if the survey instrument is to be modified over time while still permitting comparisons, we contend that the alternative and superior analytical techniques that are available should be used." (p.74) The results of the Rasch analyses are reported in greater detail in Curtis (1999) and are similar to those of Waugh (1998): eight of the 25 items misfit the measurement model, but that the 17 remaining items do form a coherent measure. This, in spite of evidence from exploratory and confirmatory factor analyses confirming a single underlying factor and five separate factors (as identified in the CEQ structure), nested within that overall CEQ factor. In particular, Rasch analysis suggests that the overall perception of course quality by recent graduates of Australian universities is most strongly influenced by (only) three of the five CEQ factors—good teaching, generic skills, and clear goals (after Curtis & Keeves, 2000).

Rasch Measures as Grist for the Analytical Mill

The analysis of the CEQ data can be taken much further than that for the SFT data (above) because the graduates responding to the CEQ survey provide considerable demographic data (age, sex, mode of study, English-speaking background, employment status, etc.) while SFT data are deliberately kept identifier-free to encourage authentic responses. In order to ascertain whether there are differences among course types, Curtis undertook a two-way analysis of variance using individual GSI scores as the criterion measure and both course type and institution as categorical variables. The Graduate Satisfaction Index (GSI) is merely a linear transformation of the Rasch logit scale, centered on a mean of 500 with each logit rescaled to 100 units (see later in this chapter). The ANOVA revealed differences among broad fields of study: Nationally, students of the humanities and social sciences (GSI mean = 527.06; SD = 104.02) were much more satisfied that those studying engineering (GSI mean = 476.14; SD = 73.21) or architecture (GSI mean = 480.90; SD = 82.34). In other words, the GSI for any institution could be regarded as a function of its student × course mix: "taking the mean GSI for all graduates of an institution would bias the institutional score in favor of those universities with high proportions of humanities graduates and against those with high proportions of engineering graduates" (Curtis & Keeves, 2000, p. 76). Correcting for the course mix of each institution allowed for GSI comparisons to be based on actual versus expected GSIs rather than on means across institutions. This revealed a higher proportion of Australian universities to be performing close to course-weighted GSI expectations than would be obvious from the results of traditional analyses. Using Rasch-based GSI interval-level scores along with indicators of student demographics for 2- and 3-level Hierarchical Level Modelling revealed characteristics at the individual student levels as being implicated. Moreover, controlling for both institutional-level, and student-level characteristics provides for findings that are unexpected in the light of earlier, traditional statistical analyses, showing the benefit of using genuine interval level measures for further appropriate statistical analyses: "Multilevel analysis has permitted influences of variables that were previously confounded to be disaggregated. For example, in earlier studies (e.g., Johnson, 1997), it was reported that employment status at the time of completing the CEQ did not influence graduates' perceptions of their courses. By separating effects at individual and course levels, we have been able to show that employment status is significant. In the past, its influence has been masked by course type because of different rates of graduate employment from different courses" (Curtis & Keeves, 2000, p.81).

COMPUTERIZED ADAPTIVE TESTING (CAT)

The Rasch model has been indispensably useful in situations using computerized adaptive testing (CAT). CAT involves a special sort of computer-based test in which the difficulty of test items administered is specifically tailored to the ability level of the current test taker—thereby providing an individualized examination for each person. CAT operates on the principle that items that are too easy or too difficult for the candidate contribute little information about the test taker's ability.

There are two key elements at the heart of a well-developed CAT system. The first is a large bank of accurately calibrated items that cover a wide range of difficulties. The second is a test item presentation algorithm that determines the next item to be presented on the computer screen to the current test taker. Both of these elements derive considerable benefits from the application of Rasch measurement. The construction of calibrated item banks that provide for the presentation of almost unlimited versions of person-specific tests is a consequence unique to Rasch measured CATs. Moreover, when the intent is to operationalize another benefit of Rasch measurement, the item-selection algorithm is constrained to present items at the 50% probability of success for the current test taker, based on the success or failure on the current item. The presentations might follow, say, a 0.2 logit increase in difficulty with a successful response or a similar decrease in difficulty following an incorrect response to keep the future items well targeted for the respondent.

This type of flexible testing situation, then, quickly hones in on the test taker's demonstrated ability level with fewer questions, hence maximizing information and limiting both the amount of testing time and the number of test items exposed to any one examinee. When on-target information is maximized in this manner, the standard error measure is minimized and the test can be much shorter without sacrificing reliability. Furthermore, tests are more secure because two different students might take two entirely different tests when the test items have been previously equated. When an adaptive test is delivered from a Rasch-calibrated item bank, the estimates of test-taker ability are statistically equivalent across all exams whether the test taker has been administered easy or hard items. This level of generality is essential for CAT.

CATs are currently used for human resources selection examinations, high-stakes certification and licensure examinations, large-scale admissions testing, diagnostic testing, aptitude tests, and achievement tests. Adaptive testing is particularly appropriate for heterogeneous populations and/or testing scenarios that cover a wide range of ability. The practical implementation of CAT based on Rasch measurement principles should incorporate aspects of testing that reflect more that just the technically optimal generation of scores. For example, setting the success-rate part of the delivery algorithm at 50% can provide the candidate with a rather unsatisfactory testing experience: Half the items encountered are beyond the candidate's ability. The experience of 80% success can be much more satisfying for candidates, and is equally easy to operationalize with a Rasch measurement approach. The penalty in terms of test length is about 20% longer tests for those near the pass/fail point (depending on the stopping rule). Further, the adoption of strict maximum information rules in CAT leads to "tracking" (many examinees end up taking the same path through the test) so a certain amount of item selection randomization (with a small penalty in test length) is advisable. Similarly, the diagnostic opportunities that can derive from the Kidmap interpretation of "unexpected failures" (see chap. 12) can disappear under maximum information delivery of CAT.

There are a number of topics related to CAT that are often canvassed in the literature. They include the level of confidence in the pass/fail decisions made from CATs, the equivalence of test items, and targeted tests, as well as the role of CAT in certification and licensure. Researchers have addressed whether examinees should be retested on items exposed to them in previous test administrations. Bergstrom and Lunz (1992) demonstrated that only half as many test items were needed to achieve the same level of pass/fail decision confidence with a CAT as with a paper-and-pencil test and that ability estimates were not affected when the targeted difficulty of a test was altered (Bergstrom, Lunz, & Gershon, 1992).

Although the traditional threats to test security, such as cheating on test items or even stealing parts or all of a test, draw interest from CAT administrators and researchers, Rasch-modeled CAT research provides particular insights into testing problems posed by guessing and student misrepresentation of ability. In the context of the development of a sound-file-enhanced CAT to measure second language ability, Stahl, Bergstrom, and Gershon (2000) suggested that incorrect responses to items at the 40% probability level (in contrast to the 50% Rasch expectation) might be appropriate to flag the possibility that a respondent had deliberately missed answering questions correctly in order to be streamed into an easier second language course.

In general, the development and maintenance of a large calibrated item pool for CAT is a large task, as is administering the exam and reporting the results, and usually remains outside the experience of many researchers because of the resources (especially in terms of the software and hardware required). The UK's foremost developer of educational testing, the Curriculum, Evaluation and Management Centre (CEM Centre) at the University of Durham has recently released CADATS (Computer Assisted Design, Analysis and Testing System, www.cemcentre.org/CADATS) which places Rasch-based CAT development and delivery tools within the financial and technological reach of independent researchers. The Bergstrom and Lunz (1992) paper provides detailed Rasch-informed insights into the issues involved in moving from a paper-and-pencil test to computer adaptive format.

JUDGED SPORTING PERFORMANCES

Some Olympic Games events provide the quintessential example of how we have come to accept routinely, and even passively, subjectivity in judgments of human performance. Although, performance-enhancing drugs aside, there is rarely any dispute about who wins gold in, say, the 1,500-m freestyle, the 100-m track, or the team bobsled, a few of us can be drawn into the occasional argument about the medal winners in platform diving or on the beam. Better still, let's take the winter Olympics women's figure skating as an example of a judged event. For the first skater about to go out on the ice, the announcer dramatically whispers something to the effect, "She must be upset because being the first skater on this program puts her at a disadvantage." Surely, we have all wondered why, in the attempts to at least create *the appearance* of objectivity in judging, we could openly admit and accept that the order in which one skates actually influences the judges' ratings! Even if you haven't noticed that particular example of lack of objectivity in the rating of performers, you would really be hard-pressed not to admit what appears to be nationalistic or political alliance biases among the judges, where judges tend to favor skaters from their own countries (e.g., Eastern Bloc judges rate Western Bloc skaters less favorably and vice versa). In spite of these phenomena having been well documented in the literature (Bring & Carling, 1994; Campbell & Galbraith, 1996; Guttery & Sfridis, 1996; Seltzer & Glass, 1991; Whissel, Lyons, Wilkinson, & Whissell, 1993), the judgment by median rank approach has been maintained as the best method for minimizing this bias (Looney, 1997) because it is held to minimize the effect of extreme rankings from any one judge in determining any skater's final score.

The median rank approach has two problems, however (Looney, 1997). First, the judges are required to give different ratings to each skater, that is, no two skaters may receive the same score from the same judge. This violates the principle of independence of irrelevant alternatives (Bassett & Persky, 1994; Bring & Carling, 1994), meaning that each skater, rather than being rated independently, is compared directly with others who skated before her. This can result in a situation where skater A is placed in front of skater B, but can then be placed *behind* skater B once skater C has performed (see Bring & Carling, 1994, for an example; Looney, 1997). It is then clear why it is unfortunate to be the first skater—the judges tend to "reserve" their "better" scores in case they need them for a later performer! Second, the subjective meanings of the scores may differ from judge to judge, that is, "a 5.8 may represent the best skater for Judge A, but the third best skater for Judge B" (Looney, 1997, p. 145). This variation in meaning is what we refer to in chapter 8 when discussing how some judges are routinely more severe or lenient than others—a judge effect that certainly cannot be corrected simply by calculating the median score.

   In an attempt to illustrate how one could create a set of objective, interval-level measures from such ordinal-level rankings, Looney (1997) ran a many-facets Rasch analysis for the scores from the figure skating event from the 1994 Winter Olympics. Many will recall this controversial event in which Oksana Baiul won the gold medal over Nancy Kerrigan, who won silver.

   Looney (1997) obtained scores from the nine judges' ratings of 27 skaters on both components: Technical Program (composed of required elements and presentation) and Free Skate (composed of technical merit and artistic impression). Rasch analysis allowed her to calibrate these scores on an interval scale, showing not only the ability ordering of the skaters, but also the distance between each skater ability estimate. With many-facets Rasch analysis, Looney was also able to estimate judge severity and component difficulty (the component elements nested within each of the two items) in the same measurement frame of reference.

   Although in most of the examples throughout this book we place more interest in the ordering and estimation of items (i.e., to examine how well our survey/examination is working), here the researcher was far more interested in estimations based on the ordering of the skaters and the severity of the judges. Of course, valid component ordering is a prerequisite to the interpretation of the other facets, but the emphasis here is more on the placement of persons (given the preset required components and their rating scales) and the impact of the judges on those placements.

   The Rasch estimates showed remarkably good fit to the model for all facets of the measurement problem: the four skating components, the judge ratings (with the exception of the judge from Great Britain), and skater ability (with the exception of Zemanova, the lowest ranked skater). Consequently, Looney would have been justified in feeling confident of her interpretation of the Rasch-based placements. By estimating all of these facets in an objective frame of measurement, summing these judge ratings, and weighting each component its appropriate item weight, Looney found the top four skaters in order to be Kerrigan, Baiul, Bonaly, and Chen (Looney, 1997, p. 154). (The Olympic medals went to Baiul [Ukraine], Kerrigan [USA], and Chen [China], with Bonaly fourth.)

   Upon closer examination of the fit statistics for the judges, Looney discovered that judge idiosyncrasies did not affect the results of the Technical Program, but they did affect the results of the Free Skate. Since the Free Skate holds more weight in determining the final placement of skaters, these judge idiosyncrasies subsequently affected who won the gold medal. In fact, Looney (1997) concluded:

> All of the judges with an Eastern block or communistic background not only ranked Baiul better than expected, but ranked Kerrigan worse. The same trend was seen for Western Block judges. They ranked Baiul worse and Kerrigan better than expected. When the median of the expected ranks is determined, Kerrigan would be declared the winner. Before the free skate began, all the judges knew the rank order of the skaters from the technical program and the importance of the free skate performance in determining the gold medal winner. This may be why some judging bias was more prevalent in the free skate than in the technical program. (p. 156)

Looney's investigation of the effect of judges' ratings on the final placement of skaters objectively validates what a chorus of disbelieving armchair judges had suspected. The median rank system cannot remove the effect of judge bias in close competitions because it focuses on between-judge agreement. The many-facets Rasch model (see chap. 8), however, shifts that focus to within-judge consistency (Linacre, 1994, p. 142) so that individual judge effects, including bias, can be detected and subsequently accounted for in the final placement decisions.

PREDICTING BASKETBALL SUCCESS

When Mike Linacre was working at the MESA Psychometric Laboratory (University of Chicago), he attempted to create a set of objective measures for predicting the success and failure of NCAA Division I men's basketball teams. The measures were created using the paired-comparisons method (by using the log odds of a win for a home team [H] over a guest team [G]), using only the win–loss records for each team, the opponent, and whether the games were at home or on the road (Linacre, 1999c, p. 18):

$$Log \frac{\text{Probability of Win by H}}{\text{Probability of Loss by H}} = \text{H's Proficiency} + \text{Home Court Advantage} - \text{G's Proficiency}$$

The MESA group downloaded a list of teams from the Web, along with accurate daily results. For those teams with perfect records at the start of the season, MESA imputed scores for wins against notional bad teams and losses against notional good teams (Linacre, 1999c). (This harks back to the ideas raised in chapter 9 for calculating estimates for perfect scores on a multiple-choice test.) Using this process, MESA was able to publish daily measures for the entire basketball season. These orderings were compared to those posted by the Associated Press (AP).

Both MESA's and AP's orderings were very similar for the top 20 teams. However, MESA provided estimates for all 315 teams, thereby providing more accurate predictions for more teams. One of the most interesting inconsistencies between the AP rankings and the MESA rankings was shown in the predictions for the New Mexico team. New Mexico was consistently ranked in the top 25 by AP. Apparently, AP's ranking was based on a series of wins at the start of the season and further strengthened when they beat a 13th-ranked team (Arizona). What AP apparently did not figure into this ranking, however, was the fact that these initial wins were against weak teams and with the home-court advantage, and that the Arizona victory was an unexpected result (i.e., showed misfit in the MESA analysis). Using an objective measurement system, MESA rated New Mexico in approximately the 75th spot (Linacre, 1999c). This placement was later reinforced when New Mexico was defeated by number 242 (Hawaii). Furthermore, MESA's predictions for wins and losses were accurate to about 72%, similar to rates of professional tipsters (Linacre, 1999c). However, MESA made predictions for every team for every game of the entire basketball season, not just for select games.

LINKING PHYSICAL FUNCTIONING SCALES

In the long term, the use of the Rasch model to perform joint calibration of measures of the same underlying construct will be an extremely productive means to further our scientific endeavors. The following example of linking physical functioning scales demonstrates a key step toward an indispensable goal in human science research: the creation of universal measures. Again, the need for universal measures in the human sciences is made obvious from research in the physical sciences, and made possible by fundamental measurement techniques grounded in Rasch analysis. Take, for example the measurement of temperature that we have used previously. It is still the case that most everyday reports of temperature are scale dependent: 32 °F, 0 °C, and 276 °K refer directly to the particular temperature scale being used, in these cases, degrees of Fahrenheit, Celsius, and Kelvin, respectively.

In the same way, creating universal measures in the human sciences would help us to avoid unnecessary duplication of efforts in variable construction and move research toward the construction of common metrics for specific constructs, much as in the physical sciences. One aim of "psychosocial metrology," as Fisher described it, would be the establishment of a single measurement scale of units for each human variable of interest: a logit-based equal-interval set of values that would apply regardless of which appropriate test was used with any appropriate subject (Fisher, 1993, 1999, 2000).

The most prominent work in creating universal measures in the human sciences has been done with physical functioning scales. This work begins by linking various physical functioning scales with one another, then gradually builds a common item pool with specific units. The linking study by Fisher, Eubanks, and Marier (1997) serves as a model of a single step in this ongoing process.

Fisher et al. (1997) pointed out that physical functioning often is used as a medical rehabilitation index, but argued that the use of such tests is restricted when a patient's score interpretation is dependent on which physical functioning test the patient took. They thus undertook the step of linking the physical functioning sub-scales of the Medical Outcomes Study Short Form 36 (SF-36; Haley, McHorney, & Ware, 1994; McHorney, Haley, & Ware, 1997; Stucki, Daltroy, Katz, Johanneson, & Liang, 1996) and the Louisiana State University Health Status Instruments–Physical Functioning Scale (LSUHSI–PFS; Fisher et al., 1997). The SF-36 has a 10-item physical functioning scale with three ordered categories yielding 20 distinctions, whereas the PFS has 29 items and six ordered categories yielding 145 distinctions.

The linking process depended, in the first instance, on the theoretical argu-ment that the two scales to be equated represent the same underlying construct or variable. Then, each set of items was analyzed separately using Rasch analysis. Linking examines the extent of the concurrence between the two scales; that is, can a common meaningful interval scale be constructed?

The methodology used to answer this question consisted of using two types of linking methods to compare both scales in terms of their item difficulties, person measures, mean square and standardized fit statistics, as well as separations and reliabilities. The first linking procedure compared estimates from the separate scale analyses (steps for conducting common item linking are outlined in chapter 5 of this volume). The second procedure was a cocalibration, or combining all data from both scales. The cocalibration provided a common metric from which it was possible to anchor the difficulty estimates in any subsequent set of separate scale analyses. Estimates from these comparisons are then compared in the same manner as the first linking procedure. The authors used both approaches to link-ing in order to examine the effect of the different numbers of items and rating-scale points for the two scales and whether the items were positioned in meaningful relation to one another. Once equivalence was established between the scales, inspection of the combined item set showed that measures on one scale could be translated directly to the other scale, as is done routinely with the Celsius and Fahrenheit temperature scales.

Of course, it takes more than this first set of steps to establish a universal metric, but in the field of medical rehabilitation, the future is very promising indeed. Fisher (1997) had reported earlier that the construct of physical functional independence shows a remarkable measurement convergence across a wide range of instru-ments, samples, and areas of physical functional independence. He emphasized the importance of this opportunity to build scale-free measures in transforming the economics of health care to evidence-based preventive care. This effort shows the way in which each of our own human science disciplines can benefit from the establishment of a common meaning (i.e., a common metric) for behaviors, attitudes, symptoms, and abilities.

DIAGNOSIS IN HEALTH SCIENCES

Perkins, Wright, and Dorsey (2000) illustrated the use of Rasch measurement to produce a clear, simple picture of the relation between laboratory abnormalities in the diagnosis of gout. Ninety-six sets of medical record observations were submitted for analysis—half for patients diagnosed with gout and half for nongout patients. Each observation had values recorded for indicators usually considered in the diagnostic process for gout: uric acid, gender, age, diabetes, hypertension, weight, height, body surface area, nephrolithiasis, diuretics, cholesterol, triglyceride, blood urea nitrogen, and creatinine. Rasch measurement techniques were used in an attempt to establish a single dimension for diagnosing gout. Because blood chemistries in mg/dl, height, and weight are recorded as continuous variables, each of the physical science data points (X) was rescored linearly to its nearest integer code, using the conversion Y = (X − Min. Value)/((Max. Value − Min. Value)/9). The resultant coding, which simplifies the physical science metrics to 10 equal-size steps, has a monotonic relation with the original physical science variables (see later this chapter).

Usual Rasch analysis procedures (estimates and fit indices) were followed by the deletion of items that did not contribute useful information. In this case, Perkins et al. (2000) then used the WINSTEPS principal component analysis of measure residuals to identify significant relations among the diagnostic items (see the end of chap. 12). The plot of factor loadings of residuals against the Rasch item measures in Figure 10.7 shows a clear separation of the male corpulence cluster from the blood chemistry cluster. Note that the gout diagnosis is located in the center of the blood chemistry cluster at the bottom. The triglyceride variable was also removed from the measurement model because person separation was improved by setting aside triglyceride information (see chap. 11). In the end, a medical variable defined by the three blood chemistries (uric acid, blood urea nitrogen, and creatinine) was established, proving the best linear variable for predicting gout that the data could support. This allows the probabilities for gout diagnosis to be read off for any particular blood chemistry results, as well as the identification of both gout and nongout patients who do not fit the gout variable.

APPLICATIONS TO PHYSICAL THERAPY

Throughout this book we have emphasized the advantages of the Rasch measurement model over classical test theory in many ways. Because one of our greatest emphases has been on using the model to establish the construct validity of an instrument, it seems appropriate to end this chapter with an exceptional example of such an application. We briefly summarize a study by Campbell, Kolobe, Osten, Lenke, and Girolami (1995), in which they examined the construct validity of the Test of Infant Motor Performance (TIMP). Their article was proclaimed the best published in the journal *Physical Therapy* for that year (Linacre, 1996).

The TIMP is intended for use by physical therapists to detect deviations from an infant's normal path of development. These detections must be made as early as possible in order that effective interventions can be quickly implemented. Detection of deviations involves close contact between the therapist and baby, during which the therapist observes "both spontaneous and provoked actions of babies ranging in age from premature to 4 months old" (Linacre, 1996). The therapist then rates these actions according to a strict protocol learned during training.

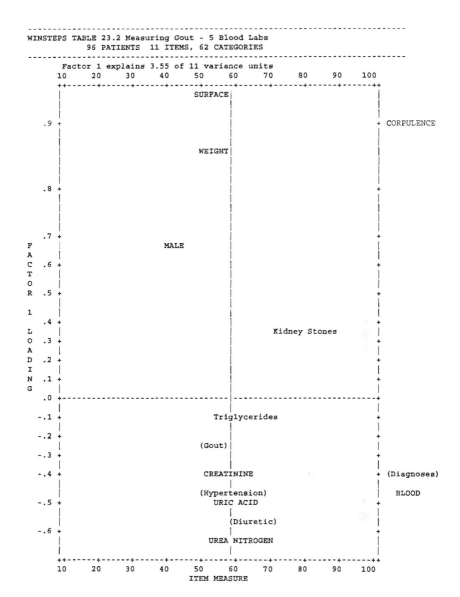

Figure 10.7.   WINSTEPS map of Rasch residual principal components.

Using therapist ratings of videotaped babies of a variety of ages, impairment levels, and racial origins, Campbell et al. (1995) constructed measures with a many-facets Rasch model. They plotted measures of development separately for normal and high-risk children. The comparison of the two sets of measures revealed that although high-risk babies start lower on the scale and grow more slowly, the difference was slight, indicating the critical importance of precise measurement at this stage (Campbell et al., 1995). Moreover, their research provided empirical validation of a key theory of fetal development: The plots revealed that 7.5 months after conception is a pivotal point in motor development.

Converting Logits to Meaningful Units

Throughout this book we have explained the transformation of raw scores to logits (log odds units), and have expressed the locations of persons and items as points along this logarithmic scale. We should not finish this chapter on practical applications of the Rasch models for measurement without addressing issues relating to the units in which we could report our subsequent scales and measures. The concept of logits is confusing, and is not readily interpretable by the non-Rasch user (Smith, 2000). Furthermore, logits contain both negative numbers and decimals (Wright & Stone, 1979)—numbers that are quite dissimilar from the original response options (e.g., in Likert-type surveys). Therefore, conversion of logits to more user-friendly scales is recommended for optimal communication of Rasch results to lay audiences. Conversion of logits to more meaningful units is a straight-forward process that will become practiced more often as common meanings can be recognized across scales.

Choosing a new scale for presenting results should be tied into meaningful *reference points* along the measure. For example, the item hierarchy might contain qualitative reference points, such as developmental stage demarcations, minimal competency, mastery, or pass/fail points for exams. If the person hierarchy is more readily interpretable than that for the items, as in the case of normative scales (e.g., IQ), then the new scale should reflect meaningful differences among persons. These reference points on the new scale are then converted to familiar numerals such as 50 or 100 or probability points (e.g., 25%, 50%) of passing/failing/achieving/not achieving (Wright & Stone, 1979).

Conversion of logits to meaningful units occurs the same way we learned how to transform scores (e.g., z and T scores) in our introductory statistics course. Note that each old score (in logits) can be seen as having a relationship to the mean score (in logits) and its distance from that mean, expressed in terms of standard deviations (+0.6SD; −3.2SD), and so on. So:

Old score = old mean + distance from mean (expressed in terms of old SD)
New score = new mean + distance from mean (expressed in terms of new SD)
The new mean is the location factor and the new SD is the ***spacing factor***, thus:
New score = location factor + distance (spacing factor)

After these spacing and location factors have been determined, the new person measures, item calibrations, and standard errors are converted for reporting purposes according to the following formulas (modified from Wright & Stone, 1979; Smith, 2000):

New measure = location factor + (spacing factor * person measure) (for PERSONS)
New calibration = location factor + (spacing factor * item measure) (for ITEMS)
New standard errors = (original standard error * spacing factor) (for PERSONS and ITEMS)

One easy way to make these transformations is to use the scaling function provided in WINSTEPS software (Linacre & Wright, 2004) to do the calculations. The online manual (found at www.winsteps.com) provides step-by-step instructions for rescaling under a variety of conditions. The formulas used next are described in detail in chapter 8 of Best Test Design (Wright & Stone, 1979) and in Smith (2000), an article dedicated to the rescaling issue in Rasch measurement.

Rescaling the Children's Empathic Attitudes Questionnaire (CEAQ) provides illustrative examples of the conversion of logits to user-friendly scores for reporting.

Children's Empathic Attitudes
Questionnaire–Score Reporting Examples

The children's Empathic Attitudes Questionnaire (CEAQ) was developed to measure empathy of late elementary and middle school aged children (Funk, Fox, Chan, & Brouwer, 2005). The initial instrument was piloted and revised on four separate occasions. At each administration, items were revised according to their difficulty levels and fit statistics, resulting in a 16-item version with three response options for each (no, maybe, yes). The CEAQ findings in this chapter are based on the responses of 213 fifth, sixth, and seventh graders across two school systems (one urban and one suburban).

Figure 10.8 shows the keymap (omitting one misfitting item) ordered from the easiest to the most difficult to endorse (empathize with) items. Easiest items include those related to perceived immediate harm, whereas the most difficult items to endorse were related to identifying with others' feelings or problems when unable to relate to the reason. The line drawn through the mean of the responses depicts the average child as most likely to respond "yes" to perceived immediate harm, such as being upset at seeing an animal hurt. The average child in this sample (mean person value = +1.02 logits) would most likely answer between "maybe" and "yes" when identifying with familiar problems, such as "I would feel bad if my mom's friend got sick." The more difficult items to empathize with would most likely receive answers of "maybe," such as "Seeing a kid who is crying makes me feel like crying." Few in this sample would be expected to respond "no" to any of the questions. This suggests that either the least empathic

MORE EMPATHY

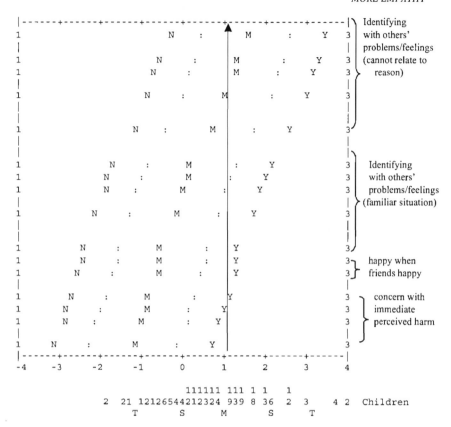

Figure 10.8.   Keymap of CEAQ on original logit scale.

(e.g., antisocial) children are not represented in this sample or that situations requiring more empathy might be added to the CEAQ.

Norming on the Sample

The first score-conversion example involves norm-referenced user scaling. This sets the average person measure to zero, and the person sample standard deviation to 1.0. The desired standard deviation (1.0) must be divided by the reported standard deviation found in the sample. WINSTEPS Table 3.1 provides the summary statistics needed to make the conversion (see the screen shot in Table 10.3). The reported mean of 1.02 and standard deviation of 1.04 for persons are highlighted by a box in the summary output.

TABLE 10.3
WINSTEPS Summary Statistics

```
TABLE 3.1 INPUT: 213 PERSONS, 16 ITEMS
           MEASURED: 213 PERSONS, 16 ITEMS, 3 CATS 3.37
```

SUMMARY OF 211 MEASURED (NON-EXTREME) PERSONS

	RAW SCORE	MODEL COUNT	MEASURE	MODEL ERROR	INFIT MNSQ	INFIT ZSTD	OUTFIT MNSQ	OUTFIT ZSTD
Mean	37.6	16.0	1.02	.46	1.00	-.2	1.05	-.1
S.D.	5.5	.6	1.04	.11	.43	1.2	.64	1.2
Max.	47.0	16.0	3.87	1.03	2.37	3.0	6.14	3.3
Min.	19.0	7.0	-1.97	.39	.31	-2.8	.27	-2.5

```
REAL RMSE  .52  ADJ. SD  .90  SEPARATION 1.75  PERSON RELIABILITY  .75
MODEL RMSE .48  ADJ. SD  .92  SEPARATION 1.93  PERSON RELIABILITY  .79
S.E. OF PERSON MEAN = .07
```

The WINSTEPS commands for making this conversion are calculated as follows:

USCALE = (wanted S.D. of 1.0)/(reported S.D. of 1.04); *this is the spacing factor*
UPMEAN = 0; *this is the location factor*

And the actual commands for the control file are:

USCALE = .96
UPMEAN = 0

Figure 10.9 shows the new output with the mean of the person distribution set at zero and SD the at 1.0.

Choosing the standard error of measurement of the original scale as the spacing factor (rather than the SD) will provide a distribution such that person locations that are more than 2 (SEM) units apart will differ significantly ($p < .05$) on the variable (Smith, 2000).

The SEM is approximated by using the formula (Wright & Stone, 1979):

$$SEM = 2.5/\sqrt{L}$$

(where L is the total possible score on a test)

In this questionnaire, there are 16 items, with a "3" or a "yes" as the highest score per question. Thus, L = 3 × 16 items = 48. SQRT L ($\sqrt{48}$) = 6.93

Thus, the SEM = 2.5/6.93 = .36

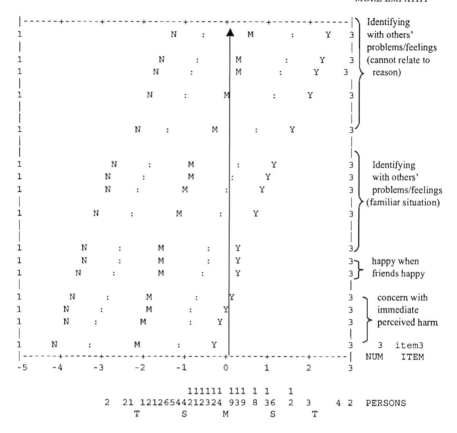

Figure 10.9.   Keymap of CEAQ with persons centered at a mean of zero and standard deviation of 1.0.

The rescaling commands for the WINSTEPS control file are then:

USCALE = .36
UPMEAN = 0

Figure 10.10 shows the new keymap with one unit equal to the approximate SEM for the questionnaire. Note that almost all the children in the sample are within 2 SEM of one another, indicating the only significant differences in empathy between the few children who "topped" "out" on the CEAQ and the rest of this sample. This is consistent with the low separation statistic (G) of 1.75. (See pp. 284–285).

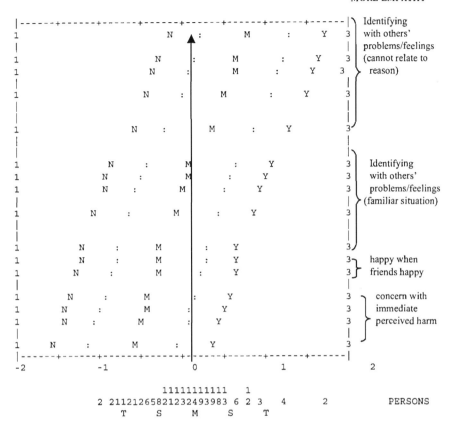

Figure 10.10. Keymap of CEAQ with persons centered at a mean of zero and SEM of 1.0.

Scaling From 0 to 100

Some users find it easier to interpret numbers on a more familiar scale (e.g., 0 to 100) so that negative numbers are eliminated. One might want the lowest reportable person measure to be 0 and the highest to be 100. Table 20 from the WINSTEPS output (see Table 10.4), shows the extreme values are −5.05 and +5.12. Calculating the values for making this conversion:

USCALE = (wanted range) / (current range)
USCALE = (100 −0) / (5.12 − (−5.05)) = 100 / 10.17 = 9.83
UMEAN = (wanted low) − (current low * USCALE) = 0 − (−5.05 * 9.83) = 49.64

TABLE 10.4
WINSTEPS Table 20 Showing of Extreme Values (Table 20)

TABLE 20 INPUT: 213 PERSONS, 16 ITEMS
         MEASURED: 213 PERSONS, 16 ITEMS, 3 CATS

TABLE OF MEASURES ON COMPLETE TEST

SCORE	MEASURE	S.E.	SCORE	MEASURE	S.E.	SCORE	MEASURE	S.E.
16	-5.05E	1.84	27	-.80	.40	38	.94	.42
17	-3.81	1.03	28	-.64	.40	39	1.12	.43
18	-3.06	.74	29	-.48	.39	40	1.31	.45
19	-2.60	.62	30	-.33	.39	41	1.52	.46
20	-2.26	.55	31	-.17	.39	42	1.74	.49
21	-1.97	.51	32	-.02	.39	43	1.99	.52
22	-1.73	.48	33	.13	.39	44	2.29	.56
23	-1.52	.45	34	.28	.39	45	2.64	.63
24	-1.32	.44	35	.44	.40	46	3.11	.75
25	-1.14	.42	36	.60	.40	47	3.87	1.03
26	-.96	.41	37	.77	.41	48	5.12E	1.84

The WINSTEPS rescaling commands follow:

USCALE = 9.83
UMEAN = 49.64
UDECIM = 0; *to show no decimal places in report*

Figure 10.11 shows the rescaled output with the lowest person score at 0 and the highest person score at 100. It is just a convenient coincidence that the mean for the new person distribution locates near 50.

Because Figure 10.11 does not include the extreme scores of 0 and 100, we can doublecheck the accuracy of our commands by looking at our new Table 20, as depicted in Table 10.5.

Scaling Based on a Meaningful Reference Point

Choosing a meaningful reference point on the CEAQ variable based on the item content and not the person average, yields several likely transition points. A point of high empathy would indicate where a child would be predicted to respond either "yes" or between "maybe" and "yes" on all but the most empathic items. Figure 10.8 shows that a location of approximately +2 logits would satisfy that condition.

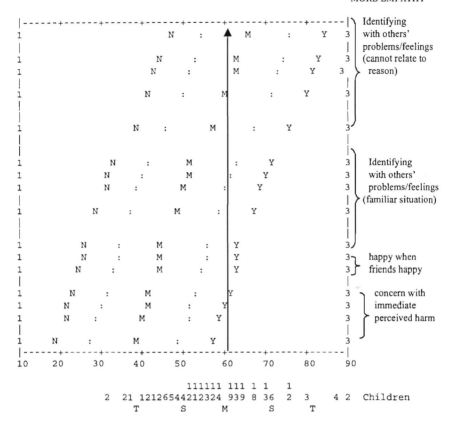

Figure 10.11. Keymap of CEAQ with scaling from 0 to 100.

To give this transition point a new value (say, 500), and to have 100 given to the lowest reported measure, we use the transition point of +2.0 (from Fig. 10.8) and the lowest reported measure of −5.05 (from Table 10.4).

Then:

USCALE = (500−100)/(2 − 5.05)
USCALE = 400/7.05 = 56.73
UMEAN = 500 − (2) * 56.73 = 386.53

TABLE 10.5
CEAQ Person Scores Converted From 0 to 100

Score	Measure	S.E.	Score	Measure	S.E.	Score	Measure	S.E.
16	0.E	18.	27	42.	4.	38	59.	4.
17	12.	10.	28	43.	4.	39	61.	4.
18	20.	7.	29	45.	4.	40	63.	4.
19	24.	6.	30	46.	4.	41	65.	5.
20	27.	5.	31	48.	4.	42	67.	5.
21	30.	5.	32	49.	4.	43	69.	5.
22	33.	5.	33	51.	4.	44	72.	6.
23	35.	4.	34	52.	4.	45	76.	6.
24	37.	4.	35	54.	4.	46	80.	7.
25	38.	4.	36	56.	4.	47	88.	10.
26	40.	4.	37	57.	4.	48	100.E	18.

This makes the cut point equal to 500 (from 386.53 + 2 (56.73)) and the lowest score equal to 100 (from 386.53 − 5.05 ∗ 56.73). The results of that rescaling are shown in Figure 10.12, with a line drawn from the reference point at a score of 500.

To better understand the effects of the conversions demonstrated here, we take a moment to remind readers of how a scale conversion with which we are more familiar would look in summary form. Table 10.6 provides a summary of the relationships between three temperature scales, harking back to the exemplar we introduced very early in this edition. Rather ironic, is it not, that the negative values that critics can't seem to get their minds around with logit values ("How can a child have −2.84 logits of cognitive development?") do not seem so preposterous in measuring temperatures? Minus 10 is really cold but not too difficult to comprehend.

Note that interesting temperature related events (e.g., freezing water, boiling alcohol) have locations on all three scales. Not only do the orders of events remain the same, but the intervals between events on each scale maintain their

TABLE 10.6
Some Comparisons Between Temperature Scales

Fahrenheit °F	Celsius °C	Kelvin °K	Qualitative Descriptor
212	100	373	Boiling Water
173	78.5	351.5	Boiling alcohol
32	0	273	Freezing water
−175	−115	158	Freezing Alcohol
−460	−273	0	Absolute Zero

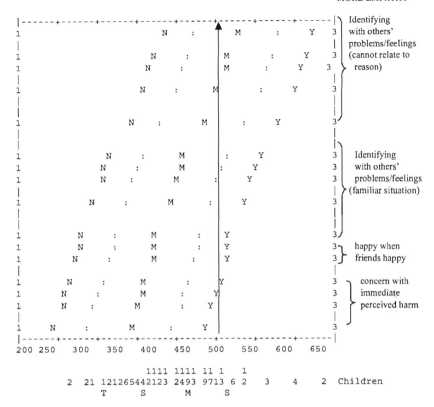

Figure 10.12.   Keymap of CEAQ with scaling based on meaningful reference point set at 500.

values across scales. If we are told that another temperature-related event (e.g., boiling iodine) has a particular value on one scale (i.e., 184 °C) the locations for that event on the other scales can be calculated by using a conversion similar to those used before with the CEAQ.

Table 10.7 summarizes the effects of the various rescaling options used with the CEAQ in this chapter. We've taken the liberty of rounding down the values in columns 4 and 5 to whole numbers. Take a moment to track the values of, say, the average child, across the scales to see the effect of the conversion process.

Although it is true that analyses based on the use of the Rasch family of measurement models do have potential required by the researcher who faces the pragmatic task of trying to make a silk purse of measures out of a sow's ear of underconceptualized data, the future for many of the human sciences lies in the

TABLE 10.7
Some Comparisons Between Converted CEAQ Scales

Logits	Norming on the Sample	SEM of 1.0	Scaling 0 to 100	Meaningful Reference Point	Qualitative descriptor
+3.87	2.74	1.39	87	606	Highest score
+2.06	1.0	.74	69	503	+ 1 SD
+2.0	.94	.72	69	500	Maybe or Yes
+1.02	0.0	0.0	59	444	Average child
0.0	−.98	−.36	49	386	Item mean

intelligent application of Rasch measurement to the theory–practice nexus of empirical research. Our key argument remains: Empirical research must incorporate the principles and procedures of Rasch modelling if researchers are to derive the benefits of fundamental measurement necessary for the development of rational quantitative human sciences. Substantive theory about the human condition provides detail of empirical outcomes that are subjected to the requirements of genuine measurement. Discrepancies between anticipated findings and the actual empirical outcomes are mutually informative: Theory informs practice—and practice informs theory.

CHAPTER ELEVEN

Rasch Modeling Applied:
Rating Scale Design

The process of responding to a rating scale should be viewed as a communication between the test developer's intentions (as expressed in the items and their associated response categories) and the respondents' record of their attitudes, behaviors, or achievement on the construct of interest. It is common knowledge that the way each rating scale is constructed has a great influence on the quality of data obtained from the scale (Clark & Schober, 1992). That is, some categorizations of variables yield higher quality measures than other categorizations (Linacre, 1999a; Wright & Linacre, 1992). Thus, not only should rating scales reflect careful consideration of the construct in question, but they also should be conveyed with categories and labels that elicit unambiguous responses. Even after great care has been taken to develop an unambiguous rating scale, the assumptions about both the quality of the measures and the utility of the rating scale in facilitating interpretable measures should be tested empirically.

This chapter expands on the analysis of rating scale data presented in chapter 6 by discussing guidelines for investigating empirically the utility of rating scales in the development of high-quality measures. Such investigations give explicit consideration to the influence of both the number and the labeling of categories in this process. We address these issues to demonstrate specifically how the design of rating scales has a large impact on the quality of the responses elicited, and to show how the Rasch model provides an appropriate framework for carrying out such investigations.

NUMBER OF CATEGORIES

Say, for example, respondents are asked to rate the extent to which they agree with the statement, "My boss is supportive of my work." Both the type of elicited responses and the inferences made about perceived supervisor support will depend on how many and what kind of response options are provided. We examine the following three options:

Option A		Disagree		Agree	
Option B		Disagree	Neutral	Agree	
Option C	Strongly disagree	Disagree	Neutral	Agree	Strongly agree

Option A is designed as a yes or no (dichotomous) type: My boss is either supportive or not. Option B allows for a middle of the road response to be included so respondents are not forced into choosing either of the extremes. Option C allows for more definition to the variable of interest (i.e., it depicts perceived support as a continuum). By designing rating scales as in the options, the test developers are conveying their ideas about perceived support to the respondents. The respondents are now required to express their perceptions within the restrictions imposed by this scale, and to the extent that the respondents can communicate effectively their perceptions within those restrictions, the quality of the measures will be enhanced. We should remember that the categorization that works best for communication with the respondent might not be the one that works best for analysis. The ideas we introduce here for thoughtfully collapsing categories are often the most useful way to bridge this divide.

At this point, we go beyond the careful design of the rating scale and begin to question how well our scale actually worked. Do the respondents need more categories to express themselves (as provided in Option C)? Will they actually use more categories if more categories are offered as alternatives? Will the number and type of categories preferable for respondents also work best for the measurement analysis? These questions focus on the important empirical issue: What is the practical number of response categories for the optimal measurement of this variable? This solution often lies in collapsing rating scale categories.

A considerable amount of research literature examines the question of how to determine the appropriate number of rating scale categories. Typically, the criterion for judging the optimal number has been the reliability of the responses. Results have shown mixed conclusions, with the following range of assertions about reliability: that it is independent of the number of response categories (Bendig, 1953; Brown, Widing, & Coulter, 1991; Komorita, 1963; Remington, Tyrer, Newson-Smith, & Cicchetti, 1979), or that it is maximized with a 7-point scale (Finn, 1972; Nunnally, 1967; Ramsay, 1973; Symonds, 1924), a 7-point scale plus or minus two (Miller, 1956), a 5-point scale (Jenkins & Taber, 1977; Lissitz & Green, 1975; Remmers & Ewart, 1941), a 4-point scale (Bendig, 1954b), or a 3-point scale (Bendig, 1954a).

Here is a common 7-point scale as an example:

Option D	Strongly disagree	2	3	4	5	6	Strongly agree

Would this rating scale communicate more effectively than Options A through C? Is it actually useful to add more response categories, or do the distinctions between, say, five and six categories now become blurred, hence introducing confusion for the respondents and ultimately lowering the meaningfulness of the scores (Fox, Gedeon, & Dinero, 1994)?

There is research suggesting that although the addition of response categories generally increases reliability, it does so only if these additional categories are not arbitrary (Linacre, 1995; Wright & Linacre, 1992). As explained by Chang (1994), the increase in the number of response alternatives might introduce error by allowing respondents to draw more freely on divergent frames of reference. In such a situation, it is difficult for a "common language" (Lopez, 1996) to be shared between the respondent and the investigator via the rating scale. In short, two people might perceive the same level of supervisor support, yet one may check a 5 and the other a 6, simply because the introduction of too many response options muddles the definition of the variable in question. With Options A or B, the category definition and meaning is much more exact than it is in Option C.

The fact is, there is no definitive optimal number of response categories that applies to all rating scales. Whereas five response categories might work for accurately measuring one construct, a simple yes-or-no type of response might be best for another. It is therefore the job of the test developer to determine empirically the optimal number of response categories every time a new rating scale is developed or when an existing rating scale is used with a new population. Thus, the analyst must discover empirically, rather than merely assert, the optimal number of rating scale categories for measuring a given construct (Lopez, 1996).

CATEGORY LABELS

A different, but closely related, empirical question involves the labeling of these response categories (Dunham & Davison, 1990; Frisbie & Brandenburg, 1979; Klockars & Yamagishi, 1988; Lam & Klockars, 1982; Lam & Stevens, 1994; Ory, 1982; Spector, 1976). Variation in labeling includes choice of category labels, use of anchors, and positive and negative packing of the scale, to name a few.

Consider options E and F as follows:

Option E	Strongly disagree	2	3	4	Strongly agree
Option F	Strongly disagree	Disagree	Somewhat agree	Agree	Strongly agree

Option E is ambiguous in that it is missing labels for several categories, whereas Option F is stacked, or positively packed, in its labeling of responses because it includes three "agree" options but only two "disagree" response options.

Rating scale Examples A through F all encompass certain assumptions about how the construct is perceived by the respondents, and how that perception can be communicated best through the rating scale. We argue that these assumptions can and should be routinely tested empirically. The principles for investigating the quality of the measures is similar for both assumptions, and the Rasch model provides a set of diagnostics to help us with this task.

RATING SCALE DIAGNOSTICS

The strategy for determining the optimal number of response categories requires examination of Rasch measurement diagnostics. Statistics guide us in assessing how the categories are functioning to create an interpretable measure. Here we fall back on the principles espoused throughout this volume: Do we have reliable data for persons and items? Do the categories fit the model sufficiently well? Do the thresholds indicate a hierarchical pattern to the rating scale? Are there enough data in each category to provide stable estimates?

If any problems are diagnosed in the existing rating scale, a general remedy is to reduce the number of response options by collapsing problematic categories with adjacent, better-functioning categories, and then to reanalyze the data. Diagnostics from the new analysis then are compared with those from the original analysis, and a determination is made to see whether the collapsing helped to improve variable definition. At no stage would we ever "go so far as to blindly recommend collapsing categories." Thoughtful *post hoc* investigation of rating scale category functioning is commended to those who wish to clarify the meaning or their collected data, especially in the cases where investigators intend to improve data collection procedures in subsequent iterations of the research enterprise. The goal is to produce the rating scale that yields the highest quality measures for the construct of interest. The WINSTEPS software provides a wide variety of output formats that are virtually indispensable for investigating rating scale quality.

CATEGORY FREQUENCIES AND AVERAGE MEASURES

The simplest way to assess category functioning is to examine category use statistics (i.e., category frequencies and average measures) for each response option (Andrich, 1978c, 1996; Linacre, 1995, 1999a). Category frequencies indicate how many respondents chose a particular response category, summed for each category across all items. These category frequencies provide the distribution of responses across all categories, allowing a very quick and basic examination of rating scale use.

Two features are important in the category frequencies: shape of the distribution and number of responses per category. Regular distributions such as uniform, normal, bimodal, slightly skewed distributions are preferable to those that are irregular. Irregular distributions include those that are highly skewed (e.g., distributions having long tails of categories with low responses; Linacre, 1999a). However skewed distributions are common in the real world of clinical data, with the most interesting patients located somewhere in that long tail.

Categories with low frequencies also are problematic because they do not provide enough observations for an estimation of stable threshold values. Such

TABLE 11.1
Category Frequencies and Average Measures for
Well-Functioning Four-Category Rating Scale

Category Label	Observed Count	Average Measure
1	63	−1.03
2	341	+0.34
3	884	+1.57
4	1,179	+3.12

infrequently used categories often indicate unnecessary or redundant categories. Hence, these are the categories that should be collapsed into adjacent categories. Exactly how these collapsing decisions should be made is detailed later in the chapter. The recommended minimal number of responses per category is 10 (Linacre, 1999a).

Average measures are useful for "eyeballing" initial problems with rating scale categories. They are defined as the average of the ability estimates for all persons in the sample who chose that particular response category, with the average calculated across all observations in that category (Linacre, 1995). For example, if for Category 1, the average measure were recorded as −1.03, that −1.03 can be interpreted as the average ability estimate, or logit score, for persons who chose Category 1 on any item in the questionnaire. These average measures are expected to increase in size as the variable increases. They increase monotonically, indicating that on average, those with higher ability/stronger attitudes endorse the higher categories, whereas those with lower abilities/weaker attitudes endorse the lower categories. When this pattern is violated, as indicated by a lack of monotonicity in the average measures, collapsing categories again is a possibility.

Table 11.1 shows sample output for a well-functioning four-category (three-threshold) rating scale. The category frequencies (i.e., the observed count) show a negatively skewed distribution, with at least 10 responses in each category. Average measures appear in the next column. The average measure for Category 1 is −1.03, meaning that the average agreeability estimate for persons answering 1 across any item is −1.03 logits. For the persons who answered 2 on any item, the average agreeability estimate is +0.34 (i.e., these persons are more agreeable on average than the persons who answered 1). We can see that these average measures function as expected (i.e., they increase monotonically across the rating scale).

THRESHOLDS AND CATEGORY FIT

In addition to category frequency and the monotonicity of average measures, other pertinent rating scale characteristics include thresholds, or step calibrations, and category fit statistics (Lopez, 1996; Wright & Masters, 1982). As explained in chapter 6, step calibrations are the difficulties estimated for choosing one

TABLE 11.2
Thresholds for a Well-Functioning Four-Category Rating Scale

Category Label	Threshold
1	None
2	−2.05
3	−0.01
4	+2.06

response category over another (e.g., how difficult it is to endorse "strongly agree" over "agree"). Like the average measures, step calibrations should increase monotonically. Thresholds that do not increase monotonically across the rating scale are considered disordered.

The magnitudes of the distances between adjacent threshold estimates also are important. Threshold distances should indicate that each step defines a distinct position on the variable. That is, the estimates should be neither too close together nor too far apart on the logit scale. Guidelines recommend that thresholds should increase by at least 1.4 logits, to show distinction between categories, but not more than 5 logits, so as to avoid large gaps in the variable (Linacre, 1999a). Diagnostics presented in Table 11.2 illustrate that our rating scale meets these criteria.

One visual method of inspecting the distinction between thresholds is to examine the probability curves, which show the probability of endorsing a given rating scale category for every agreeability–endorsability (B–D) difference estimate. Each category should have a distinct peak in the probability curve graph, illustrating that each is indeed the most probable response category for some portion of the measured variable. Categories observed to be "flat" on the graph are useful if they span a large portion of the variable. If, however, these flat categories are overshadowed and redundant with other categories, they might not aid in defining a distinct point on the variable. Therefore, problematic thresholds that are disordered or too close will show up visually, often with flat probability curves spanning small sections of the measured variable.

The graph in Figure 11.1 illustrates the probability of responding to any particular category, given the difference in estimates between any person ability and any item difficulty. For example, if a person's ability were 1 logit lower than the difficulty of the item (−1 on the x-axis), that person's probability of endorsing a 4 is close to 0, of endorsing a 1 or a 3 is close to 0.2, and of endorsing a 2 is close to 0.55 on that item. This person therefore is most likely to endorse Category 2 on this item. For persons with ability estimates higher than the given item difficulty (e.g., +3 on the x-axis), the most probable response is a 4. This graph shows that each response category in turn is the most probable across some section of the variable.

The threshold estimates in Table 11.2 correspond to the intersection of rating scale categories in Figure 11.1. Each threshold estimate represents a distinct point on the measured variable. Thus, each response category is the most probable category for some part of the continuum. It should be noted that each threshold estimate from Table 11.2 is represented visually by the intersection of probability curves in Figure 11.1, the point at which there is an equal probability of choosing either of two adjacent response category options. For example, the first threshold in Table 11.2 is −2.05. A vertical line drawn from the intersection of the 1 and 2 probability curves in Figure 11.1 intersects with the x-axis at −2.05. You should take a few minutes to find the corresponding point in Figure 11.1 for each of the other two thresholds seen in Table 11.2.

Fit statistics provide another criterion for assessing the quality of rating scales. Outfit mean squares greater than 2 indicate more misinformation than information (Linacre, 1999a), meaning that the particular category is introducing noise into the measurement process. Such categories warrant further empirical investigation, and thus might be good candidates for collapsing with adjacent categories. Table 11.3 shows the fit of each rating scale category to the unidimensional Rasch model, meeting the criterion of mean square statistics less than 2.0 (Linacre, 1999a).

The rating scale diagnostics discussed earlier include category frequencies, average measures, threshold estimates, probability curves, and category fit.

These diagnostics should be used in combination. Typically, they tell the same story in different ways. For example, if one category has a very low frequency, the thresholds are likely to be disordered, and the probability curves will not have distinct peaks for each of the rating scale categories. Likewise, the average mea-

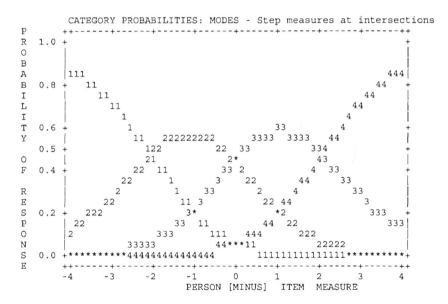

Figure 11.1.   Probability curves for a well-functioning four-category rating scale.

TABLE 11.3
Category Fit for a Well-Functioning Four-Category Rating Scale

Category Label	Outfit Mean Square
1	1.10
2	1.11
3	0.81
4	1.02

sures might be disordered, and the fit statistics will be larger than expected. This will not be the case in every situation, but these diagnostics, when used in combination, are very useful in pointing out where we might begin to revise the rating scale to increase the reliability and validity of the measure.

REVISING THE RATING SCALE

When rating scale diagnostics indicate that some categories were used infrequently or inconsistently by respondents, adjacent categories can be combined and the data reanalyzed. The aim here is to eliminate noise and improve variable clarity (Fox et al., 1994; Linacre, 1999a; Wright & Linacre, 1992). Look again at the example in Option D at the beginning of the chapter. Do we understand the intended difference between a 5 and a 6 on this rating scale? Is it possible that given two respondents with the same attitude, one might circle 5 and the other might circle 6? If respondents cannot make a distinction between the meaning of Categories 5 and 6 and hence use them in an inconsistent manner, unreliability is introduced into the measure, and category diagnostics will show us where we went wrong in the development of the rating scale. On the basis of this information, collapsing categories together will, in most cases, improve the representation and interpretation of the measure.

Revision of the rating scale should come at the pilot phase in the development of the measure, because the subsequent measures and their diagnostics might not correspond to those based on the original scale. Just as item format and content are pilot tested in the first phase of measure development, so should the number and type of rating scale categories. The collapsing of categories can be used in an exploratory manner, to investigate the best fit between diagnostics and respondent use, with the optimal categorization being used in the final phase of the instrument development. Of course, there is no guarantee that the newly collected data will substantiate the final category choice.

AN EXAMPLE

In this example, 221 elementary science teachers were asked to rate the frequency with which they used different pedagogic strategies for teaching science (e.g.,

TABLE 11.4
Diagnostics for Problematic Rating Scale

Category Label	Observed Count	Average Measure	Infit Mean Square	Outfit Mean Square	Threshold Calibration
1	190	−2.08	0.77	0.83	None
2	207	−0.86	0.93	1.01	−1.51
3	179	0.15	1.13	1.88	−0.36
4	7	1.71	0.33	0.90	3.57
5	113	1.18	1.45	1.47	−1.70

writing reflections in journals, developing portfolios, working to solve real-world problems, engaging in hands-on activities). The rating scale categories were labeled as follows:

1	2	3	4	5
Never	Rarely	Sometimes	Often	Always

The rating scale diagnostics are shown in Table 11.4 and Figure 11.2. The first obvious problem we see in Table 11.4 is that Category 4 has only seven observations in all, across all prompts. This problem also is reflected in the average measure values, the step calibrations, and the probability curves. The average measures for categories 4 and 5 are disordered. Respondents who endorse "always" (category 5) on average have lower measures (agreeability estimates) on this variable than do respondents who endorse "often." This is counterintuitive, and also is reflected in the threshold calibrations, in which thresholds 3 and 4 are disordered, and in Figure 11.2, in which the probability curve for category 4 is flat (i.e., it never is the most probable category).

These problems with the rating scale impede our interpretation of the construct frequency of pedagogic strategies. When it is easier on average to endorse "always" than to endorse "often," we have direct empirical evidence that our rating scale is not being used by respondents in the way we intended. This suggests collapsing of rating scale categories to see if that would improve variable construction and interpretation.

GUIDELINES FOR COLLAPSING CATEGORIES

The first and foremost guideline in collapsing rating scale categories is that what we collapse must make sense (Wright, 1996; Wright & Linacre, 1992), that is, collapsing is never thoughtless or arbitrary. That is, will the new pivot point between, say, agree/disagree and rarely/often responses be based on something substantive? In the example described, our infrequently used category was labeled "often." Does it make sense to collapse this category with "sometimes"? Does it make sense

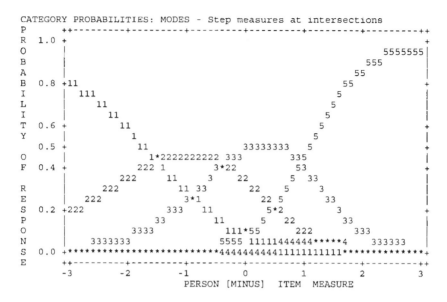

Figure 11.2.   Probability curves for a problematic rating scale.

to collapse this category with "always"? In this particular example, there does not seem to be a compelling substantive reason to do either, so which do we do? Do we collapse the "often" category up or down?

A second guideline for collapsing data indicates that we should attempt to create a uniform frequency distribution (Linacre, 1995, 1999a). This suggests that Category 4 should be joined, or collapsed, into Category 5. The software codes for collapsing Category 4 upward into Category 5 are "12344," indicating that we want to analyze four categories instead of five, with the last two categories (4 and 5) being analyzed as the same response (4 and 4). The complete software commands are found at the end of the chapter.

Table 11.5 and Figure 11.3 present the results from this recategorization of the variable (i.e., with "frequently" and "always" treated as the same response). With

TABLE 11.5
Diagnostics for 12344 Collapsing

Category Label	Observed Count	Average Measure	Infit Mean Square	Outfit Mean Square	Threshold Calibration
1	190	−2.5	0.72	0.79	None
2	207	−0.83	0.97	0.92	−1.74
3	179	+0.79	0.88	1.35	−0.12
4	120	+1.96	1.39	1.31	+1.86

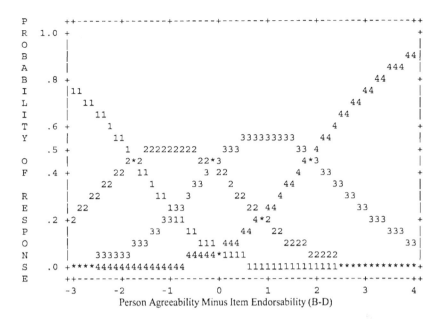

```
P       ++------+-------+-------+-------+-------+-------+-------++
R   1.0 +                                                        +
O       |
B       |                                                     44|
A       |                                                  444  |
B    .8 +                                               44      +
I       |11                                           44        |
L       |  11                                       44          |
I       |    11                                   44            |
T    .6 +      1                                 4              +
Y       |        11               333333333    44              |
     .5 +          1  222222222    333       33 4               +
O       |           2*2         22*3          4*3               |
F    .4 +          22  11        3 22        4     33           +
        |         22      1      33    2      44     33          |
R       |       22        11   3     22     4        33         |
E       | 22              133        22 44        33            |
S    .2 +2              3311           4*2          333         +
P       |              33    11       44    22          333     |
O       |         333       111 444       2222           33|
N       |    333333      44444*1111        22222                |
S    .0 +****444444444444444    11111111111111************+
E       ++------+-------+-------+-------+-------+-------+-------++
          -3      -2      -1      0       1       2       3       4
              Person Agreeability Minus Item Endorsability (B-D)
```

Figure 11.3.   Probability curves for 12344 collapsing.

four categories instead of five, we now have enough observations in each of the response categories. The average measures and step calibrations are now monotonic, and the probability curves show that each category represents a distinct portion of the underlying variable. Thus, collapsing Categories 4 and 5 has improved our rating scale diagnostics.

In addition to the guidelines found in the literature, we would also suggest collapsing the original Category 4 downward into Category 3 for comparison purposes (12334). We suggest this because the guidelines for collapsing are just that—guidelines. This is a common precept for Rasch modelling: Analysis is undertaken to develop and measure the meaning of a concept in practice. There can be no fixed rules to which we must adhere whereby the meaning or significance of a result becomes completely void when an arbitrary value is passed. Therefore, it is important to remain scientific about our investigations and explore several categorizations before settling on the preferred one. So, Table 11.6 and Figure 11.4 are included to show the results from collapsing Category 4 downward into Category 3 (12334).

It is clear that the collapsing improved category definition in both cases. Collapsing each way (12344 then 12334) resulted in monotonic step ordering and distinct category definitions. But how do we know which is the better of the two?

When comparing several categorizations of the same rating scale, we also can look at indicators other than category diagnostics. For example, we can assess the quality of the various reliability and validity indices for the variable, and compare

TABLE 11.6
Diagnostics for 12334 Collapsing

Category Label	Observed Count	Average Measure	Infit Mean Square	Outfit Mean Square	Threshold Calibration
1	190	−2.49	0.72	0.79	None
2	207	−0.84	0.94	0.90	−1.74
3	186	+0.83	0.87	1.27	−0.15
4	113	+1.91	1.43	1.34	+1.88

these across each categorization (Lopez, 1996; Wright & Masters, 1982). Chapter 3 argues that person and item separation should be at least 2, indicating that the measure separates persons, items, or both into at least two distinct groups. Table 11.7 shows that categorization 12344 yielded the higher reliability for both persons and items.

With respect to validity, we can look at both the item order and fit. That is, does one categorization of the variable result in a better ordering of the underlying variable, one that is more consistent with the theory that generated the items in the first place? Do more items misfit with one categorization than another? These reliability and validity issues are addressed in previous chapters, but the same

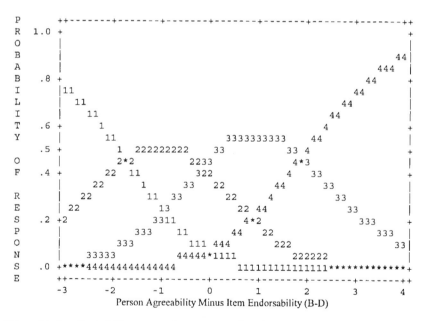

Figure 11.4.   Probability curves for 12334 collapsing.

TABLE 11.7
Comparison of Three Categorizations

Categorization	Average Measures	Fit	Step Calibrations	Person Separation	Item Separation
12345	Disordered	< 2.0	Disordered	1.36	6.91
12344	Ordered	< 2.0	Ordered	2.06	8.23
12334	Ordered	< 2.0	Ordered	1.90	8.16

principles apply here as well. Here they help us gain a fuller picture of how we can best define the rating scale. Thus, whereas the rating scale diagnostics help us in determining the best categorization, knowledge of Rasch reliability and validity indices tells us how the measure is functioning as a whole.

THE INVARIANCE OF THE MEASURES ACROSS GROUPS

A final step in investigating the quality of the new measure is to compare the estimates across two or more distinct groups of interest (e.g., male/female, Christian/Jewish, employed/unemployed, married/divorced/never married) to examine whether the items have significantly different meanings for the different groups. This is called differential item functioning (DIF). We take the same example as before, the reported frequency of pedagogic strategies among elementary science teachers. Suppose we want to compare the frequency of use with that of a sample of mathematics teachers. We can use the data from both groups in the Excel spreadsheet for common item linking, plotting item estimates for science teachers against those for mathematics teachers to examine whether the frequency of usage is significantly different for science and mathematics teachers. Any difference in the frequency of pedagogic strategies between the groups can be examined more closely to see why any particular strategy was not rated the same for both groups (Fig. 11.5).

Examination of DIF follows the same procedures as those outlined in chapter 5 on invariance. Comparing persons across two tests to determine the invariance of the ability estimates, however, DIF (based on common item linking principles) models the invariance of item difficulty estimates by comparing item estimates across two or more samples. The procedure requires that item difficulties be estimated for each sample separately, and that the item calibrations be plotted against each other.

The model for invariance of item estimates is represented by a straight line with a slope equal to 1 (i.e., 45°) through the mean item difficulty estimates from each sample (i.e., 0 logits for each). Control lines show which items do not display invariance within the boundaries of measurement error, across the person samples (see Wright & Masters, 1982, pp. 114–117). Given that the model requires that relative item estimates remain invariant across appropriate samples of persons (see chap. 5), items revealing DIF should be investigated closely to

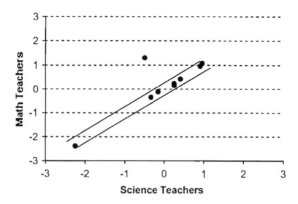

Figure 11.5.   Differential item functioning (DIF): math versus science teachers.

determine what might be inferred about the underlying construct, and what that implies about the samples of persons detected. In achievement testing, for example, DIF is regarded as *prima facie* evidence of item bias. However, it takes detailed knowledge about the construct and the samples of relevant persons to determine just what can be learned from DIF, how it can be avoided, and whether it should be. The evidence of DIF might just be the very information that is central to your investigation.

Software Commands

```
WINSTEPS:
&INST
TITLE='Collapsing Categories'
NI=15
ITEM1=5
NAME1=1
MODEL=R
CODES=12345
NEWSCOR=12334
RESCOR=2
&END
Item 1
Item 2
  .
  .
  .
Item 15
END NAMES
```

Line 1 contains a command that must begin every WINSTEPS file.

Line 2 provides a title for the output.

Line 3 indicates the number of items in the test.

Line 4 identifies the starting column for the data.

Line 5 identifies the starting column for the person identification number.

Line 6 specifies the rating scale model.

Line 7 identifies all possible rating scale scores in the data set.

Line 8 specifies the new codes, joining categories 3 and 4 together to make a four-category rating scale.

Line 9 tells the program to do the rescoring for all of the items in the scale.

CHAPTER TWELVE

Model Fit and Unidimensionality

It is in vain to do with more what can be done with fewer.

—William of Occam

It would be difficult to deny the claim that the most contentious issue in Rasch measurement circles is that of fit. Outside Rasch measurement circles, we continue to perplex the rest of the psychometric world by insisting that our task is to produce data that fit the Rasch model's specification rather than talk of fit in what others consider to be the conventional way (i.e., how well the model fits the data). Of course, the concept of fit must be considered hand-in-hand with that of unidimensionality. The concept of unidimensionality reflects the Rasch model's focus on the process of fundamental measurement, and it is essential that our data fit the model in order to achieve invariant measurement within the model's unidimensional framework. Indeed, the benefits and properties of Rasch measurement exist only to the extent that the data fit the model's demanding requirements. This is consistent with the position emphasized throughout this text: even in the most complex measurement situations, individual attributes should be measured one at a time.

The Rasch model is a mathematical description of how fundamental measurement should operate with social/psychological variables. Its task is not to account for the data at hand, but rather to specify what kinds of data conform to the strict prescriptions of fundamental measurement. There is no doubt, however, that mathematical models do not hold exactly in the real world. Instead, they describe an unattainable idealization, just as they do in all sciences. Check for the existence of genuine Pythagorean right-angled triangles. Empirical data describe what the imperfect real world is like. In Rasch measurement, we use fit statistics to help us detect the discrepancies between the Rasch model prescriptions and the data we have collected in practice.

TABLE 12.1
Some Actual or Observed Scores (*xni*) From Table 2.3 (Ordered)

Persons	Items					Person Total
	i	a	b	. . .	g	
J	1	1	1		1	9
C	1	1	1		0	8
E	1	0	1		0	7
. . .						. . .
H	0	1	0		0	2
Item Total	11	10	7	. . .	1	

THE DATA, THE MODEL, AND RESIDUALS

In a number of places so far, we have used an item–person matrix to show the interactions between person ability and item difficulty. Each cell in the complete matrix would have an entry, *xni*, representing the actual observed score (x = either 0 or 1) that resulted when Person n took Item i. Table 12.1 shows a portion of the ordered matrix of actual observed scores from Table 2.3, where schoolchildren A–N answered math questions *a-l*. When we order that matrix according to the difficulty of the items and the ability of the persons, we have the opportunity to compare the Rasch model prescriptions with what we actually find in the data set. The estimation procedure in Rasch analysis has two distinct phases: first, calibration of the difficulties and abilities; and second, estimation of fit.

In the dichotomous model, the Rasch parameters, item difficulty and person ability, are estimated from the pass-versus-fail proportions for each item and each person. (The pass/fail proportion = number correct/number incorrect: $n/[N - n]$.) For item difficulty, the estimate is calculated from the proportion of the sample that succeeded on each item. Person ability is calculated from the proportion of items on which each person succeeded. The result of that iterative process is a set of all the item calibrations (i.e., one for each item) and a set of all possible person measures (i.e., one for every possible total score).

If we then take a second, same-size but empty matrix, we can substitute the estimated Rasch person measures in place of the $n/[N - n]$ proportion for each person and the Rasch estimated item measures in place of the n/N proportion for each item (see the ability and difficulty estimates in Table 12.2). Given that there is a direct monotonic curvilinear transformation of $n/[N - n]$ proportions into logit values, the items and persons maintain their exact orders. Next, we take the corresponding pair of parameter values for, say, Person n and Item i and substitute those values into the Rasch model (Formula 3 in Appendix A), thereby obtaining an expected response value, E_{ni}, for that particular item–person pair (i.e., the expected response value E when Person n encounters Item i). By repeating that calculation for every item–person pair and entering the resultant value in the

TABLE 12.2
Rasch Expected Response Probabilities (E_{ni})
Based on Item and Person Estimates

| Persons | Items | | | | | Ability Estimate |
	i	a	b	. . .	g	
J	0.26	0.50	0.77		0.95	+1.52
C	0.20	0.40	0.70		0.94	+1.19
E	0.12	0.27	0.56		0.89	+0.58
. . .						. . .
H	0.02	0.04	0.14		0.50	−1.52
Difficulty Estimate	+2.59	+1.59	+0.32	. . .	−1.52	

appropriate cell, we use the Rasch model to generate a complete matrix of expected response values based on the previously estimated person and item calibrations. Table 12.2 shows the Rasch-modeled correct response probabilities (E_{ni}) for Persons J, C, E,...,H encountering Items i, a, b,..., g (E_{ni} is the expected response value for Person n on Item i).

RESIDUALS

The difference between the actual observed score in any cell (x_{ni}—Table 12.1) and the expected response value for that cell (E_{ni}—Table 12.2) is the response residual (y_{ni}—Table 12.3). If the expected response value for a cell is high, say, estimated at 0.95 (i.e., $E_{Jg} = 0.95$), then we can calculate the unstandardized residual in which the actual score is 1 (x_{Jg}—we observed that Person J actually scored 1 on Item g). So capable Person J performed as expected on rather easy Item g and scored 1 (i.e., $x_{Jg} = 1$). Then $y_{Jg} = x_{Jg} - E_{Jg} = 1 - 0.95 = +0.05$ (a small residual), whereas if Person J had unexpectedly scored 0 for Item g (i.e., $x_{Jg} = 0$), then $y_{Jg} = x_{Jg} - E_{Jg} = 0 - 0.95 = -0.95$ (a large residual). For the first case the residual is low, indicating that the actual response was close to the model's expectation. The alternative scenario, with the much larger residual, indicates that such an actual performance would be quite different from the Rasch modeled expectation.

It then is easy to imagine a third similarly sized matrix that for each person–item pair contains the score residual for that cell (y_{ni}) when the expected response value (E_{ni}) is subtracted from the actual score (x_{ni}). Table 12.3 is a matrix of response residuals (y_{ni}) derived from Table 12.1 actual scores (xni) and Table 12.2 expected response values (E_{ni}). When the person's ability is the same as the item's difficulty, the residual value will be +0.50 if the answer given is correct ($1 - 0.50 = +0.50$) or −0.50 if the person gets that item wrong ($0 - 0.50 = -0.50$). Whereas residual values range from −1 to +1, negative values are always derived from incorrect (0) responses and positive residual values from correct (1) responses.

TABLE 12.3
Matrix of Response Residuals ($y_{ni} = x_{ni} - E_{ni}$)

Persons	i	a	b	...	g	Residual Total (Person)
J	0.74	0.50	0.23		0.05	low
C	0.80	0.60	0.30		−0.93	high
E	0.88	−0.27	0.44		−0.89	high
...						...
H	−0.02	0.96	−0.14		−0.50	modest
Residual Total (Item)	high	modest	low	...	high	

There is an obvious problem (one frequently encountered in statistics) in trying to aggregate a total residual score for any item or any person. Because any actual score (x_{ni}) will be either 0 or 1, and every expected response value (E_{ni}) will be a decimal fraction ($0 < E_{ni} < 1$), the residual will always a negative fraction for all actual scores of 0 and a positive fraction for all actual scores of 1. Just adding those residual values for any item or person string results in totals of 0.0 for every person and every item. However, squaring those residual values will result in all positive values (e.g., $+0.05^2 = +0.0025$ and $-0.95^2 = +0.9025$). These squared residual values can then be aggregated by summing along any relevant item residual column or any person residual row. Although the expected residual is an impossible-to-achieve 0, residual values outside of ±0.75 are seen as unexpected. In practice, each raw residual (y_{ni}) is standardized by using the variance of that residual, and it is the standardized residual (z_{ni}) that is used to calculate fit statistics.

FIT STATISTICS

Rasch suggested the use of chi-square fit statistics to determine how well any set of empirical data met the requirements of his model. Rasch analysis programs usually report fit statistics as two chi-square ratios: infit and outfit mean square statistics (Wright, 1984; Wright & Masters, 1981).

Outfit is based on the conventional sum of squared standardized residuals, so for Person n, each standardized residual cell is squared and the string of those squared residuals, one for each and every item encountered by Person n, is summed and its average (mean) found by dividing by the number of items to which person n responded, hence "mean squares."

Infit is an information-weighted sum. The statistical information in a Rasch observation is its model variance, that is, the square of the model standard deviation of the observation about its Rasch expected value. This variance is larger for well-targeted observations and smaller for extreme observations. To calculate infit, each squared standardized residual value in the response string, say, the residual z_{ni} for each of the items encountered by Person n, is weighted by its variance and then summed. Dividing that total by the sum of the variances leaves the differential effects of the weightings in place.

Therefore, infit and outfit statistics are reported as mean squares in the form of chi-square statistics divided by their degrees of freedom, so that they have a ratio scale form with an expected value of $+1$ and a range from 0 to positive infinity. Infit and outfit mean square values are always positive (i.e., > 0). In this form, the mean square fit statistics are used to monitor the compatibility of the data with the model.

An infit or outfit mean square value of $1 + x$ indicates 100x% more variation between the observed and the model-predicted response patterns than would be expected if the data and the model were perfectly compatible. Thus, an infit mean square value of more than 1, say, 1.30 (i.e., $1 + 0.30$) indicates 30% (100×0.30) more variation in the observed data than the Rasch model predicted. An outfit mean square value of less than 1, say, 0.78 ($1 - 0.22 = 0.78$) indicates 22% (100×0.22) less variation in the observed response pattern than was modeled.

The idea of the response string showing more variation than expected is a concept with which most are comfortable. This happens when a person's responses are more haphazard than expected: A capable person gets easier items unexpectedly wrong (e.g., 0010011110, where items are ordered easiest to most difficult), or a less able person gets harder items unexpectedly correct (e.g., 1101000110).

EXPECTATIONS OF VARIATION

However, the Rasch model is a stochastic or probabilistic model and from that viewpoint, a perfect Guttman response pattern, 1111100000, is unrealistically and unexpectedly perfect and shows too little variation (i.e., much less variation than the Rasch model predicts). A Guttman response string would have a mean square value considerably less than 1. According to the probabilistic principles incorporated in the heart of the Rasch model, a more realistic and expected response pattern would look more like this: 1110101000, and the mean square fit value would be much closer to $+1$. (All of these exemplar response strings have a score of five answers correct.)

Infit and outfit statistics also are reported in various standardized forms (e.g., t or z) in which their expected value is 0. For example, both of these mean square fit statistics can be transformed into an approximately normalized t distribution by applying the Wilson-Hilferty transformation. These normalized versions of the statistics are referred to as the infit t and the outfit t in QUEST (Adams & Khoo, 1992, p. 79). When the observed data conform to the model, the t values have a mean near 0 and a standard deviation near 1. Using the commonly accepted interpretation of t values, infit and outfit t values greater than $+2$ or less than -2 generally are interpreted as having less compatibility with the model than expected ($p < .05$). Normalized or standardized infit and outfit statistics could have either positive or negative values. Negative values indicate less variation than modeled: The response string is closer to the Guttman-style response string (all easy items correct then all difficult items incorrect). Positive values indicate more variation than modeled: The response string is more haphazard than expected (Table 12.4).

TABLE 12.4
Fit Statistics and Their General Interpretation

Mean Squares	tz	Response Pattern	Variation	Interpretation	Misfit Type
> 1.3	> 2.0	Too haphazard	Too much	Unpredictable	Underfit
< 0.75	< −2.0	Too determined	Too little	Guttman	Overfit

We must emphasize here that underfit to the model (i.e., erratic responses or noise) and overfit to the model (i.e., determinacy or Guttman style response pattern) have different implications for measurement. Underfit degrades the quality of the ensuing measures. Underfitting performances are those that should prompt us to reflect on what went wrong. Overfitting performances might mislead us into concluding that the quality of our measures is better than it really is. In many practical measurement situations in the human sciences, it is quite likely that overfit will have no practical implications at all. The technical implications are smaller standard errors and inflated reliability, so take some care there. With a strong developmental theory such as Piaget's, we might expect rather muted fit indicators (overfit): Preoperational thought strictly precedes concrete operational thought, which is the logically necessary precursor of formal operational thought, and so forth. In physical rehabilitation we would not be surprised if indicators for standing, stepping, walking, and climbing stairs exhibited overfit. Development of these skills is expected to be heavily interrelated. One of the regular candidates for overfitting is the last typical item on a consumer satisfaction survey, "In summary, how would you rate....?" Statistically and substantively, it adds little to our knowledge, but it doesn't do any harm to our findings. The last of the mandatory SFT items (see chapter 10; Bond, 2005a), "Overall, the quality of this staff member's teaching was..." produces the predicted overfitting indicators: Infit Mn Sq.: 0.54; Outfit Mn Sq.: 0.54. On the other hand, including a question such as "This teacher's punctuality was..." results in underfit: Infit Mn Sq.: 1.53; Outfit Mn Sq.: 1.57. While the question about "punctuality" was included in the SFT at the time of its development for important reasons, it is clear that "punctuality" taps some other aspects of university life other than just those tapped by the remaining SFT items (i.e., Item 13 "Punctuality" is not related to the good teaching construct as are other SFT questions). Adding responses to such a question to give an overall satisfaction score would spoil the measure. In fact, SFT reporting procedures eschew the calculation of a total satisfaction score. Further, it is the case that eliminating the underfitting items shifts the fit frame of reference, and often leads to the overfitting items falling into line.

Even the term overfit and underfit cause problems for some readers in this field. Underfit refers to noisy or erratic item or person performances, those that are not sufficiently predictable to make useful Rasch measures. Underfit is detected when the fit statistics are too high to meet the Rasch model's requirements (i.e., over the fit cutoffs). Overfit reflects item or person performances that are almost too good to be true; they yield Gutmann-like response patterns. Overfit is detected when the fit statistics are too low to meet the Rasch model's expectations (i.e., under the fit cutoffs). In essence, for items, this indicates a lack of local independence, that is, the items are not working independently of each other, as in the summary survey item. So, a number of questions based on the same information (a paragraph of prose, a diagram, or one of Piaget's tasks) might overfit (exhibit too good fit statistics) because they lack local independence. (In an important sense, rather than talking about *fit* statistics, perhaps we should talk about the estimation of *misfit*. For any cells in which the empirical data do not match the Rasch model prescription, the difference between the data and prescription, the residual, contributes toward *misfit*. But, conventionally, we use the term *fit* statistics, so we will stay with that.)

Our conception of misfit must include the idea that every response string is actually possible in practice, although some response strings are more probable than others. Although the Guttman pattern remains the most probable, all other patterns are probable, although some are highly improbable. The Rasch model, as a probabilistic or stochastic model, regards the perfect Guttman pattern as too rigid. The Rasch expectation is that there is a zone of uncertainty or unpredictability around the person's level of ability. Linacre and Wright (1994a) described the following response strings and provided infit and outfit mean square values for each (Table 12.5).

The interpretation of fit statistics, more than any other aspect of Rasch modeling, requires experience related to the particular measurement context. Then, "[w]hen is a mean-square too large or too small? There are no hard-and-fast rules. Particular features of a testing situation, for example, mixing item types or off-target testing, can produce different mean-square distributions. Nevertheless, here, as a rule of thumb, are some reasonable ranges for item mean-square fit statistics" (Wright, Linacre, Gustafsson, & Martin-Loff, 1994; Table 12.6). Unfortunately, many readers will scour this text merely to cite the page to support that the fit values they have reported are within some acceptable bounds. Our guidelines are much more equivocal: fit statistics should be used to assist in the detection of problem item and person performances, not just to decide which items should be omitted from a test. Indeed, omitting the overfitting items ($t < -2.0$ or Mn Sq. < 0.70) could rob the test of its best items—the other items are not as good as these.

For fit mean squares, we expect values close to one when the data fit the model. But how close is good enough? Now, our interpretations of mean-squares indicators do not take sample size into account, although it is easy to demonstrate that mean squares fit statistics will get closer and closer to 1.0 just by increasing sample size. But, of course, the standardized (transformed) versions of fit statistics (z or t) are designed to take sample size into account (using the mean and variance of the mean-squares statistic). So, problem solved, except as we have already argued, no set of data can have perfect fit to the Rasch model. The consequence is that even the smallest amount of misfit must become significant (i.e., > 2.0) when the sample size becomes large enough. Margaret Wu (personal communication, 2004) expressed that these characteristics of Rasch residual-based fit statistics place us in a dilemma. If we use mean-square fit values to set

TABLE 12.5
Diagnosing Misfit

Response Strings Easy ... Items ... Hard	Diagnosis	Infit Mean Square	Outfit Mean Square	Fit Type
111 ... 0110110100 ... 000	Modeled	1.1	1.0	Good Fit
This would be regarded as an ideal Rasch model response string.				
111 ... 1111100000 ... 000	Deterministic	0.5	0.3	Overfit
Is an example of a Guttman or deterministic pattern. Note that the outfit and infit mean square statistics are too low to be believed.				
011 ... 1111110000 ... 000	Carelessness	1.0	3.8	Underfit
This suggests carelessness with an easy item.				
000 ... 0000011111 ... 111	Miscode	4.3	12.6	Underfit
This response string is too bad to be believed and suggests that the responses might be miscoded.				
111 ... 1111000000 ... 001	Lucky guessing	1.0	3.8	Mixed
On the other hand, unexpected success on the most difficult item suggests lucky guessing.				
111 ... 1000011110 ... 000	Special knowledge	1.3	0.9	Mixed
This highly improbable pattern suggests the presence of special knowledge, either the knowledge that is missing in the string of failures or special knowledge that allowed the unexpected string of successes.				

TABLE 12.6
Some Reasonable Item Mean Square Ranges for Infit and Outfit

Type of Test	Range
Multiple-choice test (High stakes)	0.8–1.2
Multiple-choice test (Run of the mill)	0.7–1.3
Rating scale (Likert/survey)	0.6–1.4
Clinical observation	0.5–1.7
Judged (where agreement is encouraged)	0.4–1.2

criteria for accepting or rejecting items on the basis of fit, we are likely to declare that all items fit well when the sample size is large enough. On the other hand, if we set limits to fit t values as a criterion for detecting misfit, we are likely to reject most items when the sample is large enough.

So while a set of general guidelines like those above will be helpful for researchers embarking on Rasch modeling, a considerable bibliography of relevant material exists. Articles published by Smith (e.g., 1991a, 1994, 2000) provide good starting points for a more thoroughly informed view of issues concerning fit statistic interpretation.

FIT, MISFIT, AND INTERPRETATION

In chapter 4, we alerted you to the use we would make of ICCs from the BLOT to help us reflect on the idea of misfit. Figure 12.1 contains an interesting representation of fit for actual person performances (the *jagged* empirical ICC) against the Rasch modeled expectations (the *smooth* model ICC) for Item 4— the BLOT item at the midpoint on the BLOT item/person logit scale (0.0). The BLOT item output in Table 4.1 gives the following summary for Item 4:

Item	Estimate	Error	Infit MnSq	Outfit MnSq	Infit t	Outfit t
4	0.00	0.22	1.00	0.88	0.0	−0.4

Both infit and outfit mean square values are reported as close to the expected 1.0 and the standardized versions of those fit statistics, and infit and outfit t are close to the expected zero values. The smooth curve in Figure 12.1 is the single ICC for Item 4 from Figure 4.4 and models the expected performance of the interaction between persons and that item when the performances fit perfectly to the Rasch model (an impossible expectation). The plotted points on the jagged curve represent the actual performances of 150 students from chapter 4 and were selected from the output options in WINSTEPS. To understand fully the potential meaning of this graph, it is worth thinking through the steps involved in producing the plot of actuals.

First of all, the B–D calculation for each person is made: BLOT Ability B – Item 4 difficulty (D). In this case, D_4 (conveniently) = 0.0. Persons with close to the same B–D values are grouped together (in this case, at intervals of 0.4 logits) and the

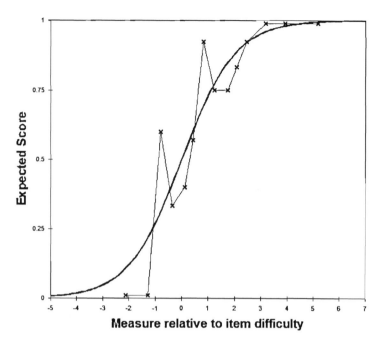

Figure 12.1.   Actual person performance versus theorietical ICC for an item
with good fit: BLOT 4 (again).

actual scores for every person in each group (i.e., 0, 1, 1, 0, 0,...) are totaled and the
mean value (total/n) calculated. Each plotted point then represents the mean score
($0 \leq x \leq 1$) on the vertical axis for the group of students with ability estimates within
±0.2 logits of the location on the horizontal axis. Indeed, WINSTEPS actually plots
the mean score (on y) against the mean of the measures within the interval (on x).

Now the plotted points of mean actual responses from each of 14 groups of
students, grouped at intervals of 0.4 logits intervals along the BLOT ability–difficulty logit scale show quite remarkable proximity to the Rasch modeled expectation of performances (the ICC). Yes, this is a slight deviation away from the
modeled curve, where the mean ability for student groups that are around −1.0
and +1.0 logits relative to the item difficulty, but this is the sort of actual versus
model match that yields the fit statistics above. In other words, this is the degree
of variation of actual around expected that the Rasch model predicts.

Now the actual versus theoretical comparison in Figure 12.2 paints a much less
favorable picture for BLOT Item 21, the most difficult of the BLOT set.

The segment of output for Item 21 from Table 4.1 shows its fit characteristics
to be poor from any perspective: Every one of the four fit indicators is noticeably
higher than expected by the Rasch model, although some might say that an Infit
MnSq value of 1.27 isn't too bad. Performances on this item are more erratic than
expected; although the Rasch model does predict correctly about 100 out of 150

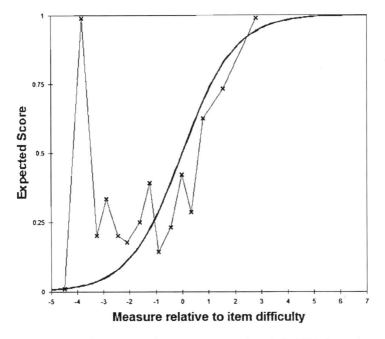

Figure 12.2. Actual person performance versus theoretical ICC for an item with poor fit: BLOT 21 (again).

responses. Poor fit means that the performance of about 50 students on BLOT Item #21 cannot be predicted comfortably by what is known about those persons' performance on the BLOT test overall (BLOT ability estimate).

Item	Estimate	Error	Infit MnSq	Outfit MnSq	Infit t	Outfit t
21 2.	33 0.	2 1.	27 1.	75 2.	6 3.	4

So how is that revealed in Figure 12.2? The smooth curve is the single model ICC for Item 21 from Figure 4.4, and the plotted points represent the actual performances of the sample of 150 students from chapter 4. Again, the figure comes from the output options in WINSTEPS. Note that this time, the value on the horizontal axis is the calculated B (BLOT ability) – D (Item 21 difficulty) as Item 21's difficulty estimate is +2.33 logits (i.e., not 0 as for Item 4). If we covered the eight plotted points on the left side of the graph, we could conclude, rather generously, that the able groups of students to the right perform close to the Rasch model's expectation: not wonderfully so, but "good enough for government work." Now cover that right side of the graph and look on the left at the summaries of groups of person performances on BLOT Item 21 for the less able portion of the BLOT sample. These students perform above expectations almost right across the board, so the probabilistic expectations of success that we have derived from the Rasch model for persons and items don't hold up here—especially where the less able two-thirds of the students meet with the most demanding item. Indeed, while the expectations of success should increase from left to right across the graph (following the expectation encapsulated in the ICC), for the less able students, the actual success rate hovers around 0.25, more or less. Could that be related to the fact that there are 4 response choices for Item 21? Could we draw the inference that the able students actually try to solve this item using the (formal operational thinking) ability that gets them high-ability estimates overall, but that the others, simply guess? High-ability students rely on that ability; for lower ability students, when the going gets tough, guess; at least that way you have a 25% chance of success!

We can change the focus for examining fit from looking at individuals items to looking at the performance of individual persons. We should expect to be able to diagnose persons in a manner that corresponds with our diagnoses of items above. The kidmap for Student 1 (Fig. 12.3) summarizes that student's performance according to the Rasch model's expectations. In the kidmap option in the QUEST software, the item difficulties are displayed in the usual Rasch fashion, with the easiest items at the bottom of the map and the most difficult items at the top. The items located on the left side of the map are those on which this particular child was successful, and the items on the right side of the map are those that the child did not complete successfully. The child's ability estimate of $-.40$ logits is plotted in the center column, with the dotted line on the left indicating the upper bound of the ability estimate (ability estimate plus one standard error: $b_n + s_n$) and the dotted line on the right indicating its lower bound (ability estimate minus one standard error: $b_n - s_n$). The fit index, an infit mean square value of 0.92, indicates a pattern of performance that closely approximates the predicted Rasch model response pattern based on the child's ability estimate: The expected fit value is $+1.0$. Item 10.3 is correct despite a less than 50% probability of success, whereas Item 7.2 is incorrect, a little against the Rasch expectation of a slightly more than 50% probability of a correct response. The 0.92 infit mean square value indicates a performance close to that predicted by the Rasch model, and the kidmap corroborates that visually.

The infit mean square value of $+1.78$ for Student 16 indicates that the pattern of responses shown in the Figure 12.4 kidmap is more haphazard than the Rasch model would expect for an estimated ability of $+.45$ logits. Following the principles outlined in the previous interpretation, we can detect the unexpected responses made by Student 16: Item 3.3 is the only item that the student gets unexpectedly correct, but the difficulty estimate of this item step is so close to the upper bound of the estimated ability for Student 16 that it could be just disregarded in terms of affecting misfit. The items that are unexpectedly incorrect, however, paint a different picture: These are the source of the misfit, estimated at 78% ($1.78 - 1.0 \times 100\%$) more variation than the Rasch-modeled expectation. Given that the items unexpectedly incorrect for Student 16 are relatively on-target for the student's ability, the impact of this performance shows up more clearly in the weighted (infit) statistics than in the unweighted (outfit) statistics (Table 12.7).

```
Middle School Math Project
------------------------------- K I D M A P --------------------------------
Student #1                                          ability:    -.40
  group:    all                                     fit:         .92
  scale:    all                                     % score:   40.00

------------Harder Achieved --------------------Harder Not Achieved --------



                                             18.3

                                             18.2



                                             23.3


                                             8.3
                                             3.3      23.2
                                             3.2       4.3      22.3
                                             8.2      21.3
                           10.3              4.2      22.2
                                             9.3      21.2
                                            17.2
.............................10.2.........   2.3      11.3
                           14.3              9.2      19.3
           16.3    14.2     2.2             12.3      19.2
                           15.3      XXX    11.2      20.3
                                             7.3      12.2
                           16.2    ..................................................
                            6.3
                   20.2    15.2              7.2
                            6.2

                            5.3
                    1.3     1.2

                            5.2

                           13.3


                           13.2




     4.1      3.1      2.1      1.1
------------Easier Achieved --------------------Easier Not Achieved --------
     Some items could not be fitted to the display
=================================================================================
```

Figure 12.3.   Kidmap for Student 1 showing good fit to the model (Infit mean square = .92).

```
Middle School Math Project
------------------------------- K I D M A P-------------------------------
  Candidate: 16                                    ability:      .45
  group:    all                                    fit:         1.78
  scale:    all                                    % score:    62.22

------------Harder Achieved ----------------------Harder Not Achieved --------
                                        |  |
                                        |  |
                                        |  |
                                        |  |
                                        |  |
                                        |  |
                                     18.3
                                     18.2


                                     23.3


                                        8.3
                            3.3      23.2
............22.3.....4.3.....3.2..........
                                        8.2     21.3
        22.2      10.3     4.2
                          9.3   |XXX|   21.2
                                        17.2
        11.3      10.2     2.3   . . . . . . . . . . . . . . . . . . . . . . . .
                          9.2   |  |   14.3     19.3
                  12.3     2.2         14.2     16.3     19.2
                  20.3    11.2         15.3
                  12.2     7.3
                                       16.2
                          6.3
                  20.2     7.2         15.2
                          6.2

                          5.3
                   1.3     1.2

                          5.2

                         13.3


                         13.2




          4.1      3.1     2.1     1.1   |  |
------------Easier Achieved ----------------------Easier Not Achieved --------
  Some items could not be fitted to the display
===============================================================================
```

Figure 12.4. Kidmap for Student 16 showing inadequate fit to the model (Infit
mean square = 1.78).

TABLE 12.7
Case Statistics for Students 1 and 16

Case ID No.	Actual Score	Possible Score	Ability (Logits)	Error	Infit Mean Square	Outfit Mean Square	Infit t	Outfit t
01	18	23	−0.41	0.30	0.93	0.68	−0.19	−0.17
16	28	23	+0.45	0.30	1.78	1.50	2.41	0.82

But how can this be of value diagnostically to the investigator? A comparison between the two kidmaps is a good place to start. Student 16 (est. = +0.45) was completely unsuccessful at a group of items that were well within that student's ability (revealed by this testing). Student 1 (est. = −0.41) has considerably less ability overall, as revealed by this investigation, but this student was able to successfully complete all the items in groups 14, 15, 16, and 19. In terms of Table 12.5, the response pattern of Student 16 is consonant with that shown as "special knowledge missing." To the child's teacher, however, this indicates the possibility of a developmental gap in this child's understanding of fundamental mathematical concepts. Of course, the teacher first would ensure that the child actually was present at school on the occasions when this material was covered in school lessons before going on to investigate further the reasons behind this apparent deficiency.

New teaching that did not account for this lack of understanding would not be as effective as teaching that first successfully undertook learning experiences aimed at remediation.

There is an interesting sidelight to these kidmaps and the issue of fit that could help us further understand the qualitative–quantitative nexus in the investigation of human behavior. The original researcher who had undertaken the qualitative interview of each student in this middle school mathematics investigation asked the data analyst to explain the meaning of the Rasch output. During that process, Kidmaps 1 and 16 were generated solely on the basis of the fit statistics shown in the group output. Kidmap 1 was chosen as the first student in the output with unremarkable fit values, whereas Kidmap 16 was chosen as the first in the sample where misfit seemed apparent. The segments of output for those two students are shown in Table 12.7. When shown what the high misfit values for student 16 revealed in terms of unexpected errors in the response pattern, the interviewer took out the handwritten case notes for that student. The top of the page was annotated with an expression of the interviewer's surprise that an apparently capable student had performed so poorly on a whole group of obviously easier questions. The investigator was both surprised and delighted that the misfit values had alerted the data analyst to a case on quantitative grounds that the investigator had noted while conducting the qualitative interview.

FIT: ISSUES FOR RESOLUTION

Notwithstanding the important distinction raised earlier about the relation between the data and the Rasch model, Rasch analysis procedures share a number of general features with other data-modeling techniques. After the initial estimation of approximate item difficulties and person abilities, these initial values are used to estimate improved difficulty and ability estimates. This iterative process is repeated for the purpose of reducing the marginal totals of item and person residuals to as close as possible to zero. Generally speaking, WINSTEPS estimation iterations continue until the largest marginal residual is less than the default level of 0.5 score points (while the largest change in any person or item estimate is less than 0.01 logits). The default value in QUEST is a 0.005 logit change in estimate value. Iterations cease when marginal residuals are acceptably small, or when the biggest change in any estimate is too small to matter. However, although marginal residuals are very small, individual response residuals can remain large. It is these that form the basis of fit analysis.

This leads to a rather counterintuitive paradox: A test made up of two equal-size, but unrelated, sets of items can produce more acceptable fit estimates than a test attempting to measure one attribute that includes a small number of poorly constructed items. Think of it this way. In the example of the "two different halves" test, there is no single underlying attribute on which person performance is being measured. The estimation iterations simply will be repeated until the default change in residual values is recorded, and perhaps all items will "fit." For a well-constructed test, in which two or three items are not working as well as the others, the underlying latent attribute is defined, psychometrically, by the performances of the persons on the large number of items. The interactions between the persons and the large number of good items will dominate the estimation process. When the residuals are reduced as far as possible for the bulk of the data set, the two or three less adequate items will show evidence of misfit. This is the caution behind using the process of common-person linking between BLOT and PRTIII in chapter 5. One alternative is to pool the data and conduct one analysis of all the data. In the original investigation, both techniques were used.

This leads us back, conveniently, to the value of theory-driven research. Misfit indicators are likely to be less reliable when data collection devices have been assembled haphazardly. How can data analysis be expected to discriminate between equally poor items? It is not unreasonable to suggest, however, that misfit indicators could be very useful in helping the investigator understand where the theory-driven measurement intentions went astray in empirical practice: A small number of less satisfactory items might be detected against a backdrop of a larger number of successful items.

MISFIT: A FUNDAMENTAL ISSUE

"Refereeing papers for European journals, in particular, reveals to me that our Rasch colleagues in Europe usually require a broader range of fit indicators than we have in the US and Australia, and are often more stringent in the application of misfit cutoffs" (Bond, 2005b, p. 336). For those who wish to conduct other, perhaps more rigorous, tests of fit, the most appropriate reference is that of Fischer and Molenaar (1995). In part of the next chapter, we review the relation between the Rasch measurement model and the requirements for fundamental measurement in the social sciences following the prescriptions for axiomatic conjoint measurement (Luce, 1995; Luce, Krantz, Suppes, & Tversky, 1990; Michell, 1999). We also look at Karabatsos's (1999a) arguments maintaining that axiomatic measurement theory helps to decide which IRT models actually contribute to the construction of measures, and that axiomatic tests, rather than residual fit statistics, are more informative about the violation of the unidimensionality principle. Indeed, Karabatsos argues, following Cliff (1992), that the axioms of conjoint measurement require the parallel item characteristic curves (ICCs) that are central to Rasch measurement.

IN THE INTERIM

One interesting sidelight to come from the never-ending search for ways to detect important deviations from the important undimensionality requirement of Rasch modeling has been the application of factor analysis techniques to the residual matrices (Wright, 1996). If the Rasch-modeled person–item interaction information extracted from the data matrix leaves a random dispersion of residuals, then the claim is that the solution accounts for just one dimension. The presence of factor loadings in the analysis of residuals would suggest the presence of more than one underlying test dimension. WINSTEPS facilitates this analysis and interpretation in its Tables 23.3 and 24.3, Principal Components Analysis of Residuals, which decomposes the matrix of item or person correlations based on residuals to identify other possible factors (dimensions) that might be affecting response patterns (Linacre, 1998; Smith, 2000). Alternatively, CONQUEST software (Wu, Adams, & Wilson, 1998) provides methods for assessing whether a single Rasch dimension, or two or more closely related Rasch dimensions, provide the most parsimonious summary of data–model fit.

DETECTING MULTIPLE DIMENSIONS

One of the distinctive features of the Rasch approach to scientific measurement has been revealed by the insistence that our attempts at making measures should proceed by one clearly theorized construct at a time. That is, the Rasch model requires that measures must be unidimensional. But, of course, that underlies our problem. How do we know when we have established a undimensional measure suitable to our measurement purposes? All attempts at summarizing data are compromises; many would claim that the only strictly unidimensional test is the single-item test, and even that one item might be revealed as tapping more than one underlying trait (e.g., reading the prompt, (a) calculating the answer, (b) writing the response, etc.). Generally, practitioners of Rasch measurement rely on the indicators of misfit to reveal the extent to which any item or person performance suggests more than one underlying latent trait is at work.

Given our current knowledge of the possible inadequacies of fit indexes for this purpose and our deeper understanding of the nature of scientific measurement structures (chap. 1; 13) it would be remiss of us not to reflect on the possible consequences of treating two or more dimensions as one or to suggest how recent developments in the field can help us deal with this potential problem. We adopt a two-pronged approach: The first looks at how we can use factor analytical approaches to help us detect extraneous dimensions in our data; the second will outlines how a more sophisticated Rasch-based model makes comparisons between multidimensional and unidimensional measurement structures.

So, the identification of possible multiple dimensions within a data set must remain one of the main focuses of measurement construction in the human sciences. Given that factor analysis still remains the single most common statistical tool for diagnosing dimensionality, it is no wonder that our understanding of underlying measurement constructs remains so limited. In practice, factor analyses, due to their sample dependency and use of ordinal-level data, provide dimensionality information that is only partially replicable across other samples of interest, and further perpetuates the notion that scientific measures can be developed and diagnosed using correlational methods.

FACTOR ANALYSIS—PROBLEMS AND PROMISE

Factor analyses are based on correlations of sample-dependent ordinal-level data, typically requiring complete data matrices for analysis. Not only are complete data sets unrealistic for most investigations (Wright, 1996), but the solutions to missing data problems result in data loss (using casewise deletions) or distortions of the data matrix (using pairwise deletions or missing data imputation).

The major problem is that factor analysis does not require the construction of linear, interval-level measures or factor scores from the outset, and hence the factor sizes and factor loadings rarely are reproduced when new sets of relevant data are reanalyzed with the same procedure (Wright, 1996). Furthermore, even though the confirmation of a factor structure is based on its reproducibility with another data set, the confirmation procedure includes neither fit statistics nor standard errors for loadings (Wright, 1996).

This dependence on sample-dependent correlations, without analysis of fit or standard errors, severely limits the utility of factor analysis results. It continues to appear as if factor analysis is an obligatory step in establishing the validity of a measure, but yet few seem to be able to explain how the results help in understanding or improving the measure. Factor analysis is far removed from the idea of constructing a linear measure and often serves as a compulsory yet misleading exercise in the construct validation process. Thus, two major concerns with factor analysis are: It does not provide information on which items and which persons work towards defining a useful yardstick (i.e., it does not serve to construct linear measures), nor on the extent to which they do so (e.g., using fit indices, standard errors). Rather, it identifies correlations with the underlying variable, but not *locations* on it (Schumacker & Linacre, 1996). It does not provide a defensible framework (i.e., it is based on sample-dependent correlations) for understanding the magnitude of and relations among possible subscales. This leads to a variety of possible, yet arbitrary, interpretations of the resulting factors.

RASCH FACTOR ANALYSIS

Rasch factor analysis (first introduced by Wright in 1996) can be a somewhat misleading term, but, simply put, it involves, first, a regular Rasch analysis procedure (using the ordinal-level descriptive data to construct a linear measure), followed by a factor analysis of the (ordinal-level) residuals that remain after the linear Rasch measure has been extracted from the data set (Linacre, 1998). A factor analysis of these residuals is used to identify any common variance among those aspects of the data that remained unexplained or unmodeled by the primary Rasch measure. This use of factor analysis procedures, (i.e., after a linear variable has been constructed), can be quite informative because it provides information supplemental to understanding what common variance in the data is not accounted for by the linear Rasch measure under investigation.

Linacre (1998) suggested three stages to the investigation of data dimensionality. First, any negative-point biserial correlations (from traditional statistics) should be examined to identify potentially problematic items. Second, misfitting persons and items should be diagnosed using Rasch fit indicators. Third, these procedures should be followed by the examination of dimensionality using Rasch Factor Analysis. If any substantial and interesting dimension is identified from the Rasch Factor Analysis, the researcher should consider creating a separate measure for this dimension (Linacre 1998).

The identification of common variance in the residuals is not always meaningful. Both the size of the factor (that is, the amount of variance for which it accounts) and the nature of the factor (reflection of response styles or item content, e.g., Linacre, 1998) need to be considered in assigning importance to additional dimensions that might emerge. The nature of any additional dimension must be assessed by the researcher. Hopefully, that reflection will be theoretically driven, but, realistically, it is often based on pragmatic reasoning. For example, one easily can conceptualize a mathematics test functioning as a single dimension even-though it contains items on both subtraction and addition. Others might find it useful to construct two different measures—one of subtraction ability and one of addition ability. Wright and Stone (2004, p. 20), using characteristics of stones (i.e., rocks, etc.), illustrate some of the decisions that one might make:

> Principal component analysis of stone residuals might identify a subset of stones that has something in common. When we examine these stones, we might find that smooth stones are harder to lift than rough stones of similar weight, which would produce a telltale set of similar residuals. This would identify a secondary and probably unwanted variable of smoothness operating in our men/stones data and give us the opportunity to decide whether or not we want to measure stones on two variables (i.e., weight and smoothness) or control the intrusion of smoothness by ensuring that all of the stones that we use to build our strength/weight measure are equally smooth. When constructing a strength/weight yardstick we would then take care to use stones of similar smoothness in order to clarify our definition of strength/weight. Principal component analysis of men residu-

als might also show a second variable—this time the effect of wet hands on lifting. The natural resolution of this disturbance to the construction of a strength/weight yardstick is to control for hand wetness.

ANALYSIS OF A PSYCHOTHERAPY MEASURE—AN EXAMPLE

The Symptom Checklist 90 Revised (SCL-90-R; Derogatis, 1975, 1994) is one of the most commonly used psychological assessment instruments today. The instrument consists of a checklist of symptoms on a 5-point Likert scale, ranging from (0) *not at all* distressed to (4) *extremely* distressed, for symptoms the patient might have experienced over the past week. The SCL-90-R is composed of nine symptom subscales and three global indeces. The subscales include Somatization, Obsessive–Compulsive, Interpersonal Sensitivity, Depression, Anxiety, Hostility, Phobic Anxiety, Paranoid Ideation, and Psychoticism. The three global indices of distress/psychopathology are the Positive Symptom Total Index (number of symptoms), Positive Symptom Distress Index (intensity of distress), and the Global Severity Index (calculation of both number of symptoms and intensity of distress). As with many psychological inventories, clinicians interpret the scores based on responses to individual items as well as scale scores (Derogatis & Savitz, 1999).

As with the factor analysis of other psychological instruments, investigations into the dimensionality of this inventory have resulted in mixed support for the hypothesized subscale structure of the SCL-90-R (Derogatis & Savitz, 1999). What has been consistent, however, is the finding of relatively high inter-correlations among the subscales (ranging from .59–.67; see Dinning & Evans, 1977, Holcomb, Adams, & Ponder 1983, Clark & Friedman, 1983. This evidence pointed toward the potential utility of the factor analysis of the Rasch model residuals to investigate the dimensionality of the checklist. If the "subscales" are so highly intercorrelated, might they work together to form a single meaningful yardstick that measures global distress? If so, we could develop an equal-interval measure that would remain invariant (within standard error) for diagnosing distress levels and then measuring change in those levels over time. The Rasch Factor Analysis could be used to detect any substantial and meaningful variance that was not captured by that primary global distress yardstick. "Therefore, we performed a Rasch factor analysis, that is, an analysis of response residuals among items in order to see if we could find any evidence for the presence of unsuspected secondary variables, after removing variance due to the primary 'Distress Yardstick'"(Wright & Stone, 2004).

A team of researchers, in the beginning stages of instrument investigation, used data from two different psychotherapy outcome studies on process-experiential therapy (Greenberg, Rice, & Elliott, 1993; Elliott, Watson, Goldman, & Greenberg, 2004), both conducted at The University of Toledo. The first group of clients was recruited through a depression study and all were diagnosed with major depressive disorder or related affective disorders. The second group was a naturalistic sample, in therapy for a variety of Axis I and Axis II disorders (SCID-I &-II; First, Spitzer, Gibbon, & Williams, 1995).

PRINCIPAL COMPONENTS ANALYSIS OF RASCH RESIDUALS

Figure 12.5 shows the factor plot of the standardized residuals after the primary Rasch dimension has been extracted. This map plots the item measure (Rasch estimate in logits) against the magnitude of the PCA factor loading of its residual, based on the standardized residual of each item from the Rasch dimension. Thus, items that have substantial variance that remains unexplained by the primary Rasch measure have higher factor loadings (seen at the top of the map). The vertical spread of these items helps diagnose whether these items are clustered in particular levels of the measure (e.g., clustered as more or less difficult). Items that are clustered together with loadings substantially greater than zero are those requiring further investigation for measurement disturbances (Wright & Stone, 2004).

When describing secondary dimensions in the data, Wright and Stone (2004) used the analogy of identifying a *branch* of items that are distinguishable from the main stem or yardstick (p. 30). The substantiality of any such additional factor(s) is then evaluated by comparing the ratio of variance of the residual factor to that of the yardstick (Rasch measure) as a whole (Wright & Stone, 2004).

The heading in Figure 12.5 indicates that the first factor extracted from the residuals accounts for 5.7 units (items) out of 90 residual variance units (items).

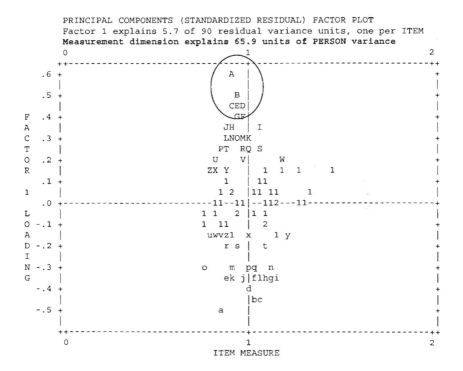

Figure 12.5.   WINSTEPS dimensionality map for SCL-90-R residuals.

Further, the yardstick (Rasch measure) dimension explains 65.9 units of the person variance. These indices are then used to calculate a *factor sensitivity ratio* (Wright & Stone, 2004) by taking the common residual units divided by the yardstick (analogous to systematic or explained variance) units. Here, dividing 5.7 (residual variance units) by 65.9 (Rasch measure variance units) yields .086; that is, 8 -9% of the yardstick stability is affected by this factor representing unexplained relations between the item residuals *after* the Rasch measure was extracted.

Table 12.8 (a truncated table from Winsteps, Linacre & Wright, 2004) lists the factor loadings, indicating six items (69, 61, 79, 21, 88, & 76) with substantial positive loadings on the factor discovered in the item residuals (i.e., with off-dimension loading of .4 or greater).

The six positive items appear to have a common meaning of *social anxiety*. These items are:

69. Feeling very self-conscious with others
61. Feeling uneasy when people are watching or talking about you
79. Feeling of worthlessness
21. Feeling uneasy with the opposite sex
88. Never feeling close to another person
76. Others not giving you proper credit for your achievements
37. Feeling that people are unfriendly or dislike you

The four items (1, 39, 49, & 40) that are substantially negatively correlated with the factor have a common meaning that could be labeled "physical anxiety."

These items are:

1. Headaches
39. Heart pounding/racing
49. Hot/Cold Spells
40. Nausea/Upset Stomach

This secondary variable identified by the Rasch factor analysis provides evidence of a small influence of another dimension that might be labeled "social distress." Nine percent of the common variance undefined by the primary distress Rasch dimension is associated with this other, albeit minor, dimension. This now provides empirical evidence for the existence of a separate subscale, and the researcher can decide if this is large enough and meaningful enough to measure separately from the main distress yardstick.

Now the original researchers can reflect on the costs/benefits of both including the social/physical anxiety items merely as part of the original Rasch dimension (potentially losing some sensitivity/validity of measurement), or excluding those items from the total score of the SCL-90-R and perhaps working towards assessing and interpreting the other dimension(s) separately. Even so, the structure revealed for this Checklist by the combination of Rasch analysis and the PCA of the Rasch item residuals stands in considerable contrast to the originally claimed 9-factor structure: It is in vain to do with more what can be done with fewer. (William of Occam).

TABLE 12.8

WINSTEPS Output for Loadings on First Dimension of Residuals

FACTOR	LOADING	MEASURE	INFIT MNSQ	OUTFIT MNSQ	ENTRY NUMBER	I
1	.59	.90	.82	.77	A	69	69
1	.49	.93	.93	.87	B	61	61
1	.44	.90	.86	.81	C	79	79
1	.44	.97	1.05	1.18	D	21	21
1	.43	.93	1.23	1.15	E	88	88
1	.42	.94	1.08	1.00	F	76	76
1	.40	.95	.88	.83	G	37	37
1	.37	.88	.98	.93	H	83	83
1	.36	1.05	.98	.95	I	70	70
1	.33	.89	.75	.72	J	41	41
1	.32	.97	.94	.88	K	90	90
1	.31	.87	.77	.74	L	36	36
1	.30	.98	.91	.81	M	80	80
1	.30	.92	.95	.91	N	18	18
1	.29	.90	.92	.87	O	77	77
1	.27	.84	.77	.73	P	54	54
1	.27	.98	.95	.90	Q	43	43
1	.26	.97	1.15	1.04	R	22	22
1	.25	1.06	.97	.84	S	50	50
1	.23	.88	1.02	1.08	T	89	89
1	.21	.83	.82	.79	U	26	26
1	.21	.96	1.02	.98	V	68	68
1	.19	1.18	1.20	1.23	W	73	73
1	.17	.79	.81	.80	X	29	29
1	.16	.87	.85	.80	Y	32	32
1	.14	.79	.85	.87	Z	28	28
1	.14	1.08	1.56	1.62		84	84
1	.14	1.19	1.18	1.90		63	63
1	.14	1.44	1.23	.70		16	16
1	.13	1.26	1.15	1.01		7	07
1	.11	1.06	1.20	1.48		85	85
1	-.52	.86	1.31	1.50	a	1	01
1	-.47	1.04	1.11	1.16	b	39	39
1	-.43	1.04	1.17	1.13	c	49	49
1	-.40	.99	1.08	1.27	d	40	40

Note. Factor 1 is the principal component analysis of standardized residual correlations for items (sorted by loading). Factor 1 explains 5.7 of 90 residual variance units, one per ITEM Measurement dimension explains 65.9 units of person variance.

257

It is important, when examining and ultimately identifying these extra dimensions, to remember that unidimensionality is always provisional and a data set manifests one dimension so long as it is productive to think of it that way (Linacre, 1998 p. 268). This rather pragmatic approach to identifying unidimensionality is consistent with Ben Wright's reference to dimensions as *useful fictions*—that is, any yardstick (or residual dimension) is identified only to solve a problem at hand.

Furthermore, the dimension is only as useful as it remains current in what it is meant to help explain, and within acceptable standard errors (i.e., measures need recalibration over time). These dimensions or useful fictions are based on constructs (ideas) that researchers theorize (posit) to be helpful in understanding complex human phenomena and solving practical problems. These useful fictions are only supported by data (different data and mathematical solutions can tell a variety of stories about the data), and should never be confused as confirmed reifications of the construct under investigation.

One Dimension, Two Dimension, Three Dimension, Four...

When the first hints of multidimensional Rasch modelling entered the discussions of Rasch SIG members and participants of the International Objective Measurement Workshops, many died-in-the-wool Rasch enthusiasts were given to raising eyebrows and making dismissive comments, much in the same way as when the first uses of Rasch Factor Analysis were reported as helping to determine the dimensionality of data sets. After all, it was almost an act of faith that Rasch analysis had replaced factor analysis, particularly for the determination of unidimensionality, so how could avid proponents of the Rasch model even contemplate the use of factor analysis in the context of examining dimensionality? Now, the role of what is called RFA—factor analysis of Rasch residuals to check the dimensionality of the residuals of the data set not explained by the single Rasch dimension—is not without controversy in Rasch measurement circles and, of course, the idea of a multidimensional Rasch model seems to deny the basic measurement principle espoused from the outset of this volume: Measurement should proceed one variable at a time.

In an overly simple introduction to one context in which a multidimensional approach could be used to capitalize on many Rasch measurement principles, we could focus on some of the constraints and problems that might be encountered in conducting a large comparison of educational achievement. Let us presume to see, say, mathematics, science, and written language achievement each as a single dimension in the Rasch measurement sense. We could set out carefully to construct the sort of Rasch calibrated unidimensional measurement system for each curriculum area, in turn: math, science, and language. We could ensure that fair comparisons could be made across examination contexts of different curricula and even different languages by keeping the strictest interpretation of Rasch measurement principles of calibration, invariance, and linking foremost in the minds of the assessment teams. We could, alternatively, consider that there was a more general construct, "educational achievement," that was the focus of our investigation and with rather more relaxed criteria in mind construct a sufficiently unidimensional test of that single variable instead.

You can hear the cries already: Mathematics, language, and science are separate dimensions. Some will even contend that the individual components of mathematics (or language) need to be tested separately. The counterargument is also compelling: Treating each achievement test as separate and unrelated (even at the level of the individual respondent) discards a lot of potentially important information about the ways in which, say, mathematics, language, and science might be related in the context of overall educational achievement for any child or sample of children.

Somewhere in between those two extremes (individual, unrelated, single Rasch dimensions for each component subject and one Rasch dimension called educational achievement) lies another conceptualisation of the measurement possibilities. Each of the separate dimensions is regarded as a unidimensional ability, but the multidimensional model used for the analysis of PISA data specifically recognizes that the achievement scores in the different subject domains are highly correlated. Because the Rasch model can make use of data from only one subject area at a time, it must ignore the correlated information that could be obtained from test performances in other subject areas when tests are given at about the same time. The evidence from the PISA 2000 assessment shows that the cognitive dimensions assessed in that international testing program were highly correlated (Table 12.9).

The model applied to the PISA data is a generalised form of the Rasch model: the mixed coefficients multinomial logit model (MCMLM; Adams, Wilson, & Wang, 1997). It is implemented in ConQuest software (Wu, Adams, & Wilson, 1997). Applying a variety of constraints in the ConQuest control lines, the variety of Rasch models already described in earlier chapters can be used on a variety of data. While a review of the possibilities of the MCMLM and ConQuest are beyond the scope of this chapter, two features will be of interest to those undertaking Rasch analysis in closely related domains. In a paper presented at IOMW—Cairns—2004 (Wu & Adams, 2004), Wu reported simulated data generated to represent the relationship between two related (correlation = 0.8), but not identical single dimensions (Fig. 12.6).

Consistent with our earlier warning in Chapter 5, the recovered correlation between estimates calculated on the basis of two separate unidimensional analyses was 0.34 (without correction for attenuation due to errors of measurement). When the relationship was directly estimated in a multidimensional analysis using MCMLM, the recovered correlation was reported at 0.73. In light of Endler's findings of consistently high intercorrelations between BLOT scores and achievement in Australia and the US (Endler & Bond, 2001; Endler, 2004), the application

TABLE 12.9
Correlations Between Cognitive Dimensions Assessed
in the PISA Testing Program

Scale	Reading	Science
Mathematics	0.819	0.846
Science	0.890	

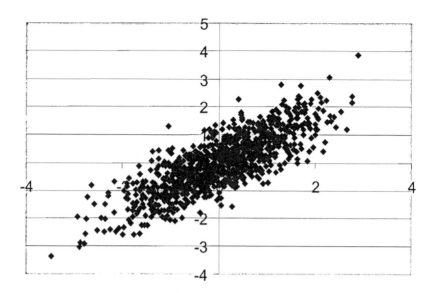

Figure 12.6.   Plot of generating abilities on the two dimensions (Wu & Adams, 2004).

of the MCMLM to the US data, in particular, appears promising. Correlations calculated between the Oregon State Scores (OSS) and the BLOT ability estimates revealed strong relationships between the cognitive level of these students and their achievement in the state-mandated mathematics, reading, and literature, and science tests. Of the 84 correlations performed, 77 correlations were found to be significant at $p < 0.01$ and more than 50 of these r values exceeded 0.70, even though the Rasch estimates were calculated on separate analyses (by Endler for the BLOT and a testing company for the OSS) and the correlations were not corrected for attenuation. If the uncorrected correlations between the two single Rasch dimensions are already so high, what might we expect if the raw cognitive development and achievement data are subjected to multidimensional analyses using the MCMLM instantiated in ConQuest software?

The issue of dimensionality remains central to those interested in developing genuinely scientific measures in the human sciences. The benefits of the Rasch model for measurement apply only to data that fit the model, but of course, no data ever can, fit perfectly. Fit statistics remain rather imperfect ways to detect lack of adherence to the unidimensionality requirement of measurement. In spite of the requirements of journal editors and contributors for unambiguous interpretation of indicators of misfit, the routine application of cutoff criteria for acceptable fit statistics always risks undervaluing the theory driven process of developing measures in the human sciences.

CHAPTER THIRTEEN

A Synthetic Overview

Those who are enamored of practice without science are like a pilot who goes into a ship without rudder or compass and never has any certainty where he is going. Practice should always be based on a sound knowledge of theory.
—Leonardo da Vinci (1452–1519, Notebooks)

The human condition is, by almost any definition, exceptionally complex. Although we remain amazed at the range of individual differences that distinguish each and every one of us from the others, one of the purposes central to the human sciences has been the generation of laws and theories to describe the common features of human existence. It seems as though those of us who try to understand the human condition must struggle to deal with the tension that exists between trying to describe, explain, measure, and predict the common attributes of human beings on the one hand, and appreciating and accounting for idiosyncratic individual differences on the other.

Although many paradigms exist across the human sciences for studying and explaining the human condition, the work presented in this book is essential to the position that psychology, for example, is a quantitative rational science. In spite of the many other paradigms that contribute to our understanding of human nature, social interaction, health, behavior, intellectual development, and school achievement, it is not unreasonable to claim that, in the 20th century, the social sciences have been dominated by those determined to quantify the important aspects of human behavior.

There are those who appear willing to accept all human behavior at its face value: What you see is what you get (wysiwyg). Latent trait theorists, however, regard observable behavior merely as the outward indicator of human states that remain, for the most part, at least invisible and perhaps unknowable. It would not be difficult to defend the idea that it is impossible for me to know myself, and even more so, for me to understand my fellows. When the day at the beach or the park is spoiled by bad weather that had not been predicted, we are somewhat consoled by the meteorologists' claim that weather systems are far too complex to predict accurately. Yet we express our disappointment that the behavior of a particular person cannot be predicted from what we already know about that person's past and the current situation. Although we might, in a moment of frustration, complain that the weather seems to have a mind of its own, few of us really would believe that. Although most of us would admit that, unlike the weather, humans have the capacity to influence their own behavior, we remain frustrated at the attempts of psychology, philosophy, sociology, medicine, and so forth, to predict human outcomes in the way that we expect the physical sciences to predict and explain the behavior of objects.

In his text, *Measurement in Psychology: A Critical History of a Methodological Concept*, Michell (1999) argued that measurement in psychology has failed because psychologists, unable to meet the stringent requirements of measurement as it existed in the physical sciences, invented their own definitions of what psychological measurement would be. He maintained that these definitions ignore two fundamental steps in the measurement process. First, it is necessary to argue that the particular human trait under investigation is, in fact, quantifiable. Second, it then is necessary to construct a measure of this trait so that the numbers indicating the variety of values of the trait may be subjected lawfully to the mathematical computations that we routinely use in statistical analyses. It is not good enough, Michell claimed, to allocate numbers to behavior, and then to assert that this is measurement.

Indeed, Michell argued that psychology must remain a mere pseudoscience if it does not deal with the almost complete absence of fundamental measurement from its discipline. It is not sufficient to allocate numbers to events merely on the basis of some accepted conventions such as the nominal, ordinal, interval, or ratio scales of Stevens (1946) that were designed to allow psychology to appear scientific when, in fact, it is not.

CONJOINT MEASUREMENT

Duncan Luce and his colleagues have outlined the principles and properties of conjoint measurement that would bring the same sort of rigorous measurement to the human sciences as the physical sciences have enjoyed for a considerable time. It seems that many psychologists are determined to avoid the work required to implement fundamental measurement as the cornerstone of a quantitative rational science of the human condition (e.g., Luce, 1972; Luce & Tukey, 1964; Suppes, Krantz, Luce, & Tversky, 1989). They seem determined to be satisfied with Stevens's (1959) convention, peculiar to their own world, that measurement is the allocation of numbers according to a rule (p. 19), and to accept at face value his distinction between the nominal, ordinal, interval, and ratio scales.

This, of course, is unwelcome news to those countless thousands who teach courses in measurement and statistics, who have spent lifetimes doing quantitative research based on the Stevens principles, or who have millions of dollars invested in testing procedures that produce mere numbers and not measures. The argument is that all the sophisticated statistical analyses conducted in psychology, in educational outcomes, in medical rehabilitation, for example, are wasted if the data that form the input for these analyses do not adhere to the principles of fundamental measurement common in the physical sciences and described for us by Luce and Tukey (1964).

For those who have listened to Ben Wright from the University of Chicago as he made his expositions on Rasch analysis, Michell's critique of quantitative psychology is not news at all. Wright's ever-present teaching aid was a 1-foot rule that he carried around in his back pocket and used as his model of what measurement in the physical sciences is like, and what measurement in the human sciences must be like. It is clear that, at least for the present, the Rasch model is the only technique generally available for constructing measures in the human sciences. Andrich (1988), Fisher (1994), Perline, Wright, and Wainer (1979), Wright (1985, 1999), and others have demonstrated that the Rasch model produces the sort of measurements we expect in the physical sciences when it is applied to measurement construction in the social sciences. The claim is that the Rasch model instantiates the principles of probabilistic conjoint measurement to produce interval measures in which the principles of concatenation apply.

> In 1992, however, Norman Cliff decried the much awaited impact of Luce's work as "the revolution that never happened," although, in 1996, Luce was writing about the "ongoing dialogue between empirical science and measurement theory." To me, the "dialogue" between mathematical psychologists and the end-users of data analysis software has been like the parallel play that Piaget described in pre-schoolers: they talk (and play) in each other's company rather than to and with each other. Discussion amongst Rasch practitioners at conferences and online revealed that we thought we had something that no-one else had in the social sciences—additive conjoint measurement—a new kind of fundamental scientific measurement. We had long ago carefully and deliberately resiled from the S. S. Stevens (1946) view that some sort of measurement was possible with four levels of data, nominal, ordinal, interval and ratio; a view, we held, that allowed psychometricians to pose (unwarrantedly) as scientists. (Bond, 2005b, p. 337)

This volume is then, in part, a small contribution to some sort of productive communication between theoreticians who study what measurement in the human sciences could, nay, should, be like and those involved in the foot-slogging of day-to-day research who have heard whispers of a "better way" or who have some suspicion that a better way must exist. The claim we are making is that the construction of fundamental measures is the first task in any of the human sciences in which real quantification is required. This is not to suggest that the Rasch model supersedes all that we learned in our statistics courses at college. The use of the Rasch model is, however, the precursor of any statistical analyses we want to conduct. It could be argued that the term "psychometrics" is terminally flawed, that the current practices have a lot to do with the "psycho" and very little to do with the "metrics." We can highlight the problem by looking at one of the classic texts used in postgraduate measurement classes, that of Hays (1994). In the Introduction to his book, *Statistics*, he explains:

> Controlled experimentation in any science is an attempt to minimize at least part of the accidental variation or *error* in observation. Precise techniques of measurement are aids to scientists in sharpening their own rather dull powers of observation and comparison among events. So-called exact sciences, such as physics and chemistry, thus have been able to remove a substantial amount of the unwanted variation among observations from time to time, place to place, observer to observer, and hence often are able to make general statements about physical phenomena with great assurance from the observation of limited numbers of events. . . . In the biological, behavioral, and social sciences, however, the situation is radically different. In these sciences, the variations between observations are not subject to the precise experimental controls that are possible in the physical sciences. Refined measurement techniques have not reached the stage of development that have obtained in physics and chemistry . . . And yet the aim of the social or biological science test is precisely the same as that of the physical scientist—arriving at general statements about the phenomena under study. (p. 4)

Hays then follows on with the rest of his text, explaining how the statistics part is performed and relegating the measurement part to oblivion. His position seems to be that, because measurements of human phenomena are underdeveloped, we should drop that agenda and get on with the doable task of executing inferential statistical analyses. Of course, Hays is not peculiar in this regard. His approach to measurement, or his lack of approach to measurement, is quite typical in the field. Michell (1997) lists a large number of standard texts in the field in which the measurement aspect of research is so treated. The general approach is that because the sort of measurement taken for granted in the physical sciences is beyond the reach of the human sciences, psychology's own idiosyncratic view of what measurement is will have to suffice.

The relegation of measurement to the sidelines is lamented by Pedhazur and Schmelkin (1991):

> Measurement is the Achilles' heel of sociobehavioral research. Although most programs in sociobehavioral sciences . . . require a medium of exposure to statistics and research design, few seem to require the same where measurement is concerned . . . It is, therefore, not surprising that little or no attention is given to the properties of the measures used in many research studies. (pp. 2–3)

Unfortunately, neither the authors nor those who quote them (Kieffer, 1999) seem to understand that an essential property of useful measures is the linearity and additivity inherent in measures used in the physical sciences.

Our claim is a much stronger one: The construction of measures is a prerequisite of statistical analyses. The standard for scientific measurement is that which has been the servant of the physical sciences. Those measurement principles can be applied to the human sciences via probabilistic conjoint measurement. Currently, the Rasch model is the only model that provides for the construction of measures meeting these criteria. Rasch modeling does not replace statistical analysis; it precedes it.

Therefore, those involved in the measurement of latent traits must deal with two difficulties. First, latent traits are not directly observable; only their consequent behaviors are. Second, measurement is not the mere allocation of numbers to events, but the result of a deliberative process.

MEASUREMENT AND ITEM RESPONSE THEORY

Of the few textbooks that deal with the Rasch model, most tend to lump it together with two- and three-parameter models under the general heading, Item Response Theories. In that context, the Rasch model is referred to as the one-parameter item response theory (IRT) model. But the 1-PL, 2-PL, 3-PL models are so called because the test items are characterized by one, two, or three parameters, and the sample of persons by a distribution. The persons are not individually parameterized as in the Rasch model. This has important implications for the concept of measurement invariance, because those IRT models are not "person-distribution-free" (see chap. 12). The two-parameter IRT model includes a parameter for item discrimination, and the three-parameter IRT model adds parameters for both item discrimination and guessing. Proponents of the two- and three-parameter models contend that data fit generally improves when these techniques are used. We should not be surprised that this is often, though not always, the case. The values of the second and the third parameters of these models are introduced or manipulated expressly for that purpose: to maximize the fit of the model to the data.

The Rasch model, however, is used for another purpose: the construction of fundamental measures. In this context, fit statistics are used to indicate where the principles of probabilistic conjoint measurement have been sufficiently realized in practice to justify the claim that the results can be used as a measurement scale with interval measurement properties. In this case, the Rasch model question is: How well do the empirical data fit to the measurement model requirements? Can the scale yield invariant–interval level measures? For the two- and three-parameter IRT models, there is another focus: How can the additional parameters be manipulated to maximize the fit of the model to the data? How can the empirical data be most completely explained? Indeed, as we see later in this chapter, it is precisely the addition of the extra parameters that robs the data output of its fundamental measurement properties.

In this context, the comments of a longtime Rasch critic, Harvey Goldstein (1979), are both informative and illustrative: "'The criterion is that items should fit the model, and not that the model should fit the items.' This is an extremely radical proposal"

(p. 15). Goldstein's comment presupposes that the sole objective of data analysis is to manipulate the data analytical procedures until the amount of variance that cannot be explained is reduced to a minimum. This approach to quantification is shared by many factor analytical techniques as well as the two- and three-parameter IRT models. From this perspective, the primacy of the empirical data is paramount. The task of data analysis is to account for the idiosyncrasies of the data.

From the fundamental measurement perspective, the requirements of the measurement model are paramount. The idiosyncrasies of the empirical data are of secondary importance. The measurement ideal, encapsulated in the Rasch model, has primacy. The researcher's task is to work toward a better fit of the data to the model's requirements until the match is sufficient for practical measurement purposes in that field. But, of course, it is the so far unresolved challenge for Rasch measurement to demonstrate that the procedures for determining whether the matrix of actual response frequencies (x_{ni}) adheres sufficiently to the Rasch measurement prescriptions really do satisfy these key conjoint measurement axioms. Rasch measurement is not there yet, but many proponents of Rasch measurement are addressing these issues—issues on which most psychometricians, both those from the CTT and general IRT fields, appear to remain silent. Just try raising these issues in a broader forum: Silence or dismissal are regular responses.

Would you like an interval scale with that?

No doubt a number of our learned colleagues will continue to regard our presentation of the ideas in this volume as parochial and tendentious rhetoric (e.g. van der Linden, 2001). How serious is Goldstein when he refers to Rasch measurement, in print, as "Una Tecnica Mafiosa" (2004, p. 4)? While we work to set apart some distinctive features of the Rasch model for the construction of invariant measures, Goldstein describes Rasch analysts thus:

> Most obviously the favourite technique of this psychometric subset, a group that displays certain characteristics of a mafia, is something called the "Rasch model,' named after a Danish mathematician George Rasch. This, and certain limited generalizations of it (typically the "2-parameter" model) have come to be known under the title "Item Response Theory" (Lord, 1980), although the term "theory" is something of a conceit since it is really just a special case of a statistical model that is widely used by social and other researchers to summarise a wide variety of data. I shall refer to it simply as an item response model (IRM). (p. 4)

Goldstein apparently subscribes to an alternative view: that many models (especially the other IRT models) have such features. Another pervasive view is that traditional statistical approaches in the social sciences provide all the techniques sufficient for understanding data quantitatively. In other words, the Rasch model is nothing special and anything outside the scope of traditional statistics produces little or no extra for all the extra work involved: special software, Rasch workshops, and books such as this one. In a large scale empirical comparison of IRT (including Rasch) and CTT item and person statistics in mandated achievement testing, Fan (1988) concluded that the intercorrelations between person indicators and between item indicators across Rasch, 2PL, 3PL IRT and CTT models were so high as not to warrant the extra effort of latent trait modeling.

Because the IRT Rasch model (one parameter IRT model) assumes fixed item discrimination and no guessing for all items, the model only provides estimates for item parameter of difficulty. Because item difficulty parameter estimates of the Rasch model were almost perfectly related to CTT-based item difficulty indexes (both original and normalized), it appears that the one-parameter model provides almost the same information as CTT with regard to item difficulty but at the cost of considerable model complexity. Unless Rasch model estimates could show superior performance in terms of invariance across different samples over that of CTT item difficulty indexes, the results here would suggest that the Rasch model might not offer any empirical advantage over the much simpler CTT framework. (Fan, 1998, p. 371)

Novices to Rasch measurement might ask, "How could that possibly be the case?" The explanation is really quite simple but goes to the very heart of the distinction canvassed in this volume between Rasch measurement on the one hand and general IRT- and CTT- based analyses on the other. Fan revealed, "As the tabled results indicate, for the IRT Rasch model (i.e., the one parameter IRT model), the relationship between CTT- and IRT- based item difficulty estimates is almost perfect" (p. 371). Of course, for both CTT and the Rasch model, N (number correct) is the sufficient statistic for the estimation of both item difficulty and person ability. However, for the Rasch model there is a crucial caveat: To the extent that the data fit the Rasch model's specifications for measurement, then N is the sufficient statistic. In light of the attention paid to the issues raised about Rasch model fit and unidimensionality in chapter 11, it is not so easy then to glide over the telling result of Fan's analyses: "Even with the powerful statistical test, only one or two items are identified as misfitting the two- and three-parameter IRT model. The results indicate that the data fit the two- and three-parameter IRT models exceptionally well" (Fan, 1988, p. 368). Or, should that be, the 2PL and 3PL models that were developed accounted for these data very well? Fan went on to report, "The fit of the data for the one-parameter model, however, is obviously very questionable, with about 30 percent of the items identified as misfitting the IRT model for either test." (Fan, 1988, p. 368). Then, according to our approach to the fit caveat, only about 70% of the items might be used to produce a Rasch measurement scale in which N correct would be the sufficient statistic. Fan continued, "Because there is obvious misfit between the data and the one parameter IRT model, and because the consequences of such misfit are not entirely clear (Hambleton et al., 1991), the results related to the one-parameter IRT model presented in later sections should be viewed with extreme caution" (Fan, 1988, p. 368). From our perspective, "[V]iewed with extreme caution" would be better written as "dismissed as irrelevant to evaluating the value of the Rasch model."

Given that the second and third item parameters (slope and guessing) are introduced into the 2PL and 3PL IRT models expressly for the purpose of reducing the variance not accounted for by the item difficulty parameter alone, we reasonably could expect (but do not always get) better fit of the 2PL and 3PL IRT models to the data. Let us not be equivocal about how proponents of the Rasch model, rather than the authority cited by Fan, above, regard the role of fit statistics in quality control of the measurement process: "Rasch models are the only laws of quantification that define objective measurement, determine what is measurable, decide which data are useful, and exposes which data are not" (Wright, 1999, p. 80). In other words, by this view, the results showing failure to fit the Rasch model should not merely be viewed with extreme caution, they should be dismissed out-of-hand for failing to meet the minimal standards required for measurement. Readers might wish to judge for themselves the extent to which Fan actually treated the Rasch results with extreme caution—but at the very minimum, unless the data for 30% of misfitting items are removed from the data analysis adopting the Rasch model the resultant Rasch versus IRT versus CTT comparisons remain misleading, invidious, or both.

And would you like an invariant interval level measurement scale with that? One along which both the person abilities and the item difficulties can be located simultaneously? Such that the estimation of item difficulties is independent of the distribution of the abilities of the persons in the sample and vice versa? Would you like inbuilt quality control techniques to estimate the precision of each location as well as the adherence of each person and item performance to the requirements for measurement?

CONSTRUCT VALIDITY

The foregoing discussion highlights another important issue for our consideration. The primacy of empirical data over the theoretical model in the sphere of measurement often is accompanied by a parallel regard for the primacy of data over substantive theory. This perspective has its philosophical roots in positivism, but often reveals itself in practice as short-sighted pragmatism. In this regard, Rasch practitioners often have been as guilty as any other. It frequently is the case that data have been collected in an undisciplined manner, using a poorly crafted instrument, and that Rasch measurement techniques are brought to bear on the assembled mess with the aim of making a silk purse out of a sow's ear. Although it has been possible to develop quite useful measurement outcomes from this technique, it does not capitalize on the role that Rasch measurement can and should play as a tool of construct validity. From Bond (2005): "Our research results ... (see Bond, 2001; Bond, 2003; Endler & Bond, 2001) convince me that the thoughtful application of Georg Rasch's models for measurement to a powerful substantive theory such as that of Jean Piaget can lead to high quality measurement in quite an efficient manner. No wonder I publicly and privately subscribe to the maxim of Piaget's chief *collaborateur*, Bärbel Inhelder,

"If you want to get ahead, get a theory."
—Karmiloff-Smith & Inhelder, 1975

In his American Psychological Association (APA) presentation, *Construct Validity: A Forgotten Concept in Psychology?*, Overton (1999) detailed the importance of Fisher's (1994) claim that the Rasch model is an instrument of construct validation. The term "construct validity," introduced by Cronbach and Meehl (1955) according to Overton, is the "extent to which [a] . . . test [or score] may be said to measure a theoretical construct or trait." Construct validation should serve to focus our "attention on the role of psychological [or other guiding] theory" (Anastasi & Urbina, 1997, p. 126).

Therefore, given some theoretical claim about a construct, the Rasch model permits the strong inference that the measured behaviors are expressions of that underlying construct. Even in the text quoted earlier, construct validity then becomes a comprehensive concept that includes the other types: content validity, face validity, concurrent validity, and so on (Messick, 1989, 1995). In the research world, where empirical data has primacy, the process of validating tests involves showing their concurrence with existing data collection devices. It is the process of induction that leads us from the data we have collected to the summary statements or explanations we can make about them (Overton, 1998a, 1999). A decade ago, Messick reminded us that "validation is empirical evaluation of the meaning and consequences of *measurement*" (1995, p. 747, emphasis added). But, acting as specialist reviewers for a broad range of journals, reveals that attention to construct validity is not as common as those involved in theory-driven enquiry might hope. It seems there is a whole approach to scale development which might be summarized thus: Poll a convenience-sample of subjects for whom the scale under development has some personal relevance. Construct a large set of self-report indicators based on the list derived from the sample. Trial this with a broader relevant sample and discard the items with poor Rasch measurement credentials. Then assert success at developing a "fundamental measure" of the condition under investigation.

The first edition of the current volume revealed that the Rasch–Messick link has been quite a rich source of ideas for those interested in the validity/measurement nexus (e.g., Fisher, 1994; Wilson, 1994). At the same time, Smith (2001) outlined a range of psychometric indicators of reliability and internal consistency from Rasch analysis in order to draw direct one-to-one correspondences between the eight facets of construct validity identified by Messick (1995) and inferences drawn directly from the theory and practice of Rasch measurement. The argument canvassed in Smith (2001) and Bond (2004) is that the Rasch measurement approach to the construction and monitoring of variables is directly amenable to the issues raised in Messick's broader conception of construct validity. Indeed, Rasch measurement instantiates an approach to assessment which can be described, borrowing Messick's own words, as a "comprehensive view of validity [which] integrates considerations of content, criteria, and consequences into a construct framework for empirically testing rational hypotheses about score meaning and utility" (Messick, 1995, p. 742; after Bond, 2004).

In the situation positing a substantive theory about human behavior, educational achievement, or post-trauma rehabilitation, the role of the investigator is to identify an appropriate construct or latent trait, and to use that construct as a guide in deciding which observable aspects of the human condition should be operationalized as part of a data collection device. The investigator's understanding of the construct will allow for the prediction of the measurement outcomes to a considerable extent. Given that the measurement of the construct is the first goal, the investigator will ensure that the test items, prompts, observational checklists, or the like, both validly represent the theoretical construct and meet the requirements for fundamental measurement.

Overton (1998a) used the *Drawing Hands* illustration of the famous graphic artist M. C. Escher to show the dialectical nature of the theory–practice interface. As the right hand draws the left, the left hand simultaneously draws the right. As theory tells the investigator how to go about the data collection process, the result of that process informs about theory. The process of construct validation works at the interface between the development of a data collection device and the empirical data so collected. Rasch measurement works hand in hand with the investigator to determine the extent to which the data actually measure the construct under examination.

THE RASCH MODEL AND PROGRESS OF SCIENCE

Michell (1999) asserted that it is the lack of attention to fundamental measurement in psychology that has hampered its development as a science during the 20th century. It is not the case, however, that the construction of measures will, in and of itself, pave the way for progress in the human sciences. Too often, those working in research methods, data analysis, and even Rasch measurement are called on to give advice after the data have been collected, sometimes even after the first few attempts at data analysis have failed. Instead of being involved in the research methodology and instrument design process from the very beginning, number crunchers often are called in at the last minute to advise a soon-to-graduate doctoral student on how to analyze and present the results of the data already collected. In another scenario, a colleague, an external contracting agency, or a professional licensing board rushes in to take last-minute advice on how to save a project that, on reflection, looks rather poorly conceived from the start.

These one-shot research projects, it seems, are going nowhere. They are designed merely to satisfy some course requirement or to fulfill some institutional reporting obligation or the like, and often are one-time research consultancies. We have Rasch measurement colleagues who insist that their non-negotiable requirement for becoming involved in such post hoc situations is that Rasch measurement techniques will be used to see what sort of measures can be constructed (salvaged?) from the assembled data. This is a well-grounded, but rather pragmatic, approach to the situation. Indeed, much of the advice given in the preceding chapters is quite applicable under these circumstances, which involve knowing how to make a silk purse out of a sow's ear.

However, where researchers have a long-term commitment to a substantive area of research with human subjects, in which they are consulted at the conceptualization of the project, the approach can be somewhat different. In these circumstances, wherein researchers intend for their work to have some impact in the area under investigation, their understanding of the substantive (theoretical) area can work hand in hand with the Rasch models of fundamental measurement toward progress in that area of human science. Whereas Michell (1999) castigated psychologists for their persistence in avoiding the scientific measurement imperative, Mauran (1998) warned us that although measurement might be a necessary condition for scientific investigation, without a substantive theoretical orientation, it will never be sufficient.

The contrast between the pragmatic use of the Rasch model and its incorporation at the very beginning of a research project became clear in the graduate measurement course we taught together in the College of Education at the University of Toledo. Most of our students had made considerable progress in doctoral programs. Some, in fact, were taking their last courses before writing and defending their dissertations. In the measurement course, they were required to demonstrate competency with appropriate use of Rasch analysis software, and to demonstrate sufficient understanding of Rasch measurement principles for drawing reasonable conclusions and inferences from the data they had analyzed. For those students considering their dissertation proposals, we urged each to look at one small but important area of understanding, and to work toward advancing the state of the field in that area.

For the measurement coursework assessment, any minimally satisfactory data set was fair game. As long as a modest-size item–person data matrix was available, Rasch modeling could be used to see the quality of the measures, if any, that could be constructed from the existing data. For the most part, practical considerations ruled while short timelines existed. For dissertation purposes, however, students started consulting us about how fundamental measurement principles could be built into projects they already had in mind, or how measures could be constructed in their particular fields of interest. Some students, of course, made the best of both worlds, using the measurement course assessment requirement as the trial for the investigative devices they were intending to develop in their doctoral research projects. In a stark over-simplification we could advise thus: If you merely want to finish your dissertation of fulfill the contractual obligations of your research funding, then whatever number-crunching appeals to you will often suffice. But, if you have a long-term commitment to your research topic; if you want to make a real difference; and if you are willing to undertake the iterations and reflection essential to the development of theory-driven measures, then choosing to use the Rasch model as your ideal for what measurement should be like in the human sciences is probably a very good start.

BACK TO THE BEGINNING AND BACK TO THE END

It was obvious to Ben Wright, in seeing some early presentations of Rasch measurement applied to Piagetian theory, that the apparent ease with which these developmentalists were able to develop a variety of data collection techniques to produce person and item measures, was, in part, because of their reliance on a broad, thoughtfully constructed developmental theory expressed in thousands of Piagetian chapters and journal articles. To the developmentalists, it seemed as though the chief strength of the Rasch approach to data analysis came primarily from the role that ordinality played in the construction of item and person measures. Indeed, for developmentalists, Guttman scaling held out a promise for developmental assessment that was only ever rarely satisfied in empirical practice (Kofsky, 1966). With hindsight, we can see that the key problem of the Guttman ordering for developmental studies was its deterministic or true-score nature. Clearly, the observation and recording of human performance is plagued by both systematic and random errors. A deterministic ordering model, like that of Guttman, has expectations that rarely can be met in empirical practice.

To developmentalists, the Rasch principles incorporate the attractive ordering features of the Guttman model and complement them with a more realistic probabilistic, or stochastic, framework. Indeed, this takes us back to the beginning work on this volume, which was intended to be a sort of self-help book for developmental and educational psychologists who were trying to make some measurement sense of their data. However, a confluence of originally quite diverse circumstances shows that the value of the Rasch model is not coincidental. Neither is it of benefit only to developmental and educational psychologists. The benefits to those who use Rasch modeling in constructing fundamental measures of some aspect of human existence derive from the model's expectation that good measurement should satisfy the axiomatic principles of conjoint measurement (Luce & Tukey, 1964).

It is clear from the work of Andrich (1988), Fisher (1994), Michell (1999), Perline, Wright, and Wainer (1979), and others that the axioms of conjoint measurement theory provide the only satisfactory prescription for scientific measurement and that, in terms of widespread application to the human sciences, Rasch measurement is the only game in town. In a brief but elegant American Educational Research Association paper, Karabatsos (1999a) succinctly summarized the axioms of conjoint measurement: where extensive measurement is achieved and when the requirements of transitivity, connectivity, monotonicity, restricted solvability, positivity, associativity, and the Archimedean condition are satisfied. As Karabatsos (1999a) concluded:

> The properties of extensive measurement are the logical rules underlying explicit physical measurement. Obviously, in situations where measurements are not directly observable, such as achievement or intelligence, the structures are not explicit. *But this does not mean that structure cannot be used to verify the measurement of latent traits.* The theory of additive con-

joint measurement makes fundamental measurement a possibility in the social sciences, where all observations are ordinal. Within the psychometrics framework, this theory proves that when the axioms of independence and double cancellation are satisfied, then the numbers assigned to persons and items represent a common linear (interval) style, measured on a single dimension. Furthermore, person measurement is independent of the items used, and item calibrations are independent of which persons they measure. (pp. 8–9)

By constructing a 5 × 7 conjoint matrix of Rasch-correct response probabilities based on an ordered set of five-person ability estimates and seven-item ability estimates, Karabatsos (1999a) was able to demonstrate the independence of items in relation to persons, arguing that such independence is a necessary condition for the double cancellation proof that is central to conjoint measurement. By demonstrating the double cancellation requirement for the set of correct response probabilities based on Rasch person and item estimates, Karabatsos was able to conclude that such independence, a basic requirement of measurement invariance, was the basic property of the Rasch measurement model.

However, it would be just as unexpected for any real data from the human sciences observation to satisfy the deterministic conjoint measurement axioms as it would be for them to attain a perfect Guttman structure. "However, because the axioms of additive conjoint measurement define measurement linearity, they should be considered as rules which data must statistically approximate" (Karabatsos, 1999a, p. 12).

Using simulated data to generate 100 4 × 4 conjoint matrices for each of the Rasch, two-parameter (2PL), and three-parameter (3PL) models, the theoretical probability values for each of the 300 matrices were checked for violations of the independence and double-cancellation axioms of conjoint measurement. Karabatsos (1999a) concluded:

There is strong support that almost 100% of the time, the parameters of the 2PL and 3PL violate interval scaling. On the other hand, the theoretical probabilities of Rasch models will always support a stable, interval scale structure. If the intention is to construct stable interval measurement, data should approximate uniform item-characteristic curves. The argument that 2 PL and 3 PL are advantageous because they are less restrictive alternatives to Rasch models (Hambleton & Swaminathan, 1985; van der Linden & Hambleton, 1997) does not recognize the connections between linear measurement requirements and uniform ICCs [Item Characteristic Curves] . . . This study is not needed to prove that Rasch models satisfy conjoint measurement axioms. However, it seems that the field of item response theory does not recognize the mathematical requirements of measurement. (p. 18)

The question that we called "fit" in the previous chapter could now be considered fruitfully in terms of the extent to which actual response probabilities in any Rasch-modeled data sets violate the conjoint measurement axioms. Details of the necessity and requirements of conjoint measurement are canvassed in several places (Cliff, 1992; Fisher, 1994; Michell, 1986, 1990, 1997, 1999; Narens & Luce, 1993).

CONCERNS OVER USING THE RASCH MODEL WITH REAL DATA

From the perspective taken in developing the arguments contained in this text, we are now in a much better position to react to concerns expressed about the use of the Rasch model in educational and other human science measurement spheres. These concerns are variously expressed, but the following concerns, based loosely around excerpts from a number of measurement discussion lists, will serve to illustrate. The first concern has its primacy in the role of test specifications in the assessment process. This concern goes something like this: It does not matter at all how well scored and how statistically sophisticated the results are, if the test is not valid, in the sense that it does not measure what it was intended to measure, it cannot be reliable. Moreover, in the final analysis, validity is determined by panels of experts in the subject area(s) being tested or by the final end users of whatever is being tested.

Furthermore, according to this concern, it follows that before we examine the fit of test items to the Rasch model, we should first examine the fit of the Rasch model to the test framework. It is obvious that in the case of many assessment devices, the construct the test is supposed to assess is multidimensional. For example, nearly all mandated state education assessments in writing and mathematics reflect multidimensional constructs. From this viewpoint, the candidates and the items or tasks are supposed to involve more than a single dimension, and sometimes more than a small number of dimensions. The same can be said of tests in many other domains such as medical licensure and professional certification testing.

The perception is that test developers then "fit a Rasch model to the test data" from the apparently multidimensional assessment specification and promptly delete the items that do not fit the model. The claimed result is that test developers, wedded to the Rasch model, have sacrificed content validity in favor of the Rasch model requirement, because the original argument for content validity was based on the test framework, and the internal structure of the test no longer reflects the test framework. The consequence is held to be a set of scale scores with wonderful technical properties but no validity.

Under any circumstances, we should always be concerned about the applicability of Rasch measurement to the rich concerns of school achievement or any other human attribute. However, following up on the school achievement thread for simplicity, whenever we make a decision either to measure and compare the achievement levels of different individuals in a particular area of school achievement, or to measure and monitor any individual's growth or development in an area of school achievement over time, we already have made the main assumption of Rasch measurement. Not only that, but we also have placed ourselves in a situation wherein a method for testing and validating this Rasch measurement assumption is essential.

When researchers, examination boards, licensing authorities, rehabilitation specialists, survey analysts, and so forth, summarize any human attribute in a single score, they always face a risk of being misled if the data collection and analysis process is not supervised by a unidimensional measurement model capable of identifying threats to meaningful comparison, and perhaps the need for augmentation by some qualifying descriptive data.

Such supervision is especially important if comparisons are to be made across different instruments, which explains why serious attempts to measure, say, school achievement (e.g., the Program for International Student Assessment) insistently specify such a model (G. N. Masters, personal communication, January 26, 2000: posting to the Rasch measurement electronic forum [rasch@acer.edu.au]).

One of the distinct pleasures of writing a volume such as this, or of developing widely used software as WINSTEPS, is the consequent invitations to conduct introductory Rasch measurement workshops or to speak to measurement–oriented colleagues at professional meetings. That often involves fielding questions about the Rasch model and, more particularly, fielding the objections that colleagues have about Rasch measurement and the claims of its proponents. WINSTEPS developer Mike Linacre reports that, in his lengthy experience, the objections to the Rasch model could be regarding as falling into three rather neat categories:

1. The Rasch model doesn't have the theoretical properties that it is claimed to have;
2. The Rasch model has those properties, but is an idealization that cannot work in the real world; and
3. The Rasch model might work sometimes in the real world, but it won't/can't work for my data.

The first of these, that the Rasch model doesn't have the claimed theoretical properties, is often the result of a misunderstanding. The actual claim is that Rasch person and item estimates are forced to be linear and interval by the Rasch model. But the mathematical properties of Rasch estimates can be seen to parallel those of the three sides of Pythagorean right-angled triangles (Fisher, 1998). The values in each case (Rasch estimates and lengths of sides) are computed according to certain rules (those of Rasch and Pythagoras) , and so the calculated values *must* meet the requirements set out in those rules. The following reflection is apt at this point:

So far as the laws of mathematics refer to reality, they are not certain. And so far as they are certain, they do not refer to reality.
—Albert Einstein, *Geometry and Experience*

Perhaps, even a sentence from recent literature might be allowed:

Though there never was a circle or triangle in nature, the truths demonstrated by Euclid would for ever retain their certainty and evidence.
—Monica Ali, *Brick Lane,* 2003

The second objection accepts that Rasch estimates are linear, but what remains open to dispute is how well those Rasch estimates actually represent the empirical data from which they were calculated. This strikes to the very heart of the scientific endeavour, because, as in all science, there is a mismatch between theoretical results and empirical data. Linacre often responds at this point with his favorite quote,

> Science does not, so far as we know, produce theories which are true or even highly probable. Although rare, it sometimes happens that a theory exactly predicts an experimental outcome. When that desirable result is achieved, there is cause for general rejoicing. It is far more common for the predictions deduced from a theory to come close to reproducing the data which constitute a specific problem, but with no exact coincidence of results.
>
> Empirical problems are frequently solved because, for problem solving purposes, we do not require an exact, but only an approximate, resemblance between theoretical results and experimental ones. (Laudan, 1997, pp. 23–24).

Finally, although the admission that these two objections don't hold might be secured, the final is often more personal. Even if it is couched as the Rasch model will not work for all data, that is often masking a more personal claim: that the Rasch model will not work for *my* data. Granted; but if the Rasch model won't work for your data, then neither will raw scores! This is because the Rasch model can be derived from the requirement that raw scores (N) be the sufficient statistic for linear estimation.

> . . . *for anyone who claims skepticism about "the assumption" of the Rasch model, those who use unweighted scores are, however unwittingly, counting on the Rasch model to see them through. Whether this is useful in practice is a question not for more theorizing, but for empirical study.*

—Ben D. Wright (1977)
Misunderstanding the Rasch model.
Journal for the Educational
Measurement, 14(2), 97–116.

APPENDIX A

Technical Aspects of the Rasch Model

RASCH FAMILY OF MODELS

Dichotomous Model

Georg Rasch developed a mathematical model for constructing measures based on a probabilistic relation between any item's difficulty and any person's ability. He argued that the difference between these two measures should govern the probability of any person being successful on any particular item. The basic logic is simple: all persons have a higher probability of correctly answering easier items and a lower probability of correctly answering more difficult items. For example, the simplest member of the Rasch family of models, the dichotomous model, predicts the conditional probability of a binary outcome (correct/incorrect), given the person's ability and the item's difficulty. If correct answers are coded as 1 and incorrect answers are coded as 0, the model then expresses the probability of obtaining a correct answer (1 rather than 0) as a function of the *size* of the difference between the ability (B) of the person *(n)* and the difficulty (D) of the item *(i)*.

The starting point for creating measures begins with a calculation of the percentage correct for each person (the number of items successfully answered divided by the total number of items) and each item (the number of persons successfully passing the item divided by the total number of persons) when the test is administered to an appropriate sample. These raw score totals are ordinal level data, yet they are both necessary and sufficient for estimating person ability (B_n) and item difficulty (D_i) measures as shown by Andersen (1973), Douglas and Wright (1986), and Wright and Douglas (1986).

The first step in estimating B_n (the ability measure of person *n*) is to convert the raw score percentage into odds of success, which are estimated by calculating the ratio of each person's percentage correct *(p)* over the percentage incorrect $(1 - p)$. For example, a raw score of 40% correct is divided by the percentage incorrect $(1 - p)$, that is, 60%, to obtain the ratio 40/60. The natural log of these odds (ln 40/60 = -0.4) then becomes the person ability estimate. The procedure is exactly the same for items, estimating D_i, (the difficulty measure of item i) that is, dividing the percentage of people who answered the item correctly by the percentage of people who answered the item incorrectly and taking natural the log of that value.

These item difficulty (D_i) and person ability (B_n) estimates then are expressed on a scale of log odd ratios, or logits. The average logit is arbitrarily set at 0, with positive logits indicating higher than average probabilities and negative logits indicating lower than average probabilities. The Rasch model calculations usually begin by ignoring, or constraining, person estimates, calculating item estimates, and then using that first round of item estimates to produce a first round of person estimates. The first round of estimates are then iterated against each other to produce a parsimonious and internally consistent set of item and person parameters, so that the B–D values will produce the Rasch probabilities of success described more fully later. The iteration process is said to converge when the maximum difference in item and person values during successive iterations meets a preset convergence value. This transformation turns ordinal level data (i.e., correct/incorrect responses) into interval-level data for both persons and items, thereby converting descriptive, sample dependent data into inferential measures based on probabilistic functions.

Once we have estimated ability (B_n) and difficulty (D_i), the probability of correctly answering an item can be expressed mathematically as the general statement:

$$P_{ni}(x = 1) = f(B_n - D_i) \tag{1}$$

where P_n is the probability, x is any given score, and 1 is a correct response. This equation therefore states that the probability (P_n) of Person n getting a score (x) of 1 on a given item (i) is a function (f) of the difference between a person's ability (B_n) and an item's difficulty (D_i).

By using the Greek symbols commonly used in statistics to indicate the parameters being estimated as opposed to the values calculated, the formula is expressed as follows:

$$\pi_{ni}(x_{ni} = 1) = f(\beta \pi_n - \delta_i) \tag{2}$$

where π (pi) represents response probability, β (beta) denotes person ability, and δ (delta) stands for item difficulty.

Given B_n and D_i, we then can expand upon Equation 1 to demonstrate that the function (f) expressing the probability of a successful response consists of a natural logarithmic transformation of the person (B_n) and item (D_i) estimates. This relationship can be expressed mathematically as follows:

$$P_{ni}(x_{ni} = 1/B_n, D_i) = \frac{e^{(B_n - D_i)}}{1 + e^{(B_n - D_i)}} \tag{3}$$

where P_{ni} ($x_{ni} = 1/B_n$, D_i) is the probability of person n on Item i scoring a correct ($x = 1$) response rather than an incorrect ($x = 0$) one, given person ability (B_n) and item difficulty (D_i). This probability is equal to the constant e, or natural log function (2.7183) raised to the difference between a person's ability and an item's difficulty ($B_n - D_i$), and then divided by 1 plus this same value. Therefore, for example, if a person's ability is estimated at 3 logits and the difficulty of the item at 1 logit, then

$$P_{ni}(x = 1/B(3), D(1)) = \frac{2.7183^{(3-1)}}{1+2.7183^{(3-1)}} = \frac{2.7183^2}{1+2.7183^2} = 0.88 \qquad (3.1)$$

and the person has an 88 % chance of successfully passing the item.

If that same person ($B = 3$) were given an item with a difficulty estimate of 2 logits ($D = 2$), the expected probability of correctly answering that item would necessarily be lower than 0.88:

$$P_{ni}(x = 1/B(3), D(2)) = \frac{2.7183^{(3-2)}}{1+2.7183^{(3-2)}} = \frac{2.7183^1}{1+2.7183^1} = 0.73 \qquad (3.2)$$

(i.e., the probability would be 73%).

By following the same procedure in Equations 3.1 and 3.2, we can see how an item perfectly targeted for that person, (i.e., an item with a difficulty estimate [e.g., $D = 3$] equal to the ability estimate of the person [$B = 3$]), results in a 50/50 chance of that person successfully passing that item:

$$P_{ni}(x = 1/B(3), D(3)) = \frac{2.7183^{(3-3)}}{1+2.7183^{(3-3)}} = \frac{2.7183^0}{1+2.7183^0} = 0.50 \qquad (3.3)$$

Similarly, encountering a more difficult item (e.g., $D = 4$) would result in a less than 50/50 chance of passing:

$$P_{ni}(x = 1/B(3), D(4)) = \frac{2.7183^{(3-4)}}{1+2.7183^{(3-4)}} = \frac{2.7183^{-1}}{1+21.7183^{-1}} = 0.27 \qquad (3.4)$$

Table A.1 shows the probabilities of passing an item for a variety of difference values between B_n and D_i. If the values in the ability – difficulty ($B_n - D_i$) column are placed in Equation 3, the probabilities of success will match the $P_{ni}(x = 1)$ column in Table A.1. Note that when item difficulties are greater than person abilities (negative $B_n - D_i$ values), persons have a lower than 50% probability of correctly answering the item. Likewise, when item difficulties are lower than person abilities (positive $B_n - D_i$ values), persons have a higher than 50% probability of correctly answering the item.

Parameter Separation

Parameter separation implies that one set of parameters (e.g., the items) can be estimated without knowing the values for the other set (e.g., the persons). This is

TABLE A.1
Probability of Agreeing With an Item
for Various Differences Between Item Difficulty
and Person Ability

$B_n - D_i$	$P_{ni}(x = 1)$
−3.0	0.05
−2.5	0.08
−2.0	0.12
−1.5	0.18
−1.0	0.27
−0.5	0.38
0.0	0.50
+0.5	0.62
+1.0	0.73
+1.5	0.82
+2.0	0.88
+2.5	0.92
+3.0	0.95

taken advantage of in the estimation procedure known as Conditional Maximum Likelihood Estimation. To demonstrate the calculation of the relationship between the abilities of two persons (i.e., B_n and B_m) independent of the actual difficulty value for an item (D_i):
Now

$$B_n - D_i \cong \log (F_{ni}/F_{in})$$ where F_{ni} is the count of successes by Person n on Item i; and

$$B_m \cong D_i \cong \log(F_{mi}/F_{im})$$

so

$$B_n\text{-}B_m \cong \log(F_{ni}/F_{in}) - \log(F_{mi}/F_{im}) \qquad (4)$$

So that the relationship between B_n and B_m can be estimated without knowledge of the difficulty of Item i.

The ability of the Rasch model to compare persons and items directly means that we have created person free measures and item free calibrations, as we have come to expect in the physical sciences, abstract measures that transcend specific persons' responses to specific items at a specific time. This characteristic, unique to the Rasch model, is called *parameter separation*. Thus, Rasch measures represent a person's ability as independent of the specific test items, and item difficulty as independent of specific samples within standard error estimates. Parameter separation holds for the entire family of Rasch models.

Rating Scale Model

The rating scale model is an extension of the dichotomous model to the case in which items have more than two response categories (e.g., Likert scales). For example, if an item has four response choices (0 = strongly disagree, 1 = disagree, 2 = agree, 3 = strongly agree), it is modeled as having three thresholds. Each item threshold (k) has its own difficulty estimate (F), and this estimate is modeled as the threshold at which a person has a 50/50 chance of choosing one category over another. The first threshold, for example, is modeled as the probability of choosing a response of 1 (disagree) instead of a response of 0 (strongly disagree), and is estimated with the following formula:

$$P_{ni1}(x = 1/B_n, D_i, F_1) = \frac{e^{(B-[D_i+F_1])}}{1+e^{(B-[D_i+F_1])}} \tag{5}$$

where P_{ni1} is the probability of person n choosing "disagree" (Category 1) over "strongly disagree" (Category 0) on any item (i). In this equation, F_1 is the difficulty of the first threshold, and this difficulty calibration is estimated only once for this threshold across the entire set of items in the rating scale. The threshold difficulty F_1 is added to the item difficulty D_i (i.e., $D_i + F_1$) to indicate the difficulty of Threshold 1 on Item i. Given that $B_n-(D_i + F_1)$, has the same value as $B_n- D_i - F_1$, and helps to show more easily the shared bases of the Rasch models, the latter is used in the following explanations of the rating scale model.

Modeling subsequent thresholds in the rating scale follows the same logic. The difficulty of endorsing Category 2 (agree) instead of Category 1 (disagree) is modeled as follows:

$$P_{ni2}(x = 2/B_n, D_i, F_2) = \frac{e^{(B_n-D_i-F_2)}}{1+e^{(B_n-D_i-F_2)}} \tag{6}$$

where B_n is the person ability, D_i is the difficulty of the entire item, and F_2 is the difficulty of the second threshold, estimated across all items. Thus, the general form of the rating scale model expresses the probability of any person choosing any given category on any item as a function of the agreeability of the Person n (B_n) and the endorsability of the entire Item i (D_i) at the given Threshold k (F_k) (Wright & Masters, 1982).

$$P_{nik} = \frac{e^{(B_n-D_i-F_k)}}{1+e^{(B_n-D_i-F_k)}} \tag{7}$$

Furthermore, if these probabilities are converted to odds, parameter separation can be demonstrated for the rating scale model as well:

$$\ln\left(\frac{P_{nik}}{1-P_{nik}}\right) = B_n - D_i - F_k \tag{8}$$

By using the Greek symbols commonly used in statistics to indicate the parameters estimated (as opposed to the values calculated), the formula is expressed as:

$$\ln\left(\frac{\pi_{nik}}{1-\pi_{nik}}\right) = \beta_n - \delta_i - \tau_k \tag{9}$$

where β_n is the person ability, δ_i is the item difficulty and τk is the difficulty of the kth threshold.

The thresholds for a set of rating scale items can be depicted as the intersection of item probabilitiy curves for each response option (see Fig. A.1). Figure A.1 shows F_1 as the threshold for choosing Category 1 over Category 0, F_2 as the threshold for choosing 2 over 1, and F_3 as the threshold for choosing 3 over 2. The x-axis expresses the difference between person ability (B_n) and item difficulty (D_i). So, for example, a person whose agreeability is 3 logits lower than the endorsability of the item as a whole ($B_n - D_i = -3$), has a greater than 80% chance of choosing Category 0. If, however, a person's agreeability is, for example, 3 logits higher than the endorsability of the item ($B_n - D_i = 3$), Category 3 is clearly the one most likely to be endorsed.

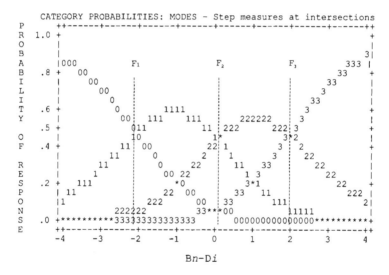

Figure A.1. Category probabilitycurves for a rating scale item with three thresholds.

Partial Credit Model

The partial credit model can be seen as a version of the rating scale model in which the threshold estimates, including the number of thresholds are not constrained, that is, they are free to vary from item to item. When the partial credit model is used to model rating scale data, it allows each item to vary in its threshold estimates. Whereas the rating scale model used one set of threshold estimates that applies to the entire set of items (an example was depicted in Fig. A.1), the partial credit model provides a set of individual threshold (k) estimates for each item (i):

$$\ln\left(\frac{P_{nik}}{1-P_{nik}}\right) = B_n - D_{ik} \tag{10}$$

Therefore, the D_{ik} replaces the ($D_i + F_k$) from Equation 8, signifying that in the partial credit model, each set of threshold estimates is unique to its own individual item (i.e., Threshold k for Item i), instead of being estimated as a separate set of threshold estimates (F_k) for the entire set of items.

The partial credit model allows not only for an Empirical test of whether the distances between response categories are constant for each item, but, more importantly, it allows the option for each item to vary in its number of response categories. A test or survey, for example, could comprise a mix of response formats, with some questions having two response options, some five, and some seven. This model could be ideal for situations in which partial marks are awarded for answers such as essay examinations.

Many-Facets Rasch Model

The many-facets Rasch model adds yet more flexibility for estimating fundamental aspects of the measurement process. If we can imagine another aspect of the testing process (in addition to person ability and item difficulty) that might systematically influence persons' scores, for example, individual raters, specific tasks within an item, time of day the test is given, and method of testing (paper and pencil versus computer), we can estimate the impact of that facet on the measurement process. A difficulty estimate for each facet is calibrated, for example, the severity (C), of Rater j. This severity is considered in the probability estimate of any person (n) responding to any item (i) for any category threshold (k), for any rater (j):

$$P_{nikj} = \frac{e^{(B_n - D_i - F_k - C_j)}}{1 + e^{(B_n - D_i - F_k - C_j)}} \tag{11}$$

and is a function of the ability of the person (B_n), the difficulty of the item (D_i), the difficulty of the threshold (F_k), and the severity of the rater (C_j).

This model adheres to the principles of parameter additivity:

$$\ln\left(\frac{P_{nikj}}{1-P_{nikj}}\right) = B_n - D_i - F_k - C_j \tag{12}$$

The symbols for the Rasch family of models are summarized in Table A.2.

TABLE A.2
Notation for the Rasch Family of Models

Values Calculated	Parameter Estimated	Definition
B	β (beta)	Person ability/measure
D	δ (delta)	Item difficulty/calibration
F	τ (tau)	Category threshold/calibration
C	λ (lambda)	Facet difficulty
P	π (pi)	Probability
n		Person
i		Item
k		Threshold
j		Facet
x		Response

RASCH MODEL ASSESSMENT

Reliability Indexes

In the Rasch model, reliability is estimated both for persons and for items. The *person separation reliability* (R_P, Wright & Masters, 1982) is an estimate of how well one can differentiate persons on the measured variable. That is, it estimates the replicability of person placement across other items measuring the same construct. The estimate is based on the same concept as Cronbach's alpha. That is, it is the fraction of observed response variance that is reproducible:

$$R_P = \frac{SA_P^2}{SD_P^2} \tag{13}$$

The denominator (SD_P^2) represents total person variability, that is, how much people differ on the measure of interest. The numerator (SA_P^2) represents the reproducible part of this variability (i.e., the amount of variance that can be reproduced by Rasch model). This amount of variance that is reproducible with the Rasch model is called the *adjusted person variability* (SA_P^2). The adjusted person variability is obtained by subtracting error variance from total variance ($SD_P^2 - SE_P^2 = SA_P^2$). This reproducible part then is divided by the total person variability (SD_P^2) to obtain a reliability estimate for persons (R_P), with values ranging between 0 and 1 (Wright & Masters, 1982).

An alternative index for estimating the spread of persons on the measured variable is the *person separation index* (G_P). This is estimated as the adjusted person standard deviation (SA_P) divided by the average measurement error (SE_P), where measurement error is defined as that part of the total variance that is not accounted for by the Rasch model:

$$G_P = \frac{SA_P}{SE_P} \qquad (14)$$

Thus person reliability is expressed in standard error units (Wright & Masters, 1982, p. 92). Reliability is estimated in the same manner as for persons, with item variance being substituted for person variance:

$$G_I = \frac{SA_I}{SE_I} \qquad (15)$$

Fit Statistics

Because the Rasch model is a strict mathematical expression of the theoretical relation that would hold between all items and all persons along a single underlying continuum, no items and persons will ever fit the model perfectly. We are interested, however, in identifying those items and persons whose patterns of responses deviate more than expectation, resulting in fit statistics for all persons and all items in the data matrix.

The estimation of fit begins with the calculation of a response residual (y_{ni}) for each Person n when each Item i is encountered. That is, how far does the actual response (x_{ni}) deviate from Rasch model expectations (E_{ni}) (Wright & Masters, 1982)?

$$y_{ni} = x_{ni} - E_{ni} \qquad (16)$$

Because there are too many person–item deviations, or residuals (y_{ni}), to examine in one matrix, the fit diagnosis typically is summarized in a fit statistic, expressed either as a mean square fit statistic or a standardized fit statistic, usually a z or t distribution. Additionally, these two fit statistics are categorized further into (a) those that have more emphasis on unexpected responses far from a person's or item's measure (outfit statistics), and (b) those that place more emphasis on unexpected responses near a person's or item's measure (infit statistics).

The outfit statistic is simply an average of the standardized residual (Z_{ni}) variance, across both persons and items. This average is unweighted. That is, it is not influenced by (multiplied by) any other information. This results in an estimate that gives relatively more impact to unexpected responses far from a person's or item's measure (Wright & Masters, 1982):

$$\text{outfit} = \frac{\Sigma Z_{ni}^2}{N} \qquad (17)$$

The infit statistic, on the other hand, is a weighted standardized residual, in which relatively more impact is given to unexpected responses close to a person or item's measure. Residuals are weighted by their individual variance (W_{ni}) to lessen the impact of unexpected responses far from the measure:

$$\text{infit} = \frac{\Sigma Z_{ni}^2 W_{ni}}{\Sigma W_{ni}} \tag{18}$$

When these infit and outfit values are distributed as mean squares, their expected value is 1. Guidelines for determining unacceptable departures from expectation include flagging items or persons as misfits when mean square infit or outfit values are larger than 1.3 for samples less than 500, 1.2 for samples between 500 and 1000, and 1.1 for samples larger than 1000 (Smith, Schumacker, & Bush, 1998).

When reported simply as standardized t values, the fit statistics have an expected mean of 0 and a standard deviation of 1. Here the recommended cutoff for flagging misfits includes t values outside of ± 2.0 (Smith, 1992).

The four types of fit statistics (mean square, t, infit, outfit) can be used separately or in combination for making fit decisions. Generally speaking, more emphasis is placed on infit values than on outfit values in identifying misfitting persons or items. The issues surrounding the estimation and interpretation of misfit are more thoroughly canvassed in chapter 12. Table A.3 provides a summary of symbols and definitions for the model assessment formulas.

TABLE A.3
Notation and Definition for Model Assessment

Notation	Definition
R_P	Person reliability index; bound by 0 and 1
SA_P^2	Person variance, adjusted for measurement error
SD_P^2	Person variance, unadjusted
SE_P	Standard error for persons
SA_P	Standard error for persons, adjusted for measurement error
G_P	Person separation index; in standard error units
R_I	Item reliability index; bound by 0 and 1
SA_I^2	Item variance, adjusted for measurement error
SD_I^2	Item variance, unadjusted
SE_I	Standard error for items
SA_I	Standard error for items, adjusted for measurement error
G_I	Item separation index; in standard error units
y	residual
x	Observed score
E	Expected score from the Rasch model
Z_{ni}	Standardized residual for each person on each item
W_{ni}	Variance for an individual across a given item

APPENDIX B

Getting Started

While many of our readers of the first edition told us that they found themselves off to a good start for understanding and applying Rasch analysis to their own data, some of our more experienced colleagues advised us to give our readers more detail about how actually to get started on that process. The steps are rather simple when one sits down with the owner of the data. A few checks to see that the data file is ready to run. Perform the analysis. After a quick flick through a few data tables to make sure we're talking about good output, we pull up the variable map, the Wright map we have used in almost every chapter to summarize how the data have performed under the scrutiny of the Rasch model. Invariably it is the representation of the item and person performances along the same unidimensional continuum that attracts the most interest. Then follow the questions: What's Item x? Should it be the easiest? Why would Item y be so much harder than all the others? Items w, x, and z all locate in the same place—is that right? Why? And is Person A really the smartest of all these kids on this test? So much smarter than all the others? Really? Why's that? And this group of respondents here, does it make sense for them all to be estimated at the same ability level? Did you think that your test would be too easy/difficult for this sample? Why's that? Looks like we need some more children (items) that are less/more able (difficult) than the children (items) you have in this data set? Is that possible? Why/not? Why's that?

DATA INPUT

One of the essentials for getting started is constructing the data file. One carry-over from mainframe computing days has been a tendency, at least in early iterations of Rasch software, to allocate single data rows to individual cases and single data columns to individual items. In those times, data were read in from punch cards or magnetic tapes or large floppy discs, but in essence each data set was a rectangular text (or ASCII) file—cases horizontally and items vertically – with each cell containing just one ascii character. The data files we provide on the accompanying CD for the analyses contained in chapters 3 to 7 follow these same requirements. All of the data files in those chapters were typed one character at a time by the researcher into word processor files. The data files were saved as text-only files with .txt or .dat as the file extension. Here is that segment of the data file from the BLOT analysis in chapter 4, again: rows = cases; columns = items (no ID and no empty cells in that file). That's the simple way to begin.

```
11111111110110101101011111111011111
11111111111111111111111111101111111
11010111111111011111011111101011111
11111111111111111111101111111111111
11111111111101111111011111111111111
11111111111110111101011111111111111
11111111111101111111011111111111111
11111111111111111111111111101011111
11111111111111111111111101111111111
11011111011111011111011111000110111
11111110111111111111011011111101111
11111110111111111111111111101001111
11111111111111011111010111101111111
11111111111110111110111111111111111
11111111111110111110111111111111111
11111111111110111111011111101110111
etc.
```

Many researchers now use spreadsheets (e.g., Excel) or other statistics packages (e.g., SPSS) for setting up data files or they want to use parts of such files (say from a larger data set) to start the Rasch analysis process. If you use Quest, then you must export the data or do a "Save as" in a text-only file format; WINSTEPS, for example, can now handle Excel and SPSS data files directly. While leaving a space in a .txt file is no problem, exporting an .xls file with blanks to .txt format will often result in the blanks going missing; the data file conflating and the item columns losing their meaning (i.e., item data in the wrong columns). Here are a few guidelines to help avoid that sort of problem:

1. Don't leave blank cells at all. While many use "9" as a code for missing data now, in the future you might need "9" as valid in a RSM or PCM analysis. So, use "X" for missing; "M" for multiple responses or other invalid response codes (ticked two response boxes, or response made but unscorable); "0—zero (not "O"—"oh") for incorrect or the lowest valid response value. So, 0–9 (numeric) codes for valid responses and a–z (alphabetic) codes for invalid responses.
2. Use a nonproportional (i.e., fixed pitch) font such as Courier for the .txt file, so data columns remain in line. A check of the row length well help to confirm the integrity of the data row for each case.

With a little practice and concentration it is possible to scan thousands and thousands of cases in a data.txt file by fast scrolling and watching the vertical columns and the row lengths flash by. A few minutes of tedium now can save hours of frustration later.

SOFTWARE

Each of the major software packages for Rasch analysis has its adherents, and some are just as passionate about a particular software package as we are about the Rasch model itself. We cannot respond to those who emailed or approached us at meetings to help them out by writing more user-friendly manuals for those packages. But beginners often have the same difficulty "getting into" a new Rasch software package as they had getting started in understanding Rasch measurement in the first place. Of course, we have passed on readers' comments to our colleagues involved in Rasch software development. Reactions vary from, "Just show us how to say it/do it better, and we'll fix it." to "You really have a problem if you can't understand/use/appreciate our procedures. Our very satisfied users cannot be wrong." Beginners should not be too concerned, however, if they don't get the point. Many experienced Rasch analysts have left software demonstrations, workshops, or presentations scratching their heads, muttering, "What was that all about? I didn't understand a thing." So instead of trying to be all things to all Rasch analysts, we have restricted this introduction to one piece of Rasch software: Bond&FoxSteps, a full size version of WINSTEPS, is provided free-of-charge on the CD that came with this volume. The choice of software for this purpose has been made very easy for us. As we mentioned in the foreword, Mike Linacre, WINSTEPS developer, has been very proactive in collaborating with us: Just months after the first edition of this volume was released, WINSTEPS contained the option of item data output in the form of the variable pathway that we had just introduced.

WINSTEPS installation instructions are included on the CD; so install it now on your PC if you do not already own a full copy of the program. (This version contains the full-size software and will handle all the data in the enclosed files. Mike's free student-version download, Ministeps, has data restrictions, so it does not allow all the BLOT items or all the CAIN cases to be run at once.) Most WINSTEPS functions perform very well on a Mac platform running Virtual PC. Please copy the data files we have provided for your practice onto your hard drive as well. The Facets folder, containing a free copy of Minifacs and the data file for the Guilford many-facets analysis from chapter 8 can wait until later if you like. Follow the ReadMe.txt file for the latest instructions.

FIRST ANALYSIS

We are going to take you through the first analysis and interpretation steps that we might use with a newcomer and new data set. Once you've worked through this, you should be able to repeat the steps with your own file for dichotomous data. If you open the BLOT instructions file (BLOTinst.doc) that you copied from the CD, you will find details of how to enter the BLOT.txt data into WINSTEPS:

Follow the instructions:

```
Highlight with your mouse from here >
Title = "B&F BLOT data: 35 items"
...
156 0110111001110011010101100110101100101
158 1100110111110111011111100110101111111
< to here. Then Copy.


Start WINSTEPS.
Do not answer the "Control File Name?" question.
Go immediately to "Edit" pull-down menu.
Click on "Edit/Create File with WordPad"
WordPad screen opens.
"Paste Special" as "Unformatted Text" what you just
copied above.

It should look exactly like the block in the instruction
file.
"Save as"
Go to the C:\WINSTEPS directory
File Name: BLOT.txt
Save as type: Text document
"Save"
You are about to save the document in a Text-Only format
..."
Click "Yes"

Click on Ministep or WINSTEPS on the bottom of your
screen
"Control File Name?" displays.
Press the Enter key
Find BLOT.txt in the file list.
Click on it.
Click "Open"

"Report output file name ..."
Press the Enter key

"Extra specifications ..."
Press the Enter key

WINSTEPS runs.
WINSTEPS reports "Measures constructed"
```

OUTPUT

WINSTEPS provides output in close to one gazillion tables and figures and has the option of producing journal quality graphs for many of the crucial figures. The downside of this provision is that beginners can be left wondering where to look to get the basic crucial information to determine whether the analysis was successfully executed and how well the data stood up to the scrutiny of the Rasch model

WHAT TO LOOK FOR

Throughout this book we have emphasized two crucial and interrelated aspects of the Rasch approach to genuine scientific measurement: "How much?" and, "How good?" The question, "How much was measured?" focuses on the estimates of person ability and item difficulty (and their associated measurement errors). The question of "How well was it measured?" points in the direction of the fit indicators that we use for quality control. So the very simple version is: good Rasch estimates + good fit statistics = good measurement. So while we might look at the Rasch output maps and tables one by one, it's the interrelationships between all the components that will help make decision whether any attempt at measurement is good enough for its intended purpose. So when we look at estimates, we keep fit in the back of our minds; when we look at fit, we know that the estimates must be where we need them to be.

WHERE TO LOOK

In this Bond&FoxSteps version of the WINSTEPS Rasch analysis software, we have greyed out the parts of the pull-down menus that we think are of more direct benefit to experienced users in order to focus your attention on the more crucial aspects of the output. Experience at workshops suggests that some new users get so carried away with all the different aspects of the program output that they find it hard to decide which bits really matter. This might not be as important when you are just looking over someone else's data, but a bit distracting when you really want to know whether your own data are good enough.

THE PATHWAY MAP

This gives the quickest possible summary of how the test performed (i.e. item information but no person information). In response to participants who turned up at WINSTEPS workshops armed with Bond and Fox (2001), Linacre developed the "Bubble Chart" in the "Plots" menu to report the basic item indicators in the form of the pathway introduced in the first edition. So,

```
Click on the "PLOTS" pull-down menu
Click on "Bubble Chart". The Dialog Box displays. Tick
Items (not Persons); Measures vertically; Infit;
Standardized. OK. Data point label= Entry Number. The Excel
graph displays as a Pathway.
```

The items are in measure-order along the pathway, and they spread across the pathway in the Infit Standardized central column.

INTERPRETATION

In answer to the questions about how much was measured and how well was it measured, the pathway map gives the following summary: Most of the 35 items fall on the pathway, so it seems like this "quality control" aspect of item performance is satisfactory. Performance on Item 21 is a bit too erratic (off the pathway to the right) and so is Item 30; two erratic items out of 35 isn't so bad. So, the item locations (how much) might be worth taking seriously; their fit seems ok at first glance. Thirty-five locations are calibrated with a default mean difficulty set at 0.0. Although from top to bottom they cover more than four logits, most of them are located within a band of just over two logits, spread around the zero origin. A more even spread of item locations from top to bottom would have been better: (a) to fill up the holes in the variable and (b) to reduce the number of items where the test seems to have more than enough.

THE WRIGHT MAP

```
Clicking on "12. ITEM Map" in the Output Tables pull-down
menu displays the Wright map.
```

Here the "How much?" question is answered more completely: on the right hand side of the variable map, the items are located against the logit scale in the same locations as found in the pathway map, but the locations of person performances tells us something about the existence of this ability in the sample of high school children who faced the test. They are represented by the numbers on the left hand side of the map. Each number represents 2 students on this map. They are nicely spread out over about 6 logits with more students towards the top of the map and a bit of a tail towards the bottom. By looking at the person distribution against the item distribution we learn more about the item–person relationships in relation to the underlying variable. Most of the persons are located opposite the items—so they seem well targeted by these items. However, there is a sizable group of person locations above the hardest item (21)—the test can't tell much about students with that much ability. Thus, this test will work better with kids who are less able than those at the top of the Wright map.

THE ITEM STATISTICS TABLE

This table summarizes the information provided for each item in the test. The how much question is answered by looking at the "MEASURE" column where item difficulty estimates are located and column "S.E." where the precision of the estimate is indicated by its error term.

```
Still in the "Output Tables" pull-down menu, click on
"14. ITEM Entry".
```

In order to interpret the item fit statistics, Bond&FoxSteps uses ZSTD, which corresponds to t. ZSTD means "Standardized like a z-statistic". For the practical purpose of monitoring fit in these output, t and z statistics are equivalent. "Table 14:Item Entry" gives the item information in the order the questions are on the test, 1–35. There is a one-to-one correspondence between item locations on the Wright and pathway maps and the numerical values in "Output Table:14" representing item difficulty estimates. "Output Table:13.1 Item measure" provides that information in a table where the items are ordered by their difficulty estimates—not by their item numbers: The matching of item values to map locations can be done by eye.

A scan down the columns containing the fit statistics should reveal any major "quality control" problems; many Rasch measurement practitioners keep an eye on standardized infit statistic on the first go through. The Infit ZSTD statistics for Items 21 and 30 catch the eye here, so look at the complete fit information for each more closely:

#21	1.27	2.6	1.76	3.7
#30	1.19	2.3	1.15	1.0

Now, on three out of four fit indicators, Item 21 doesn't look good (only infit mnsq of 1.27 looks ok); we'll need to find out what went wrong there. Item 30, on the other hand, does well enough on three out of four fit indicators (only the infit Zstd of 2.3 seems a bit too erratic); so, let Item 30 go for now.

CASE STATISTICS TABLE

It's not much use that the test performance is ok, if the person measures don't stand up to scrutiny so:

```
Click on the "Output Tables" pull-down menu and click on
"18: Person Entry".
```

But with 150 cases to inspect, running your eye over the fit statistics can be a bit daunting. Again, just scan the Infit Z and note those above +2.0, for starters.

Alternatively, "Output Table:6 Person Fit Order" is more user-friendly, because it orders the most pertinent persons by the size of mis-fit. Seems like the top three or four cases could cause some concern. But that makes about 2% of our candidates with performances that should not be judged just on the basis of the ability estimate alone: A bit of detective work is needed here. For example, Student 4 is a high ability candidate (est. = 3.96) but the fit stats indicate erratic performance by that candidate. The fit statistics (1.12, 0.4, 4.48, and 1.8) suggest that this very capable student missed a very easy question; that could be confirmed by looking at Output Table:6.6 (or 7.2.1 in the purchased version of WINSTEPS).

NEXT STEPS

Clearly, the test has a couple of items that need some attention. Bond&FoxSteps allows you the see the empirical versus theoretical ICCs for each item. Pull up "Expected Score ICC" in the "Graphs" menu, and find graphs 21.21 and 30.30 by clicking on "Next Curve" for a few more hints about what went wrong with Items 21 and 30. The Item 30 curves confirm what the fit statistics indicated: Apart from a few blips to the left of the red ICC curve, the jagged empirical line stays close enough to the smooth theoretical curve. Again, no cause for alarm. The graph for Item 21 shows that on-target students (between, say 2 logits above and one logit below the item's difficulty—0.0 in this figure) perform close to expectations, but those more than 1 logit less able than the item difficulty have quite surprising success rates (i.e., much higher than expectation). What did the item table say for Item 21? Hardest item, on-target students perform close to expectations (the infit is marginal), but off-target students (they must be in the less able part of the distribution to be off target for the hardest item) performed erratically. This implies that we should find a few of those kids (low estimate, but a tick for Item 21) and ask them to describe how they solved that item. Did those children guess? Did they see another child's answer? Was there a giveaway use of words that was somehow attractive to these children? From all information we have about persons and items, the practical summary is that the model correctly predicts the performance of 69% of this sample of children on Item 21 (see pp. 224–246).

GOING FURTHER

While the test characteristics alone for this analysis suggest future directions for test development, the purposes and theoretical background of the original test development should be the bases on which to choose between the options. Whatever happens, Item 21 needs a thorough reappraisal, based, firstly on an investigation of the strategies and processes used by some of the low overall test performers who were unexpectedly successful on Item 21. The new wording will need to be trialled. Is the stem ok? Is there a giveaway in one of the distracters? The output can't tell you that. You'll need to interview some of those children.

As for the problem of the clustering of many items between –1 and +1 logits, and the gaps in the item distribution above and below that zone, then the purposes of the test must be considered. If the role of the test is to measure progress along the variable, that is, to provide accurate measures all along the variable, then development of both harder and easier items is required. It's back to the drawing board; starting with the theoretical blueprint that gave rise to the test in the first place. On the other hand, if the test is to be used to distinguish those who can from those who can't (or, more pedantically, those who did from those who didn't), the concentration of items around the cutoff will be helpful and the gaps in the variable will not prove a hindrance. Theory and purpose will guide practice; the empirical results are then used to shine a light back on the former.

GETTING DATA

For the small independent researcher, the practical problems of completing several iterations of test development will often mean that tests might be left in less than their optimal form. Of course, word processing and desktop publishing now mean that even the underfinanced university researcher or health care professional can print new versions of the test booklet almost at will. However, the big testing companies have long had the financial, logistic, and equipment advantage in the data collection and data entry stakes. It takes a fair amount of financial commitment from the small research team to have scan sheets designed and printed, to have the scanning software customised for the particular test, and to pay for the scanning and data cleaning processes. No wonder the test becomes set in stone too early. No wonder that the long term fine-tuning often required to derive maximum benefit from the test development might not occur for small scale researchers. Changing test items midstream can be handled by Rasch model analytical processes, so the old CTT based reasons for using one only test format should no longer constrain these processes.

A wander through the publishers' exhibitions at a major conference will soon reveal the answer to the small team's test answer-form problems: design, printing and scanning can be handled by someone with a PC, a printer, and an office scanner with a document feeder, rather than a lid. Software such as SurveyPro from Apian (*www.apian.com*) allows paper-scan forms and online surveys to be designed (and of course, modified and then tweaked) by anyone with basic computer skills. OCR software will then scan the bubbled answer sheet when it's run through an office scanner. That way the several iterations made possible (nay, required) by the Rasch techniques we describe are not just the prerogative of the well-financed large national testing companies.

And neither is computer adaptive testing. In chapter 10 we pointed to the advantages of Rasch-based CAT for testing. Again, it once took a mainframe computer, or at least a large server and a genuine clever-person to develop and refine the item delivery algorithms necessary to run CAT, even for small surveys. Now software such as CADATS (Computer Assisted Design, Analysis and Testing System, *www.cemcentre.org/CADATS*), from the CEM Centre at the University of Durham (UK) places Rasch-based CAT development and delivery tools within the financial and technological reach of independent researchers.

FURTHER ANALYSES

The researcher committed to excellence in measurement won't stop at this point in the test refinement or data analysis process. Throughout this book we have posited the central roles of unidimensionality and invariance as the hallmarks of genuine scientific measurement in the human sciences. Two early checks on these features are available in software such as WINSTEPS. The factor analysis of Rasch measurement residuals seems a good place to start for examining whether what's left over in a data set after the Rasch dimension has been removed indicates the possibility of a second dimension or is likely to be mere noise. Invariance checks at the item-by-item level carried out using the DIF plots to compare the performances of two meaningful divisions in the sample: male and female; old and young; healthy and unhealthy, and so forth. Of crucial importance is the performance of your developed test with other suitable sample: The invariance of the item measures is the key here.

NEXT STEPS

This book was designed to introduce Rasch measurement in the context of the larger and more important theoretical issues about the nature of genuine scientific measurement for the human sciences. While many readers will be kept busy enough accommodating to the demands of the arguments and rehearsing the techniques elucidated in this volume, we expect that sooner or later most will want to venture further than the confines of these ideas. Readers who take seriously the ideas herein will have little trouble participating in Rasch-based discussions or moving onto the ideas contained in the classic Rasch measurement texts.

THE CLASSIC REFERENCE TEXTS

The following texts have been indispensable to the progress of Rasch measurement and to the writing of this book. Inevitably, each should become part of the serious Rasch practitioner's reference library.

The foundation stone of the Rasch family of models:

Rasch, G. (1980). *Probabilistic models for some intelligence and attainment tests* (Expanded ed.). Chicago: University of Chicago Press. (Reprinted 1992, Chicago: MESA Press)

This is Georg Rasch's seminal work on measurement that describes the theory, simple applications, and mathematical basis of the model. Many claim that in that prescient work, Rasch outlined the problems and principles that underlie even recent developments in Rasch measurement.

The dichotomous model reference:
Wright, B. D., & Stone, M. H. (1979). *Best test design.* Chicago: MESA Press. (Also available in Spanish)

In *Best Test Design,* Wright and Stone outline the principles of Rasch measurement and apply the analytical techniques to dichotomous data. This instructional text on Rasch measurement introduces very straightforward estimation procedures as well as more complex estimation methods. Chapter 1: "What Is Measurement?" Chapter 2: "How to Measure?" shows how to perform by hand a Rasch analysis of the "Knox Cube Test." The chapter on "How Well Are We Measuring?" introduces the concept of data-to-model fit.

The polytomous model reference:
Wright, B. D., & Masters, G. N. (1982). *Rating scale analysis.* Chicago: MESA Press.

In *Rating Scale Analysis,* Wright and Masters discuss the philosophy behind linear, interval measurement and extend the application of the Rasch model to rating scales as part of the family of Rasch models for different polytomous applications, including Poisson counts, binomial, Bernoulli trials, and partial credit responses. In keeping with the principles behind *Best Test Design,* *Rating Scale Analysis* derives the major estimation methods and investigates data-to-model fit.

The many-facets Rasch model:
Linacre, J. M. (1989). *Many-facet Rasch measurement.* Chicago: MESA Press.

Judges, tasks, time-points, and other facets of the measurement situation can be parameterized with the many-facets Rasch model. Because these extensions are hard to conceptualize and difficult to manage, they are usually avoided whenever possible. But, these extensions can be crucial, for instance, in the adjustment of candidate measures for the severity of the judges they encountered. This book outlines the theory and application of this methodology.

The most accessible account of the many European contributions to the development is found in:
Fischer, G. H. , & Molenaar, I. W. (Eds.). (1995). *Rasch models: Foundations, recent developments and applications.* New York: Springer-Verlag.

A succinct account emphasizing Rasch measurement properties:
Andrich, D. (1988). *Rasch models for measurement.* Newbury Park, CA: Sage.

Chapter 6 of the following provides a nice account of Rasch fundamentals and is worth consulting for its interesting depiction of the connection between ICCs and the Wright map:

Wilson, M. (2005). *Constructing measures: an item response modeling approach.* Mahwah, NJ: Lawrence Erlbaum Associates.

How psychologists willfully ignored the requirements for fundamental measurement and why the delusion continues to the present:

Michell, J. (1999). *Measurement in psychology: Critical history of a methodological concept.* New York: Cambridge University Press.

A succinct account of the Rasch family of measurement models:

Wright, B., & Mok, M. (2000). Rasch models overview. *Journal of Applied Measurement, 1,* 83–106.

OTHER RASCH-BASED TEXTS

Applying Rasch measurement to measuring language performance:

McNamara, T. F. (1996). *Measuring second language performance.* New York: Longman.

George Ingebo contrasts the results of Rasch methods with conventional statistics for assessing student responses to basic skills testing and shows the advantages of Rasch measurement for school district testing programs. It details linking strategies behind building large item banks:

Ingebo, G. S. (1997). *Probability in the measure of achievement.* Chicago: MESA Press.

Key papers from the International Objective Measurement Workshops have been issued in an important series of reference texts:

Wilson, M. (1992). *Objective measurement: Theory into practice, Vol. 1.* Norwood, NJ: Ablex.

Wilson, M. (1994). *Objective measurement: Theory into practice, Vol. 2.* Norwood, NJ: Ablex.

Engelhard, G., & Wilson, M. (1996). *Objective measurement: Theory into practice, Vol. 3.* Norwood, NJ: Ablex.

Wilson, M., Engelhard, G., & Draney, K. (Eds.). (1997). *Objective measurement: Theory into practice, Vol. 4.* Norwood, NJ: Ablex.

Wilson, M., & Engelhard, G. (Eds.). (2000). *Objective measurement: Theory into practice, Vol. 5.* Stamford, CT: Ablex.

This will continue as a new series from JAMPress:

Engelhard, G., Wilson M., & Garner, M. (Eds.). (2006). *Advances in Rasch measurement* (Vol. I). Maple Grove: JAMPress.

The selection of papers includes interesting applications and themed sections exploring topics such as rating scale analyses, facets-type analyses, and multidimensional measurement.

An edited volume which explores diverse applications of Rasch measurement in the health sciences.

Bezruczko, N. (Ed.). (2005). *Rasch Measurement in Health Sciences*. Maple Grove: JAMPress.

The Smith & Smith edited volume is based on the Understanding Rasch Measurement series that appeared in the *Journal of Applied Measurement*.

Smith, E., & Smith, R. (2004). *Introduction to Rasch Measurement*. Maple Grove: JAMPress.

A collection of exemplary applications of Rasch models in science education.

Liu, X., & Boone, W. (2006). *Applications of Rasch Measurement in Science Education*. Maple Grove: JAMPress.

SEMINAL PAPERS

Physicist Norman Campbell's Theory of Fundamental Measurement as described for psychologists by Thomas Reese (1943) is available at www.rasch.org/rm8.htm

Wright, B. (1967). Sample-Free Test Calibration and Person Measurement.

This presentation at the 1967 Educational Testing Service Invitational Conference launched Rasch measurement in the United States. Available at www.rasch.org/memo1.htm

Linacre, J. M., Heinemann, A. W., Wright, B. D., Granger, C. V., & Hamilton, B. B. (1994). The structure and stability of the Functional Independence Measure (FIM)^{TM}, *Archives of Physical Medicine and Rehabilitation, 75*(2), 127–132.

This paper demonstrated the efficacy of Rasch measurement in clarifying and solving measurement problems in survey and diagnosis situations. Available at www.rasch.org/memo50.htm

Ben Wright (1997). A History of Social Science Measurement.

This paper addresses the main threads in the conceptualization of measurement (as opposed to mere numeration) in the Social Sciences, and relates them to the Rasch model. Available at *www.rasch.org/memo62.htm*

OTHER RASCH PUBLICATIONS

Journal of Applied Measurement P.O. Box 1283, Maple Grove, MN 55311
Under the senior editorial hand of founder Richard Smith *JAM* publishes refereed

scholarly works from all academic disciplines that relate to measurement theory and its application to constructing variables. We must concur with Mike Linacre who describes it as it the "most authoritative journal for Rasch research."

Rasch Measurement Transactions, due to the inspiration and work of Mike Linacre, is a quarterly publication of the Rasch Measurement Special Interest Group of the American Educational Research Association. Back issues have been bound into volumes and published by MESA Press. *RMT* contains short research notes addressing many of the key issues and questions raised in the theory and practice of Rasch analysis. It is also available at *www.rasch.org/rmt*

MESA Research Memoranda by Ben Wright and several others form a collection of many of the foundational papers in Rasch measurement. The entire text of the pivotal MESA Research Memoranda are available at *www.rasch.org/memos.htm*

COMPUTER SOFTWARE FOR RASCH MEASUREMENT

Each of the software packages that follows implements estimation and fit procedures for more than one of the Rasch family of measurement models. Each of the estimation procedures has its own band of rather devoted adherents, but each has its shortcomings as well.

> JMLE: Joint Maximum Likelihood Estimation (sometimes called UCON)
> MMLE: Marginal Maximum Likelihood Estimation
> PAIR: Pairwise Estimation

Similarly, each of the Rasch software programs has its own disciples, but no one program incorporates the advantages of all the packages, or avoids the tolerable shortcomings of its own particular estimation procedure. For the members of the Rasch family of models dealt with in detail in this textbook—the models for dichotomous, partial credit, and rating scale data—the usual Rasch analytical procedures, as they are implemented in the software packages listed here, produce estimates that are generally equivalent, for all practical analytical purposes. Sometimes pragmatic considerations are foremost in the practitioner's mind: Macintosh users (only those who still have patience with OS 9 applications) have one obvious option—Quest—all the rest run on PCs; RUMM and WINSTEPS take full advantage of the Windows platform; WINSTEPS has lots of diagnostics and is the software included free as Bond&FoxSteps with this volume; Bigsteps is free; ConQuest has more analytical potential than most mere mortals can imagine; and so on. (However, adventurous Mac users can run even facets-type analyses using PC emulation software on, say, a G4 or G5.)

Australian Council for Educational Research—Melbourne

> *Quest—The Interactive Test Analysis System* (Adams & Khoo):
> *Joint Maximum Likelihood Estimation*

Quest claims to offer a comprehensive test and questionnaire analysis environment by providing access to Rasch measurement techniques as well as a range of traditional test analysis procedures. It combines a rather easy-to-use control language with flexible and informative output. Quest can be used to construct and validate variables based on both dichotomous and polytomous observations.

The Rasch analysis provides item estimates, case estimates, and fit statistics; the results from this analysis can be accessed through a variety of informative tables and maps. Traditional analyses report counts, percentages, and point-biserials for each possible response to each item and a variety of reliability indices.

Quest runs in batch mode, interactive mode, or a combination of the two. The batch mode conveniently allows a one-step submission of more routine analysis jobs, whereas the interactive environment facilitates exploration of the properties of test data. In interactive mode, Quest allows analysis results to be viewed on the screen as the analysis proceeds.

Quest allows the user to define subgroups and subscales so that analyses can be performed for any combination of subgroup and subscale. It has the usual Rasch flexibility for dealing with missing data and allows for item and case estimate anchoring to facilitate test equating and item banking. The software supports export of results to facilitate importation into database, analysis, and spreadsheet programs. The Quest Compare command provides Mantel-Haenszel and Rasch tests of differential item functioning.

Quest has been implemented on several platforms. In its desktop form it handles up to 10,000 cases and 400 items with up to 10 response categories per item. A total of 10 subgroup–subscale combinations are permitted.

ConQuest (Adams, Wu, & Wilson):
Marginal Maximum Likelihood Estimation

ConQuest is able to fit a much more extensive range of item response models than any of the other programs described here. Perhaps it is easiest to describe this package at two levels. First, at the level of Rasch analysis software, it can not only fit the standard dichotomous and polytomous Rasch models, but can be used for facets-type analyses and what ConQuest refers to as LLTM-type item response models as well. ConQuest does most of what Quest does, offering access to Rasch measurement techniques as well as a range of traditional test analysis procedures. At this level it is directly related to the content of this textbook and is suited to the entry-level Rasch measurement practitioner.

At the next level, directed specifically to those with more advanced analytical needs, ConQuest is a very versatile and powerful general modeling program that can also fit multidimensional item response models and both unidimensional and multidimensional latent regression models (i.e., multilevel models) as well as generate plausible values for the solution of difficult measurement problems. It uses a special keyword syntax to define the very wide range of item response models just described. Beyond that, it includes a method of defining special models using a design matrix approach, which makes it extremely flexible for more experienced users.

ConQuest is available for standard Windows and UNIX operating systems. It can be run from either a GUI (Windows) interface or a console interface. It combines a rather easy-to-use control language with flexible and informative output. In terms of output from Rasch and traditional analyses, as well as operation modes, ConQuest provides the same features detailed for the Quest package.

WINSTEPS.com—Chicago

WINSTEPS (Linacre & Wright):
Joint Maximum Likelihood Estimation

WINSTEPS constructs Rasch measures from simple rectangular data sets, usually of persons and items, with up to 1,000,000 cases and 10,000 items using JMLE. WINSTEPS is the basis of the Bond&FoxSteps software included free on the data file CD included with this edition. Each item can have a rating scale of up to 255 categories; dichotomous, multiple-choice, and multiple rating scale and partial credit items can be combined in one analysis. The developers of WINSTEPS use the program daily in their own work, and are continually adding new features as a result of their own experience and feedback from users. The inclusion of the pathway chart is but one example of responsiveness to user feedback. WINSTEPS is designed as a tool that facilitates exploration and communication.

WINSTEPS provides for powerful diagnosis of multidimensionality, using principal components analysis of residuals to detect and quantify substructures in the data. The working of rating scales can be examined thoroughly, and rating scales can be recoded and items regrouped to share rating scales as desired. Measures can be anchored at preset values. A free student/evaluation version, limited to 100 cases and 25 items, is available at www.winsteps.com. An earlier DOS-based Rasch program, Bigsteps, with a capacity of 20,000 persons and 1,000 items, can also be downloaded free. The Bond&FoxSteps version of WINSTEPS designed to support readers of this text is included on the free CD with the data files for analysis.

Facets (Linacre): Joint Maximum Likelihood Estimation

Facets is designed to handle the more complex applications of unidimensional Rasch measurement and performs many-facets Rasch measurement handling up to 1 million examinees and up to 255 response categories using JMLE. Facets constructs measures from complex data involving heterogeneous combinations of examinees, items, tasks, and judges along with further measurement and structural facets. All facet summary "rulers" are provided so the user can view all facets in the same frame of reference. It is designed to flexibly handle combinations of items of different formats in one analysis. Measures can be fixed or anchored individually or by group mean, facilitating equating and linking across test sessions. Quality-control fit evaluation of all measures is provided, and bias, differential item functioning, and interactions can be estimated. Weighting schemes can be implemented.

Since organizing the data for input to Facets and then interpreting its output can be challenging, it is recommended that simpler approaches be tried first. Minifacs, a free student/evaluation version of Facets, is included on the free CD with the data files for analysis and can be downloaded from www.winsteps.com.

RUMM Laboratory—Perth

RUMM 2020: Pairwise Conditional Estimation

RUMM 2020 is an interactive Rasch software package for Windows 95/98 and WinNT platforms, which uses a variety of graphical and tabular displays to provide an immediate, rapid, overall appraisal of an analysis. RUMM 2020 is entirely interactive, from data entry to the various analyses, permitting rerunning analyses based on diagnosis of previous analyses, for example, rescoring items, eliminating items, carrying out test equating in both raw score and latent metrics. The RUMM laboratory recommends 64 Mb of RAM and up to 12 Mb free hard disk space to make good use of the extensive graphic capabilities (128 Mb is a good idea for large data sets).

RUMM handles 5,000 or more items with the number of persons limited by available memory. It allows up to 9 distracter responses for multiple-choice items, a maximum of 64 thresholds per polytomous item, and up to 9 person factors such as gender, grade, age groups for group comparisons, DIF detection, and the like. The software employs a range of special Template files for allowing the user to customize analyses adding convenience and speed for repeated, related, and future analyses.

RUMM 2020 implements the Rasch models for dichotomous and polytomous data using a pairwise conditional estimation procedure that generalizes the equation for one pair of items in which the person parameter is eliminated to all pairs of items taken simultaneously. The procedure is conditional estimation in the sense that the person parameters are eliminated while the item parameters are estimated (Zwinderman, 1995). The procedure generalizes naturally to handling missing data.

RASCH MEASUREMENT ORGANIZATIONS

Institute for Objective Measurement

The Institute for Objective Measurement (IOM) is a nonprofit, tax-exempt corporation whose mission is to develop, teach, promote, and make available the practice of objective measurement. It is in the business of problem solving through education and the promotion of objective measurement.

The IOM sees itself as a "public" organization whose orientation and focus is outward to the world as well as inward to the professional growth and support of its members. Its members constitute measurement professionals who live in many countries throughout the world. While the majority of members are employed by universities and other organizations that concern themselves with some aspect of measurement, about one third of the IOM's membership are students. IOM provides support for programs in objective measurement that are far-reaching and implemented throughout various countries of the world. The IOM can be contacted by e-mail at: InstObjMeas@Worldnet.att.net or at www.Rasch.org

AMERICAN EDUCATIONAL RESEARCH ASSOCIATION

Rasch Measurement SIG

The Rasch Measurement Special Interest Group (SIG) of the American Educational Research Association is an international forum that allows Rasch measurement practitioners to place interesting measurement problems into a semi-public professional arena, as well as to share advice and techniques and to discuss theoretical and practical issues. The Rasch SIG sponsors several paper presentation sessions at each annual meeting of the American Educational Research Association. The SIG sponsors a Listserv that facilitates international discussions of measurement-related issues via e-mail. The SIG publishes *Rasch Measurement Transactions*, a quarterly newsletter that includes abstracts, reviews, and brief notes on the theory and practice of Rasch measurement. To join the SIG, go to http://www.rasch.org. Back issues of *RMT* can be accessed from this site as well. The SIG serves to maintain a sense of community among Rasch practitioners.

RASCH-BASED PROFESSIONAL MEETINGS

International Objective Measurement Workshops

The International Objective Measurement Workshops began in the spring of 1981, to develop and inspire cooperative and innovative work in the field of objective measurement as a tribute to the memory of Georg Rasch. The first workshop was held in Judd 111 at the University of Chicago by a small group of researchers, many of whom had worked closely with Georg Rasch (Ben Wright, Geoff Masters, David Andrich, Graham Douglas, George Morgan, Richard Smith, Barry Kissane, and Pender Pedler). IOMW3 was held at the same time as the American Educational Research Association meeting in the spring of 1985, and in 1989 the tradition of holding IOMW around the same time as AERA was established as a means of expediting participation.

Generally, the International Objective Measurement Workshop is held biennially at the same time and in the same city as the American Educational Research Association annual meeting. The most recent, IOMWXII, was held in 2004 in Cairns, Australia. The meeting is a gathering of researchers and practitioners interested in all aspects of Rasch and Rasch-related measurement. There are usually both research presentations (in the form of traditional-style talks and poster presentations, as well as software demonstrations) and professional development workshops on various practical approaches and analysis techniques.

Selected and edited papers presented at the IOMW have been gathered into several volumes listed above.

Pacific Rim Objective Measurement Symposia

PROMS (Pacific Rim Objective Measurement Symposium) is an annual professional meeting established at the instigation of Trevor Bond at IOMW-XII Cairns in 2004 to promote objective measurement and to contribute to the research and development of Rasch measurement in the Pacific Rim. PROMS is an annual symposium aiming to provide a forum for the sharing of new knowledge with the international community. Rasch measurement workshops are usually attached to PROMS meetings.

The first PROMS meeting, PROMS KL 2005, was successfully held at Kuala Lumpur, Malaysia June 21-23, 2005. It was hosted by the Research Centre of the International Islamic University of Malaysia. The theme of PROMS 2005 was "Quality Measurement for Quality Decisions." The symposium had attracted over 120 international researchers, practitioners, educators, and policymakers from 10 countries, including Australia, Sweden, Hong Kong, Korea, Malaysia, Palestine, Philippines, South Africa, Taiwan, and the US. Mike Linacre ran introduction to WINSTEPS/Facets software workshop at PROMS KL 2005.

PROMS HK 2006 was held in Hong Kong from June 27-29, 2006, and will be hosted by the Department of Educational Psychology, Counselling, and Learning Needs, The Hong Kong Institute of Education. The theme of PROMS HK 2006 was "Rasch Measurement: A Tool for Scientific Progress for the Asia Pacific." www.promshk.org

International Outcomes Measurement Conference

The Third International Outcomes Measurement Conference was held on the Chicago campus of Northwestern University on June 16 and 17, 2000. Hosted by IOM, the MESA Psychometrics Laboratory at the University of Chicago, and the Rehabilitation Institute of Chicago, the third conference built on the work of two previous conferences held at the University of Chicago in 1996 and 1998. The conference was organized by Allen W. Heinemann.

RASCH-BASED RESEARCH AND DEVELOPMENT ENTERPRISES

So what does the future look like for those starting in Rasch analysis? What are the prospects? A couple of possibilities might be suggested in looking at how Rasch measurement principles have become routine in some research and development areas.

The Australian Council for Educational Research

ACER has pioneered the application of Rasch measurement in large-scale educational testing programs, both in Australia with the Basic Skills Testing Program–NSW (1989), and worldwide with the PISA (1998–) projects.

Masters et al. (1990). *Profiles of learning—The Basic Skills Testing Program in New South Wales 1989*. Melbourne: ACER.

PISA: Program for International Student Assessment

PISA is an internationally standardized assessment, jointly developed by participating countries and administered to 15-year-olds in groups in their schools. It is administered in 32 countries, of which 28 are members of the OECD. Between 4,500 and 10,000 students typically have been tested in each country. PISA assessments are presently planned for 2006.
http://www.PISA.oecd.org/

Northwest Evaluation Association (OR)

The Northwest Evaluation Association (NWEA) has been using Rasch modeling in the area of educational achievement testing since the 1970s; indeed, it has been a clear leader in the application of Rasch measurement to educational assessment in the United States. As a not-for-profit agency, NWEA has created Rasch scales in reading, mathematics, language usage, and the sciences. These cross-grade scales include an achievement range from Grade 2 to Grade 10 and have been used to create item banks with thousands of items in each content area. These item banks have allowed the development of customized achievement-level tests and adaptive tests used in over 300 school districts in the United States. As a direct result of the influence of NWEA, many Oregon state educational assessments are now reported in RITS (Rasch logITS).

The assessments developed by NWEA benefit from Rasch modeling in several ways. First, the measurement instruments are designed for efficiency through the selection of items based on their difficulty estimates, resulting in tests that are optimally challenging for each student. Second, the scale is designed to measure growth throughout much of a student's education, resulting in particularly useful longitudinal data. Third, the scale is permanent, so that changes may be made in test instruments without disturbing any client school's ability to study change across time.

However, the assessments that NWEA develops are just a means to an end. The primary focus for NWEA is to help all students learn more. High-quality assessments supported by Rasch modeling help accomplish this by creating a climate in which data is valued and allows achievement data to be used to inform change at the student level, as well as change at school, state, and national levels. By using the Rasch models to create quality measurement instruments, NWEA aims to help move education past reliance on educational fads to an environment in which the structure of education continually improves by using measurement to direct change.

Details at: http://www.nwea.org

The Lexile Reading Framework

The Lexile reading comprehension framework uses Rasch measurement techniques to provide a common interval scale for measuring both reader performance and the difficulty of written text (i.e., it places readers and text on the same

Rasch scale). The Lexile limen is set so that when a reader has the same Lexile measure as a title, the reader should read that "targeted" title with 75% comprehension. The difference between a reader's Lexile measure and a text's Lexile measure is used to forecast the comprehension the reader will have with the text. A text measure 250L greater than a reader's measure predicts a comprehension drop to 50%, while a reader measure advantage of 250L over the text means comprehension goes up to 90%.

The technology of the Lexile Framework includes a graphical representation of reading development called the Lexile Map and, even more interestingly, a software program called the Lexile Analyzer that measures the difficulty of text. An approximation of a reader's measure can be inferred by getting the reader to read aloud from texts with known Lexile measures. For high-stakes decisions, specific tests can be used to provide more precision in reader location. The Lexile library lists tens of thousands of literature titles, magazines, newspapers, and textbooks, each of which has been assigned a Lexile measure. Chapter 1 of this book was measured at 1440L, placing it near the kind of text found on the Test of English as a Foreign Language (1400L), the Graduate Management Admissions Test (1440L), and the *Wall Street Journal* (1400L) on the Lexile map. Readers such as matriculants of first-tier U.S. universities read between 1400L and 1600L and demonstrate 75% to 90% comprehension of 1400L text. Reader response to the first edition would suggest that we are on target.

Details at: www.lexile.com

www.bondandfox.com

Glossary

Ability estimate The location of a person on a variable, inferred by using the collected observations.

Bias The difference between the expected value of a sample statistic and the population parameter statistic estimates. It also infers the effects of any factor that the researcher did not expect to influence the dependent variable. (See DIF.)

Calibration The procedure of estimating person ability or item difficulty by converting raw scores to logits on an objective measurement scale.

Classical test theory See True score model/Traditional test theory. True score theory is classical in the sense that it is traditional.

Common person equating The procedure that allows the difficulty estimates of two different groups of items to be plotted on a single scale when the two tests have been used on a common group of persons.

Common test equating The procedure that allows the ability estimates of two different groups of people to be plotted on a single scale when they have been measured on a common test.

Concurrent validity The validity of a measure determined by how well it performs with some other measure the researcher believes to be valid.

Construct A single latent trait, characteristic, attribute, or dimension assumed to be underlying a set of items.

Construct validity Theoretical argument that the items are actual instantiations or operationalizations of the theoretical construct or latent trait under investigation; that is, that the instrument measures exactly what it claims to measure.

Counts The simple attribution of numerals to record observations. In the Rasch model, raw scores are regarded as counts.

Deterministic Characteristic of a model that implies the exact prediction of an outcome. Deterministic models explicate the relation between the observed responses and person ability as a causal pattern; for example, Guttman scaling is deterministic—the total score predicts exactly which items were correctly answered. (Cf. Probabilistic.)

Dichotomous Dichotomous data have only two values such as right/wrong, pass/fail, yes/no, mastery/fail, satisfactory/unsatisfactory, agree/disagree, male/female.

DIF (Differential item functioning) The loss of invariance of item estimates across testing occasions. DIF is prima facie evidence of item bias.

Error The difference between an observation and a prediction or estimation; the deviation score.

Error estimate The difference between the observed and the expected response associated with item difficulty or person ability.

Estimation The Rasch process of using the obtained raw scores to calculate the probable values of person and item parameters.

Facet An aspect of the measurement condition. In Rasch measurement, the two key facets are person ability and item difficulty.

Fit The degree of match between the pattern of observed responses and the modeled expectations. This can express either the pattern of responses observed for a candidate on each item (person fit) or the pattern for each item on all persons (item fit).

Fit statistics Indices that estimate the extent to which responses show adherence to the modeled expectations.

Fundamental measurement Physicist Norman Campbell showed that what physical scientists mean by measurement requires an ordering system and the kind of additivity illustrated by physical concatenation. He called this "fundamental measurement." The Rasch model is a special case of additive conjoint measurement, a form of fundamental measurement.

Identity line A line with slope = 1, plotted through the means of two sets of calibrations for the purpose of equating them. The identity line is the Rasch-modeled relation between the two sets of calibrations.

Infit mean square One of the two alternative measures that indicate the degree of fit of an item or a person (the other being standardized infit). Infit mean square is a transformation of the residuals, the difference between the predicted and the observed, for easy interpretation. Its expected value is 1. As a rule of thumb, values between 0.70 and 1.30 are generally regarded as acceptable. Values greater than 1.30 are termed misfitting, and those less than 0.70 as overfitting.

Infit statistics Statistics indicating the degree of fit of observations to the Rasch-modeled expectations, weighted to give more value to on-target observations. Infit statistics are more sensitive to irregular inlying patterns and are usually expressed in two forms: unstandardized as mean square and standardized as t.

Infit t One of the two alternative measures that indicate the degree of fit of an item or a person to the Rasch model (the other being infit mean square). The infit t (also called standardized infit) is the standardization of fit values to a distribution with a mean of 0 and variance of 1. Values in the range of -2 to $+2$ are usually held as acceptable ($p < .05$). Values greater than $+2$ are regarded as misfitting, and those less than -2 as overfitting.

Interval scale A measurement scale in which the value of the unit of measurement is maintained throughout the scale so that equal differences have equal values, regardless of location. The 0 point on an interval scale is often regarded as arbitary or pragmatic, rather than absolute.

Invariance The maintenance of the identity of a variable from one occasion to the next. For example, item estimates remain stable across suitable samples; person estimates remain stable across suitable tests.

Item characteristic curve (ICC) An ogive-shaped plot of the probabilities of a correct response on an item for any value of the underlying trait in a respondent.

Item difficulty An estimate of an item's underlying difficulty calculated from the total number of persons in an appropriate sample who succeeded on that item.

Item fit statistics Indices that show the extent to which each item performance matches the Rasch-modeled expectations. Fitting items imply a unidimensional variable.

Item measure The Rasch estimate of item difficulty in logits.

Item reliability index The estimate of the replicability of item placement within a hierarchy of items along the measured variable if these same items were to be given to another sample of comparable ability. Analogous to Cronbach's alpha, it is bounded by 0 and 1.

Item Response Theory (IRT) A relatively recent development in psychometric theory that overcomes deficiencies of the classical test theory with a family of models to assess model–data fit and evaluate educational and psychological tests. The central postulate of IRT is that the probability of a person's expected response to an item is the joint function of that person's ability, or location on the latent trait, and one or more parameters characterizing the item. The response probability is displayed in the form of an item characteristic curve as a function of the latent trait.

Item separation index An estimate of the spread or separation of items on the measured variable. It is expressed in standard error units, that is, the adjusted item standard deviation divided by the average measurement error.

Iteration A repetition. In Rasch analysis computation, the item estimation/person estimation cycle is repeated until a specified condition (convergence criterion) is met.

Latent trait A characteristic or attribute of a person that can be inferred from the observation of the person's behaviors. These observable behaviors display more or less the characteristic, but none of the observations covers all of the trait.

Latent trait theory See Item response theory.

Likert scale (after R. Likert) A widely used questionnaire format in human science research, especially in the investigation of attitudes. Respondents are given statements or prompts and asked to endorse a response from the range of ordered response options, such as "strongly agree," "agree," "neutral," "disagree," or "strongly disagree."

Limen Threshold.

Local independence The items of a test are statistically independent of each subpopulation of examinees whose members are homogeneous with respect to the latent trait measured.

Logit The unit of measurement that results when the Rasch model is used to transform raw scores obtained from ordinal data to log odds ratios on a common interval scale. The value of 0.0 logits is routinely allocated to the mean of the item difficulty estimates.

Many-facets model In this model, a version of the Rasch model developed in the work of Mike Linacre of Chicago (esp.), facets of testing situation in addition to person ability and item difficulty are estimated. Rater, test, or candidate characteristics are often-estimated facets.

Measurement The location of objects along a single dimension on the basis of observations which add together.

Measurement error Inaccuracy resulting from a flaw in a measuring instrument—as contrasted with other sorts of error or unexplained variance.

Measurement precision The accuracy of any measurement.

Missing data One or more values that are not available for a subject or case about whom other values are available, for example, a question in a survey that a subject does not answer. The Rasch model is robust in the face of missing data.

Model A mathematical model is required to obtain measurements from discrete observations.

Muted Items or persons with infit mean square values less than 0.70 or infit *t* values less than –2 are considered muted or overfitting. This indicates less variability in the data than the Rasch model predicts and generally reflects dependency in the data.

95% confidence band In test or person equating, the interval within the control lines set by the investigator (at *p* << .05) requiring that 95% of measured items or persons should fit the model.

Noisy Items or persons with infit mean square values greater than 1.30 or infit *t* values greater than +2 are considered noisy or misfitting. This indicates more erratic or haphazard performance than the Rasch model predicts.

Nominal scale A scale in which numerals are allocated to category values that are not ordered. Although this is necessary for measurement, it is not sufficient for any form of scientific measurement. (Cf. Stevens.)

One-parameter item response model (1PL-IRT) This description of the Rasch model highlights the Rasch focus on just one item parameter—difficulty—along with the model's membership in the IRT family of data-fitting models. Such a description usually ignores the Rasch model focus on fundamental measurement.

Order The transitive relationship between values A, B, C, etc., of a variable such that A > B, B > C, and A > C, etc.

Order effect When subjects receive more than one treatment or intervention, the order in which they receive those treatments or interventions might affect the result. To avoid this problem, researchers often use a counterbalanced design.

Ordinal scale A method of comparisons that ranks observations (puts them in an order) on some variable and allocates increasing values (e.g., numerals 1, 2, 3 or letters a, b, c, etc.) to that order. The size of differences between ranks is not specified. Although this is necessary for measurement, it is not sufficient for any form of scientific measurement. (Cf. Stevens.)

Outfit statistics Unweighted estimates of the degree of fit of responses. These unweighted values tend to be influenced by off-target observations and are expressed in two forms: unstandardized mean squares and standardized *t* values.

Overfit See Muted.

Partial credit analysis A Rasch model for polytomous data, developed in the work of Geoff Masters (esp.), which allows the number of ordered item categories and/or their threshold values to vary from item to item.

Perfect score The maximum possible score a respondent can achieve on a given test by answering all items correctly or endorsing the highest level response category for every item.

Person ability See Person measure.

Person fit statistics Indices that estimate the extent to which the responses of any person conform to the Rasch model expectation.

Person measure An estimate of a person's underlying ability based on that person's performance on a set of items that measure a single trait. It is calculated from the total number of items to which the person responded successfully in an appropriate test.

Person reliability index The estimate of the replicability of person placement that can be expected if this sample of persons were to be given another set of items measuring the same construct. Analogous to Cronbach's alpha, it is bounded by 0 and 1.

Person separation index An estimate of the spread or separation of persons on the measured variable. It is expressed in standard error units, that is, the adjusted person standard deviation divided by the average measurement error.

Probabilistic Given that all the possible influences on person performance cannot be known, the outcomes of the Rasch model are expressed mathematically as probabilities; for example, Rasch measurement is probabilistic—the total score predicts with varying degrees of certainty which items were correctly answered. (See Stochastic.)

Raters Judges who evaluate candidates' test performances in terms of performance criteria.

Rating scale analysis A version of the Rasch model, developed in the work of David Andrich (esp.), now routinely used for the sort of polytomous data generated by Likert scales. It requires that every item in a test have the same number of response options, and applies the one set of threshold values to all items on the test.

Raw scores Scores or counts in their original state that have not been statistically manipulated.

Residual The residual values represent the difference between the Rasch model's theoretical expectations and the actual performance.

Segmentation When tests with items at different developmental levels are submitted to Rasch analysis, items representing different stages should be contained in different segments of the scale with a nonzero distance between segments. The items should be mapped in the order predicted by the theory.

Specific objectivity The measurement of any person's trait is independent of the dispersion of the set of items used to measure that trait and, conversely, item calibration is independent of the distribution of the ability in the sample of persons who take the test.

Standardized infit See Infit *t*.

Standardized outfit Unweighted estimates of the degree of fit of responses. The outfit statistic is routinely reported in its unstandardized (mean square) and standardized (*t* statistic) forms. The acceptable values for *t* range from –2 to +2 ($p < .05$). Values greater than +2 are termed misfitting, and those less than –2 as overfitting. Compared with the infit statistics, which give more weight to on-target performances, the outfit t statistic is more sensitive to the influence of outlying scores.

Step See Threshold.

Stochastic Characteristic of a model that expresses the probabilistic expectations of item and person performance on the construct held to underlie the observed behaviors. (Cf. Deterministic.)

Targeted The items on the testing instrument match the range of the test candidates' proficiency.

Three-parameter item response model (3PL-IRT) An item response model that estimates three item parameters—item difficulty, item discrimination, and guessing—to better fit the model to the empirical data.

Threshold The level at which the likelihood of failure to agree with or endorse a given response category (below the threshold) turns to the likelihood of agreeing with or endorsing the category (above the threshold).

Traditional test theory See True score model/Classical test theory.

True score model The model indicates that any observed test score could be envisioned as the composite of two hypothetical components: a true score and a random error component.

Two-parameter item response model (2PL-IRT) An item response model that estimates two item parameters—item difficulty and item discrimination—to better fit the model to the empirical data.

Unidimensionality A basic concept in scientific measurement that one attribute of an object (e.g., length, width, weight, temperature, etc.) be measured at a time. The Rasch model requires a single construct to be underlying the items that form a hierarchical continuum.

Validity Evidence gathered to support the inferences made from responses to explicate the meaningfulness of a measured construct through examining person fit, item fit, and item and person ordering.

Variable An attribute of the object of study that can have a variety of magnitudes. The operationalization of a scale to measure these values is termed variable construction. A variable is necessarily unidimensional.

Visual analogue scale (VAS) Scale designed to present to the respondent a rating scale with minimum constraints. Usually respondents are required to mark the location on a line corresponding to the amount they agree. The score is routinely read from the scale in millimeters.

References

Adams, R. J., & Khoo, S. T. (1992). *Quest: The interactive test analysis system* [Computer software]. Camberwell, Victoria: Australian Council for Educational Research.

Adams, R. J., Wilson, M. R. & Wang, W. (1997).The multidimensional random coefficients multinomial logit model. *Applied Psychological Measurement, 21,* 1–24.

Adey, P., & Shayer, M. (1994). *Really raising standards: Cognitive intervention and academic achievement.* London: Routledge.

Alder, K. (2002) *The measure of all things.* New York: The Free Press.

Ali, M. (2003) *Brick Lane.* London: Doubleday

Anastasi, A., & Urbina, S. (1997). *Psychological testing* (7th ed.). Upper Saddle River, NJ: Prentice Hall.

Andersen, E. B. (1973). A goodness of fit for the Rasch model. *Psychometrika, 38*(1), 123–140.

Andersen, E. B. (1977). The logistic model for m answer categories. In W. E. Kempf & B. H. Repp (Eds.), *Mathematical models for social psychology.* Vienna, Austria: Hans Huber.

Andrich, D. (1978a). Application of a psychometric rating model to ordered categories which are scored with successive integers. *Applied Psychological Measurement, 2*(4), 581–594.

Andrich, D. (1978b). Rating formulation for ordered response categories. *Psychometrika, 43*(4), 561–573.

Andrich, D. (1978c). Scaling attitude items constructed and scored in the Likert tradition. *Educational and Psychological Measurement, 38*(3), 665–680.

Andrich, D. (1985). An elaboration of Guttman scaling with Rasch models of measurement. In N. B. Tuma (Ed.), *Sociological methodology* (pp. 33–80). San Francisco: Jossey-Bass.

Andrich, D. (1988). *Rasch models for measurement.* Newbury Park, CA: Sage.

Andrich, D. (1989). Distinctions between assumptions and requirements in measurement in the social sciences. In J. A. Keats, R. Taft, R. A. Heath, & S. H. Lovibond (Eds.), *Mathematical and theoretical systems: Proceedings of the 24th International Congress of Psychology of the International Union of Psychological Science* (Vol. 4, pp. 7–16). North-Holland: Elsevier Science.

Andrich, D. (1996). Measurement criteria for choosing among models with graded responses. In A. von Eye & C. C. Clogg (Eds.), *Categorical variables in developmental research: Methods of analysis* (pp. 3–35). San Diego, CA: Academic Press.

Angoff, W. H. (1960). Measurement and scaling. In C. W. Harris (Ed.), *Encyclopedia of educational research* (3rd ed., pp. 807–817). New York: Macmillan.

Armon, C. (1984). Ideals of the good life. In M. L. Commons, F. A. Richards, & C. Armon (Eds.), *Beyond formal operations, Volume 1: Late adolescent and adult cognitive development* (pp. 357–381). New York: Praeger.

315

Armon, C. (1993). Developmental conceptions of good work: A longitudinal study. In J. Demick & P. M. Miller (Eds.), *Development in the workplace* (pp. 21–37). Hillsdale, NJ: Lawrence Erlbaum Associates.

Armon, C. (1995). Moral judgment and self-reported moral events in adulthood. *Journal of Adult Development, 2*(1), 49–62.

Armon, C., & Dawson, T. (1997). Developmental trajectories in moral reasoning across the lifespan. *Journal of Moral Education, 26*(4), 433–453.

Bassett, G. W., Jr., & Persky, J. (1994). Rating skating. *Journal of the American Statistical Association, 89*(427), 1075–1079.

Battauz, M., Bellio, R. & Gori, E. (2005), Combining interval and ordinal measures in the assessment of student achievement. Research Note.

Bejar, I. I. (1983). *Achievement testing: Recent advances.* Beverly Hills, CA: Sage.

Beltyukova, S. A., & Fox, C. M. (2002, April). *Equating student satisfaction measures using Rasch analysis.* Paper presented at the annual meeting of the American Educational Research Association, New Orleans.

Beltyukova, S. A., Stone, G. E., & Fox, C. M. (2004). Equating student satisfaction measures. *Journal of Applied Measurement, 5*(1), 62–69.

Bendig, A. W. (1953). Reliability of self-ratings as a function of the amount of verbal anchoring and of the number of categories on the scale. *Journal of Applied Psychology, 37,* 38–41.

Bendig, A. W. (1954a). Reliability and the number of rating-scale categories. *Journal of Applied Psychology, 38,* 38–40.

Bendig, A. W. (1954b). Reliability of short rating scales and the heterogeneity of the rated stimuli. *Journal of Applied Psychology, 38,* 167–170.

Bergstrom, B. A., & Lunz, M. E. (1992). Confidence in pass/fail decisions in computer adaptive tests and paper and pencil examinations. *Evaluation and the Health Professions, 15*(4), 453–464.

Bergstrom, B. A., Lunz, M. E., & Gershon, R. C. (1992). Altering the level of difficulty in computer adaptive testing. *Applied Measurement in Education, 5*(2), 137–149.

Boardley, D., Fox, C. M., & Robinson, K. L. (1999). Public policy involvement of nutrition professionals. *Journal of Nutrition Education, 31*(5), 248–254.

Bond, T. G. (1976/1995). *BLOT—Bond's logical operations test.* Townsville, Queensland, Australia: James Cook University.

Bond, T. G. (1980). The psychological link across formal operations. *Science Education, 64*(1), 113–117.

Bond, T. G. (1996, January). *Confirming ideas about development: Using the Rasch model in practice* [Videotape]. Invited address at the Human Development and Psychology Colloquium series, Graduate School of Education, Harvard University.

Bond, T. G. (2004). Validity and assessment: A Rasch measurement perspective. *Metodologia de las Ciencias del Comportamiento, 5*(2), 179–194.

Bond, T. G. (2005a). Accountability in the academy: Rasch measurement of student feedback surveys. In R. F. Waugh (Ed.), *Frontiers in educational psychology* (pp. 119–129). New York: Nova Science Publishers.

Bond, T. G. (2005b). Past, present and future: An idiosyncratic view of Rasch measurement. In S. Alagumalai, D. Curtis, & N. Hungi (Eds). *Applied Rasch Measurement: A book of exemplars. Papers in honour of John P. Keeves* (pp. 329–341). Kluwer Academic Publishers.

Bond, T. G. (2006). The central role of Rasch model invariance for educational accoun ability systems. Keynote address presented at *Methodological tools for accountability systems in education,* International Symposium of the European Commission Joint Research Centre, Ispra, Italy.

Bond, T. G., & Bunting, E. M. (1995). Piaget and measurement III: Reassessing the *method clinique. Archives de Psychologie, 63*(247), 231–255.

Bond, T. G., & Fox, C. M. (2001). *Applying the Rasch model: Fundamental measurement in the human sciences.* Mahwah, NJ: Lawrence Erlbaum Associates.

Bond, T. G., & King, J. A. (1998). *School Opinion Survey State Report.* Townsville, Australia: James Cook University. (Contracted research report with 1,200 individual site reports for Education Queensland)

Bond, T. G., & King, J. A. (2003a). Measuring client satisfaction with public education II: Making school by school comparisons. *Journal of Applied Measurement, 4*(3), 258–268.

Bond, T. G. & King, J. A. (2003b). Measuring client satisfaction with public education III: Group effects in client satisfaction. *Journal of Applied Measurement, 4*(4), 326–334.

Bond, T. G., King, J. A., & Rigano, D. (1997). *Parent and student forms for the school opinion survey.* Townsville, Australia: James Cook University.

Bond, T. G., & Parkinson, K. (2007). Children's understanding of area concepts: Development, curriculum and educational achievement. In M. Wilson, G. Engelhard, & M. Garner (Eds.), *Advances in Rasch measurement* (Vol. 1). Maple Grove, MN: JAMPress.

Bring, J., & Carling, K. (1994). A paradox in the ranking of figure skaters. *Chance, 7*(4), 34–37.

Bond, T .G., Rossi Ferrario, S., & Zotti A. M. (2005, June) Family Strain Questionnaire–Short Form for general practictioners and home-care teams, Paper presented at PROMS, Kuala Lumpur, Malaysia.

Brogden, J. E. (1997). The Rasch model, the law of comparative judgment, and additive conjoint measurement. *Psychometrika, 42*(4), 631–634.

Brown, G., Widing, R. E., II, & Coulter, R. L. (1991). Customer evaluation of retail salespeople utilizing the SOCO scale: A replication, extension, and application. *Journal of the Academy of Marketing Science, 19*(4), 347–351.

Brunel, M.-L., Noelting, G., Chagnon, Y., Goyer, L., & Simard, A. (1993). Le profil cognitif des élèves en formation professionnelle au secondaire. In P. Goguelin & M. Moulin (Eds.), *La psychologie du travail à l'aube du XXIe siècle* (pp. 121–131). Issy-les-Moulineaux, France: EAP.

Bunting, E. M. (1993). *A qualitative and quantitative analysis of Piaget's control of variables scheme.* Unpublished thesis, James Cook University, Townsville, Australia.

Campbell, R., & Galbraith, J. (1996, August). *Non-parametric tests of the unbiasedness of Olympic figure skating judgements.* Paper presented at the 1996 Joint Statistical Meetings, Chicago.

Campbell, S. K., Kolobe, T. H., Osten, E. T., Lenke, M., & Girolami, G. L. (1995). Construct validity of the Test of Infant Motor Performance. *Physical Therapy, 75*(7), 585–596.

Chang, L. (1994). A psychometric evaluation of 4-point and 6-point Likert-type scales in relation to reliability and validity. *Applied Psychological Measurement, 18*(3), 205–215.

Choppin, B. H. L. (1985). Lessons for psychometrics from thermometry. *Evaluation in Education, 9*(1), 9–12.

Clark, A., & Friedman, M. J. (1983). Factor structure and discriminant validity of the SCL-90 in a veteran psychiatric population. *Journal of Personality Assessment, 47,* 396–404.

Clark, H. H., & Schober, M. F. (1992). Asking questions and influencing answers. In J. M. Tanur (Ed.), *Questions about questions: Inquiries into the cognitive bases of surveys* (pp. 15–48). New York: Russell Sage.

Cliff, N. (1992). Abstract measurement theory and the revolution that never happened. *Psychological Science, 3*(3), 186–190.

Colby, A., & Kohlberg, L. (1987). *The measurement of moral judgment: Vol. 1. Theoretical foundations and research validation.* New York: Cambridge University Press.

Crocker, L., & Algina, J. (1986). *An introduction to classical and modern test theory.* New York: Holt, Rinehart & Winston.

Cronbach, L. J., & Meehl, P. E. (1955). Construct validity in psychological tests. *Psychological Bulletin, 52,* 281–302.

Cronin, J., Kingsbury, G. G., McCall, M. S., & Bowe, B. (2005). *The impact of the No Child Left Behind Act on student achievement and growth: 2005 edition.* Lake Oswego, OR: Northwest Evaluation Association.

Curtis, D. D. (1999). *The 1996 Course Experience Questionnaire: A Re-Analysis.* Unpublished doctoral dissertation, The Flinders University of South Australia, Adelaide.

Curtis, D. D., & Keeves, J. P. (2000). The Course Experience Questionnaire as an institutional performance indicator. *International Education Journal, 1*(2), 73–84.

Dawson, T. (2000). Moral and evaluative reasoning across the life-span. *Journal of Applied Measurement, 1*(4), 346–371.

Derogatis, L. R. (1975). *The SCL-90-R.* Baltimore: Clinical Psychometric Research.

Derogatis, L. R. (1994). *SCL-90-R: Administration, scoring and procedures manual.* Minneapolis, MN: National Computer Systems.

Derogatis, L. R., & Savitz, K. L. (1999). The SCL-90-R, Brief Symptom Inventory, and matching clinical rating scales. In M. E. Maruish (Ed.), *The use of psychological testing for treatment planning and outcomes assessment* (2nd ed., pp. 679–724). New Jersey: Lawrence Erlbaum Associates.

Dinnebeil, L. A., Fox, C. M., & Rule, S. (1998). Influences on collaborative relationships: Exploring dimensions of effective communication and shared beliefs. *Infant–Toddler Intervention, 8*(3), 263–278.

Dinnebeil, L. A., Hale, L., & Rule, S. (1996). A qualitative analysis of parents' and service coordinators' descriptions of variables that influence collaborative relationships. *Topics in Early Childhood Special Education, 16*(3), 322–347.

Dinning, W. D., & Evans, R. G. (1977). Discriminant and convergent validity of the SCL-90 in psychiatric inpatients. *Journal of Personality Assessment, 41,* 304–310.

Douglas, G., & Wright, B. D. (1986). *The two-category model for objective measurement* (Research Memorandum No. 34). Chicago: University of Chicago, MESA Psychometric Laboratory.

Draney, K. L. (1996). The polytomous Saltus model: A mixture model approach to the diagnosis of developmental differences (Doctoral dissertation, University of California at Berkeley). *Dissertation Abstracts International, 58*(02), 431A.

Ducret, J. J. (1990). *Jean Piaget: Biographie et parcours intellectuel* [Jean Piaget: Biography and intellectual development]. Neuchâtel: Delachaux et Niestlé.

Duncan, O. D. (1984a). *Notes on social measurement: Historical and critical.* New York: Russell Sage Foundation.

Duncan, O. D. (1984b). Rasch measurement: Further examples and discussion. In C. F. Turner & E. Martin (Eds.), *Surveying subjective phenomena* (Vol. 2, pp. 367–403). New York: Russell Sage Foundation.

Duncan, O. D. (2000). Repudiating the Faustian bargain. *Rasch Measurement Transactions, 14*(1), 734. Available from http://www.rasch.org/rmt/rmt141e.htm. Accessed March 15, 2000.

Dunham, T. C., & Davison, M. L. (1990). Effects of scale anchors on student ratings of instructors. *Applied Measurement in Education, 4*(1), 23–35.

Elliott, R., Watson, J. C., Goldman, R. N., & Greenberg, L. S. (2004). Accessing and allowing experiencing. In R. Elliott & J. C. Watson (Eds.), *Learning emotion-focused therapy: The process-experiential approach to change* (pp. 169–192). Washington, DC: American Psychological Association.

Endler, L. C. (1998). *Cognitive development in a secondary science setting.* Unpublished thesis, James Cook University, Townsville, Queensland, Australia.

Endler, L. C. (2004). *Is student achievement really immutable? A study of cognitive development and student achievement in an Oregon school district.* Unpublished thesis, James Cook University, Townsville, Australia.

Endler, L. C., & Bond, T. G. (2001). Cognitive development in a secondary science setting. *Research in Science Education, 30*(4), 403–416.

Engelhard, G. (1992). The measurement of writing ability with a many-faceted Rasch model. *Applied Measurement in Education, 5*(3), 171–191.

Engelhard, G. (1994). Examining rater errors in the assessment of written composition with a many-faceted Rasch model. *Journal of Educational Measurement, 31*(2), 93–112.

Fan, X. (1998). Item response theory and classical test theory: An empirical comparison of their item/person statistics. *Educational and Psychological Measurement, 58*(3), 357–381.

Ferguson, G. A. (1941). The factorial interpretation of test difficulty. *Psychometrika, 6*(5), 323–330.

Fernberger, S. W. (1930). The use of equality judgments in psychological procedures. *Psychological Review, 37,* 107–112.

Finn, R. H. (1972). Effects of some variations in rating scale characteristics on the means and reliabilities of ratings. *Educational and Psychological Measurement, 32,* 255–265.

First, M. B., Spitzer, R. L., Gibbon, M., Williams, J. B. (1995). The Structured Clinical Interview for DSM-III-R Personality Disorders (SCID-II). *Journal of Personality Disorders, 9,* 83–104.

Fischer, G. (1974): *Einführung in die Theorie psychologischer Tests* [Introduction to the theory of psychological tests]. Bern: Huber.

Fischer, G. H., & Molenaar, I. W. (Eds.). (1995). *Rasch models: Foundations, recent developments, and applications.* New York: Springer-Verlag.

Fischer, K. W., & Dawson, T. L. (2002). A new kind of developmental science: Using models to integrate theory and research. *Monographs of the Society for Research in Child Development, 67* (1, Serial No. 173), 156–167.

Fisher, R. A., & Wright, B. D. (Eds.). (1994). Applications of probabilistic conjoint measurement [Special issue]. *International Journal of Educational Research, 21*(6), 557–664.

Fisher, W. P., Jr. (1993). Scale-free measurement revisited. *Rasch Measurement Transactions, 7*(1), 272–273. Available from http://www.rasch.org/rmt/rmt71.htm. Accessed March 15, 2000.

Fisher, W. P., Jr. (1994). The Rasch debate: Validity and revolution in educational measurement. In M. Wilson (Ed.), *Objective measurement: Theory into practice* (Vol. 2, pp. 36–72). Norwood, NJ: Ablex.

Fisher, W. P., Jr. (1997). Physical disability construct convergence across instruments: Towards a universal metric. *Journal of Outcome Measurement, 1*(2), 87–113.

Fisher, W. P., Jr. (1998). Do bad data refute good theory? *Rasch Measurement Transactions, 11*(4), 600.

Fisher, W. P., Jr. (1999). Foundations for health status metrology: The stability of MOS SF-36 PF-10 calibrations across samples. *Journal of the Louisiana State Medical Society, 151*(11), 566–578.

Fisher, W. P., Jr. (2000). Objectivity in psychosocial measurement: What, why, how. *Journal of Outcome Measurement, 4*(2), 527–563.

Fisher, W. P., Jr., Eubanks, R. L., & Marier, R. L. (1997). Equating the MOS SF36 and the LSU HSI Physical Functioning Scales. *Journal of Outcome Measurement, 1*(4), 329–362.

Fisher, W. P., Jr., Marier, R. L., Eubanks, R., & Hunter, S. M. (1997). The LSU Health Status Instruments (HSI). In J. McGee, N. Goldfield, J. Morton, & K. Riley (Eds.), *Collecting information from health care consumers: A resource manual of tested questionnaires and practical advice, Supplement* (pp. 109–127). Gaithersburg, MD: Aspen.

Fox, C., Gedeon, J., & Dinero, T. (1994, October). *The use of Rasch analysis to establish the reliability and validity of a paper-and-pencil simulation.* Paper presented at the annual meeting of the Midwestern Educational Research Association, Chicago.

Fox, C. M., & Jones, J. A. (1998). Uses of Rasch modeling in counseling psychology research. *Journal of Counseling Psychology, 45*(1), 30–45.

Frisbie, D. A., & Brandenburg, D. C. (1979). Equivalence of questionnaire items with varying response formats. *Journal of Educational Measurement, 16*(1), 43–48.

Funk, J. B., Fox, C. M., Chan, M., & Brouwer, J. (2005). The Development of the Children's Empathic Attitudes Questionnaire Using Classical and Rasch Analyses. *Journal of Clinical Child and Adolescent Psychology.*

Gaulin, C., Noelting, G., & Puchalska, E. (1984). The communication of spacial information by means of coded orthogonal views. In J. M. Moser (Ed.), *Proceedings of the Annual Meeting of the North American Chapter of the International Group for the Psychology of Mathematics Education.* Madison, WI: Wisconsin Center for Educational Research. (ERIC Document Reproduction Service No. ED 253 432)

Gershon, R. (1992). Guessing and measurement. *Rasch Measurement Transactions, 6*(2), 209–210.

Goldstein, H. (1979). The mystification of assessment. *Forum for the Discussion of New Trends in Education, 22*(1), 14–16.

Goldstein, H. (2004). The Education World Cup: International comparisons of student achievement, *Plenary talk to Association for Educational Assessment—Europe: Budapest Nov 4–6, 2004*

Gori, E. (2006, February). School effectiveness: Empirical evidence and theoretical considerations in the light of Rasch-based longitudinal measures. Keynote address presented at *Methodological tools for accountability systems in education,* International Symposium of the European Commission Joint Research Centre, Ispra, Italy.

Greenberg, L. S., Rice, L. N., & Elliott, R. (1993). *Facilitating emotional change: The moment-by-moment process.* New York: Guilford Press.

Griffin, P. (2004, March). *The comfort of competence and the uncertainty of assessment.* Paper presented at the Hong Kong School Principals' Conference, Hong Kong Institute of Education.

Guild, J. (1938). Are sensation intensities measurable? In *Report of the 108th Meeting of the British Association for the Advancement of Science* (pp. 296–328). London: Association.

Guilford, J.P. (1954). *Psychometric methods* (2nd ed.) New York: McGraw-Hill.

Gulliksen, H. (1950). *Theory of mental tests.* New York: Wiley.

Guttery, R. S., & Sfridis, J. (1996, August). *Judging bias in Olympic and World Figure Skating Championships: 1982–1994.* Paper presented at the 1996 Joint Statistical Meetings, Chicago.

Guttman, L. (1944). A basis for scaling qualitative data. *American Sociological Review, 9,* 139–150.

Hales, S. (1986). Rethinking the business of psychology. *Journal for the Theory of Social Behavior, 16*(1), 57–76.

Haley, S. M., McHorney, C. A., & Ware, J. E., Jr. (1994). Evaluation of the MOS SF-36 Physical Functioning Scale (PF-10): I. Unidimensionality and reproducibility of the Rasch item scale. *Journal of Clinical Epidemiology, 47*(6), 671–684.

Hambleton, R. K., & Swaminathan, H. (1985). A look at psychometrics in the Netherlands. *Nederlands Tijdschrift voor de Psychologie en haar Grensgebieden, 40*(7), 446–451.

Hautamäki, J. (1989). The application of a Rasch model on Piagetian measures of stages of thinking. In P. Adey (Ed.), *Adolescent development and school science* (pp. 342–349). London: Falmer.

Hays, W. L. (1994). *Statistics* (5th ed.). Fort Worth, TX: Harcourt Brace.

Holcomb, W. R., Adams, N. A., & Ponder, H. M. (1983). Factor structure of the Symptom Checklist-90 with acute psychiatric inpatients. *Journal of Consulting & Clinical Psychology, 51,* 535–538.

Ingebo, G. S. (1997). *Probability in the measure of achievement.* Chicago: MESA Press.

Inhelder, B., & Piaget, J. (1958). *The growth of logical thinking from childhood to adolescence* (A. Parsons & S. Milgram, Trans.). London: Routledge & Kegan Paul. (Original work published 1955)

Jenkins, G. D., & Taber, T. D. (1977). A Monte Carlo study of factors affecting three indices of composite scale reliability. *Journal of Applied Psychology, 62*(4), 392–398.

Kaplan, D. (2004). *Sage handbook of quantitative methodology for the social sciences.* Newbury Park, CA: Sage Publications

Karabatsos, G. (1998). Analyzing nonadditive conjoint structures: Compounding events by Rasch model probabilities. *Journal of Outcome Measurement, 2*(3), 191–221.

Karabatsos, G. (1999a, July). *Axiomatic measurement theory as a basis for model selection in item-response theory.* Paper presented at the 32nd annual conference of the Society for Mathematical Psychology, Santa Cruz, CA.

Karabatsos, G. (1999b, April). *Rasch vs. two-and three-parameter logistic models from the perspective of conjoint measurement theory.* Paper presented at the annual meeting of the American Education Research Association, Montreal, Canada.

Karabatsos, G. (2000). A critique of Rasch residual fit statistics. *Journal of Applied Measurement, 1*(2), 152–176.

Karmiloff-Smith, A., & Inhelder, B. (1975). If you want to get ahead, get a theory. *Cognition, 3*(3), 195–212.

Keats, J. A. (1983). Ability measures and theories of cognitive development. In H. Wainer & S. Messick (Eds.), *Principals of modern psychological measurement* (pp. 81–101). Hillsdale, NJ: Lawrence Erlbaum Associates.

Keay, J. (2000). *The great arc: The dramatic tale of how India was mapped and Everest was named.* New York: HarperCollins.

Keeves, J. P. (1997, March). *International practice in Rasch measurement, with particular reference to longitudinal research studies.* Invited paper presented at the annual meeting of the Rasch Measurement Special Interest Group, American Educational Research Association, Chicago.

Kieffer, K. M. (1999). Why generalizability theory is essential and classical test theory is often inadequate. In B. Thompson (Ed.), *Advances in social science methodology* (Vol. 5, pp. 149–170). Stamford, CT: JAI.

Kindlon, D. J., Wright, B. D., Raudenbush, S. W., & Earls, F. (1996). The measurement of children's exposure to violence: A Rasch analysis. *International Journal of Methods in Psychiatric Research, 6*(4), 187–194.

King, J. (1993). Getting anxious about electronic learning. *Australian Educational Computing, 8*(2), 16–20.

King, J., & Bond, T. (1996). A Rasch analysis of a measure of computer anxiety. *Journal of Educational Computing Research, 14*(1), 49–65.

King, J. A., & Bond, T. G. (2000, April). *Measuring client satisfaction with public education: Meeting competing demands.* Paper presented at the annual meeting of the American Educational Research Association, New Orleans, LA.

King, J., & Bond, T. (2003). Measuring client satisfaction with public education I: Meeting competing demands in establishing state-wide benchmarks. *Journal of Applied Measurement, 4*(2), 111–123.

Kingsbury, G. (2003, April). *A long-term study of the stability of item parameter estimates.* Paper presented at the annual meeting of the American Educational Research Association, Chicago.

Kingsbury, G G., Olson, A., Cronin, J., Hauser, C., & Houser, R. (2004), *The State of State Standards: Research investigating proficiency levels in fourteen states.* Northwest Evaluation Association. (http://www.young-roehr.com/nwea/)

Klauer, K. C. (1995). The assessment of person fit. In G. H. Fischer & I. W. Molenaar (Eds.), *Rasch models: Foundations, recent developments, and applications* (pp. 97–110). New York: Springer-Verlag.

Klinkenborg, V. (2000). The best clock in the world . . . and why we can't live without it. *Discover, 21*(6), 50–57.

Klockars, A. J., & Yamagishi, M. (1988). The influence of labels and positions in rating scales. *Journal of Educational Measurement, 25*(2), 85–96.

Kofsky, E. (1966). A scalogram study of classificatory development. *Child Development, 37*(1), 191–204.

Kolmogorov, A. N. (1950). *Foundations of the theory of probability.* New York: Chelsea.

Komorita, S. S. (1963). Attitude content, intensity, and the neutral point on a Likert scale. *Journal of Social Psychology, 61*(2), 327–334.

Küchemann, D. (1979). *PRTIII: Pendulum.* Windsor, Berkshire, England: National Foundation for Educational Research.

Lam, T. C., & Klockars, A. J. (1982). Anchor point effects on the equivalence of questionnaire items. *Journal of Educational Measurement, 19*(4), 317–322.

Lam, T. C., & Stevens, J. J. (1994). Effects of content polarization, item wording, and rating scale width on rating responses. *Applied Measurement in Education, 7*(2), 141–158.

Laudan, L. (1977). *Progress and its problems.* Berkeley, CA: University of California Press.

Lawson, A. E. (1979). Combining variables, controlling variables, and proportions: Is there a psychological link? *Science Education, 63*(1), 67–72.

Levy, P. (1937). *Theorie de l'addition des variables aleatoires* [Combination theory of unpredictable variables]. Paris: Gauthier-Villars.

Likert, R. (1932). A technique for the measurement of attitudes. *Archives of Psychology, 22,* 5–53.

Linacre, J. M. (1989). *Many-facet Rasch measurement.* Chicago: MESA Press.

Linacre, J. M. (1992). *Many-facet Rasch measurement.* Chicago: MESA Press.

Linacre, J. M. (1994). Constructing measurement with a many-facet Rasch model. In M. Wilson (Ed.), *Objective measurement: Theory into practice* (Vol. 2, pp. 129–144). Norwood, NJ: Ablex.

Linacre, J. M. (1995). Categorical misfit statistics. *Rasch Measurement Transactions, 9*(3), 450–451. Available from http://www.rasch.org/rmt/rmt93.htm. Accessed March 15, 2000.

Linacre, J. M. (1996a). Year's Best Paper in *Physical Therapy. Rasch Measurement Transactions, 10*(2), 489–490. Available from http://www.rasch.org/rmt/rmt102.htm. Accessed March 16, 2000.

Linacre, J. M. (1996b). The Rasch Model cannot be "disproved"! *Rasch Measurement Transactions, 10*(3), 512–514.

Linacre, J. M. (1997). *Judging plans and facets* (Research Note No. 3). Chicago: University of Chicago, MESA Psychometric Laboratory. Available from http://www.rasch.org/rn3.htm. Accessed March 23, 2000.

Linacre, J. M. (1998). Detecting multidimensionality: Which residual data-type works best? *Journal of Outcome Measurement, 2*(3), 266–283.

Linacre, J. M. (1999a). Investigating rating scale category utility. *Journal of Outcome Measurement, 3*(2), 103–122.

Linacre, J. M. (1999b). Paired comparison measurement with extreme scores. *Rasch Measurement Transactions, 12*(3), 646–647. Available: http://www.rasch.org/rmt/rmt 1238.htm. Accessed: March 20, 2000.

Linacre, J. M. (1999c). What are the odds? Measuring college basketball. *Popular Measurement, 2*(1), 17–18.

Linacre, J. M. (2006a). *Winsteps (Version 3.61.2)* [Computer Software]. Chicago: Winsteps.com.

Linacre, J. M. (2006b). *Facets Rasch measurement computer program*. Chicago: Winsteps.com.

Linacre, J. M. (2006c). *A user's guide to FACETS MINIFAC Rasch-model computer programs*. Chicago: Winsteps.com.

Linacre, J. M., Engelhard, G., Tatum, D. S., & Myford, C. M. (1994). Measurement with judges: Many-faceted conjoint measurement. *International Journal of Educational Research, 21*(6), 569–577.

Linacre J. M. & Wright, B.D. (1989) The "length" of a logit. *Rasch Measurement Transactions, 3*(2), 54–55. www.rasch.org/rmt/rmt32b.htm

Linacre, J. M., & Wright, B. D. (1994a). Chi-square fit statistics. *Rasch Measurement Transactions, 8*(2), 360. Available from http://rasch.org/rmt/rmt82.htm. Accessed March 14, 2000.

Linacre, J. M., & Wright, B. D. (1994b). *A user's guide to BIGSTEPS*. Chicago: MESA Press.

Linacre, J. M., & Wright, B. D. (2000). *WINSTEPS: Multiple-choice, rating scale, and partial credit Rasch analysis* [Computer software]. Chicago: MESA Press.

Linacre, J. M., & Wright, B. D. (2004). *WINSTEPS: Multiple-choice, rating scale, and partial credit Rasch analysis* [computer software]. Chicago: MESA Press.

Lissitz, R. W., & Green, S. B. (1975). Effect of the number of scale points on reliability: A Monte Carlo approach. *Journal of Applied Psychology, 60*(1), 10–13.

Loevinger, J. (1947). A systematic approach to the construction and evaluation of tests of ability. *Psychological Monographs, 61*(4).

Looney, M. A. (1997). Objective measurement of figure skating performance. *Journal of Outcome Measurement, 1*(2), 143–163.

Lopez, W. A. (1996). The resolution of ambiguity: An example from reading instruction (Doctoral dissertation, University of Chicago, 1996). *Dissertation Abstracts International, 57*(07), 2986A.

Lord, F. M. (1980). *Applications of item response theory to practical testing problems*. Hillsdale, NJ: Lawrence Erlbaum Associates.

Lord, F. M., & Novick, M. R. (1968). *Statistical theories of mental test scores*. Reading, MA: Addison-Wesley.

Low, G. D. (1988). The semantics of questionnaire rating scales. *Evaluation and Research in Education, 2*(2), 69–70.

Luce, R. D. (1972). What sort of measurement is psychophysical measurement? *American Psychologist, 27*(2), 96–106.

Luce, R. D. (1995). Four tensions concerning mathematical modeling in psychology. *Annual Review of Psychology, 46*, 1–26.

Luce, R. D., Krantz, D. H., Suppes, P., & Tversky, A. (1990). *Foundations of measurement: Vol. 3. Representation, axiomatization, and invariance.* San Diego: Academic Press.

Luce, R. D., & Tukey, J. W. (1964). Simultaneous conjoint measurement: A new type of fundamental measurement. *Journal of Mathematical Psychology, 1*(1), 1–27.

Lunz, M. E., & Linacre, J. M. (1998). Measurement designs using multifacet Rasch modeling. In G. A. Marcoulides (Ed.), *Modern methods for business research* (pp. 44–77). Mahwah, NJ: Lawrence Erlbaum Associates.

Lusardi, M. M., & Smith, E. V. (1997). Development of a scale to assess concern about falling and applications to treatment programs. *Journal of Outcome Measurement, 1*(1), 34–55.

Maraun, M. D. (1998). Measurement as a normative practice: Implications of Wittgenstein's philosophy for measurement in psychology. *Theory and Psychology, 8*(4), 435–461.

Masters, G. N. (1980). A Rasch model for rating scales (Doctoral dissertation, University of Chicago, 1980). *Dissertation Abstracts International, 41*(01), 215A.

Masters, G. N. (1982). A Rasch model for partial credit scoring. *Psychometrika, 47*(2), 149–174.

Masters, G. N. (1984). DICOT: Analyzing classroom tests with the Rasch model. *Educational and Psychological Measurement, 44*(1), 145–150.

Masters, G. N. (1988). Measurement models for ordered response categories. In R. Langeheine & J. Rost (Eds.), *Latent trait and latent class models* (pp. 11–29). New York: Plenum.

Masters, G. N. (1994). Partial credit model. In T. Husén & T. N. Postlethwaite (Eds.), *The international encyclopedia of education* (pp. 4302–4307). London: Pergamon.

Masters, G. N. (2004, October). *Continuity and Growth: Key Considerations in Educational Improvement and Accountability.* Address to the joint ACE and ACEL National Conference, Perth, Australia.

Masters, G. N., & Beswick, D. G. (1986). *The construction of tertiary entrance scores: Principles and issues.* Melbourne, Victoria, Australia: University of Melbourne, Centre for the Study of Higher Education.

Masters, G. N., & Wright, B. D. (1984). The essential process in a family of measurement models. *Psychometrika, 49*(4), 529–544.

McHorney, C. A., Haley, S. M., & Ware, J. E., Jr. (1997). Evaluation of the MOS SF-26 Physical Functioning Scale (PF-10): II. Comparison of relative precision using Likert and Rasch scoring methods. *Journal of Clinical Epidemiology, 50*(4), 451–461.

McNamara, T. F. (1996). *Measuring second language performance.* New York: Longman.

Mercer, A., & Andrich, D. (1997, March). *Implications when adjacent categories do not increase the trait.* Paper presented at the International Objective Measurement Workshop, Chicago.

Messick, S. (1989). Validity. In R. L. Linn (Ed.), *Educational measurement.* New York: Macmillan.

Messick, S. (1995). Validity of psychological assessment. *American Psychologist, 50*(9), 74–149.

Michell, J. (1986). Measurement scales and statistics: A clash of paradigms. *Psychological Bulletin, 100*(3), 398–407.

Michell, J. (1990). *An introduction to the logic of psychological measurement.* Hillsdale, NJ: Lawrence Erlbaum Associates.

Michell, J. (1997). Quantitative science and the definition of measurement in psychology. *British Journal of Psychology, 88*(3), 355–383.

Michell, J. (1999). Measurement in psychology: *Critical history of a methodological concept.* New York: Cambridge University Press.

Michell, J. (2003). Measurement: A beginner's guide. *Journal of Applied Measurement, 4*(4), 298–308.

Miller, G. A. (1956). The magical number seven, plus or minus two: Some limits on our capacity for processing information. *Psychological Review, 63*, 81–97.

Mislevy, R. J., & Wilson, M. (1996). Marginal maximum likelihood estimation for a psychometric model of discontinuous development. *Psychometrika, 61*(1), 41–71.

Montag, M., Simonson, M. R., & Maurer, M. (1984). *Test administrator's manual for the standardized test of computer literacy and computer anxiety index.* Ames, IA: Iowa State University, College of Education, Instructional Resources Center.

Moos, R. H. (1979). *Evaluating educational environments.* San Francisco: Jossey-Bass.

Narens, L., & Luce, R. D. (1993). Further comments on the "nonrevolution" arising from axiomatic measurement theory. *Psychological Science, 4*(2), 127–130.

Noelting, G. (1980a). The development of proportional reasoning and the ratio concept. Part I. Differentiation of stages. *Educational Studies in Mathematics, 11*(2), 217–253.

Noelting, G. (1980b). The development of proportional reasoning and the ratio concept. Part II. Problem-structure at successive stages; Problem-solving strategies and the mechanism of adaptive restructuring. *Educational Studies in Mathematics, 11*(3), 331–363.

Noelting, G. (1982). *Le développement cognitif et le mécanisme de l'équilibration.* Chicoutimi, Québec, Canada: Gaëtan Morin.

Noelting, G., Coudé, G., Rousseau, J.-P., & Bond, T. (2000). *Can qualitative stage characteristics be revealed quantitatively?* Manuscript submitted for publication.

Noelting, G., Gaulin, C., & Puchalska, E. (1985, March/April). *Levels in the ability to communicate spatial information by means of coded orthogonal views.* Paper presented at the annual meeting of the American Educational Research Association, Chicago.

Noelting, G., & Rousseau, J.-P. (in press). *Overcoming contradiction: A dialectical theory of cognitive development.* Mahwah, NJ: Lawrence Erlbaum Associates.

Nunnally, J. C. (1967). *Psychometric theory.* New York: McGraw-Hill.

Nunnally, J. C. (1978). *Psychometric theory* (2nd ed.). New York: McGraw-Hill.

Ory, J. C. (1982). Item placement and wording effects on overall ratings. *Educational and Psychological Measurement, 42*(3), 767–775.

Overton, W. F. (1998a, June). *Construct validity: A forgotten concept in developmental psychology?* Paper presented at the Jean Piaget Society annual symposium, Chicago.

Overton, W. F. (1998b). Developmental psychology: Philosophy, concepts, and methodology. In W. Damon (Series Ed.) & R. M. Lerner (Vol. Ed.), *Handbook of child psychology: Vol. 1. Theoretical models of human development* (5th ed., pp. 107–188). New York: Wiley.

Overton, W. F. (1999, August). *Construct validity: A forgotten concept in psychology?* Paper presented at the annual meeting of the American Psychological Association, Boston.

Parkinson, K. (1996). *Children's understanding of area: A comparison between performance on Piagetian interview tasks and school-based written tasks.* Unpublished thesis, James Cook University, Townsville, Queensland, Australia.

Pedhazur, E. J., & Schmelkin, L. P. (1991). *Measurement, design, and analysis: An integrated approach.* Hillsdale, NJ: Lawrence Erlbaum Associates.

Perkins, K., Wright, B. D., & Dorsey, J. K. (2000). Using Rasch measurement with medical data. In *Rasch measurement in health sciences.* Chicago: MESA Press.

Perline, R., Wright, B. D., & Wainer, H. (1979). The Rasch model as additive conjoint measurement. *Applied Psychological Measurement, 3*(2), 237–255.

Piaget, J., Inhelder, B., & Szeminska, A. (1960). *The child's conception of geometry.* London: Routledge and Kegan Paul. (Original work published 1948)

Plake, B. S. (1998). Setting performance standards for professional licensure and certification. *Applied Measurement in Education, 11*(1), 65–80.

Ramsay, J. O. (1973). The effect of number of categories in rating scales on precision of estimation of scale values. *Psychometrika, 38*(4, Pt. 1), 513–532.

Rasch, G. (1960). *Probabilistic models for some intelligence and attainment tests.* Copenhagen: Danmarks Paedagogiske Institut.

Rasch, G. (1961). On general laws and the meaning of measurement in psychology. In *Proceedings of the Fourth Berkeley Symposium on Mathematical Statistics and Probability* (Vol. 4, pp. 321–334). Berkeley: University of California Press.

Rasch, G. (1980). *Probabilistic models for some intelligence and attainment tests* (Expanded ed.). Chicago: University of Chicago Press.

Remington, M., Tyrer, P. J., Newson-Smith, J., & Cicchetti, D. V. (1979). Comparative reliability of categorical and analog rating scales in the assessment of psychiatric symptomatology. *Psychological Medicine, 9*(4), 765–770.

Remmers, H. H., & Ewart, E. (1941). Reliability of multiple-choice measuring instruments as a function of the Spearman-Brown prophecy formula, III. *Journal of Educational Psychology, 32*, 61–66.

Rogosa, D. R., & Willett, J. B. (1985). Understanding correlates of change by modeling individual differences in growth. *Psychometrika, 50*(2), 203–228.

Rossi Ferrario, S., Baiardi, P., Zotti, A. M. (2004). Update on the Family Strain Questionnaire: A tool for the general screening of caregiving-related problems. *Quality of Life Research, 13*, 1425–1434.

Rost, J. (1996). *Testtheorie, TestKonstruction* [Test theory, test construction]. Göttingen: Verlag Hans Huber.

Scheuneman, J. D., & Subhiyah, R. G. (1998). Evidence for the validity of a Rasch model technique for identifying differential item functioning. *Journal of Outcome Measurement, 2*(1), 33–42.

Schumacker, R. E. & Linacre, J. M. (1996). Factor analysis and Rasch Analysis. *Rasch Measurement Transactions, 9*(4), p.470.

Seltzer, R., & Glass, W. (1991). International politics and judging in Olympic skating events: 1968–1988. *Journal of Sport Behavior, 14*(3), 189–200.

Shayer, M., Küchemann, D. E., & Wylam, H. (1976). The distribution of Piagetian stages of thinking in British middle and secondary school children. *British Journal of Educational Psychology, 46*(2), 164–173.

Simonson, M. R., Maurer, M., Montag-Torardi, M., & Whitaker, M. (1987). Development of a standardized test of computer literacy and a computer anxiety index. *Journal of Educational Computing Research, 3*(2), 231–247.

Smith, E. V. (2000). Understanding Rasch Measurement: Metric Development and Score Reporting in Rasch Measurement. *Journal of Applied Measurement, 1*(3).

Smith, E.V., Jr. (2001). Evidence for the reliability of measures and validity of measure interpretation: A Rasch measurement perspective. *Journal of Applied Measurement, 2*(3), 281–311.

Smith, R. (1993). Guessing and the Rasch model. *Rasch Measurement Transactions, 6*(4), 262–263.

Smith, R. M. (1991a). The distributional properties of Rasch item fit statistics. *Educational and Psychological Measurement, 51*, 541–565.

Smith, R. M. (1991b). *IPARM: Item and person analysis with the Rasch model.* Chicago: MESA Press.

Smith, R. M. (1992). *Applications of Rasch measurement.* Chicago: MESA Press.

Smith, R. M. (1994). Comparison of the power of Rasch total- and between-item fit statistics to detect measurement disturbances. *Educational and Psychological Measurement, 54*(1), 42–55.

Smith, R. M. (2000). Fit analysis in latent trait measurement models. *Journal of Applied Measurement, 1*(2), 199–218.

Smith, R. M., & Miao, C. Y. (1994). Assessing unidimensionality for Rasch measurement. In M. Wilson (Ed.), *Objective measurement: Theory into practice* (Vol. 2, pp. 316–327). Norwood, NJ: Ablex.

Smith, R. M., Schumacker, R. E., & Bush, M. J. (1998). Using item mean squares to evaluate fit to the Rasch model. *Journal of Outcome Measurement, 2*(1), 66–78.

Smullyan, R. (1978). *What is the name of this book? The riddle of Dracula and other logical puzzles.* Englewood Cliffs, NJ: Prentice-Hall.

Sobel, D. (1996). *Longitude: The true story of a lone genius who solved the greatest scientific problem of his time.* Harmondsworth, UK: Penguin.

Sobel, D. (1999). *Galileo's daughter: A historical memoir of science, faith, and love.* New York: Walker.

Spector, P. E. (1976). Choosing response categories for summated rating scales. *Journal of Applied Psychology, 61*(3), 374–375.

Stafford, E. (2005). What the pendulum can tell educators about children's scientific reasoning. In M. R. Matthews, C. F. Gauld, & A. Stinner (Eds.), *The pendulum: Scientific, historical & educational perspectives* (pp. 315–348). Dordrecht: Springer.

Stahl, J., Bergstrom, B., & Gershon, R. (2000). CAT administration of language placement examinations. *Journal of Applied Measurement, 1*(3), 292–302.

Stanbridge, B. (2001). *A radical constructivist approach to high school science teaching: investigating its potential to extend students meaningful learning through the optimisation and possible extension of their cognitive abilities.* Unpublished doctoral dissertation, James Cook University, Townsville, Australia.

Stevens, S. S. (1946). On the theory of scales of measurement. *Science, 103,* 677–680.

Stevens, S. S. (1959a). The quantification of sensation. *Daedalus, 88*(4), 606–621.

Stevens, S. S. (1959b). *Measurement, psychophysics and utility.* In C. W. Churchman & P. Ratoosh (Eds.), *Measurement: Definitions and theories.* New York: John Wiley.

Stone, G. E. (2001). Understanding Rasch measurement: Objective standard setting (or truth in advertising). *Journal of Applied Measurement, 2*(2) 187–201.

Stone, G. E. (2002, April). *The emperor has no clothes: What makes a criterion-referenced standard valid?* Presented at the fifth annual International Objective Measurement Workshop, New Orleans, LA.

Strauss, S. (2002). Stephen, a feature article on page, New scoring system would have iced the gold for the Canadians. *Globe and Mail.* Toronto, Canada, p.F6, Feb. 16 (www.rasch.org/rmt/rmt154a.htm)

Stucki, G., Daltroy, L., Katz, J. N., Johanneson, M., & Liang, M. H. (1996). Interpretation of change scores in ordinal clinical scales and health status measures: The whole may not equal the sum of the parts. *Journal of Clinical Epidemiology, 49*(7), 711–717.

Suppes, P., Krantz, D. M., Luce, R., & Tversky, A. (1989). *Foundations of measurement.* San Diego, CA: Academic Press.

Symonds, P. M. (1924). On the loss of reliability in ratings due to coarseness of the scale. *Journal of Experimental Psychology, 7,* 456–461.

Tesio, L., Granger, C. V., Perucca, L., Franchignoni, F. P., Battaglia, M. A., & Russell, C. F. (2002). The FIM™ instrument in the United States and Italy: A comparative study. *American Journal of Physical Medicine & Rehabilitation, 81*(3), 168–176.

Thorndike, E. L. (1926). *Educational psychology.* New York: Columbia University, Teachers College.

Thorndike, E. L., Bregman, E. O., Cobb, M. V., & Woodyard, E. (1927). *The measurement of intelligence.* New York: Columbia University, Teachers College.

Thurstone, L. L. (1925). A method of scaling psychological and educational tests. *Journal of Educational Psychology, 16,* 433–451.

Thurstone, L. L. (1927). The unit of measurement in educational scales. *Journal of Educational Psychology, 18,* 505–524.

Thurstone, L. L. (1928). Attitudes can be measured. *American Journal of Sociology, 33,* 529–554.

Thurstone. L. L. (1952). Autobiography. In G. Lindzey (Ed.), *A history of psychology in autobiography* (Vol. 6, pp. 294–321). Englewood Cliffs, NJ: Prentice Hall.

Tucker, L. R. (1953). Scales minimizing the importance of reference groups. In *Proceedings of the 1952 Invitational Conference on Testing Problems* (pp. 22–33). Princeton, NJ: Educational Testing Service.

van der Linden, W. (2001). Book review *International Journal Of Testing, 1*(3&4), 319–326

Van der Linden, W. J., & Hambleton, R. K. (Eds.). (1997). *Handbook of modern item-response theory.* New York: Springer.

Vogt, W. P. (1999). *Dictionary of statistics and methodology* (2nd ed.). Thousand Oaks, CA: Sage.

Wallace, J. G. (1965). *Concept growth and the education of the child.* Slough: National Foundation for Educational Research.

Waller, M. (1973). *Removing the effects of random guessing from latent ability estimates.* Doctoral dissertation, Chicago.

Warm, T. A. (1985). *Weighted maximum likelihood estimation of ability in Item Response Theory with tests of finite length.* (Tech. Rep. No. CGI-TR-85-08). Oklahoma City: U.S. Coast Guard Institute.

Waugh, R. F. (1998). The Course Experience Questionnaire: A Rasch measurement model analysis. *Higher Education Research and Development, 17*(1), 45–64.

Whissell, R., Lyons, S., Wilkinson, D., & Whissell, C. (1993). National bias in judgments of Olympic-level skating. *Perceptual and Motor Skills, 77*(2), 355–358.

Willett, J. B. (1989). Some results on reliability for the longitudinal measurement of change: Implications for the design of studies of individual growth. *Educational and Psychological Measurement, 49*(3), 587–602.

Wilson, M. (1985). Measuring stages of growth: *A psychometric model of hierarchical development* (Occasional Paper No. 29). Hawthorn, Victoria: Australian Council for Educational Research.

Wilson, M. (1989). Saltus: A psychometric model of discontinuity in cognitive development. *Psychological Bulletin, 105*(2), 276–289.

Wilson, M. (1994). Comparing attitude across different cultures: Two quantitative approaches to construct validity. In M. Wilson (Ed.), *Objective measurement: Theory into practice* (Vol. 2, pp. 271–294). Norwood, NJ: Ablex.

Wilson, M. (2002). Book review. *Applied Psychological Measurement, 26*(2).

Wilson, M. (2005). *Constructing measures: an item response modeling approach.* Mahwah, NJ: Lawrence Erlbaum Associates.

Wilson, M., & Iventosch, L. (1988). Using the partial credit model to investigate responses to structured subtests. *Applied Measurement in Education, 1*(4), 319–334.

Wright, B. D. (1977). Misunderstanding the Rasch model. *Journal of Educational Measurement, 14*(2), 97–116.

Wright, B. D. (1984). Despair and hope for educational measurement. *Contemporary Education Review, 3*(1), 281–288.

Wright, B. D. (1985). Additivity in psychological measurement. In E. Roskam (Ed.), *Measurement and personality assessment.* North Holland: Elsevier Science.

Wright, B. D. (1996). Comparing Rasch measurement and factor analysis. *Structural Equation Modeling, 3*(1), 3–24.

Wright, B. D. (1997). A history of social science measurement. *Educational Measurement: Issues and Practice, 16*(4), 33–45, 52.

Wright, B. D. (1998a). Estimating measures for extreme scores. *Rasch Measurement Transactions, 12*(2), 632–633. Available from http://www.rasch.org/rmt/rmt122h.htm. Accessed October 20, 1998.

Wright, B. D. (1998b). *Introduction to the Rasch model* [Videotape]. Chicago: MESA Press.

Wright, B. D. (1999). Fundamental measurement for psychology. In S. E. Embretson & S. L. Hershberger (Eds.), *The new rules of measurement: What every educator and psychologist should know* (pp. 65–104). Mahwah, NJ: Lawrence Erlbaum Associates.

Wright, B. D., & Douglas, G. (1986). *The rating scale model for objective measurement* (Research Memorandum No. 35). Chicago: University of Chicago, MESA Psychometric Laboratory.

Wright, B. D., & Linacre, J. M. (1989). Observations are always ordinal; Measurements, however, must be interval. *Archives of Physical Measurement and Rehabilitation, 70*(12), 857–860.

Wright, B. D., & Linacre, J. M. (1992). Combining and splitting of categories. *Rasch Measurement Transactions, 6*(3), 233. Available from http://rasch.org/rmt/rmt63.htm. Accessed March 20, 2000.

Wright, B. D., Linacre, M. Gustafsson, J-E., and Martin-Loff, P. (1994). Reasonable mean-square fit values. *Rasch Measurement Transactions, 8*(3), 370. Available from http://www.rasch.org/rmt/rmt83.htm. Accessed March 22, 2000.

Wright, B. D., & Masters, G. N. (1981). *The measurement of knowledge and attitude* (Research Memorandum No. 30). Chicago: University of Chicago, MESA Psychometric Laboratory.

Wright, B. D., & Masters, G. N. (1982). *Rating scale analysis.* Chicago: MESA Press.

Wright, B. D., & Mok, M. (2000). Rasch models overview. *Journal of Applied Measurement, 1*, 83–106.

Wright, B. D., & Stone, M. H. (1979). *Best test design.* Chicago: MESA Press.

Wright, B. D., & Stone, M. H. (2004). *Making Measures.* Chicago: The Phaneron Press.

Wu, M., & Adams, R. (2004, June). *Applications of Multi-dimensional Item Response Models.* Paper presented at the XIIth International Objective Measurement Workshops, Cairns.

Wu, M. L., Adams, R. J., & Wilson, M. R. (1997). *ConQuest: Multi-Aspect Test Software* [computer program]. Camberwell, Victoria: Australian Council for Educational Research.

Wu, M. L., Adams, R. J., & Wilson, M. R. (1998). *ConQuest: Generalised item response modelling software* [Computer software]. Camberwell, Victoria: Australian Council for Educational Research.

Wylam, H., & Shayer, M. (1980). *CSMS: Science reasoning tasks.* Windsor, Berkshire, England: National Foundation for Educational Research.

Zwinderman, A. H. (1995). Pairwise parameter estimation in Rasch models. *Applied Psychological Measurement, 19*(4), 369–375.

Author Index

Subject Index